Wolfgang Wagner

Kurt Tank - Focke-Wulf's Designer and Test Pilot

The History of German Aviation

Kurt Tank -
Focke Wulf's Designer and Test Pilot

by Wolfgang Wagner

translated by Don Cox

Schiffer Military/Aviation History
Atglen, PA

Translated from the German by Don Cox

Copyright © 1998 by Schiffer Publishing, Ltd.
Library of Congress Catalog Number: 98-85862

Printed in China.
ISBN: 0-7643-0644-8

This book was originally published under the title,
Kurt Tank-Konstrukteur und Testpilot bei Focke-Wulf
by Bernard & Graefe.

We are interested in hearing from authors with book ideas
on related topics.

Published by Schiffer Publishing Ltd.
4880 Lower Valley Road
Atglen, PA 19310
Phone: (610) 593-1777
FAX: (610) 593-2002
E-mail: Schifferbk@aol.com
Please write for a free catalog.
This book may be purchased from the publisher.
Please include $3.95 postage.
Try your bookstore first.

CONTENTS

Introduction

The numerous books on the Focke-Wulf Fw 190 which have appeared not only in Germany but in many other countries as well are a testimony to the extraordinary success of this airplane. They also indicate the respect and esteem in which its designer, Dipl.-Ing. Prof. Dr.-Ing. eh. Kurt Tank, is held - particularly by those who, in former days, had fought against this aircraft.

In addition to the Fw 190 and the world-renowned four-engined Fw 200 Condor airliner - the aircraft which paved the way for land-based commercial aviation on the North Atlantic routes, this book encompasses Kurt Tank's life as a designer of numerous aircraft which both preceded the Fw 190 or followed it in other countries, as in the case aircraft development in Argentinia and India.

Prof. Tank himself has made contributions to this book and reviewed the comprehensive data and figures tables for his aircraft - meaning that this work bears his signature. Accordingly, this book remains true to the goals which the publishing house and publisher have established for the series, now expanded to 16 volumes. Well-known designers, acting as their own authors, detail their own designs in each volume, while other writers give first-hand accounts from the memoirs of our aviation pioneers or provide detailed drawings of their work. Factory numbers or aircraft registration play a backseat role in these books; the thoughts of the designers which led to world-famous aircraft and produced the anticipated performance take center stage here. It is my hope that this second edition enjoys as much success as the first.

Dr. phil. Theodor Benecke
Bonn, summer 1991

Dipl.-Ing Prof. Dr.-Ing. eh. Flugkapitän Kurt Tank

Preface

A part of aviation history is embodied in one man whose name appears on only a few of his designs, despite the fact that those very designs have since become legendary. Prof. Dr.-Ing. eh. Kurt Waldemar Tank, whose most successful projects are still held in high esteem today, began his association with aviation on the Rhöne with a home-built glider. He later had a considerable influence on the flying boats of Rohrbach and in the 1920s grew to become one of the most successful aircraft designers. Later, as the technical director of the Focke-Wulf-Werke, he created the Fw 200 Condor, and in doing so laid the technological groundwork for today's long-range transoceanic aviation. With the Fw 190 Tank built one of the best fighter aircraft of its day - as much feared by the enemy as it was valued by its pilots. After the war, Tank constructed the Pulqui II in Argentina in the 1950s, the fastest jet aircraft of the time which - like nearly all of his designs - he test flew himself. While working for India under the most primitive conditions he, along with 14 experts from the German aviation industry and Indian engineers, designed the HF-24 in the '60s, a fighter that, had it been fitted with modern engines, would have been a match for - if not superior to - today's modern high-performance aircraft and those of the subsequent '80s generation.

With a rare clarity of mind, the 82 year-old Tank can reflect back on over 50 years of aviation development; he can recall every important event, remember the dates and technical minutae of his aircraft down to the smallest detail and is as comfortable with today's developments as he was with aviation in the '20s and '30s.

To discount Tank's influence over five decades would be to leave a gap in the technical history of German aviation, a gap which would be impossible to bridge at a later date.

Kurt Tank was an unusually talented individual. Many of his designs were masterpieces of long-range and high-speed flight. Only rarely did his designs come up short in comparison with his competitors or those of the enemy in wartime. He possessed the ability to recognize the important things and create new concepts from the ground up. He would critically analyze a situation before deciding on the optimum solution and as a rule only entrusted his prototypes to his test pilots after he'd flown them himself. One of Tank's closest colleagues, Dr. Heinz Conradis, masterfully documented his work for posterity in his postwar book "Nerven, Herz und Rechenschieber"(Nerves, Heart and Slide Rule). This current volume focuses more on Tank's influence in technical and aeronautical aspects, supplemented by data, tables and figures.

No less a person than Tank himself was the proofreader of the technical details in this book. He carefully checked both text and tables so that these, despite all-too-human minor errors, would withstand the test of history.

Wolfgang Wagner
Cologne, March 1980

9

Acknowledgements

The author wishes to express his gratitude to Theo Lässig for providing the three-view drawings and the graphic material taken from handbooks and factory drawings, Sontka Wegener for proofreading, Ursula Wagner for her comprehensive secretarial and typing work, the special archives in the Deutsches Museum (Avicentra and von Römer) with Messrs. Heinrich, Pöllitsch and Gurra, the Bundesarchiv in Freiburg - particularly Messrs. Dr. Maierhöfer, Noack and Albinus, plus the literary department of VFW-Fokker in Bremen with Dipl.-Ing. Hans Hollendieck and Helmut Roosenboom, the public affairs section of Daimler-Benz with Messrs. Günther Molter and archivist Burkhard Hülsen, the public affairs department of the Motoren- und TUrbinen-Union with Dipl.-Ing. Prestel, Heinz Egger and Mr. Deisinger, and Franz Prueschoff, Horst Burgsmüller and Mr. Bittner at Lufthansa. Special thanks go out to Dipl.-Ing. Flugbaumeister Hans Sander for supplying valuable documents and reviewing and checking manuscripts. By the same token this also applies to Dr.-Ing. Otto E. Pabst and Dipl.-Ing. Herbert Wolff. At this point I would also like to thank Otto Rohrbach for his review of the Rohrbach section, plus Dipl.-Ing. Fritz Trenkle, Wilfried Kersten and Georg Orlamünder for providing documents relating to the equipment. Without the efforts of those individuals named above and many other unnamed persons, along with the cooperation of the Bernard & Graefe Verlag it would not have been possible to have brought this work to fruition.

I owe a particular debt of gratitude to all of them.

The author
Cologne, March 1980

The Electronics Engineer becomes a Builder of Aircraft

Born in Bromberg-Schwedenhöhe on the 24th of February 1898, Kurt Tank spent his early years on the river; his father earned a living as a maintenance technician at an electrical power plant in Nakel on the Netze River in former Posen. When in 1914 the First World War broke out Tank would have gladly spent his life serving in the flying corps, but his father, himself a soldier of many years, thought the idea of flying was nonsense and stood by tradition: Kurt Tank would have to serve in the cavalry regiment of his father. He became a lieutenant, a company commander and when he returned home from the in 1918, having been wounded several times and bringing back numerous awards for bravery.

A physics book had been his most trusted companion during the war's four years. The young man's thirst for knowledge was great and he had a particular interest in hydrodynamics, the laws of theoretical fluid dynamics. He wanted to learn more, wanted to put the theories into practice by becoming a flyer. At every available opportunity he applied for reassignment to the *Fliegertruppe*, but all his attempts at a transfer were left to collect dust. None of his superiors wanted to lose the excellent soldier.

Studying now became his goal. Tank settled on the study of electro-technology, and after completing his studies at the Technische Hochschule (TH) Berlin was appointed to the Rohrbach Metallflugzeugbau in February of 1924, where a short time later he was given the task of establishing a design department for this company.

Gliding, his hobby as a student, now served to smooth the electronics engineer's way to aviation design. During the first days of 1924 Tank met Professor D.-Ing. M. Weber by chance in the train station at the Berlin suburb of Potsdam. Weber had been chairman of the mechanics department at the TH Berlin, and Tank had taken the higher mechanics elective taught by him while working towards his major. Weber took an interest in the future of this talented student and Tank told him that Professor Kloss had offered him an assistant position at the Siemens firm. Weber nodded thoughtfully, looked at Tank with a scrutinous expression and asked "Didn't you want to get involved with aircraft design? Rohrbach Metallflugzeugbau is looking for good people!" This company had asked Weber to provide them with names of young sharp-minded graduate engineers. The professor was familiar was familiar with Tank's design work

on sailplane construction with the Akaflieg Berlin and knew that he, along with seven fellow students, had founded the Akaflieg at the TH Berlin in 1919 - with the intention of preventing aviation technology at the Technische Hochschule from being hampered by the extremely restrictive stipulations of the Treaty of Versailles. As a sidenote, Dr. Adolf Baeumker, recently deceased and at the time a *Rittmeister*, actively supported the group. For a long time he was the group's patron and helper. Prof. Dr. August von Parseval, the inventor of the semi-rigid airship, also participated in the experiments with sailplane models.

Tank didn't take too much time thinking about it and quickly decided to go to Rohrbach Metallflugzeugbau instead of Siemens.

The electronics engineer brought with him both familiarity with flying as well as experience in the design of aircraft. While at the Technische Hochschule, Tank and his fellow students Hermann Winter, Werner Hinninger, Pauleduard Pank, Seppl Kutin, Viktor Gohlke, Edmund

Kurt Tank in the cockpit of an Fw 190A The aircraft designer test flew most of his airplanes himself and acted - unusual as it may seem - as something of his own test pilot.

Pfister and Georg Gillert had set up a workshop in the school's loft, where they began with the construction of two gliders. Winter worked on a tailless monoplane called "Charlotte" - named for Professor Parseval's daughter - while Tank's project was a strut-braced high-wing monoplane with a large wingspan. They attended lectures on flight mechanics and aerodynamics by Prof. Everling, on aircraft design statics by Prof. Reissner and there built up their theoretical knowledge. In 1922 they entered the Rhön Competition with the "Charlotte" which had been completed in the interim. The application form for the Rhön Competition stated: tailless monoplane from the Aeronautical Union of the Technische Hochschule Berlin, boat fuselage, stick control, wingspan 15.2 m, length 4.5 m, height 1.20 m and wing area 20 m2. Hermann Winter flew the flying wing design in the competition, but got caught in a downdraft, brushed a tree and crashed. Although only suffering minor injuries, he was treated at the hospital in Gersfeld. The students transported the wreckage on foot, using a wagon, to Gotha. The Gothaer Waggonfabrik arranged for the aircraft to be shipped back to Berlin, where it was repaired by the group.

In the meantime, Tank had continued working on his design and built a large-span shoulder-wing airplane for the 1923 Rhön Competition. The application form included the following information: Academic Flying Group of TH Berlin, "Teufelchen", wingspan 11.5 m, length 5.00 m, height 1.30 m, wing area 13.7 m2, and "Charlotte", wingspan 14.5 m, length 3.23 m, height 1.50 m and wing area 19.50 m².

But there simply was not enough space in the loft for building this plane. In addition, the students didn't have the time - after all, their studies could not be neglected. Accordingly, Tank and Gillert set out to visit the Albatros-Werke in Berlin-Johannisthal. They sought out technical directors Schubert and Robert Thelen, the latter of which had set two world records in Albatros biplanes in 1914. Despite the mutual interest in aviation Thelen, at that time

considered one of the great pilots during the early years of aviation, seemed to have little interest in building a complete sailplane for the students free of charge, particularly one which utilized wing warping wingtips in place of ailerons! Later, with the merger of Albatros and the Focke-Wulf-Werke (1932), the two men would meet again. Tank would become Thelen's boss.

The next visit was to the Luft-Fahrzeug Gesellschaft in Stralsund, which during the war had produced the famous LFG-Roland airplanes. Here Ing. Baatz showed greater understanding and arranged for the construction of the "Teufelchen" (Little Devil), as Tank called it, to be built in adherence with Tank's blueprints. With the construction of the "Teufelchen" Tank passed his preliminary exam on the way to becoming a graduate engineer. The work was graded as "very good" by Prof. Parseval and Dr. Wilhelm Hoff.

The Akaflieg went to the Rhön in August 1923 full of enthusiasm, where they represented the imperial capital with not a little pride and two airplanes, the repaired "Charlotte" and Tank's "Teufelchen". In order to acquire some flying experience Tank practiced several takeoffs in a training glider. Then he steered the "Teufelchen" down the slope as it launched itself from its rubber tether. Upon landing, he was forced to set down on rocky ground and the aircraft was badly damaged. The Berliner group was extremely disappointed, for not only was the aircraft kap*utt*, but they were now completely out of money. Back in Berlin they made preparations for their final exams. Nevertheless, the group eventually managed to repair the plane and later flew it successfully in Rositten on the East Prussian coast.

However, before Tank took up his new job at Rohrbach, he obtained his pilot's license at the Bornemann Flying School in Berlin-Staaken. His instructor was Rudolf Rienau, who was later killed in a flying accident. At Staaken, he was trained to fly the Kranich, an old twin-strutted LVG military biplane with a 74 kW/100 hp Mercedes D I engine which had been license-built by Raab-Katzenstein because of its good handling characteristics.

August 1923: Tank in the "Teufelchen" over the Wasserkuppe.

Beginnings at Rohrbach

Tank began his work at Rohrbach with theoretical research into flight performance and handling characteristics as well as practical tasks involving flight testing of the Ro III twin-engined flying boat. In addition to his activities as an engineer he also added to his license classes as a pilot and was instructed on flying boats, something which came easy for the enthusiastic glider pilot.

The testing of the Ro III - a design by Ing. Steiger, whose statics were in the hands of Dipl.Ing. Tempel and Dipl.-Ing. Hoch - showed that the forward hull suffered unacceptable stress when landing in rough seas. This was a result of the flat hull bottom ahead of the first step. Two pillows had to be laid down on the seats if the pilot was expected to withstand the impact. Often the stiffeners would break on one of the bulkhead plates during such landings. Tank proposed a cushioned keel which would bring the stress into tolerable limits. In order to reinforce his theoretical ideas, the company authorized him to carry out tow-

The Rohrbach Ro IIIa Rodra with two Lorraine Dietrich engines, each having an output of 330 kW (450 hp). Two of these flying boats were delivered to Turkey in 1926.

Rohrbach Flying Boats for Japan and Turkey

Manufacturer		Rohrbach	Rohrbach	Rohrbach
Type		Ro II	Ro III	Ro IIIa Rodra
Powerplant		Rolls Royce Eagle IX	Rolls Royce Eagle IX	Lorraine Dietrich
Performance	kW	2x265=530	2x265=530	2x330=660
	hp	2x360=720	2x360=720	2x450=900
Crew(+passengers)	2+2	2+2	2+2	
Length	m	16.50	17.20	17.20
Height	m	5.00	6.00	6.00
Wingspan	m	29.00	29.00	27.55
Wing area	m²	73.40	73.40	73.40
Aspect ratio		11.46	11.46	10.34
Weight, empty	kg	3600	3600	4680
Fuel	kg	900	1000	780
Oil	kg	60	80	60
Crew	kg	160	160	160
Load	kg	2500	2700	2010
Max. permissible load	kg	2500	2700	2010
Takeoff weight	kg	6100	6300	6690
Wing loading	kg/m²	83.10	85.83	91.14
Weight/power ratio	kg/kW	11.50	11.89	10.14
	kg/hp	8.47	8.75	7.43
	kW/m²	7.22	7.22	8.99
	hp/m²	9.80	9.81	12.26
Built		1923	1924	1925
Max. speed @ sea level	km/h	175	175	185
Cruise speed @ sea level	km/h	160	160	170
Rate of climb	m/s	2.00	2.00	2.00
Service ceiling	m	4000	4000	3000
Range	km	1300	1440	850
Max. flight time	hrs	8.00	9.00	5.00
Landing speed	km/h	110	112	110
Max. permissible load as % of takeoff weight		41	43	30
Payload as % of takeoff weight		23	23	15

ing trials with models having different keel shapes. These were initially conducted at the Preußische Schiffbau-Versuchsanstalt in Berlin, then continued in the test channel at the Hamburger Schiffbau-Versuchsanstalt using larger models. There he towed his models over thousands of kilometers in the search for the best hull shape. These experiments confirmed his ideas and led to Rohrbach flying boats adopting a keel design which distributed the landing shock over a greater period of time and greater length, thereby reducing it to acceptable levels without affecting takeoff performance.

The later developments of the Robbe I, Robbe II, Rocco, Romar and Rostra keeled flying boat series were strongly influenced by these improvements. Tank's subsequent experiments and experience with the above-named series also led to a new basic design of the wings and empennage. The constant-cord rectangular wing gave way to a much lighter tapered wing with greater taper at a relatively constant thickness. For example, the taper on the wings of the three-engined Romar giant flying boat had a ratio value of the inner depth (di) to the outer depth (do) of

$$di/da = 5/1$$

In this manner the flight handling characteristics were improved significantly, while at the same time maneuvering on rough seas was made easier.

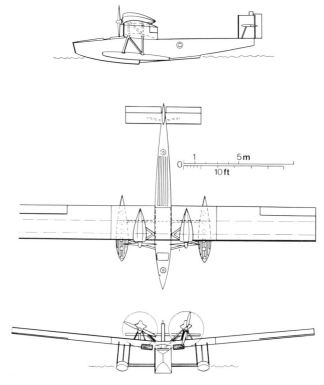

Rohrbach Ro IIIa Rodra.

The British Buy a Flying boat for Scrap

Great Britain ordered two Ro III flying boats from the British company of Beardmore in Scotland, which had acquired the Rohrbach licenses. The first boat was built in accordance with English construction guidelines at Rohrbach, while the second boat was expected to have been built under license at Beardmore. In England this special variant of the Ro IIIa (or Rodra) was designated as the Ro IV Inverness (the name of a Scottish town) and given the British registration number of N 183. Due to the constraints imposed by the Treaty of Versailles the aircraft was built in the Danish city of Kastrup, where it was fitted with two British Napier Lion engines, each having an output of 331 kW/450 hp. After final assembly and flight testing the flying boat was delivered to a British acceptance commission of the Marine Aircraft Experimental Establishment in September 1925. According to Tank, the director of this com-

mission, a certain Master of Sempill, expressed his sentiments on the aircraft at a combined dinner discussion. He could find nothing but fault with the all-metal monoplane and gave it no chance for the future. It was with this explanation that he justified the future role of the flying boat - for experimental purposes only. Once German pilots had ferried the plane to Felixstowe, the Royal Navy's test center in England, English pilots would carry out a series of flight tests with the aircraft. Following that, the Rodra would be subjected to static and dynamic loads on the ground until it succumbed to structural failure. The same fate awaited the second machine. According to the Master of Sempill, the British had no intention of pursuing this course of development further, for on the one hand metal construction led to higher empty weights and on the other hand a monoplane didn't offer the same safety as a biplane of the same weight. In actual fact the English did indeed fly biplanes as standard until well into the 'thirties.

Ro VII Robbe I

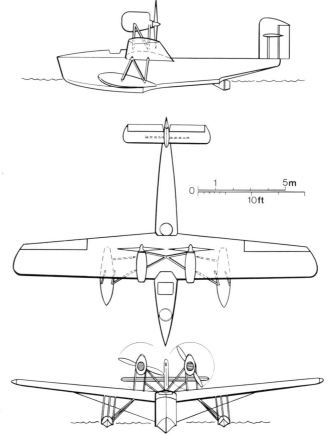

The Robbe (Seal) - a flying boat transport - clearly bore the trademark of Kurt Tank. It was the first to be fitted with pusher propellers; the high drag induced by the engines would be offset by the free airflow of the pusher prop arrangement. In addition, the propeller blades were better protected against sea spray. Tank first had measurements carried out at the test stand in the Kaiser-Wilhelm-Institut für Strömungsforschung in Göttingen to determine whether the propeller arc (which passed quite close to the wing upper surface) would be negatively affected by the boundary layer flowing off the wing. The director of the Institut für Strömungslehre, Professor Ludwig Prandtl, and his Swiss assistant Professor Ackeret, briefly participated in these experiments. As the test propeller blades crossed into the boundary layer they gave off quite a loud tone. Professor

Ro VII Robbe I. The seating of the horizontal tail unit was modified several times, thus explaining the difference between the drawing and the picture below.

In 1929 Werner Landmann set five world records in the Rohrbach Ro VII Robbe which, powered by its two 169 kW (230 hp) BMW IV engines, covered distances of 100 km, 500 km and 1000 km with loads of 500 to 1000 kilograms.

Prandtl turned to Tank and said "That is precisely the standard pitch A note". When he noticed Tank's sceptical expression, he had a tuning fork brought in, struck it when the tests in the tunnel resumed - and in fact the tone did indeed correspond to the standard pitch A.

At this time Tank had other tests carried out at Göttingen. Prof. Albert Betz had developed an impulse method by which it would be possible to measure pressure and velocity in free-flowing air both behind and in front of the model. The difference gave the actual drag of the model. Tank then evaluated a model of a standard Robbe with a normal tailplane having exposed rivet heads and another made of wood with a smooth surface. The drag of the former was some 30 percent greater. Tank obtained the approval of Dr. Rohrbach to test a taper on the Robbe's wings using a 2:1 ratio for the first time, plus add two tension cables running from the fuselage to the wing. These two measures, which Tank had discussed with chief designer Steiger, were expected to lead to a weight reduction in the wings. In addition, the tailplane was raised to keep it out of the water's spray. The improved hull design was applied, enabling the support floats to be kept smaller and lighter.

Tank played an active role in the Robbe's flight testing program and from it was able to draw considerable experience with flying boat characteristics.

Ro IX Rofix Drama

In late 1925 Turkish officers inspected the Rohrbach Werke at Kastrup and negotiated with Dr. Rohrbach for the construction of a fighter aircraft. It was agreed upon to construct two prototypes, and following their proof-of-concept a contract for a further 50 machines was expected. Tank designed a high-wing all-metal airplane with pronounced dihedral and having two streamlined shrouded cables which served to brace the wings, similar to the later Rohrbach Roland design. As Tank remembers it, the unique form of the airplane was expected to provide the pilot with unrestricted visibility on all sides. This standard requirement for all pilots had been solved in an ideal manner with the Rofix. A BMW VI served as the powerplant, which at the time had a takeoff rating at sea level of 441 kW/600 hp and cruised at 331 kW/450 hp.

Flight testing revealed that the pronounced dihedral on the first prototype (Werknummer 22), while giving the Rofix pilot unusually good visibility, also meant that the aircraft was not dynamically stable and therefore tended to "tumble", or go into Dutch rolls along the yaw and roll axes. According to a memorandum, the Rofix was also sluggish going into a spin and just as sluggish pulling out of one.

The Rohrbach Ro IX Rofix V 2 single seat fighter. The wings - at least as they appear in the photo - no longer seem to have any dihedral. This is therefore probably the second prototype, Werknummer 23, in which Paul Bäumer crashed.

Test pilot Landmann, who was a skilled long-range pilot and naval aviator and up to that point had only been involved with larger aircraft, cracked up the unfamiliar fighter on landing in January 1927. As far as can be determined, this was the second prototype and he was able to walk away uninjured. The dihedral was reduced on the first prototype and eventually given up altogether during the course of the flight test program. From the start the second prototype (Werknummer 23) had a wing which was virtually straight.

Rohrbach permitted Udet to fly this final version, who was favorably impressed with the handling characteristics and on 1 July 1927 released an evaluation of the type. However, Udet drew attention to a few shortcomings, such as the need for more effective aileron control and better lateral stability as well as the airplane's poor-quality slip handling.

After making the appropriate changes and eliminating those problems mentioned by Udet, the Rofix was test flown and put through its paces for its official certification by J. v. Koeppen of the Deutsche Versuchsanstalt für Luftfahrt. The result of the evaluation is as follows:

The good takeoff and landing characteristics enable the airplane to be operated from smaller fields.

The aircraft displays no particular problems or dangerous tendencies in any flight attitude.

It can be easily and safely flown by any pilot of average skill.

High speed and good climb rate combine with good maneuverability so that the aircraft is well suited for its intended role.

signed J. v. Koeppen
Departmental director of the Deutsche
Versuchsanstalt für Luftfahrt e.V.

Copenhagen-Kastrup, 13 July 1927

On 15 July 1927 a serious accident occurred when Paul Bäumer, a successful fighter pilot and recipient of the Pour le Mérite, spun the plane from a great height, failed to recover and was killed. The accident was a much discussed matter among the experts at the time, and even today its cause has never been clarified for the public.

Rohrbach-Metallflugzeugbau GmbH, Berlin SW 68, Friedrichstraße 203

Report No. 59

We wish to provide the following details in the matter of the crash of Mr. Bäumer on 15 July 1927 in which this renowned combat and sport pilot unfortunately lost his life:

On 15 July 1927 Mr. Bäumer carried out his sixth flight, during which he expressed his intention of spinning the aircraft from a high altitude. He began by flying rolls at about 4000 meters. Subsequently he then put the aircraft into a spin and, after recovering, continued to fly the aircraft in level flight. When he then spun the aircraft again, he failed to pull out and crashed into the sea.

As can be seen from the attached report #58 by Mr. Tank, in which he gives an expert eyewitness report of the entire event, Mr. Bäumer presumably did not take into account that fighter aircraft of this size, i.e. with such a powerful engine and large diameter propeller, have to be spun with the engine setting at half throttle vice low throttle. This is in order to prevent the control surfaces from falling into the area shadowed from the airstream, an area which is created with such a large, slow moving propeller.

In the event that inadequate control surface pressure prevents the spinning aircraft from converting to a dive - from whence a machine can be easily recovered - these heavily powered aircraft can be forcibly leveled from a spin and pulled out by applying full throttle. This characteristic of large combat aircraft with powerful engines appears to have been lost on Mr. Bäumer, since although he applied full throttle several times, he reduced the setting immediately although the aircraft visibly righted itself. To support this argument, after an absence of many years Mr. Bäumer was in the cockpit of a combat aircraft which was significantly larger than those airplanes he had hitherto flown.

The question of whether Mr. Bäumer's nerves failed him during such a lengthy spin will probably never be answered with satisfaction. In the opinion of experts, the type of injuries sustained and other circumstances indicate that Mr. Bäumer had become unconscious prior to impact. This may also explain why he did not take to his parachute despite having released his restraining belt...

For Tank, the matter had a rather unpleasant epilogue: the firm of Rohrbach was accused of levity in the construction of a fighter aircraft and had to answer these accusations in the Haus der Luftfahrtindustrie in Berlin. Tank represented Dr. Rohrbach. He was asked how he could have possibly considered laying out an aerobatic fighter as a monoplane design. Such an aircraft could and should only be a biplane. Even the DVL representative had no objection to this viewpoint expressed by Freiherr von Mallingkrod. The old fighter pilots from World War I still could not bring themselves to put their trust in the monoplane concept. Even Junkers had had serious problems with its J7 and J9 planes. At the time it was believed that the monoplane would tip over in flight. Tank, however, pointed out to the gentlemen assembled there that one of the best performing and latest fighter aircraft of the First World War, the Fokker DVIII, was a high-wing monoplane similar to the Rofix. With its 107 kW/145 hp Oberursel UR III engine it had had a climb rate of 9.80 meters per second, more than the Rofix with 441 kW/600 hp - although the latter was weatherproof and made entirely of metal. "And they, who themselves with their squadron mates had flown this aircraft on the Front, were telling me that the high-wing design was a dangerous airplane?" After that the gentlemen had little more to say.

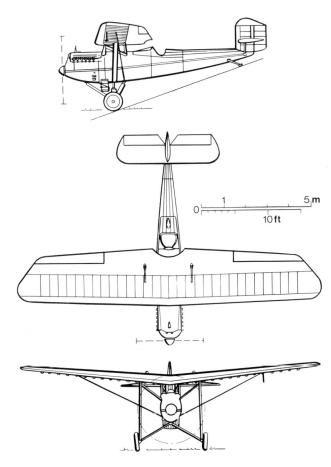

Rohrbach Ro IIIa Rodra.

Emergency Landing with the Record-Setting Ro VIIb Robbe II

The Ro VIIb Robbe II was a flying boat built for experimental and record-setting purposes. It utilized a sharply tapered wing design and had an aspect ratio of 8.40, significantly influenced by Tank's ideas. It was larger, had an enclosed cockpit and compared with Robbe I had much more powerful engines (see table) and a higher all-up weight. Experts at the time warned Rohrbach about the extreme taper to the wings and believed that because of them the flying boat would stall over onto one wing too easily. Even Werner Landmann, the test pilot, expressed his reservations about the tapered wings.

Dr. Rohrbach and Tank watched the first takeoff with much anticipation. Up to this point a reduction of 20 percent out to the wingtip was felt to be acceptable, but the Robbe II had a taper of 5:1, meaning that the chord at the

end of the wing was only 20 percent of the chord at the point where the wing joined the fuselage! In approaching a stall the airflow separated from the tip before the fuselage join, it was argued, and the aircraft would then fall over onto one wing as it stalled; there was also the danger of the aircraft then going into a spin. But Tank thought: "If the airflow separated from a rectangular wing, then the sudden increase in drag would cause forces to build up which neither the pilot nor the control surfaces could withstand. However, a wing having a tapered design such as this would enable the pilot to master these forces without difficulty because the drag would increase so little."

In a sceptical frame of mind, Werner Landmann taxied out on the maiden flight. He cautiously lifted the airplane off the water and carefully began to make the first turn. Soon, however, the people below noticed how his bias increased in favor of the plane. He made a sharp bank and, even though it was the boat's first flight, demonstrated the Robbe II's maneuverability. "Outstanding flight handling, I'm surprised", were his words upon landing.

19

Aerodynamically Refined Rohrbach Flying Boats

Manufacturer		Rohrbach	Rohrbach	Rohrbach	Rohrbach
Type		Ro VII Robbe I	RoVIIb Robbe II	Rocco Ro V	Rostra Ro XI
Powerplant		BMW IV	BMW VIa	Condor III Rolls Royce	Gnôme Rhône Jupiter VI
Performance	kW	2x169=338	2x441=882	2x478=956	2x448=896
	hp	2x230=460	2x600=1200	2x650=1300	2x610=1220
Crew(+passengers)		2+4	2+6	3+12	3+5
Length	m	13.20	15.20	18.00	15.60
Height	m	5.50	5.90	6.00	6.30
Wingspan	m	17.40	21.50	26.00	26.90
Wing area	m²	40.00	55.00	94.00	77.00
Aspect ratio		7.57	8.40	7.19	9.40
Weight, empty	kg	2000	3600	5990	4340
Fuel	kg	484	1200	1500	2450
Oil	kg	50	70	110	120
Crew	kg	160	160	240	240
Load	kg	666	650	1760	1250
Max. permissible load	kg	1360	2080	3610	4060
Takeoff weight	kg	3360	5680	9600	8400
Wing loading	kg/m²	84.00	103.27	102.13	109.09
Weight/power ratio	kg/kW	9.94	6.43	10.04	9.38
	kg/hp	7.30	4.73	7.38	6.88
	kW/m²	8.45	16.03	10.17	11.64
	hp/m²	11.50	21.82	13.82	15.84
Built		1926	1926	1927	1928
Max. speed	km/h	210	224	220	213
@ altitude	m	2000	0	0	0
Cruise speed @ sea level	km/h	180	200	170	158
Rate of climb	m/s	3.33[1]		3.00[1]	4.10[1]
Service ceiling	m	4500	4300	3200	3000
Range	km	855	1200	1300	2370
Max. flight time	hrs	4.75	6.00		
Landing speed	km/h	116	135	115	118
Max. permissible load as % of takeoff weight	40	37	38	48	
Payload as % of takeoff weight	20	11	18	15	

[1]Average rate of climb to 1000 m

The stall handling was first inadvertently demonstrated by Ernst Udet, albeit in a rather dramatic manner. He had heard of Hermann Köhl's preparations for making the first east-west Atlantic crossing and was searching for a suitably reliable aircraft for an Atlantic flight himself. During his search he paid a visit to Tank at his Kastrup branch in Copenhagen, where the Robbe II was being built (because its powerful engines violated the Treaty of Versailles) and heard that Tank was secretly planning to set long-distance records with the Robbe II. "How would it be if we com-

bined our efforts and I could use this time for preparing for an Atlantic flight?" suggested Udet.

That very evening Udet found himself sitting at the Robbe's controls with his mechanic Kern, making preparations for taking off on his first flight in a flying boat in calm seas. Tank had given him instructions beforehand, specifically pointing out that this was not some nimble little sportplane, but a heavy ship with high wing loading and high landing speeds. When making a landing, the approach had to be flown at high speeds and even with a full load would set down on the water at 135 km/h. Udet took off and all seemed to be going well at first. But on his landing approach, Tank noticed that he was flying much too slowly. His heart rose into his throat - already the heavy boat had stalled at a height of about 50 meters and smacked violently into the water. A massive plume of spray shot up and for a moment the boat disappeared completely. Then, as if nothing untoward had happened, the boat surfaced again. The only damage was a bent float brace. Tank, however, was overjoyed and forgot all about how angry he was with Udet. For now he had concrete evidence that, as the aircraft stalled, it didn't fall off onto one wing, but transitioned smoothly into a straight stall.

About three weeks later the two set out on their record-setting flight, Udet at the controls and Tank sitting to his right with tables, slide rule and charts on his knees. Tank made sure that Udet didn't pull the overloaded plane (2500 kg fuel, ballast simulating the weight of 11 passengers and cargo) off the water or climb too slowly. They anticipated a flight of ten hours, covering some 2000 km. Between Copenhagen and the Swedish coast they thrice flew a predesignated triangular course with spectators from the FAI looking on. Below, the judges marked the turning points with their stopwatches, while in the machine Tank calculated and marked with his stopwatch. His tables showed the most favorable rpm setting and speed for every part of their flight route in order to get the best performance from the two BMW VI engines without overloading them. Suddenly there was a loud noise, the engines began howling fiercely and the airplane began bucking. Using their combined strength, both pilots managed to keep the boat under control for a few moments, then suddenly it nosed over steeply. Before either knew what was happening, the huge machine struck the water's surface. "Fire!" shouted Udet, unbuckled his harness and bolted for the wing. Tank and the mechanic followed a bit more slowly and once out on the wing turned around to survey the damage: "Both propellers were gone. Emergency landing without engine power in an overloaded airplane, and it was still afloat!" In actual fact the boat had indeed suffered only minor damage. They extinguished the burning fuel, leaking from the tanks ruptured by the propeller fragments. The dream of setting a world record, of crossing the Atlantic, had vanished.

Ro VIIb Robbe II with two 441 kW (600 hp) BMW VIa engines and extremely slender wings, the aircraft in which Udet had aspirations of flying the Atlantic Ocean.

Lufthansa Tests the Ro V Rocco

The Ro V Rocco from 1927 was an elegant shoulder-wing design with a sharply tapered nose, pronounced dihedral and an aerodynamically refined fuselage shape - just as Tank had envisioned. The wing chord tapered outward along the wing. The cabin could accommodate ten to twelve passengers comfortably. The two Rolls Royce Condor engines, each with an output of 478 kW/650 hp and driving tractor propellers, were laid out like the majority of Rohrbach's flying boats - side-by-side and above the wings on supports. The coolers were located under the wings initially, but were later designed as head coolers and relocated in front of the engines. The fuel was carried in the wings, which were braced to the fuselage by two struts on each side.

The sole aircraft built, Werknummer 26, was handed over to the secret military base of Severa (from See*flugzeug-Versuchsanstalt*, or Flying boat Experimental Facility), where it was used for training flying boat pilots.

In 1929 Lufthansa assumed possession of the Rocco under the designation D-1261 to be used for experimental flights, and in May of 1929 it was sent to the E*rprobungsstelle* Travemünde. In 1932 it was written off charge.

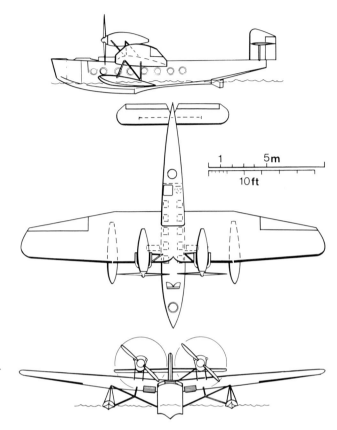

Ro V Rocco

Ro V Rocco seaplane with two Rolls Royce Condor engines, each outputting 478 kW (650 hp); Lufhansa borrowed this airplane for a time in 1929 for the purpose of carrying out a series of test flights.

Rohrbach Ro VIII Roland

Although Dr. Rohrbach was fanatically involved in the design and construction of flying boats, he achieved his greatest success with a land-based aircraft design. Close cooperation between Rohrbach, Steiger and Tank resulted in his design bureau producing for a Lufthansa order a modern, high-speed three-engined commercial airliner, the Ro VIII Roland. The construction of the design rested in the hands of chief design engineer Steiger. Tank, asked about the thinking which led to the Roland's layout as a high-wing design, replied: "We chose a semi-cantilever shoulder-wing design in order to provide the passengers with an unrestricted downward view, something which the other airplanes could not offer. We also wanted to keep the propellers as high as possible off the ground to prevent rock damage. The engines were mounted under the wings in order to achieve an uninterrupted flow of air over the upper surfaces."

Dr. Rohrbach used the Staaken four-engined monoplane as a role model. Although built in 1919, it had to be destroyed on the orders of the Allied Control Commission due to the ban on construction after the First World War.

The airplane's wings were of a rectangular design, with rounded tips and having a relatively constant chord. With an eye towards saving weight, they were braced to the fuselage underside with an aerodynamically shrouded cable. The cable was tensioned in such a way that the fluctuations in the wing spar emanating from the forces of the air and the tension balanced out as much as possible, placing a minimal load on the wing during flight.

Initially, the Roland I's cockpit was open and had dual controls. The cabin offered seating for ten passengers, was soundproofed and fitted with heating and a toilet. The landing gear, with its remarkably large wheels, was braced to the wings. The center engine was located in the fuselage nose, while the outboard engines were housed in nacelles jutting forward from the wing. During the design stages, the adjustable box coolers changed their positions often, but were always located beneath the wings. Three 235 kW/320 hp BMW IV engines served as powerplants. For ease of maintenance, the fuel was carried in the partially extendable leading edge wing sections.

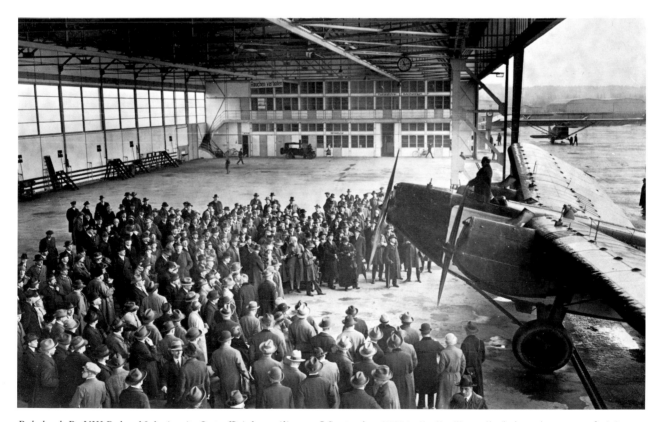

Rohrbach Ro VIII Roland I during its first official unveiling on 5 September 1926 in Berlin-Tempelhof; the twin open cockpit is seen here to good effect.

In order to seal off the last remaining aerodynamic stumbling blocks, Tank had built a cockpit canopy for the Roland, although this feature was not accepted by Lufthansa. However, when the pilot Baur complained about the cold air which the crew had to endure while making alpine crossings, Tank sent out a canopy from the warehouse. Soon the other pilots had similar canopies and it wasn't long before all Roland aircraft were flying with the planned "glass roof".

With the aircraft still under construction, Lufthansa reviewed the company documents once again and invited Dr. Rohrbach, Steiger and Tank to a meeting. During the course of the discussion Lufthansa technicians complained about the Roland's high wing loading of 80 kg/m2, saying it was too dangerous and unmanageable for the crew. Lufthansa could not accept any airplane which had a wing loading greater than 60 kg/m^2. (Today's Airbus flies with Lufthansa having a wing loading of 500 kg/m^2 to 600 kg/m^2!) Rohrbach and his engineers were astounded at Lufthansa's shortsightedness with regard to the trends in the development of larger airplanes. Dr. Rohrbach argued convincingly that for larger aircraft the wing loading increased with aircraft size in accordance with the law of similarity in ship design. Accordingly, the result of reduced external aircraft dimensions was a much more gradual increase in airframe weight with an increase in aircraft size. The extremely high payload percentage of 18 percent with a full fuel load (Airbus: 16 percent) could only be achieved

with an aircraft built to modern laws such as the Roland. Dr. Rohrbach continued by pointing out that a greater wing loading also led to an increase in speed. This became critical, for ultimately commercial airliners were still flying at cruising speeds between 140 km/h and 160 km/h. However, the Lufthansa technicians weren't interested in any of these points. They wanted to have the Roland contract annulled if a concerted effort weren't made to bring the wing loading down to 60 kg/m^2.

Deeply disappointed, the Rohrbach team left Lufthansa. Reducing the wing loading meant increasing the size of the wing. Increasing the wingspan was out of the question because work on the wing had already been completed. The costs incurred by such an action would put the company in dire financial straits. It would be just as difficult to change the established contours of the wing box as it would be to change the fuselage/wing joint. Yet Tank was able to find an alternative. Day and night he spent working on calculations and discussing the matter with chief designer Steiger,

Rohrbach Ro VIII Roland II with three 265 kW (360 hp) BMW Va engines and having an enclosed cockpit with the side panes of the canopy set quite low down on the fuselage nose.

until the two appeared to have found an acceptable solution: they increased the wing chord toward the trailing edge. This was able to be implemented without incurring any great costs. And although the wing surface area certainly increased, the drag buildup was minimal and this accordingly had only a minor effect on airspeed. Tank accordingly spent considerable time in tedious detail work removing any and all imperfections from the wing surface. As he was finishing up, he noticed the massive hole in the fuselage nose where the pilots sat. If he could succeed in closing this off, it might be possible to adhere to the calculated speed figures. As a result, Tank designed a canopy for the pilot's compartment so that the crew sat beneath and enclosed glass roof and was protected from the air draft. Not only that, but the vortices generated along the upper fuselage virtually disappeared. Rohrbach was extremely pleased with Tank's efficient work which resulted in the Roland fulfilling Lufthansa's requirements. Increasing the wing without changing its basic design and contours was a master stroke,

without which the successful Roland would have been nothing more than a stillborn child.

The Roland I was involved in a serious accident during the acceptance flights carried out by Lufthansa. Factory test pilot Hermann Steindorff was at the controls and *Flugkapitän* Polte sat unbuckled next to him as the Lufthansa representative. Steindorff insisted that Polte buckle up, which the latter reluctantly did. During takeoff the aircraft had to roll through some large water puddles. In so doing, the plane lost some of its speed, for which Steindorff attempted to compensate by applying full throttle. This in turn caused the tail to lift off on the uneven surface and the airplane tipped over on its nose. The entire nose assembly including its engine broke off and the pilots found themselves suspended high in the air - ahead of them was the windscreen and instrument panel and the engine resting on the ground. Had Polte not strapped himself in, he most certainly would have slammed into the instruments and suffered severe injuries as a result.

25

Rohrbach Landplanes

Manufacturer		Zeppelinwerke Staaken		Rohrbach	
Type		Staaken 1000hp commercial acft	Ro VIII Roland I	Ro VIII Roland II	Ro IX Rofix
Powerplant		Maybach MB IVa	BMW IV	BMW Va	BMW VI
Performance	kW	4x191=764	3x169=507	3x265=795	441
	hp	4x260=1040	3x230=690	3x360=1080	600
Crew(+passengers)		2+12	2+10	2+10	1
Length	m	16.50	16.30	16.40	9.50
Height	m	5.20	4.50	4.50	3.70
Wingspan	m	31.00	26.00	26.30	14.00
Wing area	m^2	106.00	88.00	89.00	28.00
Aspect ratio		9.10	7.70	7.77	7.00
Weight, empty	kg	6072	3365	4400	1320
Fuel	kg	1100	745	800	330
Oil	kg	100	50	55	75
Crew	kg	160	160	160	80
Load	kg	1068	945	1200	45
Max. permissible load	kg	2428	1900	2215	530
Takeoff weight	kg	8500	5265	6615	1850
Wing loading	kg/m^2	80.18	59.82	74.33	66.07
Weight/power ratio	kg/kW	11.12	10.38	8.32	4.19
	kg/hp	8.17	7.63	6.13	3.08
	kW/m^2	7.21	5.76	8.93	15.75
	hp/m^2	9.81	7.84	12.13	21.43
Built		1920	1926	1927	1926
Max. speed @ sea level	km/h	225	195	220	260[2]
Cruise speed @ sea level	km/h	180	175	180	230
Rate of climb	m/s		2.40[2]	3.00[2]	8.33[2]
Service ceiling	m	4000	5500	4600	7500
Range	km	1100	875	900	700
Max. flight time	hrs	6.00	5.00	5.00	3.00
Takeoff run	m	200			
Landing run	m	200			
Landing speed	km/h	110	100	105	105
Max. permissible load as % of takeoff weight		29	36	33	29
Payload as % of takeoff weight		13	18	18	2

[1] Average rate of climb to 1000 m
[2] 285 km/h at 3000 m

26

The Roland was soon flying the long-range routes: Berlin-Paris, Königsberg. It was employed n the difficult Alpine routes from Munich to Milan and Rome.

Experience in flight operations flowed into a follow-on development known as the Roland II, of which nine were contracted for and delivered between 1929 and 1930. The Roland II showed many significant improvements over its predecessor. The wing spar no longer ran through the cabin, but ended at the fuselage. This increased the area in the cabin considerably, which was also extended aft. The necessary measure of enclosing the cockpit under a canopy was replaced by a total glazing of the pilot's compartment, blending it fully into the contours of the fuselage profile. The center engine was lowered in order to provide better visibility from the cockpit. The engine nacelle design was changed and the outboard engine coolers were moved to the lower outboard wing sections. Finally, much more powerful BMW Va engines were employed, each having an output of 265 kW/360 hp, increasing the airplane's takeoff weight and improving its range (see tables).

The many records established by the Roland shouldn't be forgotten, either. Steindorff began 1926 with five records, with more following in the summer of 1927. In the end, the Roland set 22 records with high payloads over long distances, including endurance, altitude and speed breakers. To name but one, the Roland flew a distance of 1750 km in 10 hours and 32 minutes with a 2000 kg payload (equating to 20 passengers and their luggage).

The Ro XI Rostra Long-Range Transatlantic Flying Boat

The Robbe II came up in discussion on another occasion with the planning of yet another Atlantic crossing. One day an American by the name of Mildred Johnson called on Dr. Rohrbach and showed him numerous believable letters of intent which included a promise that an American city would pay her $10000 if she would fly across the Atlantic from Europe to the United States. A cigarette company ensured the same amount for a bit of advertising on the fuselage and wings and other promises of like nature combined to provide a sum with which it would be entirely possible to finance a transoceanic flight. Dr. Rohrbach thought of his record-setting Robbe II, which lay disassembled in a hangar. If the two BMW VI engines were traded for Jupiter VI motors and the wing center section modified appropriately, it would be possible to increase the fuel capacity by a considerable amount, making an Atlantic flight entirely within the realm of possibility. For Rohrbach and

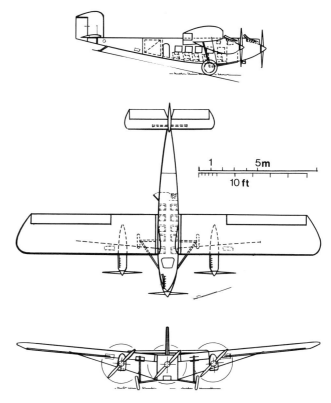

Rohrbach Ro VIII Roland I.

his flying boats this would be a great bit of advertising, which might lead to future contracts.

The application met with some initial success. Rohrbach tackled the matter, had the Robbe II pulled out of mothballs, the wing center section modified and contracted with the French for the Gnôme Rhône Jupiter VI engines. These modifications to the Robbe II led to a new name for the aircraft, the Rostra. With these changes the Ro XI showed every promise of becoming an attractive long-range, cargo or postal flying boat. It had a payload capacity of 1250 kg which it could carry over 2370 km, for its maximum permissable load was an impressive 48 percent. With full tanks the payload percentage was 15 percent of the takeoff weight. The flying boat promised excellent economic results. With reduced payload the range could even be increased to 3500 km and in an overloaded configuration it was capable of ranges which made an Atlantic crossing entirely possible.

However, after the BMW engines had been traded for the Jupiters, it was found that the new motors were not able to attain the maximum performance which the official documents from the French guaranteed. A takeoff in an overloaded configuration mandated engines which could pro-

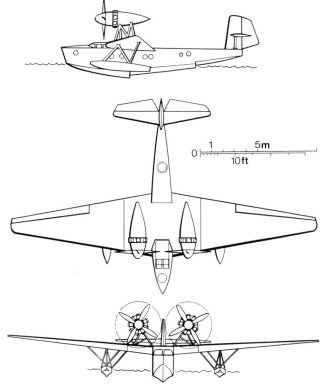

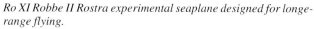

duce their maximum output. The French company sent out mechanics and engineers, but the takeoff power of the engines remained well below their guaranteed values. Rohrbach had invested 800000 RM for the purchase of the engines and the modifications. Now, however, the idea of a planned Atlantic crossing had fallen through,. Mildred Johnson had to pay nothing and the flying boat was not marketable.

In the early stages of the Rostra's construction Lufthansa showed considerable interest and would gladly have made use of the boat on a trial basis over its southern Atlantic routes (Azores-Bermuda). But this, too, would have required maximum engine performance.

Ro XI Robbe II Rostra experimental seaplane designed for longe-range flying.

Rohrbach Ro XI Rostra with two French air-cooled Gnôme Rhône Jupiter VI engine, each rated at 331 kW (450 hp).

Ro X Romar Super Flying Boat

Rohrbach and his colleagues had great expectations for the Ro X Romar flying boat. Tank praised the handling characteristics of this giant boat, with a wingspan of nearly 40 meters and an all-up weight varying between 14 to 19 metric tons; it responded to control inputs like a fighter plane and additionally demonstrated good handling qualities on takeoff and landing.

the flying boat was designed for long distance flights up to 4000 km and in addition to the four crew members could carry mail and cargo, later adding twelve passengers and their luggage as well. The pilot's compartment was to be an enclosed design from the beginning. The twelve seat cabin was laid out in a comfortable manner and equipped with heating, kitchen and toilet.

This aircraft, too, had sharply tapered wings. Riveting on the wings' surfaces was kept closely spaced along the wing spars, a feature designed to keep the boat afloat for a relatively long period of time in the event of it being damaged. Plans initially called for utilization of the BMW VI U with gearing, later designated as the BMW VIIa U improved version. In 1927/28, however, this engine was not yet ready for delivery, and the less powerful BMW VI was therefore installed. The three engines were mounted above the wings on support braces and drove four-bladed wooden pusher propellers having a diameter of 4.50 meters. The coolant water's temperature could be lowered using sea water when taxiing for long periods via intermediate radiators. The wing tanks were able to hold up to 8300 liters of fuel. The engines were started by means of a gas-pressure ignition system.

Flight testing began on 7 August 1928. The unusual location of the engines initially caused changes in trim around the pitch axis when increasing or reducing throttle. This quirkiness was eliminated by making changes to the control surfaces.

Rohrbach Ro X Romar I with three BMW VI engines having front radiators and four-bladed propellers (Werknummer 29).

Further testing was completed satisfactorily, despite the fact that minor changes had to be carried out here and there. Eventually, a problem with the aircraft yawing was corrected by enlarging the vertical stabilizer to the point where the airplane was stable in all axes. If one of the outboard engines were to fail a relief system could be activated which enabled the aircraft to continue flying straight and level without the pilot having to wrestle with the controls. Tank himself, along with other pilots who test flew the Romar, repeatedly praised the huge ship's maneuverability and its good flight handling characteristics.

Weights and Ranges for the Rohrbach Romar

Manufacturer		Rohrbach Metallflugzeugbau				
Type		Ro X Romar I				Ro X Romar II
Powerplant		BMW VI[1] 1:7.3				BMW VII aU
Performance	kW	3x515=1545				3x551=1653
	hp	3x700=2100				3x750=2250
Crew(+passengers)		4+12	4+10	4+cargo[5]	4+cargo	4+cargo
Length	m		22.55			
Height	m		8.47			
Wingspan	m		36.90			
Wing area	m²		170.00			
Aspect ratio			8.00			
Weight, empty	kg	11080	11080	11400	10575[6]	11620
Fuel	kg	6000	6815	1220	6000	6160
Oil	kg	400	360	360	360	360
Crew	kg	320	320	320	320	320
Load	kg	1200	925	1200	1245	1240
Max. permissible load	kg	7920	8420	3100	7925	8080
Takeoff weight	kg	19000	19500	14500[4]	18500	19700
Wing loading	kg/m²	111.76	114.71	85.29	108.82	115.88
Weight/power ratio	kg/kW	12.30	12.62	9.39	11.97	11.92
	kg/hp	9.05	9.29	6.90	8.81	8.76
	kW/m²	9.09	9.09	9.09	9.09	9.72
	hp/m²	12.35	12.35	12.35	12.35	13.24
Max. speed @ sea level	km/h	206	206	206	190	228
Cruise speed	km/h	128[2]	173[3]	173	165	209
@ an altitude of	m	500	0	0	0	0
Rate of climb	m/s	2.00	1.66	3.33	1.05	4.06
Service ceiling	m	2000	2600	3800	2060[7]	2800
Range	km	4102[2]	4000[3]	800	—	4066
Max. flight time	hrs	32.05	25.80	5.00	—	20.33[8]
Landing speed	km/h	106	106	106	106	106
Max. permissible load as % of takeoff weight		42	43	21	43	41
Payload as % of takeoff weight	6	5	8	7	6	
Built		1927	1927	1927	1927	1929

With a flying weight of 15300 kg the Romar required a takeoff time of 29 seconds with a headwind of 3 meters per second. At a takeoff weight of 18500 kg the Romar, even with a crosswind, lifted off so well that ultimately takeoff trials were carried out with a weight of 20000 kg with no reservations. In addition, experiments were conducted with one of the outboard engines shut down, during which the flying boat needed 40 seconds to lift off with a headwind of 2-3 meters per second. At a takeoff weight of 15000 kg the machine climbed to 1000 meters in five minutes, corresponding to a climb rate of 3.33 m/sec. According to Rohrbach's data, the fuel consumption rate was 284 kilograms per hour at a speed of 171 km/h. Subsequent flight testing by Lufthansa, however, revealed a lower cruising speed and higher fuel consumption - and a correspondingly degraded range.

Impressed with the good results of the flight test program, Lufthansa placed an order for three flying boats at the end of August 1928; it planned to utilize these aircraft to cross the Atlantic in stages via Lisbon, the Canaries and the Cape Verde Islands to Fernando Noronna, from where they would continue to Rio de Janeiro and Buenos Aires. The route was expected to be crossed with a payload of one metric ton. The price of 3618000 RM was agreed upon for the three boats, of which 1518000 RM would be financed by the Reichsverkehrsministerium.

On 11 and 13 December 1928 the Romar's much anticipated seaworthiness trials took place before representatives from the Reichsverkehrsministerium, Lufthansa and the Deutsche Versuchsanstalt für Luftfahrt. The test required a takeoff weight of 14500 kg and seas of 5. However, on that day the seas were force 6 and more. Yet the boat ac-

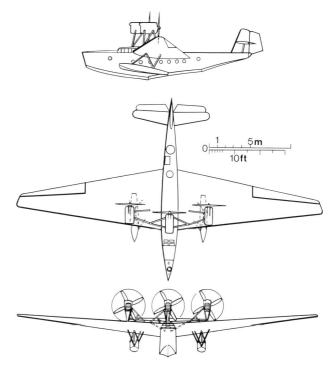

Ro X Romar I heavy lift flying boat.

quitted itself magnificently. According to Tank, at one time the heavy seas threw the boat eight or ten meters into the air. It slammed back down onto the water's surface - and held together. The flying boat later took off further out in the open sea in cross swells. The lateral forces damaged one of the struts on the starboard float. The boat leaned

[1]Based on ZFM 2/1928 p.46 according to company data:
BMW VI compression ratio 1:7.3
reduction gearing 1.6:1

max. output	kW/hp	515/700
shaft	rpm	1650
propeller	rpm	970
average sustained output	kW/hp	368/500
shaft	rpm	1530
propeller		870
fuel: benzol/gasoline		80/20
specific consumption	g/hp/h	215

[2]The speed and range values given here have been recalculated by Prof. Kurt Tank based on data for the BMW VI and Rohrbach company data (ZFM 2/1928 p.46 ff. and ZFM 1929 p.152). These calculations take into account the optimum flight configuration for maximum range and apply the continuously changing values for speed and weight.

[3]Performance, range and weight information compiled based on company data iaw ZFM 6/1928 p.152. 25.8 flying hours would correspond to an average fuel consumption of 264.14 kg/367 l at a speed of 155 km/h.
[4] With a takeoff weight of 14500 kg and in Force 5 conditions, sea trials were carried out before representatives from the Reichsverkehrsministerium, Lufthansa and the DVL in Travemünde on 11 and 13 December 1928. All the data and performance figures released by the company consistently refer to a takeoff weight of 14500 kg, which in the best case scenario resulted in a range of 800 km.
[5]Data taken from Jane's 1930 edition, p.171c and company information. Data for ranges are missing.
[6]Data for empty weight is 505 kg less than other company data. For passenger service the flying boat was only authorized a takeoff weight of 14500 kg. At higher weights it could only be used for cargo, with the passenger accommodations being removed from the cabin.
[7]Absolute ceiling.
[8]Assuming a cruising performance of 331 kW/450 hp at a fuel consumption rate of 225 g/hp/hr (equating to 303 kg/420 l for the three engines), the aircraft would therefore have an endurance of 20.33 hrs (6160:303=20.33) with a range of some 4060 km at a cruising speed of 200 km/h.

over onto the crippled side so that the right wing cut into the water, but the boat righted itself and returned to the harbor under its own power, where the bent strut was replaced. Taxiing into the harbor in rough seas in a cross wind, with towering swells smashing into the hull, was one of the most difficult situations a flying boat could face. It effectively ensured that the Romar passed its sea trials. It was certified with a takeoff weight of 15 tons in force 5 seas when carrying passengers and to 19 tons with cargo or mail in force 3 seas.

On 17 April 1929 test pilot H. Steindorff set a new world record when he lifted a payload of 6450 kg to an altitude of 2000 m. Type testing was completed at the DVL on 25 July 1929. The first Ro X Romar with Werknummer 29 and coded D-1693 was christened with the name "Hamburg", certified in July of 1929 and delivered to Lufthansa. D-1734 "Bremen" with Werknummer 30 was certified in August of that year and was also immediately pressed into service as a passenger airliner. D-1747 "Lübeck" (Werknummer 31) eventually followed its stablemates in November 1929.

Lufthansa initially carried out several test flights from Travemünde to Stockholm and back. The 1700 km long route was covered in 11 hours and 20 minutes at an average speed of 150 km/h. On 20 August 1929 there followed a five-nation flight from Travemünde along the Dutch coast to Norwich and Hull, then in an easterly direction across the North Sea to Oslo and back to Travemünde via Copenhagen. The route, totaling a distance of 2680 km, was completed in just 17 hours with an average airspeed of 158 km/h.

These figures showed that the cruising speed differed from that given by the company, which was 178 km/h, and the 154 km/h average speed actually flown by 18 km/h. Rohrbach explained that this was attributable to engines which had not yet been delivered; these engines had reduction gearing and were also more powerful. The motors currently being used had been fitted with Lufthansa's approval.

In 1929 the French government ordered a Romar II flying boat, payment which was to be charged to its reparations account, i.e. deducted from Germany's war debt. This Romar II was delivered to France in April 1931, fitted with 1.8 mm thick plates at the high-stress point on the boat hull just ahead of the first step. By that time - the machine was built two years after the Romar I - the more powerful BMW VIIa engines had become available. This engine differed from the BMW VI only in having a stronger crankshaft and roller bearings for the master connecting rod, plus improvements with the ignition system and equipment. Both motor types had variants with compression ratios of 7.3, 6.0 and 5.5. Takeoff rating for the BMW VIIa U with Farman gearing was claimed by the company (in ZFM 1928, p.593) to be 555 kW/755 hp at 1650 rpm, with the propeller having an rpm of 1024; the engine's cruise performance was 441 kW/600 hp at 1530 rpm.

The company claimed a significantly higher speed for the Romar II, a claim which was entirely believable given the fact that the engines were higher performing and the propeller effectiveness rating was certainly better given the gearing system. These factors meant that the intended range was closer to being realized, even with a significant increase in speed.

However, due to his extensive activities at Rohrbach Tank was able to see problems with the flying boat concept at an early stage, and in particular experienced its dependence on the sea state first hand. Summing up his many years of work in this aviation medium, in 1929 he stated simply: "In the international airline market the flying boat no longer stands a chance."

The difficult seaworthiness trials of the Robbe, Rocco and Romar made it clear that a flying boat is at risk when taking off and landing in force 5 gales or greater. Experiments had shown that in stormy conditions on the high seas a flying boat breaks up just as a ditched landplane does. The heavy boat's weight affects the payload able to be carried and its large hull cuts into airspeed. A landplane, designed with four or more reliable engines, would still remain airborne with 50 percent of its engines out, offering at least the same safety factor over water as a flying boat. However, a landplane was much more flexible and achieved nearly double the airspeed of a flying boat.

Looking back, Tank considers Adlof Rohrbach one of the most advanced designers of his day. Even then, his construction principles for achieving greater ranges, better economy and safety showed the way that aircraft design would have to follow over the next few decades in order to attain the success it enjoys today. Appropriately enough, even nowadays Tank reflects with fond gratitude on the six years he spent in close cooperation with Rohrbach.

Rohrbach's small production runs and the looming economic crisis, however, caused Tank to fear for the future of the Rohrbach-Werke. It was therefore understandable that the young, talented engineer and test pilot sought work with a company which focused on the design and construction of landplanes.

Model of a planned follow-on development of the Romar with two engines in tandem, giving it a total of four engines.

During a stormy night in November 1928 the Romar (Werknummer 30) tore free together with its 850 kg anchor buoy and floundered about the Pötenitzer Wieck, where it eventually beached itself and was found the next morning - unscathed.

BMW Engines of the 'Twenties and 'Thirties

Engine	Length	Height	Width	Volume	Compression	Dry weight	Start output	Sustained weight	Specific output	Consumption	Comments
	m	m	m	l		kg	@ altitude	kg/kW	g/kW/h		
# of cylinders	Bore mm	Stroke mm			Installed wt.	RPM hp	RPM hp	kg/hp	g/hp/h cruising perf.		
BMW IV 6	1.55 160	1.02 190	0.5	22.9	6 also 7.2	283 445	0-3500 1650 220 300	1.28 1450 184 250	30 0.94	5 225	The older BMW IV in the Ro VII Robbe I had a starting output of just 169 kW/ 230hp
BMW Va 6	1.795 160	1.133 190	0.635	22.92	6	317	1650 271 370	1565 235 320	1.17 0.86	299 220	High- altitude engine, could be flown 1 hr at max. output.
BMW VI 12	2.036 160	1.103 190	0.859	46.95	6	505 840	1650 515 700	0-1000 1530 368 500	0.98 0.72	306 215	1.6:1 reduction
BMW VII all 12	2025 160	1.045 190	0.846	46.95	7.3	615	1650 551 750	0 1530 441 600	1.12 0.82	306 225	With Farman 2:1 or 1.61:1 re duction gearing
BMW VI U 12	1.937 160	1.103 190	0.859	46.95	7.3	542	1700 551 750	0-1000 1530 489 550	0.98 0.72	306 225	minus hub

Intermezzo at Messerschmitt

In January 1930 Tank became director of the project department at the Bayerische Flugzeugwerke in Augsburg at a time when Messerschmitt's company was suffering the repercussions of a rash of accidents. During flight testing of the M 20 at the hands of the famous and skilled pilot Hans Hackmack the aircraft began fluttering strongly. The wing trailing edge separated, as did the rudder. Although the pilot bailed out, his parachute caught on the empennage and he was killed in the crash.

Lufthansa, which had contracted for the airplane, was quite upset about the accident and Tank found himself answering to Lufthansa director Milch, despite having absolutely nothing to do with the aircraft or the accident. Tank, however, proved that both the aircraft as well as the control surfaces clearly were in adherence with the construction guidelines of the day.

Nevertheless, the stress tolerances for rudders at the time were set too low. Tank mentioned to Milch: "At Rohrbach, had we laid out the rudders of our twin-engined aircraft in accordance with the standard stiffness requirements they would have been ripped apart in blustery weather when flying on one engine. We deliberately made them overstrong."

Shortly afterward Tank was sitting with factory test pilot Mohnicke, who had test flown the M 22, in order to learn more about the aircraft and its flying qualities. The airplane, built in 1930, was a biplane with two 389 kW/530 hp Jupiter VI radial engines mounted between the wings. It could have been an enlarged version of BFW's Marabu. The M 22 had its origins in a Reichswehr developmental contract. Such contracts were awarded from time to time to the aviation industry on a modest basis in order to keep technical pace with foreign developments and, if necessary, be able to build its own bomber. In the Soviet town of Lipetsk such prototypes were usually armed and there tested for their military suitability.

Mohnicke discussed the goals of the airplane's flight program with Tank. Afterward, he walked out to the airplane to carry out yet another test flight. Tank waited behind with Mohnicke's wife.

The pilot took off from Augsburg's old airfield and flew south toward Landsberg. Using a telescope Tank followed the unusual twin-engined biplane - so out of place in Messerschmitt's world of ultralight designs and refined aerodynamics. After awhile he heard the machine returning to base. Mohnicke approached the airfield from the south in a shallow, high-speed dive. Suddenly, Tank was horrified to see the airplane become blurred, swell up and virtually come to a standstill - it literally flew apart in the air! Once again, it was the dangerous flutter which was the culprit. A cry escaped from Frau Mohnicke's lips. Her husband jumped from the bursting wreck, but the parachute didn't open fully in time; Mohnicke fell into the trees ringing the airfield. The parachute, expanding at the last moment, draped itself over Mohnicke's body and became his death shroud.

Two major accidents in so short a time! Professor Messerschmitt was puzzled. At the time, he considered pulling out of the company and giving up aviation design altogether. It was only through the efforts of his colleagues that he was persuaded from this course of action. He could have had no idea of knowing that just a few months later, in October 1930, an M 20b (D-1930, Werknummer 443) which Lufthansa had only reluctantly purchased, would crash because of rudder structural failure and cost the life of twelve people. In April 1931 a third M 20 (D-1928) crashed, although this time most of the occupants were fortunate enough to have escaped with their lives. Subsequent investigation confirmed Tank's earlier report to Milch in which the M 20's rudder fully complied with structural soundness regulations. Yet the structural integrity was insufficient to cope with strong winds.

The Bayerische Flugzeugwerke company folded. Aviation design continued, albeit on a much more modest scale, with the Messerschmitt which had existed within the BFW.

Tank, an experienced pilot, had different ideas than Messerschmitt about aircraft construction. He was unable to unconditionally follow Messerschmitt's demands that the ultralight concept be applied as the fundamental principle in every situation. It seemed to Tank that the then-standard design load requirements were not borne out by theory and experiment when they were applied to steadily increasing aircraft weights. The consequence of this thinking was his separation from Messerschmitt in September of 1931.

A Home at Focke-Wulf

In November that same year Tank assumed director-ship of the design department and flight testing at Focke-Wulf in Bremen. In early 1932 the company numbered approximately 150 workers. With the acquisition of the Albatros company, a merger which transpired without a hitch, the Focke-Wulf Klages-Bansemir design team was joined by R. Blaser, Dr. Cassens, Dr. Müller and a host of other designers from Albatros. When Tank came over from Messerschmitt, he brought with him an engineer by the name of Mittelhüber, who was subsequently to enjoy considerable fame in the aviation design world.

Fw 39(S 39) Reconnaissance Aircraft

At first, Tank devoted all his energy to test flying, particularly those aircraft designs acquired from Albatros. His goal was to imbue those aircraft with the same qualities which were common to all the aircraft Tank evaluated: sensitive controls, the ability to respond quickly to control inputs, stability in all axes, friendly stall handling, simple take-off and easy landing characteristics. Among those airplanes which Tank so closely supervised was the Fw 39 (S 39) reconnaissance aircraft (Werknummer 98), the design for which fell to Dipl.-Ing. Bansemir. The two-seat braced high-wing airplane was of composite construction and was first built in 1931. It had an air-cooled 375 kW/510 hp Siemens Jupiter VI engine. The fuel quantity was sufficient for three hours' flight time, giving it a range of about 600 km. The radial engine was shrouded beneath a NACA cowling. The airplane's wings, which had a slight sweep, were braced by V struts.

The airplane was certified under the registration D-1708 in 1932. In 1937 it appeared as the Fw 39B with the code D-IQIM at the Erprobungsstelle Rechlin. There are also reports that it put in a guest appearance with the Deutsche Verkehrsfliegerschule (DVS). During training there, it was reputedly damaged, then later scrapped. Unfortunately, no details or data have survived. Prof. Tank had little further involvement with the type which he'd invested so much

Fw 39 (S 39), prototype of a reconnaissance design which Focke-Wulf had taken over with the fusion of Albatros.

effort without any appreciable results. For example, he was only partially successful in counteracting the rudder forces - despite several flights and a number of changes.

Fw 40(A 40) Reconnaissance Aircraft

The Fw 40(A 40) was not - as has erroneously been reported elsewhere - a follow-on development of the Fw 39, rather it was an entirely new design by Ing. Klages which actually bore a closer resemblance to Heinkel's He 46. Both aircraft were based on a requirement for a tactical recon-

naissance aircraft with good visibility. The landing gear of the high-wing design, built of wood and metal, was fitted with high-quality spats. The Fw 40 was built in 1932, carried the registration D-1908 and Werknummer 99. It was later coded D-IJEF and handed over to the Berlin test center at Staaken. Without a doubt, the Fw 40 displayed better handling characteristics than the Fw 39. It was used as a weather plane up until the mid-30s after it lost out to Heinkel's He 46 design in a competition due to the latter's excellent visibility and good flight handling. No less than 443 He 46 airplanes were built as Army reconnaissance platforms.

Fw 40 (A 40) with an uncowled Jupiter engine. It later served as a weather reconnaissance aircraft.

AL 101 as a trainer with the DVL (year of design: 1930)

Albatros L 101 Sportplane

Other Albatros aircraft which Tank flew were the L 101 and L 102. These aircraft were built by Focke-Wulf after the takeover of Albatros. The two-seat L 101 trainer was a braced high-wing design made of composite materials (metal and wood) and was powered by the 75 kW/100 hp Argus AS 8 engine. Construction was completed in 1930. The Beschaffungsamt (Office of Procurement) issued a contract for 83 aircraft of this type. The aircraft conformed to the standard Group K 5 structural requirements and was fully aerobatic certified. "A nice little sportplane with neat flight handling characteristics", was Tank's comment after his first flight. But a few changes still needed to be made.

Cheating Death in the L 102

The L 102 was a follow-on development of the L 101, having a much more powerful 176 kW/240 hp engine and wider application. Fifteen contracts were placed for the type.

To check its flutter safety, Tank pushed the plane into a dive from an altitude of 4000 m in order to hold the plane at its maximum speed for a period of time. At 2000 meters' altitude he broke through the layer of turbulence at which point the airflow would cause asymmetrical aileron oscillations and unrestrained torsional oscillations in the wings. At any moment the aileron might tear away or the wing might collapse. Tank, however, was the master of the situation: "Racing toward the ground in the shuddering craft, keeping the speed from dropping off as much as possible." And, fixed on the airfield, he plummeted earthward. As he pulled up just above the ground, the wing's torsion strap broke. With a loud bang parts of the wing began flying off. In a slip-like attitude the L 102 smacked into the ground.

A dead silence! Tank checked and found that he was still fully conscious. The wreck could go up in flames at any moment. With superhuman effort he concentrated all his strength into extracting himself from the tangled mess of wires, twisted metal and fabric. And succeeded. A mighty heave and Tank was free of the wreckage, running away from the airplane. He had apparently suffered little in the crash, for his legs and arms and hands were all working

While flying the AL 102 L (Fw 55 L) trainer, Tank suffered a broken wing during flight testing when the plane began oscillating violently during landing.

AL 102 W/Fw 55 W trainer for providing pilots with experience with seaplanes.

Manufacturer		Focke-Wulf			
Type		AL 102 L Fw 55L	AL 102 W Fw 55 W	AL 103 Experimental	Fw 47C (A 47)
Powerplant		Argus As 10C	Argus As 10C	Argus As 10C	Argus As 10C
Performance	kW	176	176	176	176
	hp	240	240	240	240
Crew(+passengers)		1+1	1+1	1+1	1+1
Length	m	8.90	9.40	11.15	10.57
Height	m	3.10	3.80	3.66	3.04
Wingspan	m	13.30	13.30	15.40[4]	17.76
Wing area	m^2	22.20	31.40	32.86	35.00
Aspect ratio		7.97		7.22	9.00
Weight, empty	kg	780	965	925	1065
Fuel	kg	160	158	100	138
Oil	kg	20	10	10	18
Crew	kg	80	80	80	80
Load	kg	160	137	335	279
Max. permissible load	kg	420	385	525	515
Takeoff weight	kg	1200[1]	1350[1]	1450	1580
Wing loading	kg/m^2	54.05	42.99	44.12	45.14
Weight/power ratio	kg/kW	6.82	7.67	8.24	8.98
	kg/hp	5.00	5.63	6.04	6.58
	kW/m^2	7.93	5.61	5.36	5.03
	hp/m^2	10.81	7.64	7.30	6.86
Built		1932	1932	1933	1932
Max. speed @ sea level	km/h	210	185	180	190
Cruise speed @ sea level	km/h	195	180	160	175
Rate of climb	m/s	4.90[2]	3.10[2]	2.70	3.80[5]
Service ceiling	m	5000	4500	4000	5000
Range	km	680	585	320	640
Max. flight time	hrs	3.50	3.25	2.00	4.00
Takeoff run	m				105
Landing run	m				164
Landing speed	km/h	88	78	80	76
Max. permissible load as % of takeoff weight		35	29	36	33
Payload as % of takeoff weight		13	10	23	18

[1]Ultimate load factor = 8
[2]Average rate of climb to 1000 m; at sea level it was 4.25 m/s
[3]Average rate of climb to 1000 m
[4]With a wing sweep of 10°
[5]Average rate of climb to 1000 m; at sea level it was 4.3 m/s

normally. In the meantime, the first members of his team had run up. They excitedly began bombarding him with questions, but Tank only muttered: "These damnable aileron flutters."

The AL 102, later also known as the Fw 55, served as a trainer for advanced students, for cross-country flying, for instrument flight training and as an aerobatic plane. The aircraft could be delivered in two versions: the Fw 55 L landplane and the Fw 55 W floatplane. In the latter configuration the type was built as a biplane, with the lower wings braced against the upper wings using N struts and supporting the wooden floats with struts as well. The additional wings and floats increased the takeoff weight from 1200 kg to 1350 kg and the wing surface area from 22.2 m2 to 31.4 m2. The floatplane was naturally slower as well.

AL 102 (Fw 55 L) trainer.

Fw A 43 Falke (A 43) high-speed touring plane and air taxi.

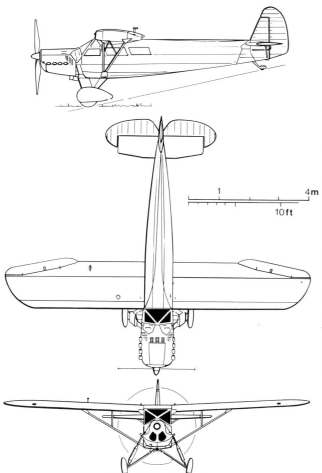

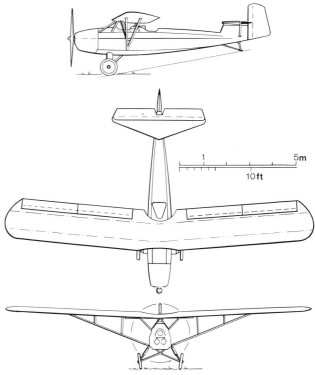

Fw A 43 Falke Modern Touring Airplane

The flight testing of the Fw A 43 Falke, a speedy commuter plane, went much more smoothly than that of the L 102. In addition to the pilot it could accommodate two passengers. It was based on the experience and ideas of Cornelius Edzard, a flight test pilot with Focke-Wulf.

The Fw A 43 Falke was a braced cabin shoulder-wing design of wood, metal and fabric construction. With its 162 kW/220 hp Argus As 10 engine the airplane attained a maximum speed of 256 km/h and a cruising speed of 215 km/h. It had comfortable seating, good downward visibility, individual ventilation and a sound-dampened cabin. The passengers could board the plane directly without the need for any type of ladder contraption.

The Falke made its debut at the 1932 Deutsche Luftsportausstellung (Dela) in Berlin. However, with the exception of Edzard's Lufttaxi business, the design had no other buyers. A glance at the chart may indicate a few of the reasons why. The fast airplane had a rather high landing speed for its day (108 km/h) and high wing loading. Without flaps or slats the machine was assuredly

41

Reconnaissance, Commuter and Sport Aircraft

Manufacturer		Focke-Wulf			
Type		Fw 39 (S 39)	Fw 40 (A 40)	Fw A 43 Falke A 43	L 101
Powerplant		Siemens Jupiter VI	Siemens Jupiter VI	Argus As 10	Argus As 8
Performance	kW	375	375	162	74
	hp	510	510	220	100
Crew(+passengers)		1+1	1+1	1+2	1+1
Length	m				8.30
8.45					
Height	m				2.30
2.70					
Wingspan	m			10.00	12.35
Wing area	m²			14.00	20.00
Aspect ratio				7.14	7.62
Weight, empty	kg		1450	750	475
Fuel	kg		265	163	90
Oil	kg		25	18	10
Crew	kg		80	80	80
Load	kg		455	139	140
Max. permissible load	kg		825	400	320
Takeoff weight	kg		2275	1150	795
Wing loading	kg/m²			82.14	39.75
Weight/power ratio	kg/kW			7.10	10.74
	kg/hp			5.23	7.95
	kW/m²			11.57	3.70
	hp/m²			15.71	5.00
Built		1931	1932	1931	1930
Max. speed @ sea level	km/h			256	170
Cruise speed @ sea level	km/h			215	150
Rate of climb	m/s			3.70[1]	2.40[1]
Service ceiling	m			5100	3600
Range	km			1050	670
Max. flight time	hrs		5.00	5.00	
Takeoff run to 20 m alt.	m			510	
Landing run fm 25 m alt.	m			580	
Landing speed	km/h			108	75
Max. permissible load as % of takeoff weight				35	40
Payload as % of takeoff weight				12	18

[1] Average rage of climb to 1000 m

The Focke-Wulf Fw A 43 Falke (1931/32) was the fastest light passenger aircraft of its day; designed for the air taxi role, it served admirably in this capacity.

not an easy plane for the casual pilot to land, and at the very least was unsuitable for beginner pilots. Tank had high praise for the tiny, sporty-looking machine, which he found a joy to fly. He even thought of how the design could be improved and recalculated the aircraft's lift distribution by taking into account an avoidable vortice which built up near the wingtip. Follow-on tests in a wind tunnel confirmed his figures. However, the appropriate design changes to the aircraft would only have been worthwhile if it had been produced in larger quantities. But there was just the prototype, Werknummer 127 and registration D-2333, which was operated successfully by Edzard's Norddeutscher Luftverkehr in Bremen.

Testing the Fw 47 Höhengeier

Before Tank could begin with new responsibilities, there was still the evaluation of an Fw 47 (A 47) weather reconnaissance plane. It had been laid out based upon the recommendations of the weather flight stations; a replacement was needed for the antiquated Junkers A 20 and A 35. The new aircraft was to have flown in any weather condition, have a good climb rate and, for rapid descent, be capable of a high sink rate. This meant an aircraft with a high degree of structural soundness with good flight stability.

The Fw 47 had been designed and built in 1937 under the direction of Professor Heinrich Focke. The Beschaffungsamt in Berlin had ordered 18 of the aircraft.

The braced, two seat high-wing composite design was powered by an Argus As 10C engine. The Argus As 10 with a Roots-type compressor was planned for a subsequent Fw 47B, which would give this variant the ability to operate at higher altitudes. The engine, however, never reached production maturity. For increasing its rate of descent and shortening the long glide approach, the airplane was fitted with braking flaps on the outer wing sections. The weather pilots soon nicknamed the plane "Höhengeier" (Alpine Buzzard). An Fw 47D variant was fitted with better equipment, to include an autopilot. In all, a total of 35 machines were built, which flew for many years as weather reconnaissance platforms.

Its good flight handling characteristics were clearly attributable to Kurt Tank, for these had not been bestowed on the design at birth. When applying strong pressure to the controls, Tank initially noticed vibrations on the brace work connecting the wooden wings with the fuselage. The appropriate corrective measures were undertaken. Professor Focke, who was especially proud of his Zanonia wing, had claimed to Tank that the wing made the Fw 47 non-spinnable - as were all of his aircraft. Although Tank found this to be true at first, he was still somewhat sceptical of the

Focke-Wulf Fw 47C, a specialized weather reconnaissance aircraft powered by an Argus As 10C engine with 176 kW (240 hp), first built in 1932. The meteorologists gave the airplane the nickname of "Höhengeier" (Alpine buzzard).

claim. Using a somewhat larger horizontal tail assembly he continued his experiments, but even then found that the aircraft could not be spun through normal stalling and rudder application. However, if he flew the plane a bit faster, pulled it up sharply and applied rudder, the Fw 47 went into a smooth spin from which it could be easily recovered. Tank subsequently demonstrated the airplane's spin characteristics for Professor Focke on several occassions.

Fw 44 Stieglitz Trainer and Aerobatic Plane

The Stieglitz was a single-strutter two-seat biplane of wood and metal construction. It later became the standard trainer of the German Luftwaffe and even today, some 46 years after it was built, is a treat for those pilots fortunate enough to fly in one of the few surviving examples. The Stieglitz had an air-cooled Siemens Sh 14A radial engine with an output of 110 kW/150 hp and was fully aerobatic.

When Gerd Achgelis became the second German Kunstflugmeister with the Stieglitz, orders for the Fw 44 followed from Bolivia, Bulgaria, Chile, China, Romania and Turkey. Countries such as Brazil, Sweden and Argentinia built the aircraft under license; Brazil even built an entire factory for construction of the type.

There was no specific requirement issued for the Stieglitz in the normal manner; it was simply based on a generic requirement from the Deutsche Verkehrs-fliegerschule for a trainer - an aerobatic biplane with good flight handling characteristics. A low-wing monoplane for training was still out of the question at that time. Tank passed the design on to Ing. Mittelhuber and provided him with the guidelines for the plane's layout. A biplane's upper wing causes little interference with the pilot's visibility if it is properly located and has a cutout over the forward seat, something which has the added benefit of making entry much easier. The downward view is better than on a low-wing monoplane. The performance of the 110 kW/150 hp Sh 14A could be utilized to its fullest and wing loading was able to be kept to a minimum.

44

The Focke-Wulf Fw A 43 Falke (1931/32) was the fastest light passenger aircraft of its day; designed for the air taxi role, it served admirably in this capacity.

The fuselage was initially found to be too short because Mittelhuber wanted to save too much weight. For construction materials steel tubing was used for the fuselage, with wood forming the basis of fabric covered wings. The leading edge was covered in plywood and the engine cowling was made of thin metal sheeting. This was aircraft manufacturing in its simplest form, something which the construction facilities and workshop at Focke-Wulf were ideally suited for and which enabled such a project to become reality in short order.

Tank had no difficulties crossing over from all-metal flying boat construction to steel tubing and wooden rib design. "After all, I'd built the "Teufelchen" in 1923, which gave me an opportunity to become intimately familiar with wooden construction. Nor did I pass obliviously by wooden sportplanes when I worked at Messerschmitt and while working there I was able to fly these types often."

Critical Vibrations with the Stieglitz

There were also problems which cropped up with the Steiglitz during flight testing when serious oscillations set in at certain speeds. Tank discusses the problem: "Sun and shadow, of all things, helped me in solving this matter. I'd just finished a test flight in a Stieglitz and, from a high altitude, raced back down toward the Bremen airfield. As I was returning, I noticed the shadow of the empennage spreading across the lower left wing, which can happen when the sun was in a particular position and the aircraft flying in a certain direction. There was nothing unusual in that. But then I saw the shadow suddenly become blurred, something which indicated vibrations. Just then, the whole airplane began vibrating, then everything started shaking, and then I found myself in a situation seldom experienced

45

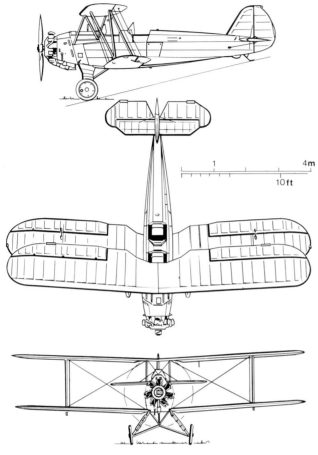

The Fw 44 Stieglitz trainer and touring aircraft.

Focke-Wulf Sport and Utility Aircraft

Manufacturer		Focke-Wulf	
Type		Fw 44J	Fw 47C
Powerplant		Siemens Sh 14a	Argus As 10C
Performance	kW	110	177
	hp	150	240
Crew(+passengers)	1+1	1+1	
Length	m	7.30	10.57
Height	m	2.70	3.04
Wingspan	m	9.00	17.76
Wing area	m²	20.00	35.00
Aspect ratio upper		7.80	9.00
lower			8.40
Weight, empty	kg	565	1065
Fuel	kg	97	138
Oil	kg	14	18
Crew	kg	80	80
Load	kg	114	179
Max. permissible load	kg	305	515
Takeoff weight	kg	870[1]	1580
Wing loading	kg/m²	43.50	45.14
Weight/power ratio	kg/kW	7.91	8.92
	kg/hp	5.80	6.58
	kW/m²	5.50	5.06
	hp/m²	7.50	6.86
Max. speed @ sea level	km/h	185	190
Cruise speed @ sea level	km/h	170	175
Rate of climb	m/s	3.40[2]	4.30
Service ceiling	m	3900	5000
Range	km	675[3]	640
Max. flight time	hrs	4.40[4]	4.00
Takeoff run	m	140	105
Landing run	m	140	164
Landing speed	km/h	80	76
Max. permissible load as % of takeoff weight		35	33
Payload as % of takeoff weight		13	18

[1]Ultimate load factor = 10.8; takeoff weight for aerobatics was 770 kg
[2]Time to climb to 1000 m was 5.5 min; to 2000 m was 12.7, to 3000 m 23.6 min
[3]At 15% throttle (n=1870 rpm); at 2050 rpm range was 585 km and endurance 3.4 hrs
[4]At 2050 rpm rate of consumption was 41 liters per hour, oil was 1.5 liters per hour

by test pilots, but which can prove extremely dangerous if you don't know the cause. I still had enough altitude to bail out if needed, so I applied more pressure on the controls to see what would happen. The vibrations eventually ceased and disappeared altogether as I slowed down for the approach. After landing I called together those personnel working on the Stieglitz and told them about the extremely strong oscillations which had announced themselves with by the presence of their shadow on the wing. This meant we knew that the vibration was not caused by the wings, something we'd assumed up until that time, but spread throughout the airframe from the empennage. As we shortly discovered, the error lay in the two elevators, which were controlled independently of each other. The cables which operated the two elevators ran from their connecting points on the elevators into the fuselage, intertwined once inside the fuselage and from there continued as a single cable to the forward fuselage. These two cables began vibrating at a point

where they still ran separately. The solution to the problem was simple: the two elevator spars were permanently joined together, so that the entire elevator assembly now functioned as a single unit. In so doing, the cause of the vibration was eliminated."

The Stieglitz was in production for many years and acquitted itself admirably in air force training schools both at home and abroad. The Fw 44A variant was first built in 1932. A 44B from 1933 included improvements to the airframe. Some of these Fw 44Bs were fitted with 99kW/135 hp Argus As 8B inline engines in 1934 and were given the designation Fw 44C; only eight of these were built.

When large-scale production got underway in 1934, Tank had the design reworked with particular consideration for simplification of production. In addition, the lubricant system was modified for upside-down flight. The fixed lines in the oil tank were replaced by flexible lines with a weight attached, so that oil could be drawn out regardless of the attitude the plane was in. For this purpose, a floatless carburetor designed for upside-down flight was also employed. This modified variant was designated the Fw 44D. Because of the flood of contracts the D-variant was built for a time under license at Bücker and Siebel.

An Fw 44E was another experiment with fitting an Argus As 8B engine. The Fw 44F, built in 1934, boasted formation lights and a high-power light for landing at night. An Fw 44J had the somewhat more powerful Siemens Sh 14A, with an output of 118 kW/160 hp. It was in production from 1936 on. A new engine, the Bramo 325 with NACA cowling, was experimentally fitted to the Fw 44J. And finally, in 1937 an Fw 44M was evaluated with an American inline engine, the Menasco C-4S with 110 kW/ 150 hp.

However, of all the engines which had been fitted to the Stieglitz, none of them had better reliability than the Siemens Sh 14A. This 7-cylinder radial engine had been on the market with the Sh 14 designation since 1929 and at that time had an output of 84 kW/115 hp at 1700 rpm. The Sh 14A, built in 1932, greatly contributed to the Fw 44's reliability and had a larger bore and more cooling ribs. It had a compression ratio of 1:5.3, a weight per unit of power of 0.83 kg/hp and a fuel consumption rate of 230 g/hp/hr. It had an output of 110 kW/150 hp at 2200 rpm. The more powerful Sh 14A-4, in use from 1936 on, had a higher compression ratio of 1:6.2, a weight per unit of power of just 0.78 kg/hp and an output of 118 kW/160 hp - as mentioned earlier.

Focke-Wulf(Albatros) AL 103 with Adjustable Wings

With production of the Fw 44 well underway, in addition to his other responsibilities Tank devoted his efforts to testing the experimental AL 103. The aircraft's wing sweep and dihedral could be changed, which offered enticing possibilities for a designer and his test pilots. The Deutsche Versuchsanstalt für Luftfahrt (DVL) had previously contracted with Albatros for such a design for the purposes of researching increased stability and carrying out suitable test flights. Focke-Wulf took over the responsibility of the airplane's design, which was similar in planform to the AL 102, with changes naturally being chiefly in the area of the wings.

AL 103 experimental and research aircraft with wings which could be adjusted in their dihedral and sweep.

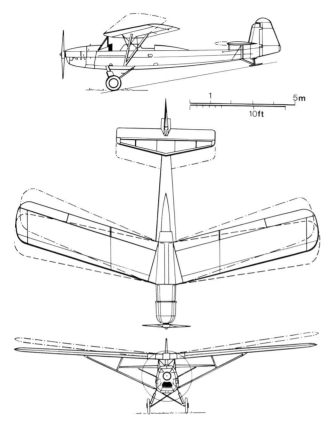

Focke-Wulf AL 103.

The prototype was built in 1933. The braced high-wing design with its Argus As 10C had a rectangular wooden wing, tubular steel fuselage covered in fabric and was laid out so that it was as stable as possible in all three axes. The wing sweep could be altered on the ground from 10° to 20° and the dihedral from 0° to 8°. Furthermore, the tailplane could be adjusted forward and backward. It was possible to shift the plane's center of gravity by moving lead plates, each weighing 15 kg, located inside the fuselage. The fuel tank was fitted at the center of gravity, so that consumption would not affect the trim configuration.

According to Tank, the test flights were carried out at different rpm settings ranging from full throttle to idle. Various sweep configurations were conducted at 0° dihedral, as well as different dihedral settings at constant sweep angles.

Very pronounced pressure built up on the elevator controls with a sweep of 20°.

Tank Attracts Qualified Experts

Tank devoted his resources to another important task at that time. In early 1933, political changes seemed to pave the way for a change in the state of aviation affairs in Germany. Unlike the former give and take approach on the part of the government, sport and commercial aviation would henceforth be encouraged to the same degree as it was in other countries, particularly in France. Tank saw the chance to develop a technically refined product, such as a commercial airliner made of metal, and not just tiny crates using antiquated construction methods of wood and steel fabric covered frames. An indispensable prerequisite for this, however, was a highly qualified staff of engineers, both in the developmental department as well as in manufacturing.

Tank was able to persuade the financial director of the company, Dr. rer. pol. Werner Naumann, that the time was ripe for investing if the company wanted to reap the benefits later. Tank became the company's technical director and was given a green light for his plans. The success of the Stieglitz and the numerous contracts from all over the world made his efforts that much easier. Hans Schubert came to Focke-Wulf from Heinkel and became the operational director; Tank was also able to attract the likes of Faehlmann, G. Mathias, W. Kaether, F. Haberstolz, E. Kosel and other technical experts. Various technical departments eventually sprang up, preparing, advising and expanding themselves within the design bureau; each had its own specific work cut out for it, each provided a critical building block for the new aircraft type. Each department functioned basically independently. The guidelines for the program were reviewed on a weekly basis during joint conferences attended by technology and operation department heads, chaired by Tank. All plans and problems were discussed in an open forum at these meetings. After listening to unresolved problems, Tank virtually always came to a clear solution by laying out the steps which had to be covered. This method was an integral part of his work method which enabled him to exercise strict control over the horizontally structured organization which consisted exclusively of department chairmen with Kaether as the organizational supervisor and Schubers as the operational supervisor.

Fw 56 Stößer, Trainer and Predecessor of the Stuka

Enjoying a success similar to that of the Stieglitz, the Stößer was a strutted high-wing design powered by a 176 kW/240 hp Argus engine. The idea for the Stößer came from Tank after the RLM requested proposals for a single-seat trainer for training advanced pilots in 1933. He assigned Oberingenieur Rudolf Blaser the responsibility of constructing the type. Blaser had come from Albatros and was intimately familiar with high wing designs and composite construction. Design layout rested in the hands of Ingenieur Mittelhuber. The resulting composite material high-wing Fw 56 had a two-piece wing, each section being braced by a V-strut. The wing was attached to the fuselage by N-struts. Downward and upward view from the cockpit was simply outstanding. The empennage made use of an extension forward of the tailplane, on which rested the horizontal control surfaces. This design feature was reminiscent of the empennage of former Albatros designs such as the L 82, L 100 and L 101.

The first Fw 56a (V1) prototypes incorporated and elliptical wing made of fabric covered wood. The fuselage consisted of steel tube construction with an oval framework design. The aircraft took off on its maiden flight in November of 1933. No significant defects were noticed on its first flight, the only initial change being the removal of the raised fairing behind the cockpit. Although it certainly added aesthetic qualities to the design, it inhibited the pilot's visibility aft. Furthermore, it was found that the extended cantilever single-leg landing gear caused some problems at first due to the fact that the shocks were too stiff.

The second Fw 56b (V2) prototype had wings made of fabric-covered metal and was fitted with a landing gear having better cushioning and somewhat larger spatting for the wheels. The V2 was also experimentally fitted with a variable-pitch propeller. Alternatively, the V3 reverted back to the wooden wing and yet another redesign of the undercarriage, which this time had only the oleo struts shrouded. By this point Tank was heavily involved in the details of the design. The aircraft was given a thorough wringing out by him in 1934. A flyoff between the Stößer, the Arado 76, Heinkel He 74 and the Henschel Hs 125 saw the choice being made in favor of the Stößer. Deciding factors were the robust and simple construction, plus the high structural load factor of 14. It should be noted that, at the time, Focke-Wulf and indeed the entire aviation industry felt that any future fighter would be a high-wing design.

The Stößer's cockpit was deliberately laid out to be as comfortable as possible. The rudder pedals were adjustable so that even small pilots would have no trouble flying the airplane. Visibility from the cockpit was incomparably better than on biplanes. Takeoff was so straightforward that the operational handbook stated: "No particular recommendations are needed for takeoff procedures". The aircraft had no ground-loop tendencies. With full throttle, a pilot simply lifted the tail off and after a run of 150 to 180 m - depending on the wind - the aircraft lifted itself off at a speed somewhere between 90 and 100 km/h. It was recommended to fly level for a bit until reaching 130 km/h. Then the airplane would climb away at 8 meters per second, reaching 1000 meters in 2.2 minutes, 2000 meters in 4.7 minutes

Fw 56b V2 Stößer with spatted landing gear.

Focke-Wulf Fw 56A Stößer in its final production form.

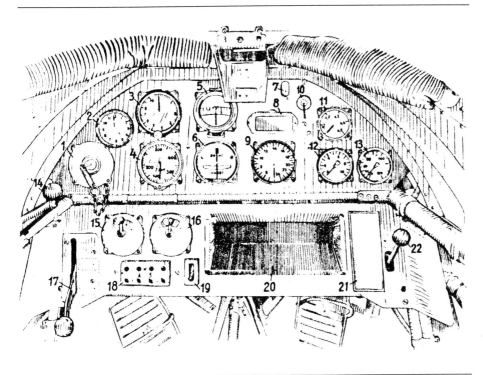

Cockpit of the Fw 56 Stößer.

1 Starter switch
2 Clock
3 Altimeter
4 Airspeed indicator
5 Compass
6 Turn and bank indicator
7 Plug for Revi gunsight
8 Compass deviation table
9 RPM indicator
10 Pitot tube warmer switch
11 Fuel pressure gauge
12 Oil pressure gauge
13 Oil temperature gauge
14 Spoiler activator
15 Calibration
16 Feedback
17 Fuel cock lever
18 Fuze box
19 Generator switch (main switch)
20 Map case
21 Model plate
22 Hand pump

and 3000 meters in 7.8 minutes. With full throttle and in level flight with a fixed-bladed propeller, the Stößer could attain 270 km/h at sea level with an rpm setting of 2250 and 265 km/h at an altitude of 1000 meters. At cruise setting (1880 rpm), the aircraft reached 245 km/h at sea level. At full throttle the plane had a tendency in level flight to drift to the right.

When diving, the throttle was reduced and the aircraft bunted over into a vertical dive. Speeds of up to 480 km/h were permissable in a dive. The vertical dive, during which the airplane followed control inputs flawlessly, was an unforgettable experience for every pilot who plummeted through 1000 m or 2000 m for the first time. It was recommended to trim the aircraft tail heavy prior to making a dive. A pilot then had only to push forcibly on the controls and the machine would recover of its own accord when he eased off again. The Stößer must have left a lasting impression on virtually every pilot who had the opportunity to fly it due to its ease of control and good flight handling. When landing at speeds of 120 to 130 km/h the majority of pilots, who at the time were more familiar with flying biplanes, would first overshoot the runway if they didn't activate the spoiler; thanks to the Stößer's good aerodynamic design the aircraft would soar for quite a distance. The spoiler, located just behind the leading edge in the wing's center section upper surface, reduced lift and greatly increased the rate of descent without changing the trim configuration. The glide angle and rate of descent could be controlled at will by fine adjustments with the spoiler. Accordingly, the moment the spoiler was either fully or partially retracted the

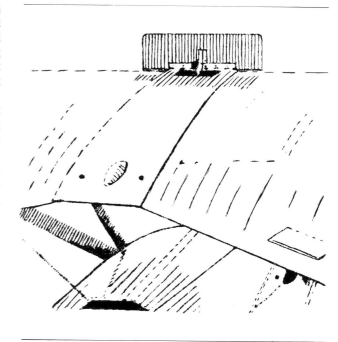

The Stößer's descent angle could easily be adjusted and controlled by this simple adjustable spoiler located above the wing.

The pleasing lines of Heinkel's competing He 74b.

Another of the Stößer's competitors was the classy low-winged Henschel Hs 125.

descent rate decreased just as quickly as it had increased. Corrective trimming was not necessary. The machine touched down at 90 km/h and, with the aid of its brakes, could be brought to a stop after a rollout of 250 to 300 meters.

The first pre-production prototype, designated Fw 56A-01, was the V4. It had several changes and improvements over the initial prototypes. The engine cowling had an improved shape, the exhaust piping was changed because exhaust fumes would sometimes get into the cockpit under certain conditions.

As the table shows, the airplane had a high payload capacity of 66 kg. It would have been possible to utilize this capacity for armament of some type. Because it was impossible to have predicted the rapid advancement in aerodynamic refinement at the time, there was consideration given to using the Stößer for defending the country in addition to its role as a trainer for aspiring fighter pilots. The V4

was accordingly kitted out with two 7.9 mm MG 17 guns mounted over the engine. Fw 56A-02 (V5) had only a single machine gun.

In 1934 the Stößer was thoroughly tested in Rechlin, and in the summer of 1935 a decision was made in favor of the Fw 56 even though its Ar 76 and He 74 competitors were virtually on par with it. Production of the Fw 56A-1 began a short time later, and no less than 445 aircraft were built. Gerd Achgelis received great acclaim in 1938 following his flight demonstrations in the US with a special variant fitted with an improved 198 kW/270 hp Argus As 10E rated at 2100 rpm and driving an Argus variable-pitch propeller. This special civilian variant was designated the Fw 56A-2. Although externally the handsome high-wing design gave the impression of being a delicate machine, it was also ideally suited to the role of dive bomber training. The aircraft could withstand the most strenuous pullouts, even if the motor occasionally was not able to withstand the rpm settings higher than rated.

The Arado 76, the third competitor for an advanced trainer.

When Udet became chief of the Technisches Amt, he finally had the opportunity to convince many notable officers of the value and importance of dive bombing. Accordingly, he invited the chief of the general staff, General Wever, and his staff to a dive bombing demonstration. For this display, he discussed the matter in detail with Tank and used a specially equipped type with cement bombs attached to shackles located underneath the wings. In addition, the aircraft had been fitted with a special sight. Udet placed 40 percent of his bombs within a small radius. No one could contradict the fact that this result was many times better than dropping bombs from a level flight profile.

A short time later (1936) initial contracts for the construction of a dive bomber went out to four aviation companies. In the competition between Arado, Blohm und Voss, Heinkel and Junkers, the Ju 87 emerged the victor. It was also a milestone for a fair method of conducting tactical warfare; it was now possible to strike exclusively military targets with precision.

It was no wonder that the Stoßer soon supplemented its initial role as a training aircraft for fighter pilots by becoming the ideal training platform for apprentice dive bomber pilots. All told, around 900 to 1000 aircraft were built. Unfortunately, all postwar attempts to find and restore a Stößer have met with failure.

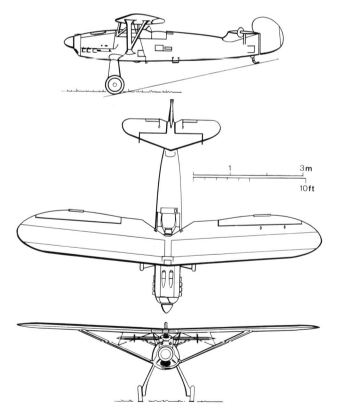

Fw 56 Stößer single-seat trainer.

The Stößer and its Competitors

Manufacturer		Focke-Wulf	Arado	Heinkel	Henschel
Type		Fw 56 Stößer	Ar 76	He 74	Hs 125
Powerplant		Argus As 10C	Argus As 10C	Argus As 10C	Argus As 10C
Performance	kW	176	176	176	176
	hp	240[1]	240	240	240
Crew		1	1	1	1
Length	m	7.60	7.20	6.45	7.30
Height	m	2.60	2.55	2.20	2.30
Wingspan	m	10.50	9.50	8.15	10.00
Wing area	m^2	14.00	13.34	14.95	14.00
Aspect ratio		7.88	6.76	4.44	7.14
Weight, empty	kg	755	750	790	695
Fuel	kg	72	76	75	82
Oil	kg	12	11	14	11
Crew	kg	80	80	80	80
Load	kg	66	153	58	107
Max. permissible load	kg	230	320	227	280
Takeoff weight	kg	985[2]	1070	1017	975
Wing loading	kg/m^2	70.36	80.21	68.02	69.64
Weight/power ratio	kg/kW	5.60	6.08	5.78	5.54
	kg/hp	4.10	4.46	4.24	4.06
	kW/m^2	12.57	13.19	11.77	12.57
	hp/m^2	17.14	17.99	16.05	17.14
Built		1934	1934	1934	1934
Max. speed @ sea level	km/h	278[3]	267	280	280
Cruise speed @ sea level	km/h	255	220	250	250
Rate of climb	m/s	8.40	7.20	6.40	8.33
Service ceiling	m	6200	6400	4800	7000
Range	km	385	470	375	500
Max. flight time	hrs	1.50	2.14	1.50	2.00
Takeoff run	m	168			
Landing run	m	233			
Landing speed	km/h	90	100	88	90
Max. permissible load as % of takeoff weight		23	30	22	29
Payload as % of takeoff weight		6	14	5	11

[1]Rate of consumption was 66 liters per hour.
[2]Weight of airframe was 342 kg, engine 304 kg, equipment 99 kg, total weight empty was 755 kg
[3]Maximum speed in a dive was 480 km/h at 2600 rpm

Fw 57 - First All-Metal Focke-Wulf Design

Tank sought out a contract for an all-metal aircraft with the intent of introducing modern construction methods into his company. On the other hand, he was aware that such a contract would of necessity lead to momentous changes throughout the entire company. Not only the engineers in the design department, but also the construction technicians, jig design, material quality control, the supervisors and workers on the control line - all would have to rethink everything anew. He had hoped for a civilian offer, but something quite different was in store.

In 1933 the Technische Abteilung (C-Amt) within the growing Luftfahrtministerium became involved in the trend in weapons development. Research led to the controversial theory to have heavy combat strike aircraft precede bomber formations in order to clear the way - especially in the immediate target area - and beat down the enemy's defenses. Many officers considered this concept absurd and there was talk of "advanced lost rabble". The strike aircraft weren't just expected to clear the airspace, but would also serve as escorts for the bombers, as light bombers or as recce platforms. The C-Amt envisioned a twin-engined, three-seat heavily armed machine built using the latest construction methods. An appropriate request to tender was issued in 1934 to Focke-Wulf, Henschel, AGO, Dornier, Bayerische Flugzeugwerke and Gotha. The recommended engines were the DB 600 or the Jumo 210. In place of a civilian aircraft, Tank was now forced to deal with a high-performance strike fighter.

The AGO firm designed a project Ao 225, a twin-engined low wing aircraft with two Jumo 210 engines, Gotha had a twin-fuselage aircraft with project number 3001 and 3002 with two DB 600 engines, Henschel offered an Hs 124 with two BMW 132Dc engines. This Henschel project, a cantilever mid-wing metal design bore some similarity to Focke-Wulf's Fw 57 proposal, both of which were contracted for. Messerschmitt's proposal did not meet the bid requirements and the firm therefore bowed out of the competition.

Accordingly, under the direction of Dipl.-Ing. Bansemir, for the first time in Focke-Wulf's history an all-metal airplane was guilt. The V1 prototype took off on its maiden flight in mid-1936 with Tank at the controls; the aircraft was a cantilever, twin-engined low wing design with retractable undercarriage and landing flaps and also incorporated a gunner's station in the nose with two 20 mm MG FF cannons and an electrically operated, traversible rearward firing turret housing a 20 mm Mauser cannon. A total of three prototypes were built.

The Fw 57 with DB 600C engines. This protoype was Focke-Wulf's first all-metal aircraft design, a new role for Tank's engineering and assembly team.

Fw 57 Strike Bomber and its Hs 124 Competitor

Manufacturer		Focke-Wulf	Henschel
Type		Fw 57 Kampfzerstörer[1]	Hs 124
Powerplant		DB 600C	BMW 132Dc
Performance	kW	2x669=1338	2x647=1294
	hp	2x910=1820	2x880=1760
Crew		1+2	1+2
Length	m	16.40	14.50
Height	m	4.00	3.75
Wingspan	m	25.00	18.20
Wing area	m²	73.57	54.60
Aspect ratio		8.49	6.06
Weight, empty	kg	6805	4250
Fuel	kg	990	1340
Oil	kg	15	15
Crew	kg	250	270
Load	kg	250	1355
Max. permissible load	kg	1505	2980
Takeoff weight	kg	8310	7230
Wing loading	kg/m²	112.95	132.41
Weight/power ratio	kg/kW	6.21	5.59
	kg/hp	4.57	4.11
	kW/m²	18.19	23.70
	hp/m²	24.74	32.23
Built		1935/36	1935/36
Max. speed @ sea level	km/h	365	363
Cruise speed @ sea level	km/h	300	300
Rate of climb	m/s		3.80[2]
Service ceiling	m	9000	7900
Range	km	1550	1820
Max. flight time	hrs	5.00	6.00
Takeoff run	m		260
Takeoff run to 20 m altitude	m		540
Landing run	m		128
Landing run from 20 m altitude	m	250	
Landing speed	km/h	110	100
Max. permissible load as % of takeoff weight		18	41
Payload as % of takeoff weight		3	19

[1]Projected data
[2]Average rate of climb to 1000 m

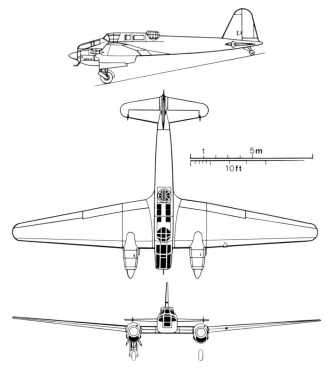

Fw 57 bomber, first built in 1936.

The Fw 57 V1 had many teething troubles and was lost when the pilot made an emergency landing on swampy ground. The flight test program continued with the Fw 57 V2 and V3, but were unable to provide satisfactory results. Without a doubt, the airplane was - with its empty weight of 6800 kg - a truly heavy machine. Numbered among the teething troubles were deficiencies with the new DB 600 motors having an output of 669 kW/910 hp. Tank considered the flight handling to be within normal parameters.

Simply put, the Fw 57 was a heavy crate - a study object for Tank and his team. A follow-on development was abandoned when the RLM soon dropped the controversial idea of a heavy strike aircraft and Messerschmitt prevailed with his concept of a light, two-seat strike fighter - which he later realized with the Me 110.

The Henschel Hs 124 V2, with air-cooled BMW 132 Dc engines, was a direct competitor of the Fw 57.

When Flugbaumeister Hans Sander returned to Focke-Wulf from Rechlin in 1937 with a bundle of valuable experience, what should he find waiting for him but this Fw 57, parked at the edge of Bremen's airfield. Nobody was interested in flying the airplane anymore. However, one day Sander, the youngest test pilot at Focke-Wulf, was assigned to deliver the Fw 57 to a military base. For better or worse, he was now forced to acquaint himself with the machine and ferry it to its new home. His assessment: "It was a too heavy, unmanageable aircraft which offered little in the way of flying pleasure."

The young graduate engineer and aircraft builder quickly earned Tank's trust and had a significant influence on the flying qualities of the company's later aircraft designs. He had the gift of being able to pass on his flying experiences to the design bureau in the language of engineers, where his proposals were accepted with open minds and bore fruit in the changes and improvements made in the designs. Sander had survived a grueling training program as a test pilot and was used to testing a sailplane one day, an autogyro the next and a canard-wing design or multi-engined aircraft the following day. Prior to beginning his employment at Rechlin, Sander had worked for a year and a half in Focke-Wulf's workshops and rose to the highest ranks in the aviation industry.

Fw 58 Weihe, Twin-Engined "Band-aid Bomber"

The Fw 58 Weihe (kite, nicknamed the "Leukoplast-Bomber", or Band-aid Bomber) was conceived in 1934 at the instigation of the RLM; it was a multi-role aircraft with two 176 kW/240 hp Argus As 10C engines. The Weihe had hydraulically activated retractable landing gear and landing flaps - at the time all the typical trademarks of a modern airplane. Those who have sat at the controls of a Weihe and experienced the plane's outstanding flight handling characteristics will reflect back with some melancholy on this beautiful machine. The Weihe remained in production until the war's end. The Luftwaffe mainly used the type in its B2 schools as a trainer, medevac and liaison aircraft. The blind flying schools utilized them for instrument flight training and for instructing observers and bomber gunners.

The wing loading, as emphasized by Tank, was deliberately kept low so that the rookie pilot, expected to become familiar with twin engined flying as well as the operation of landing flaps and retractable undercarriage, would not become overloaded. On the other hand, the low wing loading meant that the aircraft suffered from a certain handicap when used for instrument flying in that its large wingspan made it sensitive to gusts.

In production for over ten years, its many applications spawned a plethora of different variants which more or less displayed major changes.

Focke-Wulf Fw 58 V5 passenger plane for Hansa Luftbild, 1939.

Fw 58A-series

Prototypes V1 through V23 were built from 1935 to 1939. A-series aircraft were both civilian and military versions. The civilian Fw 58A-0 (Werknummer 1198) served as Kurt Tank's liaison aircraft (registration D-ALEX). The A-1 series were examples of military training planes for instrument and radio training, of which 14 machines were built (1937).

Fw 58B-series

The B-series boasted aerodynamic refinements. The fuselage was covered with wooden paneling to a point beyond the cockpit. The military version had only a single pilot's seat in order to provide room for the prone gunner in the A-Stand (nose position). The six Fw 58B-0 production machines were military trainers, as were the Bw 58B-1 and B-2, of which 641 aircraft were produced from 1937 to 1938 by various manufacturers (Fieseler, Gotha, Miag, Blohm & Voss). Today's observer will note that the range, particularly for the A and B-series, seems to be quite limited; ap-

parently, however, auxiliary fuel tanks were fitted in short order.

An Fw 58B-3 special variant was fitted with two single-step metal floats, which increased its weight to 3350 kg. An Fw 58 BSN served as a trainer for air-sea rescue training.

Fw 58C-series

The C-0 to C-2 series were likewise utilized as trainers and for military applications. The Fw 58C-0 and C-1 had unglazed noses and served as instrument trainers. They were not fitted with gunner stations, these being replaced by radio and DF equipment, plus an all-weather landing system. The Fw 58C-2 was fitted with auxiliary tanks for increased range. The C-3 was a B-3 converted by Blohm & Voss, which in turn was employed as an air-sea rescue plane and crew training. The type had the more powerful HM 508D engines (first manufactured in 1938). Approximately 553 aircraft of the C-series were produced. Individual sub-variants of the Weihe were kitted out with various radio and navigational equipment. The B and C-series chiefly made use of the FuG 3/a radio navigation set, the Peil G 5, the Fu Bl 1 radio landing system and the Ei V1a intercom.

Fw 58B2, 1937, trainer and instructional aircraft.

Armament carried on the various models included:

A-Stand(nose): MG 15 with three twin drums (each holding 75 rounds).
A Lot-Fernrohr (Lotfe) bombsight was used for bombardier training.

B-Stand(dorsal): MG 15 with three twin drums (each holding 75 rounds).

Additionally, bomb magazines for 3x50 kg or 6x10 kg bombs could be fitted.

Fw 58D and E-series

The Fw 58D-1 was a communications aircraft, at least one of which was produced as a liaison aircraft for the Zeiss company. E-1 through E-3 series (1939) flew as weather or specially modified winterized aircraft with appropriate equipment and skis, as well as multi-role experimental aircraft. For example, the E-2 was experimentally fitted with Argus As 401 rated at 202 kW/275 hp. About 15 of this type were built.

Cockpit of the Fw 58C-1, 1937, with dual controls for instrument flight training.

Commuter Aircraft: Fw 58F-series

The Fw 58F-1 through F-10 were yet more commuter types for companies, the RLM and for high-ranking officers. They were produced in the timeframe from 1939 to 1941; their numbers were estimated at 15. A few were fitted with auxiliary fuel tanks, which increased the F-4's and F-5's fuel capacity to 445 kg and gave these an endurance of five hours' flying time and a range of 1170 km.

Air-Ambulance and Specialized Types: Fw 58G-series, H and J

The Fw 58G-1 through G-3 series aircraft, of which 23 aircraft were built, were medevac and specialized airplanes, one variant of which (G-2) was used for testing winter equipment. An Fw 58 V18 was trial-fitted with a nose wheel in 1938. In 1939 the aircraft, designated the Fw 58H was equipped with a Hirth engine having a system for reducing the fuel consumption rate. Two of these Hirth-engined aircraft were sold to Hungary and delivered in December of 1939 by Hans Sander. The Fw 58J-1 was modified from the V15 as a liaison aircraft in 1938.

For Export and Commercial Aviation: Fw 58K-series

The unique K-series variants deserve mention as well. The K-1 through K-10 series were variants destined primarily for the export market and were produced from 1938 to 1942. KA-2 through KA-8 airplanes were delivered to Hungary as prototypes for license-manufacture there, while the KG-2 went to Bulgaria for the same purpose. Four KB-3 were sold to Hungary and Bulgaria for the sum of 140386 RM.

The Fw 58KE-1 through KE-3 were built as multi-purpose aircraft; a KJ-1, costing 93230 RM, served Lufthansa as a photo airplane. Two KL-1 (3100 and 3101) were fitted with 206 kw/280 hp Hirth 508Db-1 engines and delivered to Lufthansa as cargo transports. Six Hirth-powered KL-2 series machines were built for Lufthansa in 1939, with two additional aircraft following the initial delivery.

An Fw 58 V13 with two supercharged 206 kW/280 hp Hirth 805D engines was utilized as a prototype testbed. These aircraft had cantilever single strut landing gear, a take-off weight increased to 3600 kg and, with their variable-pitch propellers, reached speeds of 270 km/h.

The KO-1 was a civilian photo plane (1970) built in 1939. The Fw 58 KP-1 was to have been employed as a weather reconnaissance aircraft, but in 1940 was converted to the Fw 58 KQ-1 commuter plane (3329).

Record-Setting Exports

The high numbers of Stieglitz, Stößer and Weihe aircraft produced and exported pushed Focke-Wulf to the top of German aircraft manufacturers in the export market for a time prior to World War II. The Weihe was built under license in Brazil (25 aircraft) and Hungary, and sold to Bolivia, Bulgaria, China, Denmark, Holland, Romania and Sweden. The number of aircraft built for the home market is estimated at 1700, while foreign sales amounted to about 300; in all, a total of approximately 2000 Fw 58 of all variants were built.

At the Weihe's Controls

The Fw 58 Weihe's performance in the air and its handling characteristics were quite good thanks to Tank's personal involvement in the flight testing program. Taking off, the airplane consumed a total of 200 meters of runway at full throttle, with the required length dropping to just 150 to 180 meters when using flaps; by today's standards it made an excellent short-takeoff aircraft (STOL). It lifted free at 100 to 110 km/h. Red lights illuminated as the landing gear retracted. If the engine rpm dropped from its cruising speed of 1880 rpm to 1200 rpm, a shrill warning signal for the landing gear sounded in the cockpit.

The Weihe had the best climb rate at 135 to 140 km/h and 1650 rpm. At these settings, the rate was 4.70 meters per second at sea level. After climbing it was trimmed for level flight. A rudder wheel or trim knob served to counter lateral drifts or could be employed when flying on a single engine. At full throttle and with no gunner positions, a closed aircraft could attain a speed of 250 km/h. The landing gear was not to be extended at speeds greater than 160 km/h. When flying on only one engine, the airspeed dropped off to 160 to 180 km/h with full throttle applied to the running engine. The airplane could bank smoothly over the running engine as well as maintain its altitude. During training, banking over the standing engine was prohibited, but this too could be done without problems.

In calm weather the aircraft was stable in all axes and ideally suited for instrument flying. In gusty weather, however, instrument flying became difficult due to the fact than the Weihe's large wingspan, large wing area and low wing loading (at about 60 kg/m2) made it a job to fly. Given

these constraints, it was recommended that cross-country flights be carried out at higher altitudes.

The Weihe had good stall handling characteristics. With the throttle reduced, the speed cut to 90 km/h and a tug on the controls, the rear fuselage began shaking. When the controls were pushed back, the shaking immediately let up and the machine began building up speed rapidly. If the pilot continued to pull the nose up, he felt a nudge and the wings dropped away. The plane then rapidly picked up speed again and immediately responded to control inputs.

When landing, the approach was made along the down-wind leg with the airspeed reduced to 160 km/h and the landing gear extended. After locking in place - they extended by gravity - three green lights illuminated on the instrument panel. On the base leg the pilot reduced the speed to 150 km/h and lowered the flaps halfway. These were fully extended on final and the speed throttled back to 130 km/h. At this point the aircraft became somewhat nose heavy and it was recommended that a bit of trim be applied to offset this effect. Touchdown occurred at around 80 to 90 km/h. Thanks to its good brakes, the rollout was short at around 160 to 200 meters.

Flight with Shattered Wings

For a long time the Weihe was Tank's favorite plane. He used D-ALEX as his personal transport and kitted it out with all the most modern navigational equipment then available. Nevertheless, it was in this airplane that he came within a hair's breadth of losing his life. It was in November of 1941. Tank was flying with some of his colleagues from Paris to Bremen after a meeting on the Fw 300, which had been developed in France at SNCASO under the direction of Dipl.-Ing Bansemir. Northwest of Brussels the radioman passed the warning: "Enemy aircraft in the vicinity of Brussels". Tank thought it was probably bombers and continued flying. Suddenly, he noticed a pair of airplanes, which he first took to be Me 109s, coming at him from the port side. Then he saw four winking flashes in the planes' wings and recognized them now as Spitfires, shooting at him. But they'd led his airplane too much and the rounds overshot. He noticed the RAF roundels as they pulled up over him. "They'll be coming back again", commented Tank and pushed his plane's nose down in an attempt to escape by flying low to the ground. But it was too late. One of the Spitfire pair was already on his tail, firing away. Parts of the left wing shattered and flew apart. The aileron broke away and the leading edge of the wingtip was torn to ribbons. When the British flyers saw the parts flying off, they broke off their attack and disappeared.

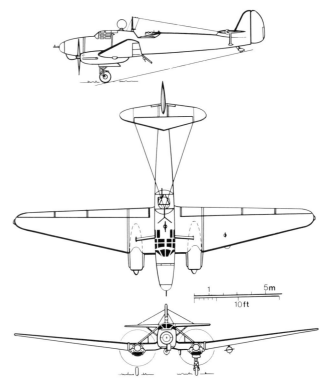

Fw 58B Weihe trainer.

Tank's colleagues were white as ghosts, but as if by a miracle the plane continued flying. Both engines were still running, but the Weihe lagged to port and threatened to dip over onto its left wing. Tank had the colleague sitting next to him hold the aileron controls. The radioman called Hilversum and asked to have the area cleared for an emergency landing. The plane could not be banked anymore and the landing had to be made from the direction they were approaching the airfield.

After 17 anxious minutes Hilversum was spotted. Tank nudged the nose in the direction of the field, lowered his airspeed and dropped the undercarriage. The whole time, the damaged wing was trying its best to drop away. He called out once again: "Buckle up!", gave it full throttle to counter the craft's desire to whip around to port, cut off the right engine and set the plane down on the field. Tank stood on the starbord brake and after a short rollout in which D-ALEX made a pronounced arc to the left, brought the plane to a halt. Tank shouted out: "Everybody out, the crate could catch fire at any moment." The fire department was already on the scene, however, and no ambulance was needed. The aircraft was hit 47 times. Incidentally, Tank discovered one of these bullets in his seat cushion as he was climbing out.

Fw 58 Weihe Variants

Manufacturer		Focke-Wulf				
Type		Fw 58 A-1 Training	Fw 58 A-2 Training	Fw 58 Bc MG training	Fw 58 C-2 Instrument flying	Fw 58 KJ+KL Lufthansa
Powerplant		Argus AS 10C[1]	Argus AS 10C[1]	Argus AS 10C[1]	Argus AS 10C[1]	Argus AS 10C[1]
Performance	kW	2x176=352	2x176=352	2x176=352	2x176=352	2x176=412
	hp	2x240=480	2x240=480	2x240=480	2x240=480	2x240=480
Crew(+passengers)		1+3	1+3	1+3	1+3	2+4
Length	m	14.10	14.10	14.10	14.10	14.00
Height	m	4.20	4.20	4.20	4.20	3.90
Wingspan	m	21.00	21.00	21.00	21.00	21.00
Wing area	m²	47.00	47.00	47.00	47.00	47.00
Aspect ratio		9.38	9.38	9.38	9.38	9.38
Weight, empty	kg	2258	2270	2400	2241	2400
Fuel	kg	125	125	220	330	350
Oil	kg	28	28	28	30	30
Crew	kg	80	80	80	80	160
Load	kg	437	370	185	238	660
Max. permissible load	kg	670	603	513	678	1200
Takeoff weight	kg	2928	2873	2913	2919	3600
Wing loading	kg/m²	62.29	61.13	61.98	62.11	76.59
Weight/power ratio	kg/kW	8.32	8.16	8.27	8.29	8.74
	kg/hp	6.10	5.99	6.06	6.08	6.42
	kW/m²	7.49	7.49	7.49	7.49	8.77
	hp/m²	10.21	10.21	10.21	10.21	11.91
Built		1935	1936	1937	1937	1939
Max. speed @ sea level	km/h	254	250	254	265	272
Cruise speed @ sea level	km/h	238	235	238	249	242
Rate of climb	m/s	4.70	5.00	4.70	4.90	5.00
Service ceiling	m	5400	5600	5400	5600	5400
Range	km	350	350	570	670	900
Max. flight time	hrs	1.35	1.35	2.40	2.70	4.00
takeoff run	m	200	180	200	200	200
Landing run	m	180	180	180	180	180
Landing speed	km/h	80	80	76	76	85
Max. permissible load as % of takeoff weight		23	21	18	23	33
Payload as % of takeoff weight		15	13	6	8	18

[1]Rate of consumption at 1880 rpm 150 kW/200 hp was 46 kg/hr or 63 liters/hr.

It had missed his radioman by a whisker. Tank reported the event to the airbase commander, General Christiansen (also known as Krischan) and asked if it were possible to have the plane repaired. He would need a new outer port wing section, replacement parts for the landing gear and a few more sundry items. Christiansen first wanted to have a bit of a birthday celebration with Tank, but then promised to do all he could to have the aircraft patched up. Tank himself considered this to be the most dangerous flight of his life next to the crash landing with the bursting L 102.

The next morning, when he went to inspect the damage with his own eyes and see if it could be repaired, there stood the Weihe in front of the hangar ready for takeoff. Tank and his colleagues lost their tongues for a moment! The Luftwaffe's mechanics had put the plane back together in seven hours. At nine o'clock he was back in the air with his engineers and reached Bremen safe and sound. The Reichsluftfahrtministerium, however, got wind of the incident and forbade Tank from flying the plane until it could be given a general overhaul. Furthermore, he was prohibited from ever again flying a Weihe in the combat theater. To take some of the smart out of the wound, a short time later the RLM gave him a Ju 88 as his transport. "Not a bad trade," opined Tank with a grin, "at least its faster!"

Fw 62 Shipborne Reconnaissance Aircraft

Little information has been published about the Fw 62. Built in 1936, it was the result of a contract issued by the Technisches Amt and was a two-seat seaplane designed for catapult launching from warships. In addition to Focke-Wulf, the companies of Arado, Dornier and the Gothaer Waggonfabrik also submitted proposals to fill the contract of a shipborne and coastal patrol aircraft. The latter company submitted a Project 14-012, a twin engined seaplane with two Argus As 410 engines, each outputting 341 kW/ 465 hp. Arado proposed its Ar 196. Focke-Wulf and Arado were initially awarded contracts for two prototypes.

Oberingenieur Arbeitlang, under the direction of Tank, designed a conventional, single-strutter braced biplane made of wood and metal. At Tank's promptings the float assembly was initially supported by the fuselage in order to offset the extremely hard landing impacts and reduce the amount of struts, cabling and reinforcements needed. A 646 kW/ 880 hp BMW 132Dc engine served as the motor. A second version, the V2, was fitted with a single central float.

Fw 62 V1 (D-OFWF) shipborne catapult-launched reconnaissance seaplane with two shock absorbing floats.

Unlike the V1, the Fw 62 V2 had a central shock absorbing float.

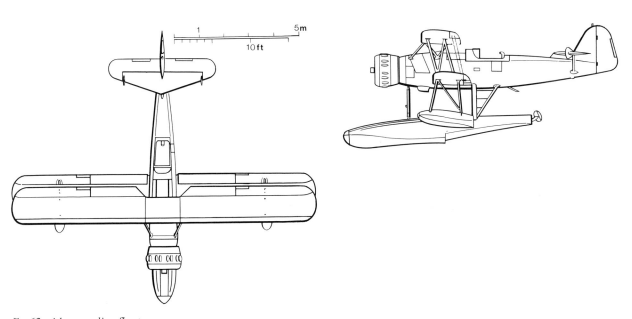

Fw 62 with centerline float.

Cockpit of the Fw 62.

The two prototypes were evaluated at Travemünde in the summer of 1937. Tank himself flew the aircraft from the forward cockpit, with Fl*ugkapitän* Stein in the aft cockpit. All testing, including catapult launching, went smoothly. Nevertheless, Arado and its more advanced low-wing cantilever Ar 196 design were awarded the final contract. Arado went on to built 520 aircraft of this type.

Catapult-launched Seaplane

Manufacturer		Focke-Wulf
Type		Fw 62 catapult seaplane
Powerplant		BMW 132Dc supercharged engine
Performance	kW	646
	hp	880
Crew		1+1
Length	m	11.15
Height	m	4.30
Wingspan	m	12.35
Wing area	m²	36.10
Weight, empty	kg	2300
Fuel	kg	254
Oil	kg	30
Crew	kg	160
Load	kg	106
Max. permissible load	kg	550
Takeoff weight	kg	2850
Wing loading	kg/m²	78.95
Weight/power ratio	kg/kW	4.41
	kg/hp	3.24
	kW/m²	17.89
	hp/m²	34.38
Max. speed @ 1000 m	km/h	280
Cruise speed @ 400 m	km/h	250
Rate of climb	m/s	10.00
Service ceiling	m	5900
Range	km	500
Max. flight time	hrs	2.00
Landing speed	km/h	90
Max. permissible load as % of takeoff weight		19
Payload as % of takeoff weight		4
Built		1937

Fw 159 Fighter, A Bigger Stößer

In 1934 the RLM's Abteilung II/Ib für Jagd- und Erkundungsflugzeuge (under the direction of Christiansen and Lahmann) approached the aviation industry with a request for tender for a single-seat pursuit fighter. The design was expected to be a modern one to replace the He 51 and Arado 68 biplanes. The specified performance figures could only be achieved using a cantilever monoplane with retractable undercarriage, variable-pitch propeller, ducted radiator and flaps for reducing the landing speeds. The concept of a refined Fw 56 Stößer suggested itself to Tank, who felt that he could improve the design by making aerodynamic improvements and employing a more powerful engine. The idea seemed all the more obvious, since the concept of a high-wing design offered several advantages. Moreover, Tank knew that when the Polish PZL P-24 single-seat fighter, a high-wing design itself, was demonstrated in Warsaw on the occasion of the 1934 Trans-Europa Flight, all those who'd observed its performance in the air and inspected it on the ground considered this design to be the optimum solution for a fighter with regard to visibility and overall performance.

Tank handed over responsibility for the Fw 159's design to Oberingenieur Rudi Blaser, who had the greatest experience and the necessary impetus to find a quick solution for the task at hand. It was known from the beginning that it would be very difficult to come up with a suitable rectraction mechanism for the undercarriage's long-legged oleos on a high-wing design. The reliable Jumo 210G with 492 kW/670 hp was selected as the engine, which initially drove a fixed-pitch airscrew. The braced single-strutter high-wing airplane was constructed entirely of metal and displayed good aerodynamic qualities. The fuel tank was sited ahead of and below the cockpit and, in the event of emergency, could be jettisoned. Unlike the Stößer, this new aircraft came equipped with landing flaps.

The V1 prototype (Werknummer 932) was finished in 1935. Prior to its first flight the landing gear retraction system was given a particularly rigorous workout. Despite this, as Flugkapitän Stein wanted to land the plane after its maiden flight, he found that the extended oleos had not locked into place. Every possible maneuver, including a loop, was tried to no avail, leaving nothing left for him to do but burn up the fuel (the V1's tank was not yet jettisonable). The airplane was wrecked upon landing, although Stein walked away with just a few minor bumps and bruises.

The reason for the landing gear's failure was simple: the engineers hadn't correctly estimated the drag and the hydraulic cylinder was not strong enough to push the strut against the drag to where it locked. Prototype number two, the V2 (933), nearly finished by this point, was therefore fitted with a much stronger cylinder.

From a flying standpoint the Fw 159 was virtually identical to the Stößer; foreign reports often cite its relatively high stalling speed stemming from the fact that its climbing speed was less than calculated and its turning radius was too great. Tank however, who had flown the type sev-

Fw 159 V2 fighter plane. Utilizing a variable-pitch propeller, the aircraft could reach speeds of 385 km/h at 4500 meters.

Fw 159 V3 during flight testing, seen with its cover plates removed.

The PZL P-24 was generally considered the best fighter aircraft at the beginning of the 1930's. For Tank, it served as something of a role model in designing the Fw 159.

The Warring Brothers: Fw 159, He 112 and Bf 109

Manufacturer		Focke-Wulf	Heinkel	Messerschmitt	Panstwowe Zaklady Lotnicze
Type		Fw 159 V2 fighter	Heinkel He 112 V2	Bf 109B V8	PZL P-24
Powerplant		Jumo 210G (Werkn. 9494)	Jumo 210G	Jumo 210Da	Gnôme Rhône 14N07
Performance	kW	492	492	528	713
	hp	670	670	720	970
Crew		1	1	1	1
Length	m	10.00	9.00	8.55	7.50
Height	m	3.50	3.85	2.45	2.69
Wingspan	m	12.40	11.50	9.87	10.58
Wing area	m^2	20.22	21.60	16.40	17.90
Aspect ratio		7.60	6.12	5.94	6.25
Weight, empty	kg	1875	1700	1505	1340
Fuel	kg	260	360	242	269
Oil	kg	27	27	27	
Crew	kg	80	80	80	80
Load	kg	8	63	296	211
Max. permissible load	kg	375	530	645	560
Takeoff weight	kg	2250	2230	2150	1900
Wing loading	kg/m^2	111.27	103.24	131.09	106.14
Weight/power ratio	kg/kW	4.57	4.53	4.07	2.66
	kg/hp	3.36	3.33	2.98	1.95
	kW/m^2	24.33	22.77	32.20	39.83
	hp/m^2	33.13	31.00	43.90	54.19
Built		1935	1935	1935	1935
Max. speed	km/h	385	485	410	408
@ altitude	m	4000	3600	0	4500
Cruise speed	km/h	363	445	465	340
@ altitude	m	2700	3600	4000	0
Rate of climb	m/s	9.80[1]	14.00	16.80	11.50[2]
Service ceiling	m	7200	8000	8200	9000
Range	km	650	1100	690	650
Max. flight time	hrs	2.00	2.80	1.50	2.00
Takeoff run	m				105
Landing run	m				275
Landing speed	km/h	95	110	120	103
Max. permissible load as % of takeoff weight		17	24	30	29
Payload as % of takeoff weight			3	14	11

[1] Average rate of climb to 6000 m
[2] Average rate of climb to 5000 m, rate of climb at sea level was 16 m/s

Ernst Udet was keenly interested in the machine. When he had business in Rechlin he often took the opportunity to fly the Fw 159. During these times the landing gear and its unique retraction manners wreaked havoc with him. It was the hydraulic system, namely, which was incapable of retracting both oleo legs simultaneously. First one strut would partially draw in, followed by the other, but then the first leg would stick back out again. In such a manner the two legs would flip-flop back and forth until slowly snuggling into the fuselage. Udet enjoyed having a bit of fun by demonstrating this "feature".

The V3 variant (D-ISXI 1246) had a Jumo 210B and a twin-blade fixed-pitch propeller, later replaced by a variable-pitch airscrew. It was armed with two MG 17s mounted over the motor and firing through the propeller arc.

During the Fw 159's flight testing phase the design department carried out work on an improved variant powered by a DB 601 engine. Blueprints were submitted in September 1936 for a light fighter with the designation of Fw 259, although no aircraft was ever actually built.

The RLM's decision came down in favor of the Bf 109, but it's difficult to say whether the Heinkel He 112 wouldn't have made the better choice despite being a more complicated design to manufacture.

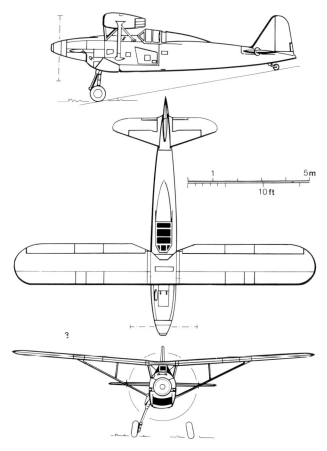

Fw 159 V3 fighter plane.

Fw 187 Falke
No Chance for the High-Speed Fighter

As mentioned before, the high-wing Fw 159's structure lacked the necessary concentration of low weight and minimal drag. With the high-performance fighter contract lost to Messerschmitt, Tank now began looking for a way to create a superior high-speed aircraft. He was convinced that he could attain this goal with a twin-engined single-seat machine.

The chief of development in the Technis*ches Amt* at the time, Oberst W. von Richthofen, approved of Tank's proposal for a high-performance airplane based on his own thinking and without involvement on the part of the Ministerium and accordingly issued a contract for three prototypes. Tank assigned the task of working out the design details to Oberingenieur Blaser, since he'd had considerable experience with the Fw 159. The main focus was on reducing drag in order to achieve a high airspeed.

The design, initiated in early 1936, revealed a cantilever low-wing planform of all-metal stressed skin construction. The wing center section, along with the fuselage center piece and engine nacelles, formed a fixed block. It was

Fw 187 V2 with Jumo 210 G engines having an output of 500 kW (680 hp). The airplane was some 225 km/h faster than the fighter aircraft then in service and about 35-40 km/h faster than the fastest single-seat fighter at the time, the Bf 109 B-0.

initially planned to utilize two 705 kW/960 hp DB 600 engines for the powerplants, but as these were not yet available in 1937 it was therefore decided to make use of the less powerful Jumo 210.

The Fw 187's undercarriage consisted of forked shock-absorbing oleos which were hydraulically retracted to the rear. The tailwheel was also retractable. Located beneath the engines were the radiators, and VDM variable-pitch propellers served as airscrews. Split flaps were designed as landing aids. The fuselage had been kept so narrow that the engine gauges were located outside the cockpit on the inboard side of the engine nacelles. With DB 600 engines, the aircraft was expected to reach speeds of 560 km/h based on calculations by the flight performance dept. (H. Wolff).

Tank test flew the V1 (Werknummer 949) with its 468 kW/635 hp Jumo 210Ds on its maiden flight in the summer of 1937. Flugbaumeister Sander later continued the flight test program. Sander summarized his experience flying the aircraft as follows:

"The Fw 187 was the first prototype that I test flew after joining Focke-Wulf as a test pilot. It was really quite a fast airplane, faster than the Bf 110 and the Heinkel He 112 with Jumo 210Ds. On its first flights the Falke attained 40speeds of 525 km/h at low altitudes; that was 225 km/h faster than the Luftwaffe's then-current frontline fighters (He 51 and Arado 68) could reach. It was some 35 km/h to

Twin-engine single-seat Fw 187 V1 fighter.

70

km/h faster than the Bf 109 with the same engine and at the same altitude. Furthermore, it had a much higher range and load, meaning that I could have set a whole series of records with the plane - something which the higher ups didn't want to see happen. With its armament of four MG 17s and two MG FF cannons installed later, the plane was the aircraft that our Luftwaffe later lacked when war broke out. For the pilots, it offered excellent all-round visibility on takeoff, landing and during flight - thanks to a large window in the fuselage floor, it even offered good downward visibility. The rudder forces were quite acceptable with adequate stability, even if their effectiveness and responsiveness was not up to the perfection achieved with the later Fw 190. This was due to a certain play and weakness in the aerodynamic counterbalance brought on by the drive in the Flettner servo tabs. Since shortly thereafter the RLM commanded that developmental work would have to stop, there was no real opportunity to effectively correct this shortcoming. When the airplane later operated as part of the Industrieschutz-Schwarm for Focke-Wulf, ballast was fitted which enabled the plane to make three-point landings with ease. The airplane could be flown on one engine virtually "hands off". There were no problems banking the plane over the running engine and, with certain caution, the same could be done over the standing engine. A bit of cross trimming lightened single-engine flight and countered the side-

slip and the resulting pull of the running engine. At first, I wasn't familiar with aerobatic flying in a twin-engined airplane. I came from Rechlin, where I'd been responsible for testing combat aircraft. As a consequence, I had little opportunity for aerobatics. The heavy inertia spawned by the outboard lying engines made aerobatic flight with the Fw 187 something entirely different than with a single engine plane such as the later Fw 190. The twin-engined, single-seat Fw 187 with its long range and load capability was actually the prototype for our fighters of today. It's common knowledge that most of the current single-seat modern jet fighters have two engines."

During the early stages of the flight test program there was a tendency for critical control surface flutter when the airplane was in a high-speed dive. Blaser then fitted a supplemental weight counterbalance to the elevators inside the fuselage in order to alleviate the problem. During one of Sander's test flights the control surfaces, then the entire plane, began vibrating at an airspeed of 735 km/h, so strongly in fact, that the pilot began entertaining thoughts of bailing out. But suddenly there was a loud bang and the vibrations disappeared. The cause of these vibrations turned out to be Blaser's "supplemental counterbalance", which had flown off when the vibrating set in. the problem was finally corrected when a counterbalance extending the entire length of the elevator span was fitted.

During the assembly process the Fw 187 V3 was converted into a two-seat "Zerstörer" attack plane.

Fw 187 V6 (CI+NY) with DB 600A engines, which utilized surface evaporative cooling and gave the plane a speed of 635 km/h at sea level.

Cockpit of the Fw 187A-0. A window in the floorboard gave the pilot good downward visibility.

Despite the aircraft's outstanding performance, the RLM stood by its refusal decision since the type was nearly twice as heavy as the Bf 109 and with its two engines would have to have been much more expensive and require more maintenance. In addition there was the matter of its higher wing loading, which was believed to be too much for the average pilot to handle.

In response to these charges, Tank reckoned that only the cost of the engines would be more. Producing the fuselage and empennage shouldn't have required much more expense than for a single-engined fighter. Without a doubt, for the defense of the Reich over friendly territory a single-engined fighter would have been much more cost-effective. However, over enemy territory a twin-engined fighter has the advantage, for in many cases it could return to base on a single engine, saving both valuable human life as well as aviation resources.

Despite its high wing loading of 164 kg/m2, Tank considered the Fw 187's flight handling characteristics to be quite good. The airplane handled like a single-engined plane and was sufficiently maneuverable. In flyoff competitions it consistently left the Bf 109 standing.

The *Technisches Amt* initially even doubted the aircraft's significantly higher airspeeds in comparison with the Bf 109, but Sander once again clearly proved this fact under even more restricted flying conditions. A precise and accurate pitot tube was needed for proving the high airspeeds claimed. For these test flights, therefore, Sander arranged for the plane to be fitted with an unusually long pitot tube joined to the nose by a streamlined, soft-skinned fair-

ing. The uninterrupted static pressure flow so far ahead of the fuselage produced flawless and accurate results.

A series of minor changes were made to the elevators on the V2 (1950). This prototype was fitted with the same engines as the V1 and received its certification in the late summer of 1937.

Udet, who soon followed Richthofen as director of the Te*chnisches Amt*, was also sceptical when it came to the Falke. In his view it was the maneuverability which made an effective fighter, not speed alone.

In the meantime, the RLM rekindled its interest in the heavy fighter and recommended that Tank build the plane as a two-seater. Prototypes V3 (1707) and V4 were accordingly converted into two-seaters while yet under construction. They were given a longer fuselage to make room for a radioman. The fuel tanks were moved to the fuselage and the engine supports were lengthened to correct the center of gravity; the taper at the rear of the engine nacelles was shortened for the same reason. This resulted in a reduced wetted wing surface. In addition, the flaps could be extended along the entire length of the wing. The engine cowlings were also modified. Armament consisted of two MG 17s and two MG FF cannons mounted in the fuselage.

The V3 was lost in a crash landing following an engine fire in the spring of 1938. From that time on the airplane was dogged by misfortune. Shortly after the V3 crash, test pilot Bauer was killed in another crash on 14 May 1938 while flying the V1. Bauer was a former parachute jump instructor, whose audacious jumping style had impressed Tank. Tank brought him to Focke-Wulf with the intention of infusing the test pilot ranks with new blood and assigned him the job of testing the Fw 187. Bauer was an excellent flyer and knew how to squeeze every drop out of the plane, especially when it came to aerobatic flying. Seldom had a twin-engined aircraft been flown so hard by a test pilot. Despite this, it was pure recklessness when Bauer - winding up a test flight - buzzed the airfield and pulled up into a loop from low level. In doing so, he lost too much speed. At the top of the loop the plane went into a flat spin - bursting apart as it unavoidably struck the hard ground. A testimony to Bauer's level-headedness and lightning-fast reaction was the fact that, during the few seconds it took to crash he was able to release the canopy and undo his harness.

Despite these setbacks, the Falke's flight test program at Rechlin had gone so well that in 1938 a contract was issued for an additional pair of two-seat prototypes, the V5 and V6. For the V6 Tank was given two of the more powerful 772 kW/1050 hp DB 600A engines, which at the time were only available in limited quantities. At the same time the RLM recommended that the V6 be fitted with surface evaporative cooling for study purposes in order to reduce

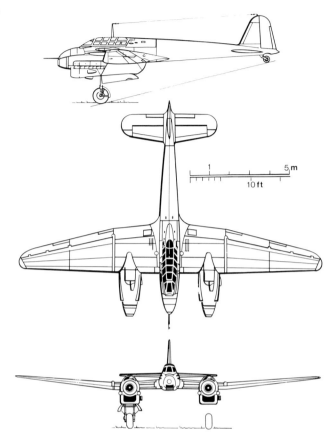

Fw 187 A-0 production variant.

the drag imposed by the radiators. For his part, Tank considered this cooling system to be ill-suited for military aircraft as it was complicated and difficult to manufacture, plus the fact that a single bullet in the wing could knock the entire cooling system out. On the other hand, the frontal and underslung radiators offered a smaller target area and were not as easily damaged. However, he had no reservations about risking such an experiment and gaining experience with this type of system.

Instead of 2x680 hp (totaling 1360 hp/1000 kW) the V6 now could draw upon 1543 kW/2100 hp; this was an engine performance boost of some 36 percent. The V6 reached speeds of 635 km/h at low level during flight testing in the spring of 1939, something of a sensational result at the time. Yet problems began cropping up with the surface evaporative cooling system, as had happened at Heinkel earlier (the He 100). With the surface evaporative cooling system the hot water from the engine was cooled by flowing through cooling tubes located beneath the skin. To divide the water from the vapor the system employed a centrifugal separator which forced the liquid/steam mixture in

Comparison of Fw 187 Twin-engined Fighter with Me 110 and Me 109

Manufacturer		Focke-Wulf	Messerschmitt	Messerschmitt
Type		Fw 187 V4 Falke	Me 110B-0	Me 109B-2
Powerplant		Jumo 210G	Jumo 210Ga	Jumo 210Ga
Performance	kW	2x492=984	2x514=1028	514
	hp	2x670=1340	2x700=1400	700
Crew		1+1	1+1	1
Length	m	11.10	12.60	8.55
Height	m	3.85	3.48	2.45
Wingspan	m	15.30	16.16	9.90
Wing area	m²	30.40	38.55	16.40
Aspect ratio		7.70	6.77	5.98
Weight, empty	kg	3700	4440	1506
Fuel	kg	500	500[3]	169
Oil	kg	54	54	54
Crew	kg	80	80	80
Load	kg	666[1]	627[1]	342[1]
Max. permissible load	kg	1300	1261	645
Takeoff weight	kg	5000	5701	2151
Wing loading	kg/m²	164.47	147.88	131.16
Weight/power ratio	kg/kW	5.08	5.54	4.18
	kg/hp	3.73	4.07	3.07
	kW/m²	32.37	26.66	31.34
	hp/m²	44.07	36.32	42.68
Max. speed @ 4000 m	km/h	500[2]	455	465
Cruise speed @ sea level	km/h	457	380	410
Rate of climb	m/s	14.50	12.50	12.00
Service ceiling	m	9250	8000	8000
Range	km	900	635	530[4]
Max. flight time	hrs	2.00	2.00	1.30
Takeoff run	m	154	400	260
Takeoff run to 20 m altitude		402	600	470
Landing run	m	448		
Landing run from 20 m altitude		726		
Landing speed	km/h	130	120	106
Max. permissible load as % of takeoff weight		26	22	30
Payload as % of takeoff weight		13	11	16

[1]**Payload:** weight difference for weapons and ammunition
[2]The data included here is derived from values obtained in August 1937 during the initial test flights in Rechlin
[3]Total fuel load was 953 kg giving a 4.00 hr duration for a range of 1220 km
[4]According to the manual the Jumo 210G had the following rates of consumption at optimal altitude:

takeoff	=215 liters per hour(155 kg/hr)
climbing and combat	=180 liters per hour(130 kg/hr)
cruising	=160 liters per hour(116 kg/hr)

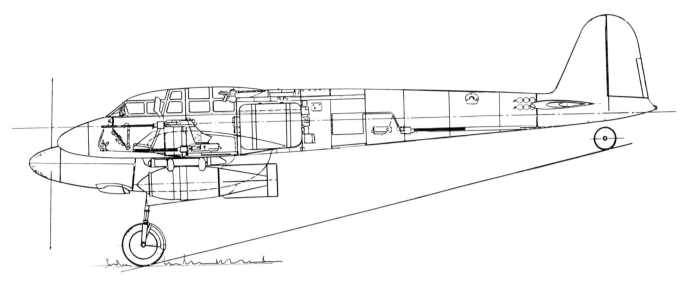

Using more powerful DB 605 engines (rated at 1084 kW/1475 hp) the Fw 187 could have been adapted into a long-range fighter or a strike bomber, carrying loads of 1000 kg and more.

a circular motion, throwing the water to the outside walls. It was trapped there and directed off, while the vapor in the middle was vented out via air louvers. The water thus cooled and separated from the vapor was then redirected back to the engine.

However, it was very difficult to achieve a smooth cooling process in all flying situations with such a system which branched throughout the wings. The flow must not be allowed to be interrupted under any condition, whether flying aerobatics, diving or with the inherent g-forces built up recovering from a dive. And here began the problems, problems which would consume a lot of time and demand a considerable expenditure of labor and resources.

In the end. the Ministry awarded Focke-Wulf a contract for a preproduction run of three aircraft (Fw 187A-01 through A-03), although the decision was eventually made in favor of Messerschmitt's Bf 110 Zerstörer - also powered by the Jumo 210G. Unfortunately, there is no surviving documentary evidence which would shed light as to why the RLM gave preference to the aircraft with the inferior performance. The table on the preceding page shows that, in comparing the Fw 187 V4 with the Bf 110B-0 and Bf 109B-2 - all fitted with the same engine - the Fw 187 was clearly superior in performance to its single- and twin-engined competitors. The Fw 187 was criticized for its narrow fuselage, too confining for the second crewman, who had the added hindrance of an extremely limited field of fire for defending himself due to the single tailfin. This could

be changed, however, but whether that would have impacted on the performance remains open to question.

The three Fw 187A-01 through A-03 preproduction aircraft exhibited a shallower canopy windscreen in addition to a handful of minor changes. After being thoroughly evaluated with full armament at Rechlin, the three were subsequently turned over to the previously mentioned Bremen Industrieschutz-Staffel. The company's test pilots operated these aircraft during air raids against the facilities. Such operations were prohibited after Dipl.-Ing. Mehlhorn, a member of the flight testing department, was killed on 10/8/1943 when attempting to land after shooting down three four-engined bombers.

The company loaned the three planes to a fighter unit in Norway during the winter of 1940. The experiences of the pilots with these high-performance aircraft were put down in a report filed with the Technisches Amt, which simultaneously called for the Fw 187's full-scale production. The unit was subsequently ordered to return the aircraft, which were being flown illegally, back to the Focke-Wulf company.

In 1942/43, as German cities nightly sank into soot and ashes, the Focke-Wulf company was awarded a contract for a twin-engined aircraft. The Focke-Wulf engineers once again pulled the dust-covered Fw 187 from out of the hangar. It served them as a prototype for a new fighter, which would have to be built of wood due to the material shortages at the time and, like its predecessor, would also meet with rejection.

Fw 189 Eule Tactical Reconnaissance Aircraft

At the war's outbreak the parasol-wing Henschel Hs 126 with its semi-enclosed cockpit was serving as the short-range and army reconnaissance platform of choice. The RLM, however, had requested a tactical recon airplane back in 1937, one which would enjoy an unbroken all-round view for self defense and room for three crew members (the third crewman was expected to serve as a rear gunner in the plane's B-Stand) in addition to having good performance characteristics.

Three companies submitted bids: Arado offered the Ar 198, a cantilever shoulder-wing design with an all-glazed lower fuselage. Blohm & Voss proposed its Bv 141 project, a design by Dr. Richard Vogt. This design utilized an asymmetrical layout with the engine at the forward end of the fuselage and the crew housed in a nacelle mounted separately on the wing starboard of the engine/fuselage.

Tank assigned Dipl-Ing. E. Kosel to design an entirely new type of aircraft. His impetus resulted in a twin-engined low-wing design with retractable gear, a twin-fuselage airplane whose extended engine nacelles also served as the tail booms. The three-man crew sat beneath an extensively glazed canopy located between the two booms and had excellent forward visibility which, as Tank noted, was unimpeded even in heavy rain. The airplane had a virtually clear field of fire aft. Two 342 kW/465 hp air-cooled twelve-cylinder Argus As 410A-1 engines served as the aircraft's powerplants.

The V1 prototype was still fitted with the somewhat less powerful 316 kW/430 hp Argus As 410 engines driving fixed-pitch propellers. Testing of the three prototypes (V1, V2 and V3) in mid-1938, went smoothly with Hans Sander at the controls, so well in fact that four additional prototypes were contracted for. There were initial problems with the aircraft suddenly pancaking on landing, the cause of which was a separation of the airflow between the crew nacelle and the tail booms. A sharper pinch to the nose profile, as had been recommended by Ing. Mathias, fixed the

Fw 189A-2 with its crew after returning from its 1500th combat mission over the Eastern Front.

Focke-Wulf Fw 189A-1 Eule, an Army reconnaissance platform powered by two Argus As 410A-1 engines (each rated at 342 kW/465 hp) driving Argus variable-pitch propellers.

problem in short order. The airplane was fully aerobatic and Tank, who'd carried out the initial flight testing of the V1 himself, flew loops, rolls and turns and spun the craft without difficulty.

The V3 served as an experimental aircraft for the planned A-series as well as a testbed for specialized equipment. It was fitted with automatic variable-pitch Argus propellers. The V4 was similar to the V3, like its forebears a reconnaissance platform, and also served as a trials aircraft. The V5 became the prototype for a B-series of trainers, having a modified canopy and dual controls. In 1939 a contract was issued for three B-0 and ten B-1 trainers. However, it came as a complete surprise to both the Ministry and the industry when the tactical reconnaissance units showed little interest in a new airplane, as their beloved Henschel Hs 126 had acquitted itself so well. For the time being, there seemed to be no rush.

An Fw 189D (V7) was to have been experimentally fitted with floats, but the contract for this variant was later withdrawn. Incidentally, the first V-types had single-strut landing gear, this design later being replaced by H-section undercarriage legs.

A C-series had been planned by the RLM as a ground attack plane and for this reason a prototype was chosen for comparison flyoffs with the Henschel Hs 129 ground attack plane. Accordingly, in 1938/39 the V1 received a much smaller, armored cockpit, increased armament in the form of dummy guns and the somewhat more powerful As 410 engine with variable-pitch propellers as had already been employed on the V2 and V3. Two different canopies, des-

ignated V1a and V1b, were experimented with. However, this variant of the airplane proved to be something of a disappointment. In 1940 the V6 was again converted into a ground attack plane. It was fitted with an armored cockpit housing two crewmen and an enormous amount of guns, including two MG 151s, four MG 17s and an MG 81Z. Fuel capacity was reduced to 198 kg (276 liters) and for communications an FuG 25 was used. In addition, the landing gear was strengthened. Takeoff weight for this variant increased from 4100 to 4610 kg.

Under tasking from the RLM, attempts to convert the Fw 189 into a ground attack platform met with unsatisfactory results due to the fact that the design simply was not laid out for such roles and the engines proved to be too weak. Its Hs 129 competitor was soon fitted with engines having nearly twice as much power.

There was often speculation that the V1 D-OPVN had been planned as a ground attack plane from the beginning. Fuel is added to the fire by the number of photos whose dates of origin cannot be confirmed showing this airplane in such a configuration. Books and magazine articles, therefore, often leave the matter open as to whether the first prototype was actually a ground attack version which was later converted to a recon aircraft.

Professor Tank has emphatically denied this claim: he would have laid out a ground attack plane with an entirely different design. Furthermore, the view from the armored cockpit was so bad that Tank would never have cleared the type for production. Even Flugkapitän Sander, who had been entrusted with the entire flight test program after Tank's

Fw 189 Eule Reconnaissance Aircraft

Manufacturer		Focke-Wulf		
Type		Fw 189A-1 Recon	Fw 189A-2 Recon	Fw 189F-1 1942 project
Powerplant		Argus As 410A-1[1]	Argus As 410A-1[6]	Argus As 411
Performance	kW	2x342=684	2x342=684	2x423=846
	hp	2x465=930	2x465=930	2x575=1150
Crew		1+2	1+2	1+2
Length	m	11.90	12.00	12.00
Height	m	3.10	3.10	3.10
Wingspan	m	18.40	18.40	18.40
Wing area	m²	38.00	38.00	38.00
Aspect ratio		8.91	8.91	8.91
Weight, empty	kg	285	2830	2800
Fuel	kg	335	335	335
Oil	kg	35	35	35
Crew	kg	270	270	270
Load(military equipment)	kg	610[2]	700	810
Max. permissible load	kg	1250	1340	1450
Takeoff weight	kg	4100	4170	4250
Wing loading	kg/m²	107.89	109.74	111.84
Weight/power ratio	kg/kW	5.99	6.10	5.02
	kg/hp	4.41	4.48	3.70
	kW/m²	18.00	18.00	22.26
	hp/m²	24.48	24.48	30.26
Max. speed	km/h	335	350	380
@ altitude	m	1700	2400	4000
Cruise speed	km/h	290	325	350
@ altitude	m	1700	2400	4000
Rate of climb	m/s	5.25[3]	6.00	8.00
Service ceiling	m	7000[4]	7300	7500
Range	km	835[5]	670	950
Max. flight time	hrs	3.00	2.16	2.70
Takeoff run	m	240	230	220
Takeoff run to 20 m altitude	m	470	450	425
Landing run	m	300	300	300
Landing run from 20 m altitude	m	570	570	570
Landing speed	km/h	120	120	120
Max. permissible load as % of takeoff weight		30	32	34
Payload as % of takeoff weight		15	17	19

[1]With automatic variable pitch propellers, 465 hp @ 3100 rpm and 1.4 ata. Climb and combat performance for the AS 410A-1 had to be reduced to 2850 rpm in 1941, apparently due to problems with the engines, which also reduced overall aircraft performance accordingly

[2]Armament consisted of 2 MG 17 + 1 MG 15
Photographic equipment and hand camera, 8.5 mm armor for pilot, FuG 17 with Ei V and Peil G4

[3]9.5 min to 3000 m with a takeoff weight of 4100 kg
18.5 min to 5000 m with a takeoff weight of 4100 kg
40.0 min to 7000 m with a takeoff weight of 4100 kg
[4]On one engine, the service ceiling was 2000 m
[5]At an altitude of 5000 m @ 2820 rpm, 230 km/h 0.6 ata, rate of consumption was 95 liters per hour (69 kg/hr)
[6]This was an improved variant of the As 410A-1 with short-term emergency boost of 356 kW/485hp at 3100 rpm

View of the cockpit of an Fw 189B trainer variant with dual controls.

first flights, is not aware of the Fw 189 being designed for anything other than a reconnaissance platform and believes that the airframe had only been made available for trials with cockpit armor. The fact that the company used the first prototypes for such unsuitable experiments indicates that these RLM trials didn't carry much weight, since the first prototypes generally undergo the most changes. The *Technisches Amt* therefore chose the Henschel Hs 129, which had been designed for the ground attack role from the outset. Presumably, the trials were nothing more than an attempt to ascertain the practicality of getting by with just a single aircraft type with a view towards economy savings.

In the summer of 1940 Focke-Wulf received the first contract for an initial production run of the Fw 189A-0 reconnaissance aircraft. It was fitted with As 410A-0 engines and automatic Argus variable-pitch propellers. Armament consisted of two forward-firing fixed MG 17s in the wing roots and two flexible aft-firing MG 15s. One of these MG 15s was located in the dorsal position (B-Stand) with the

other housed in a tail mount at the rear of the crew nacelle. Offensive armament was to have included 4x50 kg bombs carried singly on four ETC 50/VIII mounts on the wing undersides, plus two S 125 smoke generators. An FuG 17 served as communications equipment. A VHF system for voice and telegraphy, it was suitable for both air-to-ground as well as air-to-air communications. Furthermore, the A-0 was kitted out with a G 5 radio direction finding and radio compass system and an FuG 25a IFF system. The aircraft could carry either the RB 50/30, 20/30, 15/18 or 21/18 automatic camera in addition to a hand-held camera. The installed automatic cameras were driven by a continuous feed electric motor.

The V4, having a takeoff weight of 3950 kg, served as the prototype for this initial production variant. Subsequent A-series machines were initially produced in Bremen, although production later transferred to the French sites at Bordeaux and Mérignac. The A-1 series was similar to the A-0 with the exception of being equipped with somewhat more powerful As 410A-1 engines. In Bordeaux there was

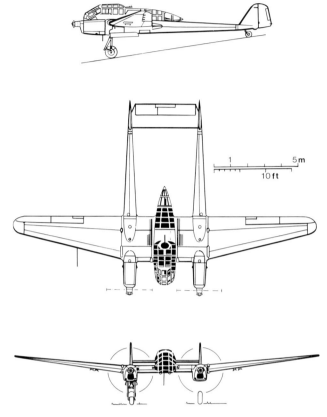

Fw 189A-2 tactical reconnaissance aircraft.

also the opportunity to experimentally fit the Fw 189 with available French engines.

An Fw 189A-1 was accordingly fitted with two air-cooled Gnôme Rhône 14M radial engines, each having an output of 514 kW/700 hp. However, the prototype was lost in a crash and only one other aircraft was built, being used by *Feldmarschall* Kesselring as a liaison plane.

Production of the A-2 began in late 1941, this variant having improved armament with the replacement of the MG 15s by two MG 81Zs. A small A-2/Trop series was fitted with equipment for operating in hot climates.

The A-3, also built in 1941, was a trainer having dual controls and closely resembled the B variants. The A-4 was in production from 1942 on, being an improved A-2 with more armor and better armament. The fixed MG 17s were replaced by MG FF cannons.

An Fw 189G variant was to have received more powerful engines, in this case the new 698 kW/ 950 hp Argus As 402. The airplane was expected to have speeds of 435

km/h at an altitude of 4500 meters. Full-scale production of the engine never materialized, however.

An Fw 189F-1 (built in 1943) was fitted with As 411 engines, which produced 423 kW/575 hp at 3400 rpm. Data for this markedly better performing variant is included along with that for the Fw 189A-1 and A-2 in the table on page 78. Production of this variant took place in the Mérignac factory, although the war's events prevented more than 17 from being built.

A total of 850 Fw 189A planes were built, chiefly as recon platforms, although a handful served as trainers, air ambulances or commuter planes. Tank, who had flown the Weihe for many years, used the faster Fw 189 for his air travels during the war.

Fw 191 Flying Powerplant

Within the first few months of the war it became apparent that a critical error had been made back in 1937 when the Luftwaffe's high command ordered the long-range Ju 89 and Do 19 designs, which had been contracted for in 1935, to be scrapped. A strike by an He 111 unit against British warships in the Scapa Flow (1939) had demonstrated that these aircraft had neither the requisite accuracy nor could they carry an adequate bomb load over longer distances. Although a contract was awarded three years later for a replacement for the blocked Do 19 and Ju 89 in the form of the Heinkel He 177, this type didn't attain front-line service until the war had almost ended. However, the Techn*isches Amt* clearly recognized the fact that the long-range aircraft concept could not be dropped entirely. In late 1939 the RLM accordingly filed a request to tender with various aircraft manufacturers for designing a medium heavy bomber in the shortest possible time. The requests were issued to Arado (Ar 340), Dornier (Do 317), Junkers (Ju 288) and Focke-Wulf (Fw 191).

The requirement was for a twin-engined aircraft that could carry a two-ton payload over approximately 1800 kilometers at a speed of 600 km/h at 7000 meters. The airplane was to have a pressurized cockpit in order to fly above the effective range of naval anti-aircraft fire. The most important point, however, was the requirement for dive-bombing capability, a point which doomed the Bomber-B program (as it was called) from the outset.

The engine choice lay with three different types, all of which were still under development. The first was the DB 604, a 24-cylinder fuel injected engine with a two-stage turbocharger and having two-ratio gearing. The engine was to have had a maximum output of 1840 kW/2500 hp at 3200

Fw 191 V1, a medium bomber pwered by BMW 801 engines, photographed during its flight testing stage.

rpm at sea level and 1764 kW/2400 hp at 3200 rpm at an altitude of 5100 meters. In 1940 an order was placed for about 30 examples of this engine, which had been contracted for on 26 February 1936. This order was reduced to six engines in 1941 and in 1942 work stopped on the type altogether in favor of the DB 608.

Development of the advanced BMW 802 was agreed upon in early 1939; in May of 1942 work came to a halt on the air-cooled 18-cylinder double radial high-altitude engine with fuel injection. The 60 liter engine had a mechanically operated two-stage charger, each stage having two-ratio gearing. The maximum pressure altitude had been estimated at 10500 meters, with the maximum output weighing in at 1889 kW/2570 hp.

The third engine proposed was Junkers' Jumo 222, then under development. The only 2000 hp performance classengine which had actually completed its initial test runup (on 24 April 1939), in March of 1940 it attained an output of 2000 rpms on the test bench. The RLM accord

Fw 191 V1 with its Multhopp landing flaps fully extended. At this setting, the flaps served as dive brakes.

ingly instructed large scale production to begin in July 1942, a bit prematurely as it turned out. On 3 November 1940 the first Jumo 222 flew in a Ju 52/3m flying test bed. Shortly thereafter several Ju 52s were regularly flying with Jumo 222s. It was then that, like with most engines, the teething troubles started appearing - a series of minor defects which caused serious problems and which could only be rectified after much tedious, continuous and laborious detailed work. Something the industry could ill afford to do at the time.

On 24 December 1941 the RLM reached the decision to stop the manufacture of the Jumo 222 since it had not been able to attain the necessary operational maturity and 2000 hp(1470 kW) was no longer acceptable.

From these three examples it's clear how the developmental period for highly complicated engines was underestimated and how the delays brought on by shortages of raw materials and the testing of substitutes were simply not taken into account at the time.

In July of 1940 the previously named companies submitted their proposals for a medium heavy bomber; Junkers and Focke-Wulf were awarded a contract for building two prototypes each. Tank assigned Dipl.-Ing. Kosel the task of coming up with the design. The initial plan was to utilize the DB 604, a water-cooled 24-cylinder X-profile engine. Preference was later given to the 24-cylinder Jumo 222, since the latter was the furthest along in the developmental process. Internally, Tank also had calculations made for using the DB 603 with 1286 kW/1750 hp since he - not unjustifiably - felt this engine had considerable developmental potential. On the other hand, he could just as easily have selected the Jumo 213. On the RLM's recommendation an Fw 191 was submitted with the DB 610 as its engines (see table) which, although offering only a minimal speed advantage over the Jumo 222, had a marked negative effect on the aircraft's range and payload capacity. With roughly the same performance capabilities, the plane equipped with the Jumo 222 would have been a simpler, lighter and smaller machine.

43567

The 24-cylinder DB 604 A engines with 1838 kW (2500 hp) @ 3100 rpm at sea level, built in 1940, was initially planned as the powerplant for the Fw 191. However, it was never put into production.

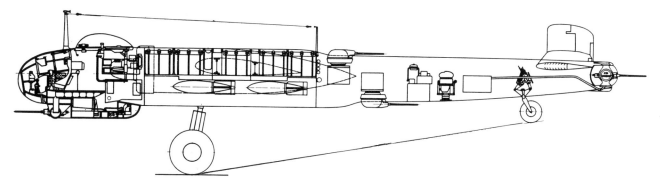

Cross-sectional cutaway of the Fw 191 showing its automatic gun turrets, military load and camera system.

At Junkers, Prof. Hertel took great pains to ensure the Ju 288 was developed as a shining example of technical refinement in which virtually all systems were automated through the use of hydraulic lines. Stimulated by this feature, the *Technisches Amt* turned to Tank and demanded that virtually all moveable components on his design be operated via electro servomotors. Tank had studied electro-engineering and was not adverse to implementing the RLM's demands. However, as a technician he was well aware of the limits of electrotechnology, particularly when plans were rolling ahead at full steam. This switch in the middle of a war to a "flying powerplant" cost a lot of time and an immeasurable amount of experimental work.

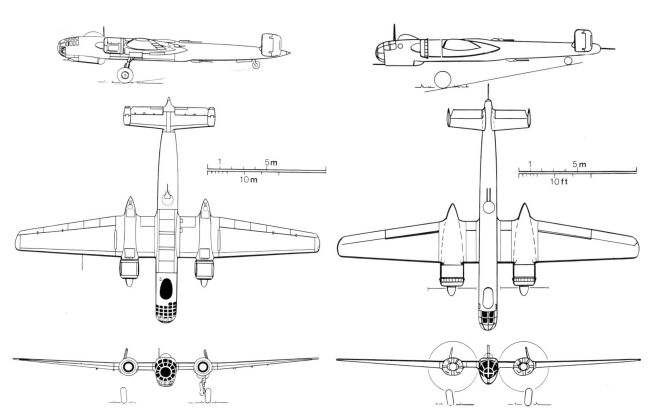

Fw 191 V1 with BMW 801 engines.

Fw 191B with two DB 610 engines.

By 1942 the two V1 and V2 prototypes had been completed. Now they stood silent, waiting on the engines. The Jumo 222, the DB 604, the BMW 802 - all the engines for advanced airplanes were not available. Even the DB 603 was not deliverable at the time. There was nothing left to do but turn back to the BMW 801.

Fw 191 Performance Using Various Powerplants

Manufacturer		Focke-Wulf			
Type		Fw 191A	Fw 191	Fw 191B	Fw 491(Fw 191C)
Powerplant		Jumo 222	DB 603	DB 610	Jumo 211J
Performance	kW	2x1470=2940	2x1286=2572	2x2168=4336	4x1044=4176
	hp	2x2000=4000	2x1750=3500	2x2950=5900	4x1420=5680
Crew		1+3	1+3	1+3	4
Length	m	18.45	18.45	18.45	18.45
Height	m	4.80	4.80	4.80	4.80
Wingspan	m	25.00	25.00	26.00	26.00
Wing area	m²	70.50	70.50	75.00	75.00
Aspect ratio		8.87	8.87	9.00	9.00
Weight, empty	kg	11465[0]	10795	16500	13923
Fuel	kg	4390	3690	4400	3540[11]
Oil	kg	350	285	500	485
Crew	kg	360	360	360	360
Load	kg	3010[1]	3010[1]	2040	4892
Max. permissible load	kg	8110	7345	7300	9277
Takeoff weight	kg	19575	18140	23800	23200
Wing loading	kg/m²	277.66	257.30	317.33	309.33
Weight/power ratio	kg/kW	6.66	7.05	5.49	5.56
	kg/hp	4.89	5.18	4.03	4.08
	kW/m²	41.70	36.48	57.81	55.68
	hp/m²	56.74	49.65	78.67	75.73
Max. speed	km/h	620[2]	585[6]	635[9]	[12]
@ altitude	m	6350	6000	6350	
Cruise speed @ 6000 m	km/h	550	480	550	
Rate of climb	m/s	6.10[3]	5.20	7.60	
Service ceiling	m	8000[4]	7900[7]	8800	
Range	km	3600[5]	3600[8]	3050[10]	
Max. flight time	hrs	7.00	7.50	6.10	
Takeoff run	m	600	720	835	
Takeoff run to 20 m	m	950	1040	1150	
Landing speed	km/h	135	130	150	135
Max. permissible load as % of takeoff weight		41	40	31	40
Payload as % of takeoff weight		15	17	9	21
Built		1940	1940	1942	1942

In the end, the V1 and, shortly afterward, the V2 flew with the much less powerful 1323 kW/1800 hp BMW 801 engines. In addition to the problems incurred when converting to electric systems, difficulties with the landing flaps also cropped up. Oberingenieur Hans Multhopp had come up with an ingenious idea of arranging three flaps in sequence, similar in concept to today's Fowler flaps. Multhopp's flaps were operated by electric motors and rods and were to have been activated on landing and takeoff, as well as being used for dive brakes. But the entire system had a tendency to begin shaking as it extended. One flap affected the other and it was not possible to smoothly land the plane using this flap system. Because of these problems and the difficulties with the electrical system (up to 40 complaints per flight), further work on the V3, V4 and V5 came to a halt.

Once senior officials were convinced by the constant accidents with the underpowered plane, the RLM called for a halt in further production of the prototypes and assigned Tank the construction of a new variant, the Fw 191 V6, which was to be fitted with a combined hydraulic-electric power system. The Multhopp flaps were replaced by normal, hydraulically-activated flaps on the V6. The RLM also now provided two Jumo 222 engines for testing purposes. The more powerful engines would have enabled the airplane to carry a 2000 kg payload over 3600 km at a speed of 550 km/h.

The V6 took off on its first flight at the end of 1942 with Jumo 222 engines, which only attained 1617 kW/2200 hp instead of the claimed 1837 kW/2500 hp. This aircraft did not meet expectations either, and development on the Fw 191 was accordingly stopped.

Today, Tank feels that the aircraft's construction was an unnecessary burden placed on Focke-Wulf's available developmental capacity, particularly since the political leadership was not sure whether priority should have been given to the dive bomber or the long-range strategic bomber. Although the formal test program was carried out by Dipl.-Ing Mehlhorn, Tank flew the Fw 191 on several occassions. His verdict: "sluggish from a flying standpoint, comparable to the Condor, too-weak engines due to the fact that the promised engines were never available."

---

[0]**Breakdown of weights:**

Fuselage	1462 kg
Landing gear	930 kg
Empennage	473 kg
Control system	118 kg
Wings	2838 kg
Basic airframe	5821 kg
Engines	4286 kg
Equipment	630 kg
Empty weight	10737 kg
Add'l equipment	728 kg
Total empty weight	11465 kg

[0]**Drag Inducing Surfaces of the Fw 191A with Jumo 222**

	Area(m^2)	C_w	fs(m^2)
Wings	70.50	0.0081	0.570
Fuselage	2.75	0.110	0.303
Empennage	16.10	0.0090	0.145
Engine nacelles (including radiators)	2x1.40	0.110	0.309
Military fittings	0.64	0.15-0.30	0.148
			fs=1.475m^2

[1]A stand MG 81Z 63 kg
B-stand ditto + MG 151 158 kg
C-stand ditto + ditto 158 kg

D-stand 2 MG 81Z 126 kg
Ammunition 505 kg
Bombs 2000 kg

Total 3010 kg

[2]Calculated performance figures
At average flying weight of 15400 kg + 1/2 fuel capacity
2x1345 kW/1830 hp at sea level 495 km/h
2x1397 kW/1900 hp at 2000 m 540 km/h
2x1323 kW/1800 hp at 4000 m 570 km/h
2x1323 kW/1800 hp at 6350 m 620 km/h
2x1051 kW/1430 hp at 8000 m 605 km/h

[3]Time to climb with a takeoff weight of 19575 kg
1000 m 2.7 min
2000 m 5.6 min
4000 m 12.6 min
6000 m 20.6 min

[4]9700 m at 15400 kg, 5600 m on only one engine
[5]At 550 km/h at an altitude of 6000 m
[6]At a takeoff weight of 14300 kg
[7]9700 m at a takeoff weight of 14300 kg, 5300 m on only one engine
[8]At 480 km/h at an altitude of 6000 m
[9]At an average takeoff weight of 19450 kg
[10]At a cruising speed of 500 km/h
[11]Two drop tanks each holding 1300 liters(1959 kg) were planned
[12]No data is available for flight performance

Four-Engined Fw 491 (Fw 491C)

To give the Tech*nisches Amt* the opportunity of benefiting from the resources already squandered on the type, the company developed a third variant which utilized engines already in production such as the Jumo 211F, the DB 605 or the DB 601A; the design was a less-refined version lacking a pressurized cabin with cut-back mechanical features. It was to have made use of many of the Fw 191's components. The weight of the four engines was some 2000 kg greater than for the two Jumo 222s, meaning that a somewhat shorter range would have to be taken into account. The *Technisches Amt*, however, showed no interest whatsoever in this proposal.

SOS...The Americans Are Coming!

Unfazed by the lack of planning which doomed the Fw 191 - electronics and one engine today, hydraulics and another engine tomorrow, and finally no engines altogether and a halt in production - on 2 June 1941 Tank turned to the Reich's senior officials with the cautionary warning that America's entrance into the war and that country's large-scale production of long-range bombers would become a threat which should not be underestimated "particularly to our production and, as a result, to the outcome of the war". Fighters in large numbers had to be produced immediately to counter this threat. Feldmarschall Kesselring didn't respond, but at a conference in Italy informed Tank that he supported his ideas, but because of strong differences with the leadership could not do anything. Feldmarschall Milch gave a trivial answer. Göring's command staff did not reply at all.

At the war's end the Americans occupied Bad Eilsen, where they found Tank and 2000 engineers still hard at work. An American colonel by the name of Ferrari searched through Tank's safe and its files and in so doing came across Tank's warning letter calling for an increase in fighter production. Ferrari then related to Tank that he had done a study back in the US in which he'd expressed the concern: "The whole bomber offensive could fail if the Germans can produce superior numbers of fighters in time." Ferrari: "It was lucky for us that your letter was ignored."

Tank's Greatest Success: Fw 190 Würger

When in 1938 Tank was awarded a contract for building a new fighter, the fighter units' conversion from the He 51 and Arado 68 biplanes to the Bf 109 was in full swing. For the pilots, it was not easy having to adjust from biplanes with low wing loading to such an aerodynamically refined plane with retractable undercarriage, variable-pitch propeller and nearly double the airspeed. The He 51, for example, had a wing loading of 70 kg/m2, while on the Me 108 (an intermediate stage airplane prior to the Bf 109 in which pilots flew with dual controls and later soloed for the first time) this value was 85 kg/m^2. This jump was just manageable for the majority of pilots. However, as they transitioned to the Bf 109 they found that the wing loading rapidly increased to 130 kg/m^2 (Bf 109D) and even to 161 kg/m^2 (Bf 109E). Oftentimes thorough instruction was lacking; there were too few pilots who had experience with the

speedy bird. Furthermore, there was no instructional material available and the pilots initially were encouraged to push and pull all its levers and buttons, especially the operational sequence for landing and taking off, so that by the time they'd had their first flight they were at least familiar with the mechanics of the new fighter, if not its handling.

The Reichsluftfahrt-Ministerium's *Technisches Amt* felt quite proud to be able to equip its front- line units with what was probably the world's best fighter. Certain reservations didn't set in until accidents with the aircraft began piling up at an alarming rate. Without a doubt, a large number of these crashes was because of the aircraft - as a result of its narrow track undercarriage the Bf 109 had a strong tendency to ground loop. During landing, it had the unpleasant quality of tipping over onto one wing if the aircraft were leveled out even a bit too high. Even as late as

Wind tunnel model of the Fw 190 V1.

September 1944 the Luftwaffe was afforded the luxury of losing 30 to 40 Bf 109s per month due to ground loop crashes, according to a statement by Oberst von Lossberg. Along with that came an extremely high number of belly landings which, although they had nothing to do with the quality of the aircraft, were very likely due to the haste with which the units had been re-equipped with the Bf 109. A few senior ranking personnel within the RLM must certainly have gotten cold feet, even though pilots were injured in these mishaps in only the rarest of cases. They laid their blame on the aircraft and appeared to have little interest in the real reasons, which most likely be found in the inadequate training.

Without a doubt, these unpleasant events had a certain influence on the RLM approaching a surprised Prof. Tank in the spring of 1938 with a contract for drawing up a new fighter plane. It was to be an aircraft which was superior to both the Bf 109 and the British Spitfire.

With his typical energy Tank dove headlong into the complex project and had the design department under the direction of Oberingenieur Ludwig Mittelhuber draft several proposals. These went to Rudolf Blaser in the construction department, who made some major changes. Thus was born the design for a fighter which utilized the water-cooled DB 601 with 864 kW/1175 hp. Another plan, which Tank saw as having the greatest chance, saw the fitting of an air-cooled Siemens BMW 139 twin radial, with an output of 1103 kW/1500 hp. The water-cooled engine, whether it be the DB 601 or the Jumo 211, wouldn't be able to match the performance of the air-cooled design after the next two years in any case. Today, Tank feels justified in stating that the Fw 190 at the front racked up more flight hours per aircraft due to the fact that the radial engine was less susceptible to damage than the Bf 109's water-cooled engine. Unfortunately, there are no statistics available which can back up this opinion.

The Butcher Bird's First Flight

On 1 June 1939, one and a half years after the initial dialog between Tank and the Technisches Amt, the V1 prototype (Werknummer 0001 D-OPZE) took off on its maiden flight with test pilot Hans Sander at its controls. The Fw 190 was a compact design, in appearance giving the impression of perfection of form, a low-wing layout with an extremely wide-track undercarriage.

Tank expressed himself thusly regarding the train of thought which led to the design's layout: "I took part in the First World War as an infantryman and cavalry soldier and saw the rough conditions a soldier was forced to live in during wartime. A piece of equipment made for combat should stress simplicity, robust construction and ease of maintenance for the average skilled personnel in its layout. It was no simple task to harmonize these ideals with extremely light construction, refined aerodynamics and good reliability. The goal could only be achieved with an extremely powerful engine. We had our eye on the air-cooled BMW 139 which had an output 239 kW/325 hp more than the most powerful water-cooled engine at the time. With this powerplant it seemed that the goal of creating a robust high-performance fighter was in sight.

The best solution appeared to be a low-wing design of compact construction, having the ability to retract the wide-track undercarriage into the wings. The next main focus of the layout was a cockpit with good all-round visibility. The radial engine offered high reliability coupled with safety, being much less prone to damage from than a water-cooled engine with its touchy and easily damaged radiator mantle.

One of the most important considerations was the approved rate of descent for the undercarriage, which at 4.50 meters per second was designed to be twice the amount specified in the requirement. This ensured that the landing gear remained trouble-free throughout the Fw 190's developmental cycle and the ever-increasing weight of the different variants. The aircraft's good flight handling characteristics were directly attributable to the large rudder and elevator dimensions and its good aerodynamic and dynamic balance. In addition, push-rods were used for the controls in place of cables - the secret of the Fw 190's responsive controls. We didn't need any trimming other than small, adjustable tabs on the ailerons which, once set properly, kept the plane stable. The Fw 190 had only a single manually-operated electrical elevator trim control. If our design succeeded it was in no small part due to the excellent cooperation between my assistant Willi Kaether and constructor Rudi Blaser, design engineer Ludwig Mittelhuber and the two test pilots Hans Sander and Kurt Mehlhorn."

Focke-Wulf Fw 190 V1 with BMW 139 twin-radial engine, rated at 1103 kW (1500 hp). Standing in front of the aircraft (from left) are Lucht, Udet and Carl Francke.   (Photo: VFW-Fokker via Eddy Creek).

For Hans Sander, taking off in the first prototype was a high point in his flying career. At 1103 kW/1500 hp the machine accelerated rapidly and had an impressive rate of climb. But the experienced pilot also found a few shortcomings on his first flight which would later cause many headaches: almost unbearable heat, particularly near the pilot's feet, inadequate cockpit seal which allowed exhaust gases to seep in so that Sander had to make use of an oxygen mask, and landing gear which did not lock properly. Once the latter two problems were overcome the machine went to the *Erprobunsstelle* Rechlin in October 1939 after just a few flights.

1103 kW/1500 hp BMW 139, the powerplant for the Fw 190 V1 and V2.

89

Fw 190 V1 D-OPZE with test pilot Hans Sander in the cockpit.

Plagued by Teething Troubles

Some of the best test pilots, including *Flugkapitän* Beauvais, flew the V1 while it was at Rechlin. To a man, they expressed their enthusiasm with the plane's good handling and its high airspeed, but were also concerned about the unbearable heat in the cockpit, which could reach temperatures of 55°C. Its speed of 502 km/h at sea level was markedly higher than the 460 km/h of the Bf 109E, just being delivered, at the same altitude. Due to the cooling problems Rechlin handed the machine back over to the company with various recommendations for a series of improvements.

The V1 was modified over the winter months. One of its most noticeable features had been the unusual engine cowling: the entire forward nacelle rotated with the airscrew. Where the propeller hub could normally be found was the intake for the cooling air. Behind the hub was located a cooling fan which was spun up by the propeller gearing and rotated inside the ring-shaped cowling at three times the speed of the propeller itself. This system didn't provide adequate cooling, however, particularly for the rear set of cylinders. Consequently, the aircraft was fitted with a NACA cowling. The cockpit was better ventilated and sealed. Following these modifications the airplane was given the Luftwaffe coding FO+LY. It was in service until 1943.

In the meantime the second prototype (V2, 0002 FO+LZ) had been made ready for its maiden flight on 1 December 1939. This aircraft had also been fitted with Focke-Wulf's new cowling design. When the V2 also showed no improvement in cooling, Hans Sander eventually began to express doubts as to whether the blower disk behind the propeller hub had any positive effect whatsoever. According to his flight log, on 6 December he chanced a flight without the blower fan. The result was even higher temperatures and the blower was quickly refitted. For test purposes BMW supplied a blower disk with adjustable blades, but this design was not able to lower the temperature at the rear row of cylinders either.

The V2 was the first to be fitted with armament and in February 1940 was ferried to the Erp*robungsstelle* Tarnewitz for firing trials. The type subsequently went to the *Erprobungsstelle* Rechlin. In September 1940 the V2 was again flown to Tarnewitz with its new RM+CB markings and there thoroughly tested by Flugbaumeister Pfister up until 1941 for weapons suitability. During these trials, the plane's armament included two 7.9 mm MG 17s with 750 rounds each in the fuselage and two 13 mm MG 131 with 470 rounds each in the wing roots. The Revi C12a gunsight for cannon was fitted, with the radio being the FuG 7a.

Even before the V1's first flight BMW had a new engine running in its test plant; although based on the BMW 139, it had undergone significant modifications and, in addition to an improvement in the cooling, had improved its performance by 74 kW/100 hp to 174 kW/200 hp. The engine was some 50 centimeters longer and 90 kg heavier than the BMW 139 and was equipped with a control system which automatically regulated mixture, ignition, turbocharger switching and other functions. The 14-cylinder twin-radial engine had exhaust ejector jets which provided about 145 kp thrust at its maximum pressure altitude, equating to approximately 247 kW/336 hp at 630 km/h.

The RLM then issued a contract for modifying the Fw 190 to accept the BMW 801. Work on the two V3 and V4 prototypes was halted as a result in anticipation of the BMW 801's test bench results. The V3 airframe was later plundered for replacement parts and the V4 served as a structural stress testbed airframe.

Fw 190 V1 in 1940 following modifications and after being fitted with a new engine cowling.

Fw 190 V5K, the fifth prototype here with the original short wings, was the first one to be fitted with the more powerful BMW 801 C-0 engine (with an output of 1147 kW/1560 hp)

Fw 190 V5 with BMW 801C

The Focke-Wulf engineers made use of the time until the BMW 801's test run-ups were completed by giving the Fw 190 design a complete reworking and evaluating the flight test results from the trials already completed. A series of structural components were strengthened; von Faehlmann and Mittelhuber in the design department moved the seat further aft, a measure necessitated by the heavy BMW 801 engine. Moving the seat back was expected to reduce the heat in the cockpit to a tolerable temperature, plus provide more room for the installation of armament. The downside to this was the fact that visibility was degraded during taxiing.

The seat itself became somewhat smaller and had armor plating fitted in order to offer the pilot some protection. In addition, the canopy was blended more smoothly into the fuselage profile. Blaser moved the leading edges of the wings a bit more forward at the roots in order to provide more weapons space in this area as well. The undercarriage attachment points on the wings were modified; Blaser moved the lower section of the wheel covers, a characteristic feature of the V1 and V2, from the landing gear

to the fuselage underside, while the tailwheel was enlarged and fitted with a pneumatic tire.

Despite these many changes the fuselage was only lengthened by 0.10 meters; however, takeoff weight with no armament climbed to 3125 kg. The extended wing roots increased the wing area only marginally, and the increased weight was therefore translated into degraded climb performance and maneuverability. As a consequence, Blaser also had a wing built with a lower weight but having a somewhat larger span and area - after it was discovered that the Fw 190, in a flyoff with the Bf 110, could not turn as tightly as the twin-engined plane. This case, too, was a testimony to the somewhat larger wingspan approach.

The V5k (0005) configuration initially possessed the short-span wing of the V1 and V2 and flew for the first time in August 1940 with Sander in the cockpit. Sander had to bring the plane back in immediately after takeoff when the engine cover over the guns came loose and threatened to break free. As he taxied in after touchdown he also ran into a tractor, damaging the plane severely. The V5g variant was fitted with the entirely new wing design having a span of 10.50 meters vice 9.56 meters and a wing area of 18.30 m2 instead of 15.00 m². The powerplant was the BMW 801C-0, a pre-production version with 1147 kW/1560 hp.

The V-5k configuration with the smaller wingspan was - as the tests had shown - only about 10 km/h faster than the configuration with the larger wing. On the other hand, the V5g proved itself to be much more maneuverable and have a better climb rate. Because the airplane had been fitted with two different wings it has often been assumed that two V5 prototypes had been built. According to Focke-Wulf's company files - and even from various other sources - there was only a single V5 with the Werknummer 0005, which along with the V-6 (0006) were the only prototypes for the A-0 series. As a side note, the V5 flipped over on 9/9/1940 and was damaged beyond repair.

Initial Production Run: Fw 190A-0

A rather large order was placed for 28 A-0 series aircraft (0008-0035), production which began in November 1940. The V6, first prototype for the production batch, was equipped with the BMW 801C-0 and for armament had two MG 17s firing through the propeller arc, two MG 17s in the wing roots and provisions for installing two MG FF cannons in the wings outboard of the propeller arc. It was also fitted with the FuG 7a. The V6 was given the designation of Fw 190A-0/U1, with the letter U indicating modification, equipment configuration or some other type of change. The first seven aircraft, Werknummer 0008-0014, were still fitted with the smaller wings due to the fact that production was too far along for major changes to be introduced. The remaining aircraft (0015-0035) were equipped with the larger wings.

These aircraft primarily served as flight, engine and weapons trials. Werknummer 0008, 0010 and 0013 - designated Fw 190A-0/U2 - were fitted with two MG 131s in the wing roots, with the MG FF cannons being dropped. Various machines were fitted with the improved BMW 801C-1 engine, which had a twelve-bladed engine cooling fan instead of the ten-bladed cooler. The large wing Focke-Wulf 190A-0/U-3, Werknummer 0021, was lost in a crash on 1 October 1941. With modifications to their engine mounts and carrying the designations Fw 190A-0/U-12 and U-13, Werknummer 0031 and 0025 through 0028 were powered by the BMW 801D production engine. They accordingly became the testbeds for the more powerful production engine. Werknummer 0022 and 0023 (Fw 190A-0/U4) were employed as trials aircraft for carrying bomb loads up to 500 kg and for tests with drop tanks and with the FuG 16Z radio homing device. Ejector seats were also installed on an experimental basis.

Fw 190A-0, Werknummer 27, was utilized for field testing.

First Prototypes of the Fw 190

Manufacturer		Focke-Wulf [1]		
Type		Fw 190 V1	Vw 190 V5K	Fw 190 V6(A-0)
Powerplant		BMW 139	BMW 801C-0	BMW 801C-0
Performance	kW	1103	1147	1147
	hp	1500[2]	1560	1560
Crew		1	1	1
Length	m	8.85	8.95	8.95
Height	m	3.95	3.95	3.95
Wingspan	m	9.56	9.56	10.50
Wing area	m²	14.88	15.00	18.30
Aspect ratio		6.14	6.09	6.02
Weight, empty	kg	2310	2415	2500
Fuel	kg	396	396	396
Oil	kg	34	34	50
Crew	kg	80	80	80
Load	kg	200[3]	200[5]	474[5]
Max. permissible load	kg	710	710	1000
Takeoff weight	kg	3020	3125	3500
Wing loading	kg/m²	202.96	208.33	191.25
Weight/power ratio	kg/kW	2.74	2.72	3.05
	kg/hp	2.01	2.00	2.24
	kW/m²	74.13	76.47	62.68
	hp/m²	100.80	104.00	85.25
Built		1939	1939	1940
Max. speed	km/h	595	630	630
@ altitude	m	4500	4500	6100
Cruise speed	km/h	500	520	570
@ altitude	m	4500	4500	6100
Rate of climb	m/s	14.00	14.00	14.00
Service ceiling	m	8600	9600	9600
Range	km	750[4]	750[4]	810[6]
Max. flight time	hrs	2.00	2.00	2.05
Takeoff run	m	300	300	300
Takeoff run to 20 m	m	600	600	600
Landing speed	km/h	130	135	150
Max. permissible load as % of takeoff weight		24	23	28
Payload as % of takeoff weight		7	6	14

[1]Data in this table was compiled from available company documents and from RLM tables and sources

[2]Takeoff power (1 min); 1103 kW/1500 hp at sea level
Maximum power (5 min); 1036 kW/1410 hp at 4500 m
Extended maximum power (30 min); 933 kW/1270 hp at 4500 m
Cruising power
845 kW/1150 hp at 5400 m
Fuel consumption rate at 5400 m was 230 g/hp/hr, equating to 264 kg/hr or 367 liters/hr

The engine weighed 800 kg
[3]No armament was fitted. The actual takeoff weight was therefore 2820 kg. It can be assumed that for at least part of the test flight program the aircraft was flown with just 1/2 its fuel capacity
[4]At economy setting at 5000 m (2.05 hr endurance). During combat and when using emergency power the range was 545 km (1.25 hr's endurance)
[5]Load = weight of armament and equipment
[6]At economy setting at 5000 m

Hans Sander, in whose hands rested the Fw 190 flight testing program, seen here in the aircraft's cockpit.

Powered by a BMW 801C, Werknummer 0018 (designated Fw 190A-0/U-5) served as the basis for testing the MG 151 machine cannon. Werknummer 0015 (U-11) had four MG 17s and two MG FF guns fitted; the MG FF's ammunition feed system underwent thorough testing on Werknummer 0030 (U-10). The first GM 1 system was trial-fitted to the BMW 801D-powered Werknummer 0031 (U-12); this system had been installed to improve the engine's high-altitude performance and will be discussed in detail later.

The above brief sampling ought to give an overview of the enthusiastic, comprehensive manner in which the Fw 190A-0's test and evaluation program was tackled.

Six of these production airplanes were flown to Rechlin in March 1941. There, too, significant problems cropped up at an early stage, mostly caused by inadequate cooling, mangled cylinders or broken oil lines. Occasionally, during high-speed test flights parts of the engine cowling came off altogether, necessitating the strengthening of this area. The cockpit canopy could not be jettisoned at higher speeds.

There were also problems with the propeller's variable pitch, a technology which was still relatively new at the time. Thanks to Tank's dynamic drive and the perseverance of his engineers and technicians, they were able to take quick action to eliminate many of these shortcomings. This they did in close cooperation with a team of technical personnel from Jagdgeschwader 26 "Schlageter" headed by Oberleutnant Otto Behrens and Fliegerstabsingenieur Battmer, who had been sent to Rechlin for the express purpose of correcting deficiencies; fifty of their solutions were passed along to the engine manufacturer and the company. JG 26 had been selected as the initial recipient of the Fw 190 and, as such, had a keen interest in the airplane. The unit was stationed in Le Bourget at the time.

The aircraft were subjected to a grueling test program at the hands of test pilots and pilots from the Schlageter Jagdgeschwader; the program included flyoffs and mock dogfights against the Bf 109 and - in particular - against captured Spitfire machines. Both from a flying standpoint as well as in its performance, the airplane proved itself to be markedly superior to all the types it flew against.

Fw 190A-1, 1941, fitted with the BMW 801C, an engine rated at 1147 kW/1560 hp.

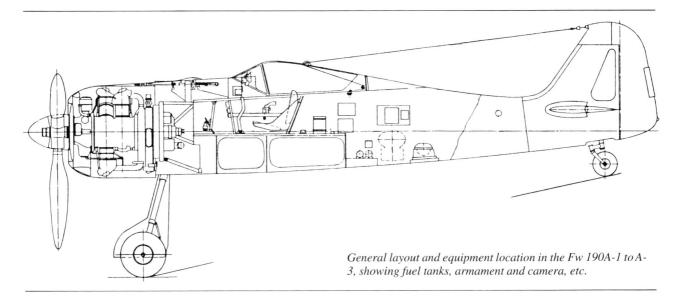

General layout and equipment location in the Fw 190A-1 to A-3, showing fuel tanks, armament and camera, etc.

Testing the Fw 190A-1 at Jagdgeschwader 26

Because of the war's change of fortunes, the two remaining units serving on the Channel Front were in desperate need of a new airplane. The Luftwaffe's other units had been transferred to the East for the attack on Russia. With-

out waiting for further testing, the RLM therefore issued a contract for 102 A-1 production aircraft as early as 1940; work on this order was to begin immediately at both the Bremen and Hamburg facilities.

The V7 served as the prototype in this case. It was comparable to the V6, or A-0, and was powered by the 1176 kW/1600 hp BMW 801C-1. The airplane was equipped with the FuG 7 radio and the FuG 25 IFF system, first built in 1939 and later replaced by the FuG 25a. Armament con-

sisted of four MG 17s and two MG FF, in addition to which the aircraft could carry 500 kg worth of bombs or a 300 liter drop tank.

The first A-1 series aircraft were delivered to Jagdgeschwader 26 in August of 1941. They in turn proved themselves to be excellent flying platforms, although they caused the pilots and ground personnel no little consternation because of incessant problems with the engines. According to a report filed by Oberleutnant Behrens on 4 September 1941, these problems could be traced back to the spark plugs, which caused a dropoff in performance and led to engine vibration, turbocharger damage and even fires in the forward engine compartment.

Improved BMW 801C-2 for the Fw 190A-2

While the A-1 was being delivered to the field, in mid-1941 production began on the 315 A-2 variants ordered by the RLM. Because of the numbers involved, Focke-Wulf was forced to permit the AGO-Werke in Oschersleben and Arado in Warnemünde to build the airplane under license.

There were only minor differences between the A-1 and the A-2. The V14 with a BMW 801C-1 engine served as the prototype for the new series. The A-2, however, had the improved 801C-2 as its powerplant. In order to show the pilot the position of the landing gear, either retracted or extended, the A-2 was fitted with a scaled rod which protruded from the upper wing surface when the gear was extended, or disappeared inside the wing when it retracted. The engine cowling was once again reinforced and fitted with push-type safety clasps. BMW improved the cooling by installing a more effective fan. In addition, the A-2 was fitted with a canopy which could be blown off by small detonating charges. It was armed with two MG 17s over the engine, two MG 151s in the wing roots and with an additional two MG FF cannons which could be optionally carried in the wings outboard of the propeller arc. Takeoff weight climbed considerably to 3850 kg.

The aircraft from this production batch were supplied to the units from October 1941 to July 1942. Its equipment included pylons for carrying bombs or drop tanks, the FuG 7 radio and FuG 25 IFF system. One Fw 190A-2/U-1 (Werknummer 0315) was also test-fitted with a Patin PKS autopilot. Such a device was extremely beneficial when flying in formation through cloud cover.

Fw 190A-2, built in 1941.

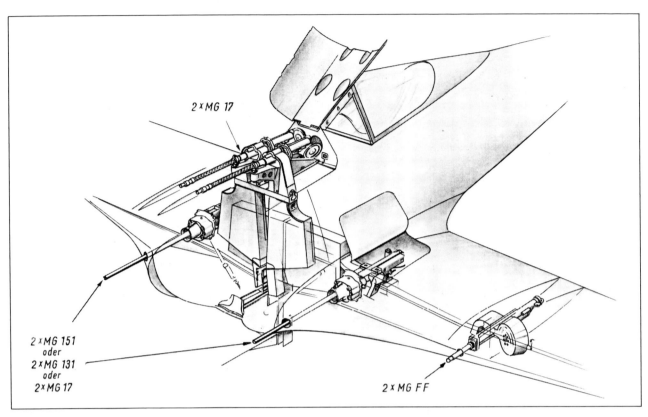

Armament layout of the Fw 190A-2. However, the gun arrangement was changed several times.

Multi-role Fw 190A-3

The two units which received the majority of Fw 190s, JG 2 and JG 26, enjoyed considerable success with the new type. According to British reports, in 1942 the two groups shot down no less than 300 enemy aircraft, of which at least 272 were the vaunted Spitfire. Frontline experience and Focke-Wulf improvements were incorporated into the next variant, the A-3 series. BMW offered what appeared to be a "grown up" variant of its BMW 801, the D-2, which could be flown at its maximum output of 1250 kW/1700 hp; BMW had also increased its compression ratio, jumping from 6.5 to 7.22, and its boost pressure. In addition, it had also changed the gearing on the engine's turbocharger drive and replaced the two-gear with a three-gear charger. Despite these improvements, the engine was restricted to combat settings and could not be flown with takeoff power.

The V14 was fitted with this engine in the summer of 1942 and put through its paces as the prototype for the A-3 series. Armament included two MG 17s over the motor and two MG FFs. The two outboard Oerlikon MG FFs could be swapped out for the MG 151 cannons with their more rapid rate of fire. Modifications to ease maintenance were made to the engine cowling.

The trials showed that the airplane was not only a remarkable fighter, but was also suitable as a long-range fighter-bomber. This variant was later designated as Jabo-Rei (from Jagdbomber- *Reichweite*, or literally fighter bomber, long-range). The prototype as well as a handful of production machines were fitted with numerous field conversion kits and tested in a variety of roles. The indefatigable design proved to be suited not just for operating in an overloaded configuration, but also as a light bomber, a reconnaissance plane, a night/all-weather fighter, a ground attack plane and even as a torpedo bomber. This led to the A-3 and subsequent A-series versions to be put into immediate large-scale production (which lasted until 1943) and be fitted out with field conversion kits for the widest variety of roles imaginable.

Other factories were incorporated into the Fw 190's manufacturing program, and the A-3 was soon rolling off the lines in great numbers at Focke-Wulf, at Arado's facilities in Brandenburg,

Landing gear of the A-series

1 Oleo strut
2 700 x 175 tire
3 Torque link
4 Compression strut cover
5 Forward spherical bearing
6 Aft spherical bearing
7 Drive motor with cyclic gear-box
8 Mechanical landing gear position indicator
9 Upper side-stay
10 Lower side-stay
11 Switch and line for electronic position indicator
12 Retraction actuator
13 Lockpiece
14 Release line
15 Tailwheel retraction cable

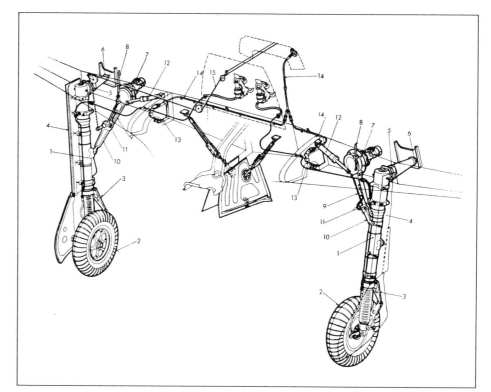

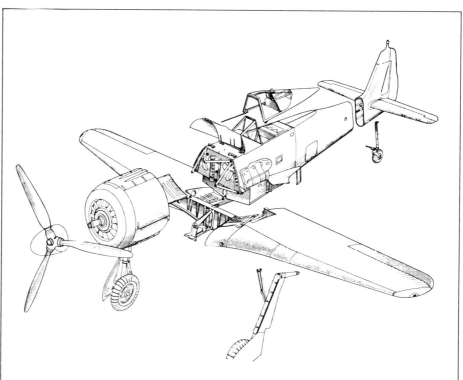

Major sub-assembly components for the Fw 190A series.

99

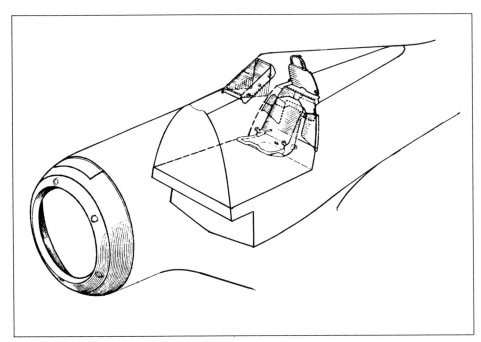

Armor protection areas of the A series.

Fw 190A-3/U7 with BMW 801D and intake filters for operations in tropical climates.

Cutaway view of the BMW 801D engine.

Warnemünde, Anklam, Rathenow, Wittenberge and Neuendorf, at Fieseler's Kassel plant and at AGO in Oschersleben and another site.

Werknummer 270, an Fw 190A-3/U-1, had its BMW 801D engine moved even more forward. Armament consisted of two MG 17s and two MG 151s which could be exchanged for two MG FFs and, with few exceptions, was retained for the entire series. Werknummer 385, an A-3/U-3, served as a recon testbed with the installation of various cameras. Experience with this aircraft led to the A-3/U4 being fitted with two RB 12.5 cameras, a smaller 7x9 automatic camera and with shackles for carrying a single underfuselage bomb. The pilot could monitor the success of his attacks using the automatic camera. Twelve of these specially-modified aircraft were delivered from October to November 1942. Three other BMW 801D-powered aircraft, Werknummer 528, 530 and 531 (designated Fw 190A-3/

U-7), incorporated weight-saving measures for testing them in anticipation of the planned B-0 high-altitude fighter series. The engines needed for this role failed to materialize at first, however. The three aircraft were eventually finished in September 1942 with just two MG 151s.

72 A-3 series airplanes (Fw 190Aa-3) were delivered to Turkey from October 1942 to March 1943 under the codename "Hamburg", where they served until 1948.

To get an idea of the effects that external loads had on the plane's airspeed, tests were carried out in a French wind tunnel in Chalais Meudon. These showed that a single pylon with a 250 kg bomb or a drop tank reduced the speed by 45 km/h at sea level and by 55 km/h at an altitude of 6500 m. Two underwing ETC bomb racks alone, with no bombs, reduced the airspeed by 13.7 km/h (2.9%) and added to the total dead weight by 64 kg. Two full drop tanks under the wings resulted in a loss in speed of 34.2 km/h (7.4%) with an additional 96 kg dead weight.

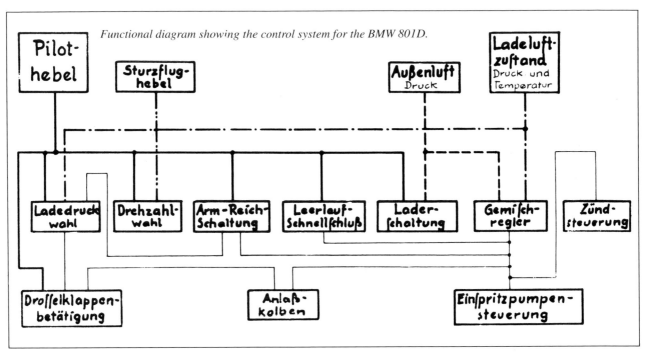

Functional diagram showing the control system for the BMW 801D.

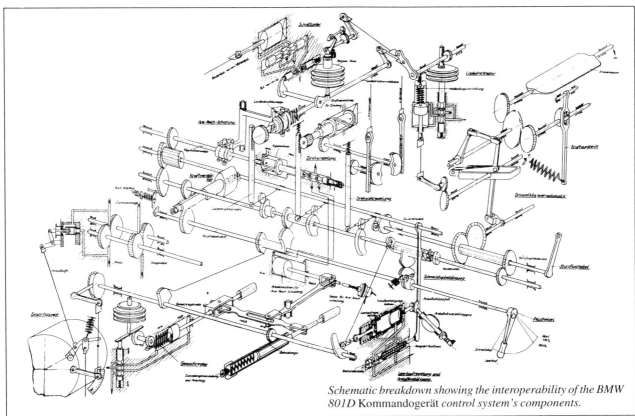

Schematic breakdown showing the interoperability of the BMW 801D Kommandogerät *control system's components.*

Dipl.-Ing. Karl Prestel was the creator of the BMW 801's Kommandogerät *control system, the heart of the engine.*

How to Steal an Fw 190

In early 1942, as the Fw 190's superiority over the Spitfire V was hammered home almost daily and their numbers increased over the Channel, the British put all their efforts into capturing an Fw 190.

In his book "Fw 190 at War", Dr. Alfred Price - with contributions from Prof. Kurt Tank and Flugbaumeister Hans Sander - describes how the British pilots initially mistook the first Fw 190s over the English Channel for Curtiss Hawks, then for captured French aircraft. They soon noticed, however, that these were dangerous enemies indeed, which in Price's own words: "...could out-run, out-climb, out-dive and out-roll the Spitfire Mark V, the best aircraft RAF Fighter Command then had available". The Fw 190 proved to be a nasty surprise for the British in the summer of 1941. It would only eventually meet its match with the Spitfire Mk IX with its more powerful engine and two-stage turbocharger; but this aircraft was still months away from reaching production maturity.

In early 1942 the English hatched an adventurous plan to discover the secret behind the Fw 190: two officers would

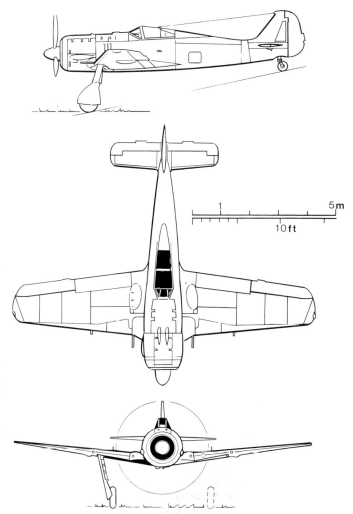

Fw 190A-3 with BMW 801D.

be dropped off on the French coast, stealthily make their way to one of the airbases near the coast and in the morning, when the engines were being run up, shoot one of the mechanics. Then, while one man provided covering fire, the other would jump into the plane, give it full throttle and race off across the field towards England.

While the details of this rather daring coup were being ironed out, the RAF was presented with an undamaged Fw 190A-3 (Werknummer 313) in June of 1942 when Oberleutnant Arnim Faber, a Staffel commander at JG 2, landed at RAF Pembrey in southern Wales by mistake. Following a dogfight, the pilot had become disoriented and thought he was landing at his base in France. In August 1942 the British Ministry of Production invited the press to an aerial demonstration with the captured Fw 190 flown by test pilots and gave the journalists all the details of the German machine. The results were published in several of the magazines at the time and are collectively summarized below.

Fw 190A-3 in Comparison with the Opposition

These articles revealed that the Fw 190 had a high rate of speed and was easy to control. Its high wing loading, however, made for long takeoffs and landing approaches. Despite the plane's two-stage supercharger its performance fell off dramatically at altitudes above 6100 meters. The 390 kg fuel capacity appeared much too low for the engine; at speeds of 500 km/h it gave the aircraft an endurance of barely one hour. If the machine were flown at full throttle for any length of time - which undoubtedly would have been the case under combat conditions - the flying time would have had to have been reduced in proportion to the consumption rate, a disadvantage which most certainly arose from the powerplant. In general, it was considered that the design was quite successful for a point defense fighter but was inadequate for offensive roles, missions which were at the heart of the RAF's Bomber and Fighter Command's philosophy. Without a doubt, much had been gleaned from the airplane, and this knowledge was incorporated into the design programs for many of the newer British aircraft.

One example of a journalist's assessment of the Fw 190A-3 can be found in the August edition of Aeroplane magazine:

"The Focke-Wulf Fw 190A is a remarkably compact and efficient fighter, heavily armed, well armored and fast. But it is not a high-level fighter - it cannot fly as high as the Me 109F - and, because of its high landing speed it is not a particularly easy machine to fly. It shows room for further development, but there is no fighting feature about it in which we cannot do better. As things stand at present the Focke-Wulf Fw 190A-3 is undoubtedly a very formidable fighter between about 16,000 ft and 24,000 ft - as good as anything else in the World at present. Above and below those heights it is less dangerous.

Technically, the most interesting feature of the design is the use of an air-cooled engine, magnificently cowled and efficiently cooled. Aerodynamically, the machine is poor; structurally it is excellent; electrically it is first class; as a production job it should be easy, as a result of much painstaking care and thought; from a flying viewpoint it is delightful, but its finish is bad, its range limited, the engine rough and its boost low.

In detail, the top speed on normal boost is 375 mph at 18,000 ft. In an emergency the throttle can be put "through the gate" and with override boost and high revs the absolute maximum for one minute is 390 mph at 20,000 ft. The speed falls off rapidly above and below this height - at 4,500 ft the top speed is 326 mph. The machine has to be brought in at 125 mph and touches down at 110 mph. The undercarriage is well forward so that severe braking is possible."

In his book "Fw 190 at War", Price reveals the effect which the appearance over the English Channel of an airplane which was superior to the Spitfire in virtually every respect up to 7000 m wrought on the decisions of the British government. Even Adolf Galland, the commander of JG 26, expressed his surprise at the plane's impact in the book's introduction, especially since the Germans had no idea of the effect the Würger was having at the time. Among other things, Galland took this occasion to characterize the Fw 190 as follows: "When I flew the Fw 190 for the first time, in 1942, I remember being greatly impressed by its high performance and its beautiful handling characteristics."

A comparison between the Fw 190 and its German Bf 109E, F-4 and G counterparts, as well as its opponents in the 1941-1942 time frame is worth examining more closely. When the Fw 190 first began flying with the units stationed along the English Channel, one of its potential enemies included the Spitfire Vb. This later expanded to include the Spitfire IX, the Mustang, the Typhoon, the Lightning, the Thunderbolt and the Spitfire F XII. The British carried out comparison flights between the Fw 190A-3 and the above-named types, specifically with production-fitted armament and load. Rechlin, too, conducted numerous trial competitions of a similar nature using captured Allied aircraft. Unfortunately, up to now only small fragmentary excerpts have come to light, barely hinting at the results and technical evaluation of these programs.

On the other hand, the original British report on their flight experience and evaluation and comparison flights with Oberleutnant Faber's Fw 190A-3 is available in its entirety. The report, dated 18 August 1942, was issued by the Air Fighting Development Unit, RAF Station Duxford. This assessment must also have served as material for Dr. Price's book. The Fw 190A-3's performance and flying qualities were described in this report as follows:

"The (Fw 190's) power unit is a BMW 801D, 14-cylinder, 2-row radial engine, fitted with a two-speed supercharger giving the best performance at 9,000 and 18,000 feet. Between 5,000 and 8,000 ft the performance of the engine falls off as it is just below the height where the two-speed supercharger comes into operation. The estimated power of the engine is 1,700 hp at the maximum power altitude of 18,000 ft. The engine oil coolers and induction system are totally enclosed by and extremely neat cowling and cooling is assisted by an engine driven fan behind the propeller.

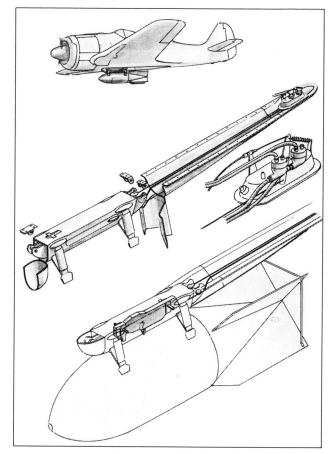

Single hardpoint, or ETC, of an Fw 190A-3, which could carry external loads up to 500 kg.

Fw 190A-3 fuselage hardpoint holding a 300-liter fuel tank.

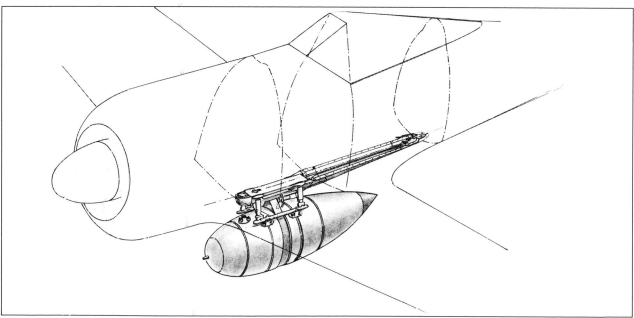

The constant speed VDM 3-bladed metal propeller is electrically operated. It is automatically controlled by an hydraulic governor and if required manually, by an electric switch on the pilot's throttle lever.

The aircraft is pleasant to fly, all controls being extremely light and positive. The aircraft is difficult to taxi due to the excessive weight on the self-centering tailwheel when on the ground.

For takeoff, 15° of flap is required, and it is necessary to keep the control column back to avoid swinging during the initial stage of the takeoff run. The run is approximately the same as that of the Spitfire IX.

Once airborne, the pilot immediately feels at home in the aircraft. The retraction of the flaps and undercarriage is barely noticeable although the aircraft will sink if the retraction of the flaps is made before a reasonably high airspeed has been obtained.

Fw 190A Series

Manufacturer		Focke-Wulf			
Type		Fw 190A-1	Fw 190A-2	Fw 190A-3	Fw 190A-5/U8
Powerplant		BMW 801C	BMW 801C	BMW 801D2[8]	BMW 801D2
Performance	kW	1147	1147	1250	1250
	hp	1560	1560	1700	1700
Crew				1	1
Length	m			8.95	9.10
Height	m			3.95	3.95
Wingspan	m			10.50	10.50
Wing area	m²			18.30	18.30
Aspect ratio				6.02	6.02
Weight, empty	kg	2522[1]	2700[6]	2845	2950
Fuel	kg	396	396	396	820[10]
Oil	kg	50	40	40	40
Crew	kg	80	80	80	80
Load	kg	727[2]	634[7]	634[9]	470[11]
Max. permissible load	kg	1253	1150	1150	1410
Takeoff weight	kg	3775	3850	3995	4360
Wing loading	kg/m²	206.28	210.38	218.30	238.25
Weight/power ratio	kg/kW	3.29	3.35	3.20	3.49
	kg/hp	2.41	2.47	2.35	2.56
	kW/m²	62.68	62.68	68.30	68.30
	hp/m²	85.25	85.25	92.90	92.90
Max. speed @ 6100 m	km/h	630[3]	630[3]	630[3]	630[3]
Cruise speed @ 6100 m	km/h	570	570	570	570
Rate of climb	m/s	15.00[4]	15.00[4]	15.00[4]	14.00[4]
Service ceiling	m	9600	9600	10600	10000
Range	km	545[5]	545[5]	545[5]	865[12]
Max. flight time	hrs	1.25	1.25	1.25	2.00
Takeoff run	m	300	360	360	560[13]
Takeoff run to 20 m	m	600	600	600	600
Landing run	m	500	500	500	500
Landing speed	km/h	157	158	162	160
Max. permissible load as % of takeoff weight		33	30	29	32
Payload as % of takeoff weight		19	16	16	11
Built		1940	1941	1941/42	1942/43

The stalling speed of the aircraft is high, being approximately 110 mph with the undercarriage and flaps retracted, and 105 mph with the undercarriage and flaps fully down. All controls are effective up to the stall. One excellent feature of this aircraft is that it is seldom necessary to re-trim under all conditions of flight.

The best approach speed for landing with flaps and undercarriage down is between 130 and 140 mph indicated, reducing to about 125 when crossing the edge of the aerodrome. Owing to the steep angle of glide, the view during approach is good and the actual landing is straightforward, the touchdown occurring at approximately 110 mph. the landing run is about the same as that of the Spitfire IX. The view on landing is poor due to the tail-down attitude of the aircraft.

The aircraft is very pleasant for aerobatics, even at high speed.

The all-round performance of the Fw 190 is good. Only brief performance tests have been carried out and the figures obtained give a maximum speed of approximately 390 mph True, at 1.42 atmospheres boost, 2,700 rpm at the maximum power altitude of about 18,000 ft. All flights at maximum power were carried out for a duration of 2 minutes only.

There are indications that the engine of this aircraft is de-rated, this being supported by the pilot's instruction card found in the cockpit.

Throughout the trials the engine has been running very roughly... The cause of this roughness has not yet been ascertained... (Flugbaumeister Sander believes that, based on his experience, this was due to dirty or damaged spark plugs as a result of intense combat. The British pilots never flew over water because they didn't trust the engine.)

The total of 115 gallons of fuel is carried in two self-sealing tanks... A total of 9 gallons of oil is carried in a protected oil tank. The approximate endurance under operational conditions, including...a climb to 25,000 ft is approximately 1 hour 20 minutes. There is a red warning light fitted...which illuminates when there is only sufficient fuel left for 20 minutes flying.

The rate of climb up to 18,000 ft...at 1.35 atmospheres boost, 2,450 rpm...is between 3,000 and 3,250 ft/min. The initial rate of climb...is high...and from a dive is phenomenal. It is considered that the de-rated version of the Fw 190 is unlikely to be met above 25,000 ft as the power of the engine...by 25,000 ft has fallen off considerably. It is not possible to give the rate of climb at this altitude.

The Fw 190 has a high rate of dive, the initial acceleration being excellent. The maximum speed so far obtained in a dive is 580 mph True, at 16,000 ft, and at this speed the controls, although slightly heavier, are still remarkably light. One very good feature is that no alteration of trim from level flight is required either during the entry or during the pull-out. Due to the fuel injection system it is possible to enter the dive by pushing the control column forward without the engine cutting.

The cockpit hood is of molded plexiglas and offers an unrestricted view all around. (A) rear view mirror...is considered unnecessary. The hood must not be opened in flight as it is understood that tail buffeting may occur and that

---

[1]**A-series breakdown of weights:**

Fuselage	248 kg
Landing gear	221 kg
Empennage	96 kg
Control system	28 kg
Wings	331 kg
Engine	1488 kg
Fixed equipment	110 kg
Total empty weight	2522 kg

[2]**A-1 payload**

4 MG 17 with ammunition	160 kg
2 MG FF with ammunition	148 kg
Add'l payload for various weapons	419 kg
Total	727 kg

[3]Average takeoff weight with 1/2 fuel (clean), 530 km/h at sea level
[4]Climbing under emergency power to 1000 m; weight of aircraft was 3775 kg without external load
in 3.5 min to 3000 m
in 8.0 min to 6000 m
in 11.5 min to 8000 m
[5]At highest allowable cruising speed at 3000 m; 535 km/h at 5000 m

810 km range (2.05 hrs endurance) at economy setting at 5000 m
[6]Includes 50 kg for armor protection
[7]Weapons = 308 kg, plus 326 kg for auxiliary fuel tanks or other loads
[8]Takeoff and emergency power blocked; figures are therefore as A-2 with emergency boost

[9]**A-3 payload**

2 MG 17	20.00 kg
850 rounds	66.00 kg
2 MG 151	84.00 kg
250 rounds	50.00 kg
	220.00 kg
Remainder for other loads	414 kg
Total	634.00 kg

[10]Normal fuel load was 396 kg + 2x 295 liters = 590 liters(424 kg), totalling 1140 liters(820 kg) carried

[11]**Payload**

Armament	220 kg
Ext. ordnance	250 kg
Total	470 kg

[12]At an altitude of 500 m
[13]With drop tanks and bomb

Navigation and Communications Systems Used in Focke-Wulf Aircraft

FuG 7: HF voice system; 2.5 to 3.75 MHz frequency range; 7 Watts transmitting power

FuG 7a: Improved FuG 7 with trailer antenna for air-to-air and air-to-ground voice communications. Radio communication also possible using speaking key and Morse code.

FuG 10: HF MW communications system (successor to the FuG 3a). HF was primarily for flight safety telegraphy communications; MW for air-to-air tactical telegraphy communications, later retrofitted with TZG 10 for voice communications

FuG 15: Also known as "Christa". VHF voice and radio homing system; replacement for FuG 16 and FuG 17; the system could only transmit or receive; unsuitable for "Y-Verfahren"

Fug 16: VHF air-to-air and air-to-ground voice system

FuG 16Z: VHF voice and radio homing system; air-to-air and air-to-ground voice communications; precision approach system suitable for other aircraft (fighter direction) and ground stands

FuG 16 ZE: VHF voice system for fighters under the direction of "Y-Verfahren" (fighter) without the ability to carry out precision approach. Range finding and voice communications can be carried out simultaneously

FuG 16SZ: Special variant of FuG 16Z, only suitable for strike fighter radio communications and approach. Functions in the overlap areas of the FuG 16 and FuG 17

FuG 16ZY: Modification of FuG 16ZE, enabling precision target approaches to be carried out

FuG 25: VHF voice and key (telegraphy) system, also used for air-to-air and air-to-ground communications. Introduced from 1939 on

FuG 25a: Ready for full-scale production from 1943 on and installed as an IFF system for friendly radars and AAA receiver frequencies in the majority of aircraft from 1944 on. Receives impulses from the ground radar systems and transmits these back as Morse code (two codes can be selected onboard, although these have to be changed on the ground using special keys), where they are shown on the radar system. Also used for bomber and fighter control (EGON-Verfahren)

FuG 125: Called Hermine, supplement (EBL 3) to FuG 16ZY for fighters for receiving beacon and ILS signals

FuG 200 Rostock: Rostock surface search radar element of the FuG 200

FuG 200 Hohentwiel: Hohentwiel surface search radar element of the FuG 200

Peil G 5: MW DF and homing system; both mechanically and electronically remote controlled. Also includes APZ 5 and PPA 2 DF supplemental systems

FuBl 1: ILS operating in the 30.0-33.3 MHz range using two selectable frequencies for VHF localizer beam and 38.0 MHz for outer and inner marker beacon transmitter

FuBl 2: Stems from FuBl 1, retro-fitted with EBL 3 calibratable receiver operating between 30.0-33.3 MHZ. FuBl 1 converted to FuBl 2 from 1942 on. Suitable for receiving VHF beacons: Knickebein, Bernhard and Hermine

Fu NG 101: Approach altimeter (developed by Siemens) with the aid of ground-based radar; area of coverage is 150 to 1000 m; FuG 101a 150 to 750 m

Ei V: Internal communications system; onboard telephone

Lorenz: HF communications system (DLH), SEZ 07535 20 W 5-15 MHz transmitter, E 24 694 4-12 MHz receiver

Lorenz TO Stand: FuG 200 radar system with VP 245 transceiver stand

170 W Langwellen-Sendeanlage: VP 257, 275 to 550 kHz (Lorenz 1937)

Above information compiled from documentation provided by Fritz Trenkle

---

there is a chance of the hood being blown off. During conditions of bad visibility and rain, or in the event of oil being thrown on the windscreen, the fact that the hood must not be opened in flight is obviously a disadvantage.

The aircraft, although extremely light on all controls, is reasonably easy to fly on instruments.

The good all-round view from the aircraft...makes the Fw 190 very suitable for low flying and ground strafing. Another good point is that the sight is depressed, which would probably help in preventing pilots from flying into the ground. In conditions of bad visibility, however, low flying is likely to be unpleasant as the hood must not be opened in flight.

The aircraft is easy to fly in formation and due to the good view, all types of formation can be flown without difficulty. The aircraft has a wide speed range which greatly assists in regaining formation, but care must be taken to avoid over-shooting as its clean lines make deceleration slow."

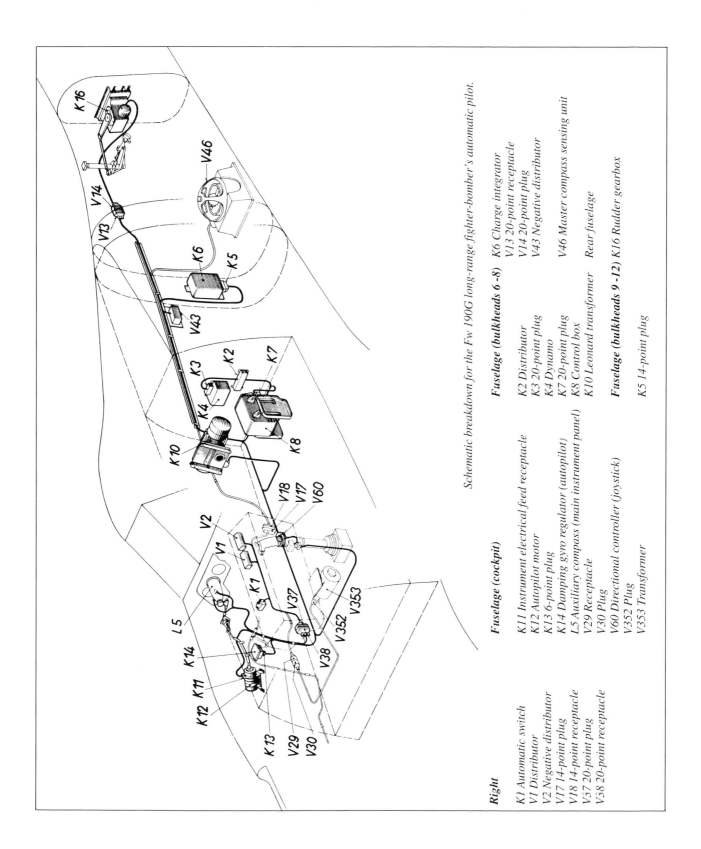

Schematic breakdown for the Fw 190G long-range fighter-bomber's automatic pilot.

Right

K1 Automatic switch
V1 Distributor
V2 Negative distributor
V17 14-point plug
V18 14-point receptacle
V37 20-point plug
V38 20-point receptacle

Fuselage (cockpit)

K11 Instrument electrical feed receptacle
K12 Autopilot motor
K13 6-point plug
K14 Damping gyro regulator (autopilot)
L5 Auxiliary compass (main instrument panel)
V29 Receptacle
V30 Plug
V60 Directional controller (joystick)
V352 Plug
V353 Transformer

Fuselage (bulkheads 6 -8)

K2 Distributor
K3 20-point plug
K4 Dynamo
K7 20-point plug
K8 Control box
K10 Leonard transformer

Fuselage (bulkheads 9 -12)

K5 14-point plug

K6 Charge integrator
V13 20-point receptacle
V14 20-point plug
V43 Negative distributor

V46 Master compass sensing unit

Rear fuselage

K16 Rudder gearbox

BMW 801C and 801D Engines of the Fw 190

Engine Type	# of cylinders	stroke (mm)	bore (mm)	capacity (ltrs)	compression	length (mm)	width Ø (mm)	height (mm)	Supercharger	type of performance	altitude m	output kW/hp	rpm ata	boost pressure	consumption rate g/hp/hr	ltrs/hr	Dry Installed Weight kg	Comments
BMW 801C-0	14	156	156	41.8	6.5	2006	1290	1290	1st gear 1:5.07 2nd gear 1:7.47 super-charger impeller Ø: 338 mm	takeoff	0	1147/1560	2700	1.32			1055	87 octane B4 fuel
										emergency	900	1176/1600	2700	1.32				
										climb	700	1073/1460	2400	1.27				
										max. cruise	1300	941/1280	2300	1.15	230	400		
										economy	1500	757/1030	2100	1.10	205	287		
										climb	4400	963/1310	2400	1.27				
										max. cruise	4500	860/1170	2300	1.15	280	446		
										economy	4700	728/990	2100	1.10	225	304		
BMW 801D-2	14	156	156	41.8	7.2	2006	1290	1290	hydraulic 2-stage high-altitude super-charger 1st gear 1:5.31 2nd gear 1:8.31 super-charger impeller Ø: 338 mm	takeoff	0	1250/1700	2700	1.42	1055			Higher performance than 801C; higher boost pressure, higher compression, 95 octane C3 fuel
										climb	700	1117/1520	2400	1.32				
										max. cruise	1200	1007/1370	2300	1.20	240	447		
										economy	1800	779/1060	2100	1.10	200	288		
										emergency climb	5700	1058/1440	2700	1.42				
										climb	5300	970/1320	2400	1.32				
										max. cruise	5500	867/1180	2300	1.20	265	425		
										economy	5400	723/985	2100	1.10	210	261		

Fw 190A-3 Versus the Spitfire Vb

In comparing the Fw 190A-3 with the Spitfire Vb, the table shows that the power loading (i.e. the weight per unit of kilowatt or horsepower) is greater for the German aircraft than for the much older and lighter Spitfire. The Fw 190's high engine performance, far better than the Spitfire's, is made clearly obvious by the aircraft's power per unit surface area. The difference in wing loading is enormous. Nevertheless, when British pilots confirmed that the Fw 190 was easy to land and takeoff, it must have meant that the Würger was indeed an exceptionally good airplane - something which was stressed in many of the British reports.

The large difference in maximum speed is plain to see. The Fw 190's maximum speed figure of 660 km/h comes from RLM sources. These also show the A-3 as having a top speed of 550 km/h at sea level with no external stores and with 1/2 fuel capacity. According to their data, the British achieved 630 km/h at an altitude of 5490 meters (18000 feet). The Fw 190 gives quite a good showing with its favorable 27 percent load to flying weight ratio and 14 percent pure payload ratio. As mentioned in the table's footnotes, company figures for foreign manufacturers include part of the equipment weight, and presumably also the ar-

mor, under the category of empty weight; although in no case does this empty weight include armament and ammunition. The weight of the weapons and of the drop tanks, in all cases and rightly so, falls under the payload category. And when the weight distribution is made roughly in accordance with this in mind, it is apparent that no other aircraft comes close to the Fw 190's values. This resulted in its capacity for carrying very powerful and heavy armament. For example, the much lighter Me 109 was not able to carry a weapons load even approximating that for the Würger. Only the Bf 109G-1/R2 with its DB 605 - and lacking any type of armor other than for the pilot's windscreen - enjoyed a better speed and climb rate in comparison with the other planes. In particular, it had enough reserves to carry a drop tank or other type of combat payload. The 14 percent payload to takeoff weight ratio, however, was achieved at the expense of the pilot's chances for survival.

But let us return to the Spitfire. It had a famous ancestor, the winner of the Schneider Trophy Race in 1931. Three times the British won the trophy with their Vickers-Supermarine aircraft at the great speed race of the 1920s. The final victory was achieved by the Supermarine S.6B having a special Rolls Royce racing engine with an output of 1727 kW/2350 hp; average speed was 547.31 km/h. Its designer, Reginald J. Mitchell, also was responsible for

Vickers Supermarine Spitfire VB with Rolls-Royce Merlin 45.

111

Fw 190A-3 and Bf 109 Comparison

		Messerschmitt			Focke-Wulf
Manufacturer					
Type		Bf 109E	Bf 109F-4	Bf 109G-1/R2	Fw 190A-3
Powerplant		Daimler Benz DB 601A	Daimler Benz DB 601E[01]	Daimler Benz DB 605[02]	BMW 801D
Performance	kW	808	992	1084	1250
	hp	1100	1350	1475	1700
Crew		1	1	1	1
Length	m	8.80	8.95	9.05	8.95
Height	m	2.50	2.60	2.60	3.95
Wingspan	m	9.90	9.93	9.95	10.50
Wing area	m²	16.40	16.00	16.00	18.30
Aspect ratio		5.97	6.16	6.19	6.02
Weight, empty	kg	1913	2184	2173[8]	2833
Fuel	kg	300	300	300	400
Oil	kg	30	30	30	50
Crew	kg	80	80	80	80
Load	kg	327[1]	246[4]	287[4]	532
Max. permissible load	kg	737	656	697	1062
Takeoff weight	kg	2650	2840	2870	3895
Wing loading	kg/m²	161.50	177.50	179.37	212.84
Weight/power ratio	kg/kW	3.28	2.86	2.65	3.12
	kg/hp	2.41	2.10	1.95	2.29
	kW/m²	49.27	62.00	67.75	68.31
	hp/m²	67.07	84.38	92.19	92.90
Built		1939	1941	1942	1942
Max. speed	km/h	555	670[5]	700[9]	660
@ altitude	m	4800	6300	6600	6900
Cruise speed	km/h	520	610	630	565
@ altitude	m	4900	4900	5500	5200
Rate of climb	m/s	14.00[2]	17.00[6]	22.00[10]	15.00
Service ceiling	m	10500	11800	12600	11500
Range	km	460[3]	525[7]	500	600
Max. flight time	hrs	1.20	1.20	1.10	1.30
Takeoff run	m	300	300	300	370
Takeoff run to 25 m	m	470	500	500	610
Landing run	m	500	600	600	500
Landing speed	km/h	145	145	150	177
Max. permissible load as % of takeoff weight		28	23	24	27
Payload as % of takeoff weight		12	9	10	14

[1]Payload includes 187 kg for 2 MG 17 with 2000 rounds and 2 MG FF with 120 rounds
[2]Average rate of climb to 3000 m (3.5 min); 5000 m (6.5 min); 6000 m (7.5 min); 9000 m (16.5 min)
[3]920 km with 300-liter/216 kg drop tank
[4]Payload includes 146 kg for 2 MG 17 with 500 rounds each and 1 MG 151 with 200 rounds

drawing up and building the first Spitfire Mk I. Powered by a 728 kW/990 hp Merlin C engine, the Spitfire first flew in March of 1936. It was with this aircraft that the English went to war in 1939, and it was this aircraft that was thrown against the Bf 109. According to British information, the Spitfire was somewhat faster and more maneuverable than the Bf 109E. On the other hand, the Emil climbed better, dove faster and had better high altitude performance. This situation changed, however, with the introduction of the Spitfire II, IIa, III, IV and V, variants which were fitted with additional tanks plus more powerful engines having better high-altitude performance and more effective armament. The Spitfire V's main rival was the Fw 190. Compared to the stocky Fw 190A-3 the Spitfire was lighter, had a bigger wing and a correspondingly much lower wing loading. The British felt the Fw 190A-3 to be an excellent fighter at low to medium altitudes, well armed and extremely maneuverable. Comparison flights between the Spitfire Vb and the Fw 190A-3 showed that the Fw 190 was on average 40 to 56 km/h faster between the altitudes of 300 to 1500 meters. The same applied for altitudes around 2700 meters. Between 3000 and 7600 meters the Fw 190A-3 was an average of 32 km/h faster with a better climb rate at all altitudes. In turning, however it was markedly inferior to the Spitfire thanks to the latter's much lower wing loading.

Spitfire IX Versus the Fw 190A-3

In late 1941/early 1942 the new Bf 109F and G variants also began demonstrating their clear superiority over the Spitfire Vb. With the improved Spitfire VII and VIII still in the testing stages, the critical situation spurred the British to fit the Spitfire Vc with Rolls Royce Merlin 66 and 70 engines, having an output of 1213 kW to 1286 kW/ 1650 hp to 1750 hp. This improved variant was designated the Spitfire IX. Although the airplane had been planned only as a stopgap measure and interim type, no less than 5665 of them were built (with 1188 being delivered to the Soviet Union).

The Merlin 70 was a high-altitude engine with a two-stage turbocharger, while the Merlin 66 on the other hand was a low-altitude engine using a supercharger to increase the low-level performance of its engine by 40 percent. Those types fitted with the engine were designed to operate at low to medium altitudes and were designated Spitfire IX LF (LF = low altitude fighter). The LF was expected to force the German fighters, increasingly specializing in low-level attacks, back up to higher altitudes. There they could be attacked by the IX HF, the variant powered by the Merlin 70 and designated HF for its high-altitude fighter role.

Comparison flights between an Fw 190A-3 and a Spitfire IX HF showed the Fw 190 to have a minor advantage between 600 and 5500 meters; from about 7600 meters upward the Spitfire was faster. The climb rate for both machines was equal to about 7600 meters. At that point the Fw 190 began lagging considerably behind the Spitfire. Diving and turning were the same as for the Spitfire Vb comparison.

---

[5]500 km/h at sea level, both data for average all-up weight with 1/2 fuel capacity and no external tanks or bombs

[6]Average rate of climb to 3000 m (2.9 min); to 6000 m it was 6.1 min; to 10000 m it was 14 min

[7]Range was 1000 km with a 300-liter/216 kg drop tank at a take-off weight of 3100 kg

[8]Minus armor and ordnance release system weighing 180 kg (for comparison with Bf 109G-1)

[9]570 km/h at sea level; 590 km/h at 12000 m

[10]Average rate of climb to 6000 m (4.5 min); to 10000 m (10.5 min); to 12000 m (17 min)

[01]**DB 601E**

Takeoff power kw/hp at alt.	Combat power kW/hp at alt.	Cruising power kW/hp at alt.
992/1350/0	900/1200/0	735/1000/0 (sea level)
970/1320/4800 (max pwr alt)	900/1200/4900	764/1040/5300

[02]**DB 605**

1084/1475/0	963/1310/0	790/1075/0 (sea level)
1003/1365/5700	948/1290/5800	830/1130/5500 (max pwr alt)

Average rate of consumption for the DB 601E was 339 ltrs/hr (244 kg/hr)

Average rate of consumption for the DB 605L was 399 ltrs/hr (287 kg/hr)

Comparison of Fw 190 and Spitfire

Manufacturer		Focke-Wulf	Vickers Supermarine	Vickers Supermarine	Vickers Supermarine
Type		Fw 190A-3	Spitfire VB	Spitfire IX LF[4]	Spitfire IX HF
Powerplant		BMW 801D	RR Merlin 45	RR Merlin 66	RR Merlin 70
Performance	kW	1250	1080	1213	1286
	hp	1700	1470	1650	1750
Crew		1	1	1	1
Length	m	8.95	9.12	9.56	9.56
Height	m	3.95	3.48	3.84	3.54
Wingspan	m	10.50	11.24	9.94	11.24
Wing area	m^2	18.30	22.50	21.48	22.50
Aspect ratio		6.02	5.62	4.60	5.62
Weight, empty	kg	2833[1]	2280	2630	2630
Fuel	kg	400	278	278	278
Oil	kg	50	23	30	35
Crew	kg	80	80	80	80
Load	kg	532	329	387	377
Max. permissible load	kg	1062	710	775	770
Takeoff weight	kg	3895	2990	3405	3400
Wing loading	kg/m^2	212.84	132.88	158.52	151.11
Weight/power ratio	kg/kW	3.12	2.77	2.81	2.64
	kg/hp	2.29	2.03	2.06	1.94
	kW/m^2	68.31	48.00	56.47	57.15
	hp/m^2	92.90	65.33	76.81	77.77
Built		1942	1941	1942	1942
Max. speed	km/h	660	602	650	670
@ altitude	m	6900	4000	6400	8400
Cruise speed	km/h	565	518	528	518
@ altitude	m	5200[2]	6100	6100	6100
Rate of climb	m/s	15.00	13.50	14.00	15.00
Service ceiling	m	11500	12000	12960	13700
Range	km	600[3]	750	650[5]	700
Max. flight time	hrs	1.30	1.50	1.50	1.50
Takeoff run	m	370			
Takeoff run to 25 m	m	610			
Landing run	m	500			
Landing speed	km/h	177	115	120	120
Max. permissible load as % of takeoff weight		27	24	23	23
Payload as % of takeoff weight		14	11	11	11

[1]The empty weight of 3200 kg originally provided by Focke-Wulf included 367 kg for weapons and ammunition. As the military equipment for foreign aircraft usually was included in data tables as part of the maximum permissable load and, in so doing, as purely military payload, this entry for the Fw 190A-3 also took the weapons/ammunition weight into account to provide a balanced comparison. It totaled 165 kg + 367 kg = 532 kg

[2]505 km/h at 1200 m. Maximum and cruising speeds at an average all-up weight with 1/2 fuel supply and no bombs
[3]2 hrs flying time at economy setting of 740 kW/1000 hp, giving it a range of 950 km in formation flight
[4]LF = low altitude fighter
[5]650 km range with economy
[6]HF = high altitude fighter

Griffon-Powered Spitfire F XII Versus the Fw 190A-3

In mid-1942, with the comparison flyoffs still underway, the English were already at work testing the prototypes of a much-improved Spitfire F XII powered by a 1275 kW/1735 hp Rolls Royce Griffon III engine. This powerplant was a follow-on development of the Rolls Royce racing engine designed for the S.6B, the 1931 Schneider Trophy winner mentioned earlier. This new engine embodied all the experience gained from the development and operation of the Merlin. The engine had much development potential and soon reached outputs of 1719 kW/2340 hp at sea level and 1558 kW/2120 hp at 3740 meters' altitude. The Spitfire XII had also stemmed from the trusty Vc variant, undergoing corresponding changes to the engine forward assembly in order to accommodate the much more powerful Griffon III and its four-bladed Rotol airscrew. The fuselage was somewhat longer and the tailwheel now of a retracting kind. According to British reports the Spitfire XII, of which 100 were completed in a great rush, was specially laid out to combat the Fw 190, for the German Würger (Butcher-bird) - as it was officially called, ruled the low-level skies over England in increasingly alarming numbers. A final measure was the reinforcement of the Mk XII's wings in order to increase its low-level speed.

While the British were preparing a major blow for the Fw 190, in mid-1942 the Mk XII prototype and its Fw 190A-3 adversary flew peacefully alongside each other. These flights showed the Spitfire XII's acceleration to be greater and its top speed to be somewhat better than the Fw 190's; the Spitfire also proved to be better at turning than its rival. All in all, the Spitfire XII enjoyed a slight edge over the Fw 190A-3 at low levels. Weather precluded comparison flights from being carried out at higher altitudes. Somewhat more powerful engines, like the BMW 801E and F already running on their test stands, would have slightly tipped the scales back in favor of the Fw. The BMW 801E had by this time reached production maturity and had been cleared for large-scale manufacture. It delivered 1470 kW/2000 hp to 1617 kW/2200 hp, but never entered production because the required tooling machinery was lacking and could not be obtained before the war's end. An interim solution, and an effective one at that, was found with the GM 1 injection system - although for years this system displayed teething troubles which had to be overcome.

Spitfire F XII Griffon

Manufacturer		Vickers Supermarine
Type		Spitfire F XII Griffon
Powerplant		Rolls Royce Griffon III
Performance	kW	1275
	hp	1735
Crew		1
Length	m	9.70
Height	m	3.35
Wingspan	m	9.93
Wing area	m²	21.48
Aspect ratio		4.59
Weight, empty	kg	2540
Fuel	kg	278
Oil	kg	36
Crew	kg	80
Load	kg	425
Max. permissible load	kg	819
Takeoff weight	kg	3359
Wing loading	kg/m²	156.37
Weight/power ratio	kg/kW	2.63
	kg/hp	1.93
	kW/m²	59.36
	hp/m²	80.77
Built		1942
Max. speed @ 5490 m	km/h	630[1]
Cruise speed @ 6100 m	km/h	586
Rate of climb	m/s	15.00
Service ceiling	m	12190
Range	km	530[2]
Max. flight time	hrs	1.20
Landing speed	km/h	135
Max. permissible load as % of takeoff weight		24
Payload as % of takeoff weight		13

[1] 598 km/h at an altitude of 1680 m
[2] At 425 km/h. The fuselage fuel load could be supplemented by tanks in the wing leading edge and wings, increasing the amount carried to 536 liters/1386 kg. The same also applies to the Spitfire IX LF and IX HF

Hans Werner Lerche, in his book "Testpilot auf Beute-Flugzeugen", discusses the German experience with the Spitfire. Among several other types, he was able to fly and evaluate the Spitfire Mk III with its Rolls Royce Merlin XX, having an output of 941 kW/1280 hp at sea level and 1088 kW/1480 hp at 3700 meters. Although built in 1939, it was considered obsolete by then, and Lerche's assessment was as follows: "The Spitfire III was, thanks to its armament (two cannons and two to four machine guns) and low wing loading, a worthy opponent while climbing and turning, while it was slower than our fighters overall." However, because there were no precise test results showing particular rpm settings at specific altitudes, it is not possible to provide a comparison with German aircraft. There are only fragmentary reports available on these test flights, some of which were carried out by the DVL and jointly evaluated with the Rechlin test team.

Mustang Ia Versus the Fw 190A-3

But let us return back to the British comparison flights. The first American fighters were made available to the British as early as mid-1942 for evaluating their suitability in the European Theater. These planes were also flown against the Fw 190A-3. Two of the most interesting of these aircraft were the Mustang Ia (P-51A) and the P-38F Lightning.

In 1940 the British wanted North American to license-build the Curtiss Hawk 87A-1 and then be able to purchase these aircraft. However, North American informed the English that it had little interest in license-building and instead offered its own design which the company claimed it could build within three months. It was under this time constraint that the Mustang was born, taking off on its maiden flight in October 1940. The company immediately was

North American Mustang II/P-51A fitted with the armament of the later F-6 reconnaissance version. This aircraft is part of the Flying Oldtimers collection at the EAA Museum and is flown annually at Oshkosh, here with Paul Poberezny at the controls.

awarded a British contract for 320 aircraft. Becausethe Allison engines were not yet available, however, it was not until May 1941 that the first production machines were delivered and the first British squadrons began operating the type in April of the following year. A further 300 aircraft were subsequently ordered.

The Mustang was the first fighter with a laminar wing profile and was initially powered by an Allison V-1710-81 engine delivering 882 kW/1200 hp. The British immediately realized that the Mustang was vastly superior to any previous American fighter; the Allison low-level engine, however, meant that it was unsuitable as a fighter in the European combat arena. On the other hand, its high speed and excellent maneuverability made the Mustang an excellent candidate for tactical low level roles. With its four cannons and four machine guns, plus its low altitude engine, the Mustang was predestined as a strike fighter. Its overall design layout, however, hinted at a superior long-range fighter; these qualities would later be demonstrated with the fitting of a different powerplant. It came at just the right time for the English, who were feeling more and more threatened by the low level Fw 190 raids.

The Mustang Ia/Fw 190A-3 comparison flights showed that both aircraft operated at virtually the same speed; only at altitudes between 300 and 4500 meters was the Mustang somewhat faster than the Würger. Of course, with an engine 34 percent more powerful, the Fw 190 had a markedly superior rate of climb. Both machines were roughly equal in a dive, and the Fw 190 again was superior with regard to maneuverability - excepting in a sustained turning fight. Without a doubt the Mustang would prove to be an extremely dangerous foe when fitted with more powerful engines.

Hans Werner Lerche flew a Mustang at Rechlin; the plane in question was a P-51B with a Packard-built Rolls Royce Merlin 68 having 1212 kW/1650 hp maximum output and 1029 kW/1400 hp takeoff performance. He praised the responsive plane's outstanding flight handling characteristics and its performance and remembers attaining a speed of 670 km/h at 7000 meters. The P-51B, however, was a later version of the Mustang, arriving in England in late 1943 and accompanying the Flying Fortresses on their 1700 km journeys to Berlin. The airplane can therefore best be compared with the later Fw 190D.

P-38F Lightning Versus the Fw 190A-3

The British also included the American twin-engined Lockheed P-38F Lightning fighter in fly-offs with the Fw 190A-3. In actual fact, the Fw 187 would have been the Lightning's true rival, although the former - as discussed earlier - was not allowed into production. Many twin-engined single-seat fighters had already been built and tested as prototypes in the West; but the only successful design was that produced by L.H. Hibbard and his engineering team -the Lockheed Lightning.

The P-38 was a twin-boom aircraft with nose gear, its cockpit located above the wing between the two engines. The prototype took off for the first time in January 1939 under the designation of XP-38 and was lost in a crash just 14 days later.

The propellers were inward-rotating in order to prevent the twin-engined plane from ground looping due to the high torque generated by the two Allison V-1710-11/15 engines (each delivering 882 kW/1200 hp). Despite this, the airplane had many problems. The P-38A, of which only a few were built, was experimentally fitted with a pressurized cockpit. The B and C models never left the drawing board and it was left to the P-38D to incorporate the experience being gleaned from the European war. The next variant, the P-38E, had more powerful armament and the P-38F was initially conceived as a recon plane.

The English ordered 143 Lightnings in 1941. Two of the first planes delivered were immediately returned after the British test flew them and found that their performance didn't live up to expectations. They subsequently were given a more powerful version, the P-38F-13-LO and 15-LO, also designated the Lightning II. The British report doesn't specify whether the Lightning used for the competitive trials with the Fw 190A-3 was one of the returned aircraft or the improved variant. It only states that the machine was armed and was flown by an experienced American Army Air Force pilot. The flyoff showed that the Fw 190 was markedly superior to the Lightning in speed and maneuverability at all altitudes up to 7000 meters. The same went for climb rate. The Fw 190 climbed better up to 7000 meters, at which point it was overtaken by the Lightning. In view of its better high altitude performance, the variant must have had an engine equipped with a high-altitude turbocharger.

Lockheed P-38F Lightning with two Allison V-1710-49/53 engines, year of service 1942.

Hawker Typhoon and Fw 190A-3: Two Bulls Hunting Each Other

Eventually, the British confronted the Würg*er* with a Hawker Typhoon armed with four cannons, an aircraft with which the British weren't altogether happy.

The Hawker company had developed a fighter in 1939; it was a low-wing design having slightly kinked wings and an inward retracting undercarriage similar to that of the Fw 190. The aircraft had been specially designed around its powerful Napier Sabre engine, a water-cooled 24 cylinder inline monster which initially had an output of 1470 kw/ 2000 hp and later achieved 1764 kW/2400 hp - the counterpart to the Jumo 222. In 1940 the Sabre I completed it 100-hour test, delivering 1617 kW/2200 hp at 3700 rpm.

The Typhoon prototype first flew in May of 1941. As with the BMW 801, engine production began too early and it now "delighted" the British with a host of problems. During the aircraft's test phase the Fw 190s (chiefly the Fw 190A-3/U1) began their low level attacks as has already mentioned several times previously. As a side note, these attack profiles had been born of necessity in order to get below the Brits' good radar umbrella. Without any type of "terrain-following" system, these aircraft literally flew at ground level and almost invariably returned to base with damage to their wings or props after having brushed bushes or telephone lines. The pilots knew: the lower we fly, the greater our chances of survival. These attacks were directed at military targets in southern England. At first the British were clueless, for the planes came in at low level without warning, struck like lightning and disappeared just as quickly. The British hoped that the powerful Typhoon would prove to be the ideal Würger hunter. Despite its teething troubles the plane was rushed into production.

118

Lightning, Mustang and Typhoon

Manufacturer		Lockheed	Norht American	Hawker
Type		P-38F Lightning	P-51A Mustang	Typhoon 1B
Powerplant		Allison V-1710-49/53	Allison V-1710-81	Napier Sabre IIA
Performance	kW	2x974=1948	882	1602
	hp	2x1325=2650	1200	2180
Crew		1	1	1
Length	m	11.54	9.83	9.73
Height	m	3.00	3.71	4.06
Wingspan	m	15.86	11.28	12.67
Wing area	m²	30.42	21.67	25.92
Aspect ratio		8.27	5.87	6.19
Weight, empty	kg	5568	2973	2995
Fuel	kg	821	491	550
Oil	kg	50	25	35
Crew	kg	80	80	80
Load	kg	700	426	510
Max. permissible load	kg	1651	1022	1175
Takeoff weight	kg	7129	3995	5170
Wing loading	kg/m²	237.31	184.36	199.46
Weight/power ratio	kg/kW	3.71	4.23	3.53
	kg/hp	2.72	3.33	2.37
	kW/m²	64.04	40.70	61.81
	hp/m²	87.11	55.38	84.10
Built		1942	1941	1941
Max. speed	km/h	636[1]	623	652[6]
@ altitude	m	7625	4575	5490
Cruise speed	km/h	536	494	530
@ altitude	m	7600	4575	
Rate of climb	m/s	13.00[2]	12.00[4]	12.00[7]
Service ceiling	m	11900	9561	10370
Range	km	850[3]	1200[5]	980[8]
Max. flight time	hrs	1.25	2.00	2.00
Takeoff run	m	730		483
Landing run	m	1035		
Landing speed	km/h	170		140
Max. permissible load as % of takeoff weight		23	26	23
Payload as % of takeoff weight		10	11	10

[1] 559 km/h at an altitude of 1525 m; 565 km/h at 3050 m; 470 km/h at sea level
[2] Average rate of climb to 3050 m
[3] 1300 km/3 hrs 45 mins at economy; with 2310 liters/1663 kg of fuel in drop tanks the range was 1650 km/2 hrs 50 mins or 2500 km and 7 hrs endurance with economy settings; maximum amount of fuel capable of being carried (for ferry flights) was 3420 liters/2462 kg, giving a range of 3400 km and an endurance of 9 hrs
[4] Average rate of climb to 1500 m(2.2 mins)
[5] At 485 km/h at an altitude of 3050 m; range was 1610 km at 375 km/h at 3050 m
[6] 602 km/h at an altitude of 1670 m
[7] Average rate of climb to 4575 m(6.2 mins)
[8] At 409 km/h at an altitude of 4575 m

Hawker Typhoon IB with 24-cylinder Napier Sabre IIA, rated at 1602 kW/2180 hp.

It had been mentioned earlier that, when the Fw 190A-1 and A-2 were assigned to Jagdgeschwader Schlageter on the Channel coast, the plane's engine had not yet reached maturity and caused many problems due to its overheating.

The British, however, not only were troubled by the as-yet unreliable engine, but also had problems with the airframe. The information found in British sources is astounding. When diving at high speeds the airplane had a tendency to shudder profoundly, and the aileron controls responded in exactly the opposite manner as their inputs.

Unfortunately, the comparison flights with the Fw 190 were not completed because the Fw 190 was having problems with its engine. At an altitude of 600 meters the Typhoon was a bit faster, but it could not fly up to its maximum speed because the heavy aircraft needed more time to accelerate. At altitudes between 2500 m, 3000 m, 5000 m and 6000 m the Typhoon proved to have a marked speed advantage. The Fw 190 showed itself to be far better at climbing, but the heavy Typhoon again demonstrated its superiority over the Würger in a dive. The Brits felt that the maneuverability of both machines was roughly equal.

The Enemy's Assessment: "An Outstanding Aircraft, Made for Pilots"

When examining evaluation reports of the Fw 190A-3 on the part of the British, it should be noted that the aircraft's engine was most likely de-rated and that the spark plugs didn't function properly. Nevertheless, the appraisal was good:

"The Fw 190 is undoubtedly a formidable low and medium altitude fighter. Its designer has obviously given much thought to the pilot. The cockpit is extremely well laid out and the absence of large levers and unnecessary gadgets is most noticeable. The pilot is given a comfortable seating position, and is well protected by armor. The simplicity of the aircraft as a whole is an excellent feature, and enables new pilots to be thoroughly conversant with all controls in a very brief period.

The rough running of the engine is much disliked by all pilots and must be a great disadvantage, as lack of confidence in an engine makes flying over bad country or water, most unpleasant.

The armament is good and well positioned, and the ammunition capacity should be sufficient for any normal fighter operation. The sighting view is approximately half a ring better than that from a Spitfire. The all-round search view is the best that has yet been seen from any aircraft flown by this unit.

The flying characteristics are exceptional and a pilot new to the type feels at home within the first few minutes of flight. The controls are light and well harmonized and all maneuvers can be carried out without difficulty at all speeds. The fact that the Fw 190 does not require re-trimming under all conditions of flight, is a particularly good point.

The initial acceleration is very good and is particularly noticeable in the initial stages of a climb or dive.

Perhaps one of the most outstanding qualities of this aircraft is the remarkable aileron control. It is possible to change from a turn in one direction to a turn in the opposite direction with incredible speed, and when viewed from another aircraft the change appears just as if a flick half roll has been made.

It is considered that night flying would be unpleasant, particularly for landing and take-off, due to the exhaust glare and the fact that the cockpit canopy cannot be opened in flight.

The engine is easy to start but requires running up for a considerable time, even when warm, before the oil temperature reaches the safety margin for take-off, and this coupled with the fact that the aircraft is not easy to taxi, makes the Fw 190 inferior to our aircraft for quick take-offs (The English were apparently unaware that we often used the cold-start method for taking off!).

The comparative fighting qualities of the Fw 190 have been compared with a Spitfire VB, Spitfire IX, Mustang IA, Lockheed P 38F, 4-Cannon Typhoon and a prototype Griffin Spitfire, all aircraft being flown by experienced pilots.

The main conclusion gained from the tactical trials of the Fw 190 is that our fighter aircraft must fly at high speed when in an area where the Fw 190 is likely to be met. This will give our pilots the chance of bouncing and catching the Fw 190 , and if bounced themselves, the best chance of avoiding being shot down.

The all-round search view from the Fw 190 being exceptionally good makes it rather difficult to achieve the element of surprise. Here again, however, the advantage of our aircraft flying at high speed must not be overlooked, as they may, even if seen by the pilot of the Fw 190 catch it before it has time to dive away.

Wing Commander,
Commanding,
A.F.D.U.
AFDU/3/20/24
9th August, 1942

Weapons and Conversion Sets

Up to this point weapons have been only discussed in the vaguest of terms, as the focus thus far has been on technical developments and the aircrafts' performance and flying qualities. Armament is only addressed insofar as it becomes necessary for understanding the text. Readers who have a greater interest in aircraft weapons should consult Manfried Schliephake's book "Die Bordwaffen der Luftwaffe von den Anfängen bis zur Gegenwart".

Attacking with bombs at low levels over long distances meant a whole new role for the Fw 190, a plane which had originally been laid out as a fighter. Included among the ordnance dropped by the Würger were so-called high-explosive bombs which a fighter carried externally on either single or multiple racks. Sights and release mechanisms for dropping and arming the bombs also formed part of the

equipment. Bombs or drop tanks were attached to lugs on the single racks (*Einzelträger*, abbreviated ET) and supported on the sides by so-called adjustable shackles. Bombs were collectively designated C-munition (C), so that the abbreviation ETC meant single rack with high-explosive bomb. The caliber of the bomb was represented by a number following the ETC designation. ETC 50 or 100 or 500, therefore, were racks for 50 kg, 100 kg or 500 kg bombs, respectively. Then there were special designations for the bombs themselves, such as the ETC 500 IXd, whereby the Roman numerals followed by the "d" identified the specific type of bomb. Based on their application, bomb racks, bombs, their associated equipment and drop tanks formed the oft-mentioned U1, U2 or U3 field or factory conversion sets. These kits were fitted to each aircraft type individually and often were changed during the course of the war.

Interlude: Fly-by-Wire with an He-111

In 1941, after a landing at Berlin-Schönefeld, Tank ran into an old acquaintance by the name of Altvater from the Siemens company. Altvater told Tank about an He 111 which was controlled by electronic impulses. Today we call this "fly by wire" - all modern fighters are controlled this way. "Would you like to fly the plane?" asked Altvater. Tank didn't have to be asked twice. He was familiar with the He 111 and had flown it before, so it was just a short time later that he was in the pilot's seat. The crew chief, who had to be intimately familiar with the machine, was for him the most important man aboard during such flights. Next to the control wheel was a knob about 8 cm in length, which could be used to control the aircraft electronically via cables.

Tank took off in the He 111 and - as agreed - pulled in behind a Bf 108 which he was expected to follow using the knob control. He was surprised at how responsive the machine was to even the slightest pressure. Because of the electronic controls it was more maneuverable than ever before, since the lag time inherent with control rods and the many guide pulleys, etc. no longer existed and the electronic impulses created by the knob were transferred to the control surfaces at lightning speeds.

The Fw 190A Workhorse

Fw 190A-4 with Water-Methanol Injection

Experience gained from the A-3 was applied to the Fw 190A-4, produced in series from July 1942 to January 1943 at Focke-Wulf, Arado, AGO and Fieseler. Externally, differing characteristics were minor: the formerly horizontal radio antenna mast on the tailfin was now vertical. Performance of the BMW 801 could not be improved, unfortunately, although this increase was urgently needed as the enemy had acquired better high-altitude engines in the meantime. It was superiority at higher altitudes which had figured prominently in British evaluation reports during the competitive fly-offs with the Fw 190. A V24 served as the prototype for the A-4 series. Its most remarkable change had actually been only a temporary solution to compensate for the engine's lack of high-altitude performance. Nevertheless, it had major significance for the development and performance capabilities of German fighter aircraft during the coming months of the war. This solution was the use of water-methanol through the MW 50 injection system.

Water, methanol or oxygen can be injected into the engine's boost air in order to temporarily increase a turbocharged engine's performance. The vaporization heat created by this process cooled the boost air. At the same time the weight of the air passing through was lowered and the pressure ratio increased. However, a temperature had to be maintained which ensured that the mixture continued the process of vaporization - for this was the only way the boost air temperature could sink.

Fw 190A-4/R6 "formation buster" with 21 cm WGr. 42 Spr. rocket launchers firing 214 caliber shells, designed for breaking up bomber formations.

The MW 50 water methanol injection system introduced on the Fw 190A-4 consisted of a mixture of 50 percent methanol, 49.5 percent water and 0.5 oil for protection against corrosion damage. Methanol, methyl-alcohol, carbinol, also know as wood spirit, is one of the simplest forms of alcohol. The MW 50 was designed for lower flight altitudes, i.e. those below the maximum pressure altitude of the engines, and its purpose was to provide a brief increase in takeoff power or, in combat or other dangerous situations, a short-duration boost in combat and emergency power. Injection led to an improved cooling inside the cylinder and worked to counter any knocking tendencies. The operating lever was linked to the throttle; if the pilot pushed the throttle lever past a certain point a pump for injecting the water methanol mixture kicked in. The BMW 801's Kommandogerät adjusted the fuel flow to the engine according to boost pressure, external temperature and altitude. By injecting water methanol into the engine the boost pressure limitation was eliminated.

However, problems arose yet again with the touchy BMW 801, particularly with the spark plugs, so that initially this boost in power could only be exploited for extremely short periods of time. It was not until later that the

Cockpit of an Fw 190A-4.

system was able to reliably deliver 10 to 20 minutes of performance. On the other hand, it seems as though the Daimler-Benz engines were much less sensitive to injection and from the outset could be operated ten minutes and longer using such a system.

Another type of system, the so-called GM 1 injection system, was employed for increasing performance of high-altitude engines. The designation GM is reputedly an abbreviation of "Göring-Mischung" (Göring Mixture) and was probably made up by someone who had a sense of humor. The mixture was "Ha-Ha", laughing gas, which utilized liquid nitrous oxide under pressure as an oxygen carrier. Injecting this mixture into the engine cooled the boost air, improved fuel combustion and giving the engine better anti-knocking properties. When the mixture was being injected, the Kommandogerät supplied the engine with additional fuel. However, the injection system was not embraced with unequivocal enthusiasm by pilots or designers. Fuel consumption increased significantly during the injection process, the system weighed a considerable amount and was a complicated mechanism.

Nonetheless, the BMW 801D-2's performance was boosted for a short period to 1544 kW/2100 hp. The system gave the aircraft an enormous power reserve. Unfortunately, it would be a long time before the two systems - the GM 1 and the MW 50 - were ready for full-scale production. And by the time they finally entered production, repeated bombing raids prevented them from being supplied on anything more than an irregular and limited scale.

The previously mentioned V24 prototype, Werknummer 561, was also the first of the Fw 190A-4 series, in production from July 1942 to January 1943. According to one source, the total number of this variant delivered was 906, while another source lists the figure at 811. The armament of the A-3 carried over to the V24. It was fitted with the BMW 801D and, for the first time, with the improved FuG 16Z, a VHF communications and homing system for air-to-air and air-to-ground with the capability of providing vector information towards another aircraft (fighter direction aircraft) and to ground transmitters. Werknummer 711 through 760 of the A-4 series were equipped with desert filters designed to absorb the sand from the intake air. Cold-climate equipment was fitted to Werknummer 761 through 810.

All A-4 series aircraft were able to carry external loads such as bombs and drop tanks. Due to an engine shortage, a series of A-4/U1 *Schlachtflugzeuge*, or ground attack planes, was produced using the older BMW 801C fitted on a temporary basis. As a weight-saving measure the fuselage side armor was dropped on the Fw 190A-4/U3, also a ground attack variant. 30 Fw 190A-4/U1 and U3 machines were supplied during the months of September and October 1943.

The Fw 190A-4/U4 was projected as a reconnaissance fighter, but was never actually built.

The A-4 was also fitted with a special field conversion kit, a so-called "formation destroyer". It consisted of a Wgr.42, a so-called lobbing device, mortar launcher, rocket launcher or also sometimes called a large caliber air-to-air rocket. These were shells of 21.4 cm caliber commonly used by the Nebelwerfer infantry troops, a spin-stabilized solid fuel rocket projectile with a 9.5 kg warhead ignited by a time-delay fuze. The projectile was fired by means of a button on the control stick. A Revi gunsight made lining up on the target easier. The launch tubes were carried beneath the Fw 190's wings. These projectiles made it possible to open fire on the bomber formations outside the bombers' defensive fire range, enabling the German fighters to "bust up" the formations.

In October 1943, Luftwaffe formations equipped with the Fw 190A-4/R6 first encountered a large-scale American bombing raid consisting of 228 four-engined "heavies" whose target was Schweinfurt. 62 bombers were shot down over German territory, 17 were lost when they crashed upon returning to England and 121 suffered damage to some degree. The scoreboard for the other side revealed a loss of 38 fighters and damage to a further 51 more. Despite this, such successes were never repeated due to the fact that the enemy changed his tactics on the very nex tmission: from then on the Americans only flew under the protection of their escort fighters.

The BMW 801D was easily accessible thanks to its fold-down shroud covers.

The Fw 190A-4/U8 was designed for carrying two 300-liter wing tanks and a 500-kg bomb under the fuselage. On the other hand, it was only armed with two MG 151s in the wing roots. This was the first fighter-bomber designed for long ranges, the so-called *Jabo-Rei*. With its additional load, the A-4/U8's takeoff weight increased to 4530 kg and the

Fw 190A-4 with a 250-kg bomb.

125

Machine Guns and Machine Cannons Used in Focke-Wulf Aircraft

MG 17: Manufactured by Rheinmetall; 7.9 mm caliber, automatic weapon; loaded by compressed air. Revi C/120 reflective gunsight, which utilized a lamp and lens to reflect a hairline cross on the glass plate. 1200 rounds/min; weapon weighed 10.2 kg. belt with 100 rounds of ammunition weighed 7.8 kg; 1200 rounds weighed 93.6 kg

MG 131: Manufactured by Rheinmetall; 13 mm caliber; weighed 19.7 kg; 900 rounds/min; belt with 100 rounds of ammunition weighed 8.5 kg; compressed air or eletronic operation

MG FF: Manufactured by Oerlikon Schweiz; 20 mm caliber; eletronic pneumatic operation; weighed 37 kg with belt feed; 530 rounds/min; 100 round drum weighed 33 kg; 100 round belt weighed 21 kg

MG 15: Manufactured by Rheinmetall: 7.92 mm caliber; weapon weighed 8.2 kg; dual drum with 75 round weighed 4.24 kg; rate of fire was 1050 rounds/min; each round weighed 12.8 g

MG 81Z: Manufactured by Mauser; 7.92 mm caliber; single weapon weighed 6.5 kg; twin unit weighed 12.9 kg; 1600 rounds/min; twin 3200 rounds/min; ammunition belt with 100 rounds weighed 7.8 kg; flex-mounted

MK 108: Manufactured by Rheinmetall-Borsig; 30 mm caliber; weapon weighed 58 kg; rate of fire was 600 rounds/min; weighed 88 kg when installed as nose armament; single belt link weighed 0.115 kg; ammunition belt with 100 rounds weighed 59.5 kg; single round weighed 480 g

MG 151/15: Manufactured by Mauser-Werke AG in Oberndorf; 15 mm caliber; weapon weighed 42 kg; rate of fire was 600 to 700 rounds/min; ammunition belt with 100 rounds weighed 16.82 kg; type of installation: fixed, free-moving, controlled, flex-mounted

MG 151/20: Manufactured by Mauser; 20 mm caliber; weapon weighed 42 kg; rate of fire was 630 to 720 rounds/min; ammunition belt with 100 rounds weighed 19.9 kg; type of installation: fixed, free-moving, controlled, flex-mounted

MK 103: Manufactured by Rheinmetall-Borsig(1942); 30 mm caliber; weighed 145 kg; rate of fire was 420 rounds/min; weight when installed as engine cannon was 165 kg; ammunition belt with 100 rounds 92 kg

MG 213C/20: Manufactured by Mauser-Werke; 20 mm caliber; weapon weighed 75 kg; rate of fire was 1200 to 1400 rounds/min(21 rounds/sec); ammunition belt with 100 rounds weighed 39.5 kg; each round weighed 0.684 kg

MG 213C/30: Manufactured by Mauser-Werke; 30 mm caliber; weapon weighed 75 kg; installed weight was 95.8 kg; rate of fire was 1100 to 1200 rounds/min(19 rounds/sec); ammunition belt with 100 rounds was 60.5 kg; single shell weighed 1.09 kg. After the war the cannon was copied in the USA as the M-39, in Switzerland as the Oerlikon 206 RK, in Britain as the Aden, in Frankreich as the DEFA 552 and in the Soviet Union as the NR-30

Rockets and Missiles

Rz 65: Manufactured by Rheinmetall-Borsig; 73 mm caliber; weighed 2.4 kg; projectile weighed 0.238 kg; 334 daN(340 kp) thrust; 0.2 sec burn time

WGr.42 Spr.: Mortar shell; 214 mm caliber; weighed 110 kg; 1720 kp thrust; 1.4 sec burn time; 320 m/sec velocity; range was 500 to 7850 m; fired at 1200 to 1400 m; fully fitted, it weighed 294 kg

WK spr.: Mortar shell; 280 mm caliber; weighed 82 kg, 50 kg of which was explosive charge; 145 m/sec velocity; range was 750 to 1925 m; fired at 1000 m

X 4 *Jägerrakete*: Manufactured by Ruhrstahl; weighed 60 kg with a 20 kg warhead; 140 kp engine thrust; 1150 km/h velocity; range was 5000 m

SG 113 *Förstersonde*: Manufactured by Rheinmetall; barrel caliber was 7.7 cm; ammunition caliber was 4.5 cm; armor piercing shell; unloaded tube weighed 48 kg

Information based on Schliephake, "Flugzeugbewaffnung"

wing loading jumped to 247 kg/m². A 4530 kg takeoff weight meant an increase in the takeoff run to 560 meters. A length of 1015 m was needed to get the plane up to an altitude of 20 meters. Takeoff was only possible from smooth grass strips, although the recommended surface was a paved runway. Initially, only two of the A-4/U8s were ordered for field testing.

One A-4/R1 command and control fighter was fitted with the FuG 16ZE (Y-method), which enabled simultaneous voice communications with and distance measuring to a ground station. The equipment set was made available to the front-line units from September 1942 for installation as needed.

Multi-role Fw 190A-5

The A-3/U1, Werknummer 270, served as the prototype for the Fw 190A-5 series entering production in November 1942. This was the first variant to have the fuselage lengthened by 15 cm; in order to compensate for the ever-increasing equipment weight the engine was moved more forward. The lengthening of the fuselage was not included in the company documentation with regards to fuselage dimensions and therefore no difference is reflected in the tables within this book. The A-3/U1 was given a thorough shake-down at Rechlin in August 1943.

All A-5 variants were fitted with an electrically-operated artificial horizon with a turn-and-bank indicator and an improved high-altitude oxygen system with automatic pressurized oxygen feed which kicked in at 10000 meters. In other respects the aircraft was virtually the same as the A-4. Due to an engine shortage, the A-5/U1s were temporarily powered by the BMW 801C which were exchanged for BMW 801Ds during general overhaul.

The A-5/U2 had a field conversion kit for "Wilde Sau" night fighting operations, with flame dampers, shrouds and plumbing for two drop tanks. It was difficult preventing the pilot from being temporarily blinded by the glare from his own exhaust. Shrouds had to be fitted over the exhaust ports on either side of the fuselage which were not susceptible to the exhaust heat and which were not unnecessarily heavy. Five aircraft thus equipped were sent to the field units for testing on 1 October 1943.

The Fw 190A-5/U3 was a ground attack platform with two MG 17s above the engine and two MG 151s in the wings. It could carry a payload of up to 1000 kg, although this figure included 400 kg for the machine guns, cannon and armor. This variant was also supplied under the designation Fw 190A-5/U3tp with hot climate equipment and served as the prototype for the later F-1 version. Like the other variants, it too was kitted out with the FuG 16Z and FuG 25 and was in production from November 1942 to September 1944.

The Fw 190A-5/U4tp was planned as a recon fighter with RB 12 cameras, had the same equipment as the A-3/U4 and at the same time was fitted with desert equipment.

Fw 190A-5 (Werknummer 1286) fighter-bomber, with an SB 1000 rack and 1000-kg bomb.

Fw 190A-5/U2 with auxiliary tanks and flash guards for night fighting operations.

Fw 190A, F and G *Umrüst-Bausatz* Factory Conversion Sets*

U1 Fw 190A-8/U1 - two seater for conversion training, also known as Fw 190S

U1 Fw 190F-8 conversion for use as *Jabo-Rei* long-range fighter-bomber

U1 Temporary fitting of BMW 801C in place of -D(A-4 only)

U2 Two 300 liter drop tanks, "blinders" above exhaust outlets, anti-dazzle covers, modifications for "*Wilde Sau*" night-fighter operations(A-5)

U2 Fw 190F-8 conversion for torpedo operations with TSA IIA system and ETC 503 racks for carrying 2x300 liter drop tanks

U3 Rack for carrying 1x 500 kg or 2x250 kg or 4x50 kg bombs, modifications to convert day-fighter to fighter-bomber(A-5, F-1)

U4 RB 12.5 camera for reconnaissance, RB 20/30, RB 50/30, RB 75/30 as needed(A-5)

U5 Upper fuselage 2xMG 17 exchanged for 2xMG 131

U8 Wing racks for two 300 liter drop tanks; fuselage rack for 250 to 500 kg bombs(A-4, A- 5)

U9 Modified to *Zerstörer* heavy fighter with two MG 131 and four MG 151(A-5)

U10 MG 17s swapped for MG 131s above the engine

U11 Two MK 103/30 mm under outer wings; rack for 250 kg or 4x50 kg, standardized R3 field conversion kit

U12 Two MG 17, two MG 151 in wing roots and four fixed MG 151 in underwing gondolas. Also trial fitted with GM 1 system (A-5, A-0)

U13 Modification of day-fighter to fighter-bomber, drop tanks and wing racks (A-5)

U14 Rack for carrying single torpedo, extended tailwheel, larger rudder(A-5)

U15 ETC 502 rack for 950 kg LT 950 torpedo; became part of R14 field conversion kit

U16 Conversion to *Zerstörer*; two MG 17, two MG 151, two MK 108 in outer wings, heavier armor, side windows fitted with armored glass, add'l fuel tanks(A-5)

U17 Conversion of day-fighter to strike fighter; two MG 17, two MG 151, rack for 250 kg bomb or rack for 4x50 kg bombs (A-5)

*Frequent changes at the factory and on the front lines meant that the actual *Umrüstsatz* conversions did not always correspond to those modifications mentioned here. This table is intended as a general reference only.

A long-range fighter-bomber (*Jabo-Rei*) was designated the A-5/U8 and carried two 300-liter underwing drop tanks and a 500 kg bomb. Conversion took place in the spring of 1943 and the machine subsequently was delivered to Rechlin for trials.

The A-5/U9 was a heavy fighter with six cannons (two MG 131s and four MG 151s), of which only two were manufactured. These were used as the prototypes for the Fw 190A-7, A-8 and F-8 follow-on variants.

Another prototype, this time for the later A-6 series, was the A-5/U10; this was the first to have two MG 131s in place of MG 17s located above the engine and firing through the propeller arc. Two of these were delivered in January 1943.

The A-5/U11, a tank-buster from 1943, carried a 30 mm MK 103 cannon and ETC rack under each wing. Only one of these was built. The Fw 190A-5 with the U9 conversion kit (802 and 816), the Fw 190A-5/U10 (861), U11 (1303) and a V51 (530765) served as armament testbeds.

These planes were fitted with a reinforced wing designed to take the different weapons and were used for a wide variety of tests involving rapid-firing heavy-caliber cannons or guns with more firepower. The V51 was to have served as the prototype for the subsequent A-7/R2 and A-8/R2 series. Most of the approximately 570 A-5 variants were manufactured in 1943.

The A-5/U12 (813 and 814) was a heavy fighter and weapons testbed having two MG 17s and no less than six MG 151s. Like the V51, the two airplanes built were used as prototypes for the A-6/R1 and A-8/R1. They were delivered to the weapons test center at Tarnewitz on 1 July 1943 and 20 August 1943.

The A-5/U13 was a long-range fighter-bomber (*Jabo-Rei*) having drop tanks, of which three examples were built. The variant was fitted with a *Kuto-Nase*, sharp blades located behind the wing leading edge inboard designed to clip blockade balloon cables encountered during low-level attacks. The U13 was also equipped with an autopilot and DF loop and an automatic camera.

Production Fw 190A, F and G *Rüstsatz* Field Conversion Sets*

R1: FuG 16ZE; VHF radio for *Y-Verfahren* method of fighter direction(Fw 190A-4/R1, A- 5/R1, B-1)

R1: 4xETC 50 racks on outer wings(Fw 190F-3 and F-8)

R1: Two WB 151/20 underwing gondolas, each holding two MG 151/20 mm machine cannons(Fw 190A-6/R1, A-7, A-8, A-9, A-10, F-3, F-8, F-15, G-3, D-9 and D-12)

R2: Two MK 108/30 mm machine cannons, one on each side either below or in the wing(Fw 190A-6, A-7, A-8, A-9, A-10, F-8 and D-12)

R3: Two MK 103/30 mm machine cannons, one mounted under each wing(Fw-190A-6, A-10, F-3 and F-8)

R4: GM 1 system for improved high-altitude performance(Fw 190A-6, A-8 and G-8)

R5: Additional 115 liter fuel tank in rear fuselage for MW 50 or long-range(Fw 190A-6, A-8, F-8, F-16, G-3 and G-8) Four tanks in wings(315 liters) (Fw 190D-12 and D-13)

R6: Two WGr 42 rocket launchers in underwing tubes(Fw 190A-4, A-5, A-6 and A-7)

R7: Additional armor for *Sturmjäger* and *Rammjäger*(Fw 190A-8)

R8: Two MK 108 machine cannons under the wings for *Sturm* aircraft (Fw 190A-8 and A-9), late 1944

R11: FuG 125 Hermine supplemental kit (EBL 3) for FuG 16ZY (from August 1943); also Patin PKS-12 autopilot, heated windscreens for all-weather fighter (Fw 190A-8, A-9, D-9, D-11, D-12, D-13, D-15, Ta 152, B-5, C-0, C-1, C-2, C-3, H-0 and H-1)

R12: FuG 125, Patin PKS-12, heated windscreens and two machine cannons in the wings for all-weather fighter (Fw 190A-8 and A-9)

R13: Equipped for night-fighting operations, flame dampers; ETC 503 for 2x300 liter drop tanks; FuG 25a and FuG 16SZ and FuNG 101 altimeter (Fw 190F-8 and F-9)

R14: Torpedo plane with ETC 502, lengthened tailwheel and reduced armament (Fw 190F-8, F-9, D-9, Ta 152C-1)

R15: BT 1400 torpedo system with ETC 502 for carrying 920 kg and 1500 kg torpedo (Fw 190F-8 and F-9)

R16: BT 700 system with ETC 501 for 2xBT 400 wings (Fw 190F-8 and F-9)

R20: Improved high compression MW 50 in fuselage (Fw 190D-11, D-12 and D-13)

R21: MW 50 system, PKS-12 autopilot and FuG 125 Hermine, plus high compression MW 50 system (Fw 190D-9, D-11, D-12, D-13, Ta 152H-1)

R25: MW 50 system in wings with 130 liter tank and R11 kit, plus Jumo 213 EB (Fw 190D- 12)

R31: GM 1 system with 280 liter tank in rear fuselage, plus 4.62 kg counterweight on the engine and MW 50 high compression system and R11 kit (Ta 152C-1 and H-1)

* Field conversion kits were subject to frequent changes in the field and at the factory.

Hans Sander used the A-5/U14 for experiments as a torpedo bomber. This variant necessitated the fitting of a lengthened tail strut with wheel and an enlarged tailfin.

The Fw 190A-5/U15 (1282) was a special variant for carrying a 950 kg LT 950 anti-ship torpedo built by Blohm & Voss. Armament was reduced to just two MG 151s in the wing roots. It was also planned to utilize two 300-liter fuel tanks under the wings. Work on the aircraft was completed in August of 1943 and it was immediately turned over to Tarnewitz. However, the torpedoes were usually damaged when they hit the water and the tests were broken off.

The A-5/U16 heavy fighter (1346) carried extremely heavy armament with two additional 30 mm MK 108 cannons in the outer wings. The A-5/U17, a ground attack plane, was later utilized as a prototype for the F-3 ground attack variant.

An A-5/R1 was, like the A-4/R1, delivered as a command aircraft with the FuG 16ZE. During production several A-5 airplanes were experimentally fitted with a reinforced and slightly enlarged wing which was later incorporated into the A-6 series. Understandably, this remarkably versatile, potentially confusing jumble of military equipment caused the all-up weight of the airplane to rise continually. It also demonstrated how the flexible the design was, being employed in the widest variety of roles.

Overloaded in the Air

One example of the wide variety of conversions carried out with the design is the A-5/U8, having 820 kg (1140 liters) of fuel and two drop tanks. Depending on the load, the variant's takeoff weight varied between 4400 kg and 4900 kg and a wing loading of 240 kg/m2 to 267 kg/m^2. The aircraft retained only the two MG 151 cannons in the wing roots, the two MG 17s and the MG FF cannons being dropped. One ETC 501 rack, capable of carrying a 500 kg load, was attached to the fuselage centerline. The two drop tanks were suspended beneath the wings and were pressurized by the engine's turbocharger. Furthermore, an electrically driven fuel pump was fitted into each wing which could be operated by the pilot from the cockpit. The drop tanks fed into the aft fuselage tank. The aircraft was not fitted with a fuel gauge for the two drop tanks. The drained tanks were released by means of a red knob on the auxiliary instrument panel. In emergency situations, both bombs and drop tanks could be jettisoned simultaneously. Once the fuel gauge showed the fuel in the aft tank to be draining (after 1 1/4 hrs flight time, according to the manual), this indicated to the pilot that the two drop tanks were empty. An available table (from the aircraft handbook) derives the takeoff weight for the Fw 190A-5/U8 from the combined total of the useful load and the fuel weight. In addition to the two drop tanks the plane could carry a 250 kg bomb as standard. Carrying such a bomb, the aircraft burned fuel at a rate of 480 liters per hour at 3000 meters' altitude at 2300 rpm and 1.20 *atas* - i.e. the maximum cruise speed for the BMW 801D, giving it a range of two to two-and-a-half hours.

The A-5's speed without water-methanol injection was, at the most, 500 km/h at sea level. Each external store caused a drop in speed of 30 km/h at sea level, so two drop tanks and a bomb effectively reduced the plane's speed by 90 km/h. Accordingly, on the outward leg of a sortie the A-5/U8 had an airspeed of 410 km/h and on the return, once all external load had been dropped, this increased to 470 km/h (the drag incurred by each of pylons was at least 10 km/h, for a total of 30 km/h). This gave the aircraft a safe range of 865 km to 900 km. Takeoffs were also permitted with a 500 kg bomb, increasing the takeoff weight to 4900 kg. With such loads, a hard-surfaced runway was highly recommended. Official documents show that RLM aeronautical engineers reckoned that, during peacetime, the plane would have a maximum endurance of 3 hrs 55 mins and a range of 1505 km at idle cruise setting and a fuel consumption rate of 260 liters/hr (187 kg/hr). A more fitting consumption rate - which can be found in any operations manual for the Fw 190 or the BMW 801 - is the maximum cruise setting better suited to actual combat conditions, for certainly no pilot would venture to leisurely fly over enemy territory at idle cruise. These manuals give a fuel consumption rate of 430 liters/hr at maximum cruise and 260 liters/hr at maximum idle cruise at an altitude of 500 meters. A machine flying in an overloaded configuration could, at best, only hope to utilize the reduced throttle setting on the return flight over friendly territory.

Today, one can only wonder how those sitting at their drafting tables in the RLM could matter-of-factly juggle figures for this fighter showing nearly double the range and excess loads of some 1000 kg. As a side note, during meetings at the RLM a suggestion was made to reduce the aircraft's armor weight, which had increased to 480 kg in the interim. This had resulted in a steady rise in the aircraft's empty weight (see A-5/U8 table).

Fw 190 Large-Scale Production

Production of the Fw 190 rose ("too late" according to Werner Baumbach) from 228 fighters in 1941 to 1850 machines in 1942, 2171 in 1943 and to 7488 aircraft in 1944. This dropped back to 1630 aircraft in 1945. In addition, there were those aircraft fitted with ground attack conversion kits, of which approximately 68 were built in 1942. In 1943 the number of ground attack planes rose to 1183, and in 1944 this increased to a further 4279 machines. The majority of production aircraft were built to the Fw 190A standard. According to Baumbach, in addition to these approximately 20000 machines another 2700 experimental and specialized aircraft were built. It appears, however, that Baumbach's statistics may not be entirely accurate if figures from BMW are to be believed - these show that from 1942 to 1945 only 13544 BMW 801 engines were produced. It should also be taken into account that this powerplant was also installed in the Ar 232, Do 217, Ju 188 and Ju 290.

Despite increased interruptions due to bombing raids, Focke-Wulf was able to effectively maintain production by dispersing the manufacturing sites and transferring the key assembly points from the western regions to eastern cities such as Marienburg, Posen and Cottbus. Tank: "And at the very end we went underground. During the war's final phases the production output of our company still amounted to 75 percent of its former maximum output. At that time Focke-Wulf employed 35,000 workers and managers. The circle of suppliers making deliveries to the manufacturer had 120,000 employees."

Fw 190A-6 Heavy Fighter

As already mentioned, the prototype for the Fw 190A-6 was an A-5/U10 with a BMW 801D and a modified R1 field conversion kit. The additional MG 151 packs housed in underwing gondolas were designated WB 151/20 (WB= Wann*enbehälter*, or tub containers). With these, the Fw 190A-6/R1 packed an enormous punch as a heavy fighter, although it suffered from the significant weight increase and reduction in speed which the armament incurred. Production began in July 1943 in the factories of Arado, Fieseler and AGO. During production minor improvements were made to the cooler's armor and from November 1943 onward the Wgr. 42 system was installed as the R6 field conversion kit. With its two air-to-air mortars, the R6 weighed in at 294 kg.

Fw 190A-6/R1 with two WB 151/20 gondolas under the wings. Most of the Zerstörer *attack variants used on the Eastern Front employed a total of six MG 151s and two MG 17s.*

The various field conversion kits have been included in a table (pages 128 and 129) in order to alleviate some of the confusion in the text, so that the "R" designation following the type should be adequate for most readers, while those having a greater interest in the technical details may consult the table provided.

The Fw 190A-6 series was fitted with the R2, R3 and R4 conversion kits in addition to the previously mentioned R1 and R6 kits. The R4 conversion set is interesting in that it anticipated the fitting of a GM 1 system for improving the engine's high altitude performance. The system's operation has already been described in detail, but it should be noted how long it took before this important piece of performance-boosting equipment actually went into production. The system was tested for the first time in an A-0/U12 in early 1941. It was not until two years later (!) that it was being installed, and even then it was on an isolated basis. The V45 and V47, Werknummer 7347 and 530115, were used for the tests.

Tje Fw 190A-6/R6 was powered by the BMW 801D2. Of the entire BMW series, only this engine was cleared for cold-starting; despite this fact, this type of starting was employed throughout the Luftwaffe with other engine types as well. During cold starting, a quantity of fuel was poured into the oil tank which served to "water down" the oil made thick from the cold weather. When starting up, this simple solution ensured the engine was supplied oil which was as thin as if it had been warmed up previously. During run-up, the fuel evaporated within the oil. In the meantime, the engine had become so warm that the oil remained thin enough without the need for the fuel mixture. However, the whole process only worked smoothly when the plane took off immediately without any long taxiing, ensuring that the engine could be brought to full military power as soon as possible and generate enough heat for the fuel to evaporate in the oil.

But back to the A-6, of which 569 examples were manufactured. One A-6/R4 was experimentally fitted with a BMW 801TS engine in July 1944 and evaluated at Langenhagen. Several higher performing engines with turbochargers and high-altitude boost systems were already running on BMW's test benches; a few had already reached production maturity and were desperately needed in the field. BMW, however, was taxed to its limits - if not overburdened - with the production of the BMW 801D. So much so, in fact, that it simply did not have the capacity to deal with setting up production runs for newer model engines. Instead of stopping developmental work on these engines,

it probably would have been better to assist the company by providing it with more manufacturing capacity.

The documentation for the BMW 801TS is quite sparse, even within the company's files. At sea level, the engine delivered 1470 kW/2000 hp on takeoff and was apparently evaluated for its high-altitude performance in conjunction with the GM 1 system in the A-6/R4. Most of the aircraft from this series found their way to the Eastern Front. Depending on the situation, they were chiefly employed as heavy fighters and fitted with the R1 through R6 conversion sets.

Fw 190A-7 Fighter

In November 1943 AGO and Fieseler began production of the Fw 190A-7, the prototype for which was the A-5/U9 with BMW 801D-2 mentioned earlier. Around 80 of these machines were built from December 1943 to January 1944. The improved FuG 16ZY homing system was utilized and the FuG 25 served as the radio. In place of the two cowling MG 17s the production A-7 was fitted with heavier 13 mm MG 131s firing through the propeller, plus a simplified intercom (no shielding) and an improved reflective gunsight (Revi). The aircraft were fitted with the R1, R2 and R6 field conversion kits. The V51(520765) served as the prototype for the Fw 190A-7/R2 and this was used to test the MK 108 30 mm machine cannon of the R2 conversion kit. Production of the A-7/R2 began in March of 1944.

Fw 190A-8 with Improved MW 50 System

The V51(530765), mentioned on several occasions already, served as the prototype for the A-8 series. A rather large quantity of 1334 examples were built in 1944. In order to fly for longer periods at emergency boost (up to ten minutes) this variant was equipped with an improved MW 50 system, plus a 115 liter long-range fuel tank located behind the pilot. This tank could be used either for the MW 50 system or as a supplemental fuel tank. The higher weight incurred by the aft tank was offset by moving the radio set and ETC 501 bomb/drop tank pylon 200 mm forward. A GM 1 system was planned for utilizing the aircraft at higher altitudes. Connecting points for the WGr. 42 mortars were also incorporated into the design.

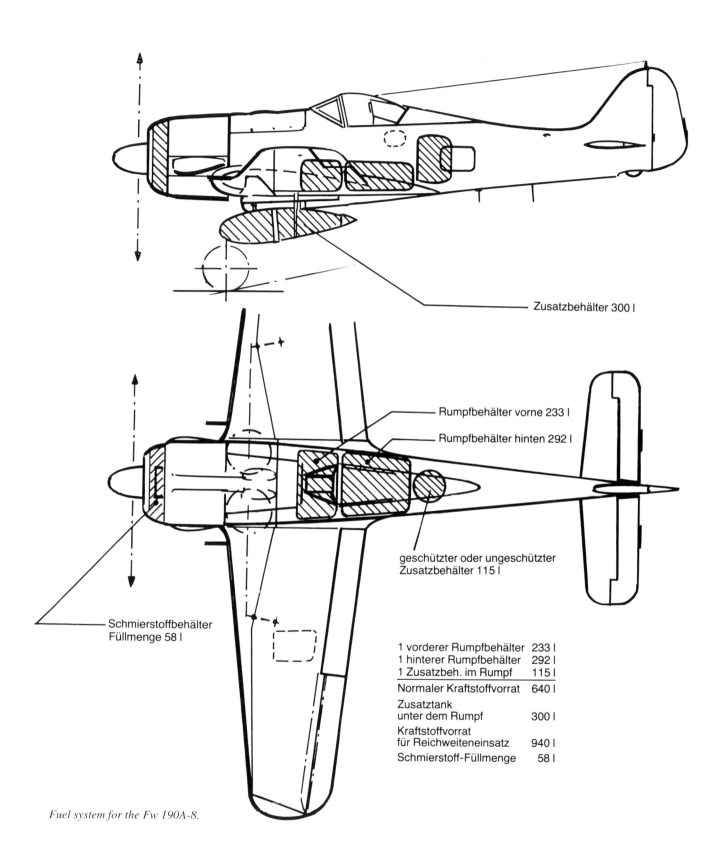

Zusatzbehälter 300 l

Rumpfbehälter vorne 233 l

Rumpfbehälter hinten 292 l

geschützter oder ungeschützter
Zusatzbehälter 115 l

Schmierstoffbehälter
Füllmenge 58 l

1 vorderer Rumpfbehälter	233 l
1 hinterer Rumpfbehälter	292 l
1 Zusatzbeh. im Rumpf	115 l
Normaler Kraftstoffvorrat	640 l
Zusatztank unter dem Rumpf	300 l
Kraftstoffvorrat für Reichweiteneinsatz	940 l
Schmierstoff-Füllmenge	58 l

Fuel system for the Fw 190A-8.

Fw 190A-8/U1, two-seat trainer version for converting Ju 87 dive bomber pilots to the Fw 190 attack plane.

Production began in February 1944 at Focke-Wulf and Fieseler and in April of 1944 at AGO and Dornier's Wismar facility. The Fw 190A-8 was fitted with the R1, R2, R3, R4, R5, R7, R8, R11 and R12 conversion kits. Production of the Fw 190A-8/R1 was abandoned due to inadequate performance. The A-5/U11 was the prototype for the A-8/R2. It was planned to utilize the 1470 kW/2000 hp BMW 801TU engine for the A-8 series. However, it was not yet available and the A-8 was therefore fitted with the BMW 801D.

The A-8/R3, the prototype for which was the A-5/U11, differed from its predecessors in having various weapons and armor combinations. A special Fw 190A-8/R7 was laid down as a Rammjäg*er* (ramming fighter), and fitted with supplemental armor. These aircraft were gathered into a specialized *Sturmstaffel*. Tank, however, wanted nothing to do with the technique of ramming; there was the very real potential that pilots could be injured or even killed by flying debris or wouldn't be able to bail out due to jammed canopies. The operation would be meaningless if both pilot and plane were lost in a ramming attack. At a conference with high-ranking officers, Tank made it plain at the time that such "oriental" tactics did not bode well. On the other hand, British sources reveal that a *Sturmverband* under the command of Major Wilhelm Moritz, IV/JG 3, on 7 July 1944 was reputed to have brought down 32 bombers with only two losses to themselves. The unit had been equipped with the Fw 190A-8/R7. After only a few months, the unit was disbanded due to the fact that the pilots (and their commanders) were totally exhausted. The pilots of these *Sturm* units must have had to fly against the enemy aircraft with utter fearlessness in the face of death, although the 400 kg of protective armor must have been of some comfort to the pilots.

The Fw 190A-8/R11 had a special radio and all-weather instrument flight system and was powered by an improved BMW 801D/TU, a D-engine having parts fully interchangeable with the 2000 hp 801E engine. Production of the A-8/R11 began at Focke-Wulf in September of 1944. Only some of the A-8 series aircraft were fitted with the BMW 801TU, for although these and other engines (like the TS) indeed delivered the promised 1470 kW/2000 hp, they were not available in even limited quantity until mid to late 1944.

A two-seat A-8/U1 version was built for converting Ju 87 pilots to the ground attack versions of the Fw 190. The type completed its first flight in early 1944; only a few of the type were built, however, since it quickly became apparent that Ju 87 pilots had little difficulty retraining on the Fw 190. Production aircraft were designated Fw 190S.

[1]Fighter, fighter-bomber and heavy fighter. Performance is based on supplemental fitting of GM 1 system, which improved combat performance above 5000 m. Weight and performance data drawn from company information (Fw Report No. 06011)
[2]Weight includes 157 kg for amor = 2743+157=2900 kg

[3]Armament and Payload

2xMG 17	kg	21
2x900 rounds	kg	140
2xMG 151	kg	84
2x250 rounds	kg	96
2xMG 151	kg	84
2x140 rounds	kg	56
fittings	kg	50
GM 1 system	kg	150
load	kg	681

[4]560 km/h at sea level.
All performance figures with no external stores (clean).
[5]510 km/h at sea level with maximum permissable cruising speed
[6]At sea level with 4100 kg takeoff weight in clean configuration
[7]Fuel consumption rate
acc. to BMW

and Rechlin reports	rpm	altitude (m)	rate (kg/hr)	altitude (m)	rate (kg/hr)
takeoff and emergency pwr	2700	0	637*	5700	520*
climb and combat	2400	0	461*	5300	388*
max. cruise	2300	0	361*	5500	361*
max. economy	2100	0	244*	5400	241*

*fuel consumption rate according to BMW + 12.5% based on Rechlin data
[8]Endurance and range of A-6 as fighter-bomber with ETC 501 + SC 500 kg bomb, average speed for ingress and return including time for climb and descent

altitude (m)	rpm	ata	rate (kg/hr)	speed (km/h)	time (hr)	distance (km)
300	2300	1.20	360	490	0.95	460
5000	2300	1.20	360	545	1.06	515
300	2100	1.10	225	440	1.52	665
5000	2100	1.10	240	510	1.44	675

[9]R2 field conversion set configuration
[10]Fuselage tank: 233 liter, + 292 liter + 115 liter supplemental tank (long-range or MW 50) = 640 liters/472 kg

[11]Load with R2 configuration

2xMK 108	kg	176
2x55 rounds	kg	65
2xMG 151	kg	84
2x250 rounds	kg	100
2xMG 131	kg	59
2x475 rounds	kg	81
MW 50 system, empty(long-range)	kg	50
Equipment	kg	233
	kg	848

[12]560 km/h at sea level, 2700 rpm
[13]500 km/h at sea level, 2300 rpm
[14]At sea level; 10 m/sec at 5500 m

Fighter and Fighter-Bomber Comparison

Manufacturer		Focke-Wulf	
Type		Fw 190A-6[1]	Fw 190A-8/R2[9]
Powerplant		BMW 801D2	BMW 801D2
Performance	kW	1272	1272
	hp	1730	1730
Crew		1	1
Length	m	9.10	9.10
Height	m	3.95	3.95
Wingspan	m	10.50	10.50
Wing area	m²	18.30	18.30
Aspect ratio		6.02	6.02
Weight, empty	kg	2900[2]	2900[2]
Fuel	kg	396	472[10]
Oil	kg	50	50
Crew	kg	80	80
Load	kg	681[3]	848[11]
Max. permissible load	kg	1207	1450
Takeoff weight	kg	4107	4350
Wing loading	kg/m²	224.43	237.70
Weight/power ratio	kg/kW	3.23	3.42
	kg/hp	2.37	2.51
	kW/m²	69.51	69.51
	hp/m²	94.54	94.54
Built		1943	1943
Max. speed	km/h	660[4]	635[12]
@ altitude	m	7000	6200
Cruise speed	km/h	600[5]	585[13]
@ altitude	m	6500	6200
Rate of climb	m/s	14.50[6]	13[14]
Service ceiling	m	10500	9600
Range	km	500[7]	615[15]
Max. flight time	hrs	1.10[8]	1.20[16]
Takeoff run	m	400	500
Takeoff run to 20 m	m	600	720
Landing run	m	500	500
Landing speed	km/h	163	168
Max. permissible load as % of takeoff weight		29	33
Payload as % of takeoff weight		17	19

[15]At 300 m and 2300 rpm
1.32 hrs and 695 km at 5000 m and 2300 rpm
2.02 hrs and 985 km at 5000 m and 2100 rpm

Fw 190A-8/U1 (S-8) trainer.

With regards to the airframe, the Fw 190A-8 was the swansong of Fw 190/BMW 801D development. Later versions differed only in equipment, armament and powerplant. Radio/navigation equipment for the A-8 included the FuG 16ZY and FuG 25. Performance figures in the table are based on new aircraft with smooth gloss coats of paint applied.

Fw 190 NC 900 in French Service

Focke-Wulf company records hint at underground production of the Fw 190 at SNCA du Centre in Cravant. The first aircraft, an A-5, is reputed to have taken to the skies on its maiden flight near the war's end, on 16 March 1945. Subsequently, the French built 64 A-5 and A-8 variants under the designation NC 900, production ceasing in the spring of 1946. These aircraft went into service with the French air force.

Delving into Transsonic Flight

Kurt Tank had always taken pains to be the one at the controls of the aircraft designed under his supervision on their maiden flights. At the least, he had become involved in the test program subsequent to the initial flights by his test pilots. With the Fw 190, however, he was so overburdened with various other projects that he left the test flights up to his pilots and limited himself to follow-on test and acceptance flights. In portraying a flight in an Fw 190A-7 he describes his own creation in detail, takes a close look at the design and compares it with other aircraft.

Tank sat in the Fw 190's cockpit, closed the hood and started the engine which the ground crewmen had warmed up earlier. He took his time checking out all the operating levers and equipment.

He then taxied out for takeoff, gradually pushed the throttle up to maximum takeoff revs, cast a scrutinous eye over the rpm gauge and boost pressure and then raced across the grass field. At 180 km/h indicated airspeed the machine lifted off by itself after a run of about 300 meters. Tank retracted the landing gear and, after reaching 230 km/h, did the same with the flaps. At 280 km/h he pulled the machine up into a climb and shot heavenward at 15 meters per second. The aircraft responded to every control input, cutting smoothly through the air. It was a joy flying such a fast bird as this. Now he had a few moments to pause and reflect.

In Rechlin Tank had once had the opportunity to fly a Russian Rata, a plane which had proven a formidable opponent during the Spanish Civil war due to its excellent maneuverability. After takeoff, a pilot had to switch hands on the control stick because the undercarriage retraction mechanism was operated by the right hand and required 22 turns of the crank lever. Certainly a most unpleasant feature when taking off in formation! When turning, a pilot had to push vice pull on the stick in order to maintain level flight, a sure sign that the aircraft was highly unstable. Tank on the other hand, when designing his aircraft, had striven to ensure the pilot could forget about operating the airplane once he'd taken off and retracted the undercarriage; instead, he could focus completely on the navigational or combat tasks at hand.

Compared with the Bf 109, the Fw 190 didn't have the dangerous tendency to ground loop when taking off. The undercarriage was of an extremely wide track layout and set well forward. Too, the Würger was able to sit on its tailwheel until the moment of liftoff. As mentioned in the introduction to this section, Tank had paid particular attention to designing a robust landing gear able to withstand high rates of descent on landing. An Fw 190 pilot who dropped onto the runway from a few meters during a landing wouldn't necessarily have damaged the undercarriage. Most importantly, however, the aircraft did not have the unpleasant habit of dropping onto one of the undercarriage legs if it were leveled off too soon, a situation which also tended to result in a ground loop.

In the interim, Tank had reached 6000 meters, and he trimmed the machine for level flight; he throttled the boost pressure back to cruise and checked to see if the machine was stable around all axes. The Fw 190 was quite easy to trim out, not requiring any input from the control stick. It flew straight and true with loose control surfaces. After aileron input the plane returned back to its neutral position. The Würger also returned to normal following a change in the yaw axis, even if Tank released the rudder. Turns with up to 70° of bank were easily and pleasantly flown. If Tank released pressure on the controls the machine returned to its original attitude. Control harmonization was good. Tank then eased up on the throttle, whereupon the plane became slightly nose heavy and went into a shallow glide. Test pilots and ground crew have really ironed out the wrinkles on this one, Tank thought. There's simply nothing to complain about here.

The stall handling was surprisingly pleasant for such a relatively heavy aircraft. Tank chopped the throttle, reduced his airspeed to 220 km/h and found he could maintain control through all rolling and yawing movements. When stalling, the airplane dropped forward, built up speed and returned control back to Tank almost immediately. It had no tendency to tip over onto either wing. However, there was no warning before entering the stall, although the experienced pilot immediately sensed he was flying in the stall regime as soon as pressure on the controls eased up.

Now Tank began spinning with the Fw 190. The plane was not easy to put into a spin; if a pilot applied rudder at about 180 km/h, the plane simply stalled over on the wing. Tank tried it and everything went just like it had on the earlier versions of his airplane. During test flights with a Ta 152 the airplane once went into a spin following a stall, but he was not able to repeat this since in all other cases the machine stalled out normally, picked its nose up and built up speed again.

The Fw 190 also stalled over onto one wing when rudder was applied while the plane was in an upside-down attitude. Once Tank unintentionally even went into an inverted spin. He was testing an Fw 190 and during a loop reached the altitude at which the automatic boost switched on. At the top of the loop the rpm briefly dropped off with a shudder, just enough to put the plane over onto its back; the machine then spun inverted for several rotations. At the time, Tank was not quite sure what was happening in this strange attitude and so put the stick and pedals in neutral. Immediately the spinning stopped, and with a half-roll he was back

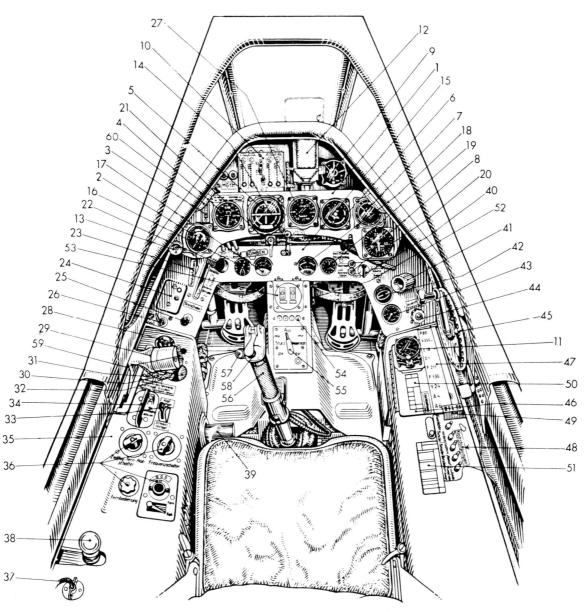

1 Main instrument panel
2 Fine and coarse altimeter
3 Pitot tube heater indicator
4 Airspeed indicator
5 Artificial horizon
6 Compass
7 Supercharger pressure gauge
8 Tachometer
9 Radio navigation gauge
10 Armament control panel and ammunition counters
11 Clock
12 Gunsight
13 Cockpit climate control knob
14 Engine ventilation flap control lever
15 Secondary instrument panel

16 Dual pressure gauge (fuel and oil)
17 Electronic oil temperature gauge
18 Electronic fuel supply gauge
19 Mechanical propeller blade pitch indicator
20 Fuel warning lights
21 Windscreen washer switch
22 Fuel cock lever
23 Manual landing gear retraction lever
24 FuG 25a control panel
25 Engine starter brushes withdrawal button
26 Stop cock control lever
27 Variometer(rate of climb/descent indicator)
28 Instrument panel illumination dimmer
29 Throttle
30 Primer switch (blocked by throttle)

31 Landing gear and flaps position indicators
32 Horizontal stabilizer trim indicator
33 Horizontal stabilizer trim switch
34 Undercarriage and flap actuation buttons
35 Left instrument panel
36 FuG 16ZY controls
37 Pilot's helmet R/T connector
38 SUM AP 20 primer fuel pump handle
39 Throttle friction knob
40 Fuel gauge selector switch
41 Flare pistol holder
42 Oxygen flow indicator
43 Oxygen pressure gauge
44 Oxygen flow valve
45 Canopy actuator mechanism

46 Flare box
47 Circuit breaker panel cover
48 Fuel pump circuit breakers
49 Starter switch
50 Operations data card
51 Compass deviation card
52 Cockpit ventilation control
53 21-cm weapons armament switch
54 Ordnance release indicator
55 ZSK bomb fusing selector switch
56 Knurled grip
57 Bomb release button
58 Wing armament firing button
59 Thumb-actuated propeller pitch control
60 Instrument panel lighting

at a normal flight attitude. In extreme situations the stick forces on the Fw 190 could reach up to 5 kg, although this was within the limits set out in the design requirements.

Once Tank was satisfied with the testing thus far, he put the airplane into a climb again with the intent of reaching 10000 meters; once at that height he checked the oxygen supply. Tank was in constant radio contact with the ground during the entire flight. Climbing to 12000 meters, where the sky was more black than blue, Tank pushed the plane over into horizontal flight, flipped it over onto its back and, reducing the throttle, went into an inverted dive. Almost straight down, he plunged back to the earth far below. The altimeter began unwinding at an incredible rate, 10000, 9000, 8000, 7000 meters... and then white flecks began flying off the wings as if they were making snowflakes. "Is the crate falling apart?" shot through Tank's mind. Yet the machine continued its dive earthward. The altimeter registered 6000 meters. It was time to pull out. The airspeed indicator showed 700 km/h, which equated to a true airspeed of 955 km/h. Cautiously, Tank pulled the machine out of its dive. At this point, powerful forces began building up, forces which could cause an airplane to rip apart. For a pilot, these forces caused his vision to go gray, blue or red, or even black out altogether, although he would remain conscious the entire time. Tank breathed a sigh of relief once he was flying horizontal again. The altimeter read 4000 meters and the g-meter showed that the forces had reached 7 g, or seven times the pull of gravity. The white flakes had been condensation buildup caused by the compression wave resulting from localized sonic speeds.

The machine performed normally in all situations and flight attitudes. No trace of flutter. It had lost little in the way of its flying qualities despite the many changes needed in order to make the airplane suitable for its wide variety of military applications.

Tank entered the downwind leg of the landing pattern, throttled back to 0.65 atas, pulled up slightly to reduce speed to 250 km/h and partially extended the landing flaps. He switched the undercarriage selector to "extended", pulled the landing gear lever and watched the undercarriage lower as the rods rose from the wing surfaces. He now gave it more throttle to maintain 220 km/h and turned in on final. Tank fully deployed the flaps and gave it a bit more throttle to keep the airspeed at 200 km/h. It was not necessary to trim the Fw 190. Even with the gear and flaps extended, no retrimming was needed (unlike the Bf 109, which then became quite nose heavy). Tank gently touched the machine down at 170 km/h. Tank climbed out of the cockpit with the satisfied feeling knowing that the field was yet again getting an improved and reliable aircraft - one which could meet all the requirements of a combat machine.

Testing Secret Weapons with the Fw 190A-8

Several sub-variants of the Fw 190A-8 were employed as testbeds. Thus, wind tunnel tests at the Graf Zeppelin research institute revealed that streamlined 250 liter drop tanks attached to the upper wing surface caused virtually no loss in airspeed - as opposed to the considerable loss of about 30 km/h per tank generated by underwing drop tanks. A large percentage of the airspeed-reducing drag was accounted for by the ETC pylons. Erprobungs-Kommando 25, later Versuchsjagdgruppe 10, conducted practical evaluations using an Fw 190A-8(380394) and, later, an Fw 190F-3(67007) and confirmed the findings of the wind tunnel testing. However, to the frustration of the designer, the RLM prohibited a conversion to these tanks in order to avoid interrupting the manufacturing flow. Problems had also reputedly cropped up during the tests with the aircraft's stability.

Other testing by the Erprobungs-Kommando related to a special armament configuration for the Fw 190A-8. Three 30 mm MK 103 cannons were combined into a single unit and a set of these upward firing oblique guns was mounted on each side of the fuselage. The weapon was to have been automatically triggered by a photo cell controller as the aircraft passed beneath a bomber. In this manner, a bomber could be engaged with little risk to the attacking pilot. The weapon itself was designated the SG 116 *Zellendusche*. However, in the middle of the war it was apparently impossible to find a practical solution for targeting and firing the system. An Fw 190 V74(733713) and a V75(582071) were employed for these tests.

The same aircraft were also used for a series of similar experiments using MK 108 machine cannons. Seven cannons were combined into a battery, designated SG 117 *Rohrblock* and this time installed in the fuselage at an 85-degree upward-firing angle along the centerline. The first shell was fired electro-optically by means of a photo cell. The recoil of the first cannon then operated the other cannons. Six Fw 190A-8s were fitted with the system.

Yet another series of tests involved the wire-guided X-4 missile built by Ruhrstahl. This air-to-air missile had been designed for targeting four-engined bombers; with this system, the fighter pilot could safely launch an attack outside the bomber's defensive field of fire. The missile was planned for use with the Fw 190 and Me 262. The device was quite interesting and modern, even by today's standards; it was based on a two-meter long spindle-shaped body whose nose housed a 20 kg warhead. Located around the body's center

were four stubby, swept fins, while its extreme aft area was fitted with four smaller guide fins. The body also housed a tank of pressurized air and, at the rear, the combustion chamber. The pilot controlled the wire-guided missile by means of a small control knob. During flight, the missile rotated at a rate of about 60 revolutions per minute. Initial trials took place at Gütersloh on 11 August 1944 using a V69(582072) and a V70(580029); these showed that firing ranges of up to 5500 meters were possible. Plans for deploying the missile operationally failed, however, when a bombing raid destroyed the factory responsible for producing the motors; there was not enough time to find a replacement source.

Fw 190A-9 with BMW 801TS, 801TU and 801TH

A series of protoypes were made available for testing the new Fw 190A-9 series and its more powerful, improved BMW 801 engine. These included V34(410230), V 35(816, BMW 801TU), V36, V72(170727, BMW 801TS), V73(733705) and V74(733713). Work on these aircraft had been completed by September 1944. Neither the BMW 801TS, 801TU nor the 801TH were equipped with exhaust turbochargers, as has often been erroneously assumed, but had only a single-stage supercharger with dual gearing. It was initially planned to utilize the BMW 801F for the A-9, but this engine was not completed until the final days of the war - and even then only a single example was available. The TS, TU and TH engines were completely interchangeable and could be swapped with the BMW 801D. Performance had increased to 1470 kW/2000 hp for takeoff and emergency power at 2700 rpm, 1.65 atas boost pressure at a fuel consumption rate of 290 g/hp/hr. The motor evidenced changes to the oil cooler, plus the armor for the cooler and oil tank had been increased to 10 and 6 mm, respectively. The exhaust system also now made use of single pipes.

Production of the Fw 190A-9 was to have begun in September/October 1944. Two versions were planned: an A-9/R11 with the TS engine for all-weather combat and an A-9/R8, also with the TS, as a *Sturm-Jäger* with thicker armor. It cannot be determined with certainty whether the A-9 ever entered full scale production in any great numbers. According to Focke-Wulf documents, a specific deadline had been set for production to begin. In addition to the previously mentioned conversion kits, it was also planned to have the airplane make use of the R1, R2, R3 and R12. However, RLM files covering actual production numbers make no mention of the A-9. It is just as likely that production was dropped in favor of the F-series, particularly since the anticipated BMW 801F never materialized and the BMW TS and TU engines were only delivered in small quantities.

The BMW 801TS/TU or TH were deliberately laid out as interim stages toward the planned 801F. The BMW 801TS caused many accidents in its early operational stages because the *Kommandogerät*'s servo valve often became stuck; as a result, the engine would not respond when throttle was applied on landing approach or during missed approaches. A provisional solution to this aggravating tendency was the fitting of a so-called "primer" which the pilot could pull in such cases.

The single BMW 801F was installed in an aircraft during the last days of the war for testing purposes. It had been designed as a replacement for the 801D and attained an output of 1764 kW/2400 hp.

Fw 190A-10 Remains a Project

The Fw 190A-10 had also anticipated the installation of the BMW 801F; it was to have carried three drop tanks and have had a payload capacity of up to 1750 kg. Furthermore, it was to have been fitted with a larger wing. Series production was planned for March 1945. Focke-Wulf records on the A-10 indicate an F-10 as well. On the other hand, RLM documentation make no reference whatsoever to the construction of the Fw 190A-10 and, as is known, the BMW 801F was never delivered. In all probability, therefore, the A-10 was never actually built.

Fw 190F-Series Strike Fighter

As mentioned earlier, from 1942 onward the Ju 87 dive bombers and ground attack variants in desperate need of replacing by a better performing aircraft. However, there was neither sufficient time nor industrial resources available for developing a new airplane from scratch. The Fw 190A's robustness and performance, plus its ability to make use of conversion kits to adapt it to a wide variety of military roles, accordingly made it a strong candidate for that replacement airplane. This was the intention behind the Fw 190A-8/U1 two-seat trainer. Formerly, most of the variants were fighter designs which had been converted to ground attack platforms through the use of conversion kits; now the planes - planned for large-scale production were to be laid down for their role as strike fighters from the outset. The undercarriage of these F-series aircraft was to be reinforced to accommodate the markedly higher takeoff weight and engine, tanks and pilot were to be better protected by armor. Armor weight was about 360 kg, while takeoff weight fluctuated between 4300 kg and 4620 kg. The F-series had intake scoops outside the engine cowling so that these might more easily be fitted with tropical filters. ETC 501 bomb racks were installed beneath the fuselage and under the wings were ER 4 racks for carrying four 50 kg boms and an automatic camera.

These relatively minor changes meant that current A-series on the assembly line could be utilized and converted accordingly. The aircraft were fitted with the strengthened wing of the A-6. Production began in May 1943 at Arado. The first Fw 190F-1 variant, of which about 30 machines were built in 1943, was a modified A-4/U3. The Fw 190F-2 was based on the A-5/U3; 271 of these were delivered. Armament consisted of two MG 17s, two MG 151s and the ETC 501 rack for carrying various air-to-ground ordnance. A large number of Fw 190F-2s were fitted with tropical equipment and operated from Italy and Tunisia.

Within this context it's interesting to note the performance loss of aircraft caused by the bomb racks, bombs and external stores - nowadays one calls these "Christmas trees" hanging from the wings and fuselage of our modern day jet airplanes, whose drag buildup with such configurations is much higher than during the WWII period due to their faster speeds. With an R1 kit on an F-3, a 4xSC 50 configuration (four 50 kg bombs on four ETC 50 racks) causes a depreciation in airspeed of 10 to 12 km/h at sea level and 20 km/h at an altitude of around 6000 meters. The loss during climbing amounted to 1.3 meters per second at 2400 rpm. Even the range was cut back by about 37 kilometers. The higher drag factor of the Fw 190F and Fw 190G has accordingly been taken into account in the performance and data table in this book.

The wings of the Fw 190F-8 ground attack variant were reinforced in the area of the landing gear. This aircraft was used in the Mediterranean theater.

Fw 190F-8/R1 with 300-l auxiliary fuel tank under the fuselage and two ETC 50 racks under each wing, each holding a 50-kg bomb.

The Fw 190F-3 ground attack plane, of which 247 were built by Arado starting in May 1943, was a follow-on development of the Fw 190A-5/U17. With the fitting of the R1 conversion kit, this variant was then designated the Fw 190F-3/R1. Only three examples of a second variant, the Fw 190F-3/R3, were built.

The Fw 190F-4, F-5 and F-6 were to have been follow-on developments of the F-3 with appropriate changes to the equipment and armament. However, these were never built, probably due to the fact that the planned BMW 801F never became available in quantity. The F-series continued with the Fw 190F-8, F-9 and F-10, for which the airframes of the A-8 and A-9 series were used.

The F-8 was an F-3 with an improved ordnance electrical system which allowed all bombs to be released individually. The wing was reinforced in the area of the landing gear. MG 131s were fitted in place of the two MG 17s over the engine. Furthermore, the F-8 carried four ETC 50 racks under the wings. Production began in March of 1944 at Arado and Dornier. The F-8/R1 and F-8R3 differed only in their conversion kit fittings. A few Fw 190F-8 examples were again used to carry out comprehensive evaluation pro-

grams for testing the use of various caliber torpedoes. The same applied for testing the installation of a variety of weapons packages such as three 30 mm MK 103s for engaging bombers. However, these did not lead to any tangible success. In all 385 F-8 variants were produced.

The F-9 was fitted with the more powerful BMW 801TS or TU. The F-10 was never built. Other variants, such as the F-15 and F-16, were yet again fitted with a strengthened undercarriage, plus the BMW 801TS or TU and conversion kits for a wide variety of roles. A V66(584002) served as the prototype for the F-15. The aircraft was cleared for flight in December of 1944 and production began in March, 1945. Series production of the F-16 was had been planned for April 1945 at Dornier. A follow-on development of the F-16/R5 called for two additional tanks, each holding 110 liters of fuel, in the wings. Prototype for this project was the V67(930516) with a BMW 801TS or TH. The FuG 16 air-to-air and air-to-ground rado was replaced by an FuG 15. The FuG 15 was only capable of transmitting or receiving and was therefore unsuitable for the Y-Ver*fahren* control system as it was unable to communicate with radar systems.

142

The Fw 190F-8/R1 ground attack plane was armed with two supplemental 130-round Mk 103/30 cannons in addition to two MG 17s and two MG 151s.

Fw 190F-8/R1 with four ETC 50 bomb racks beneath the wings and an ETC 250 rack under the fuselage, occupied by a 250-kg bomb.

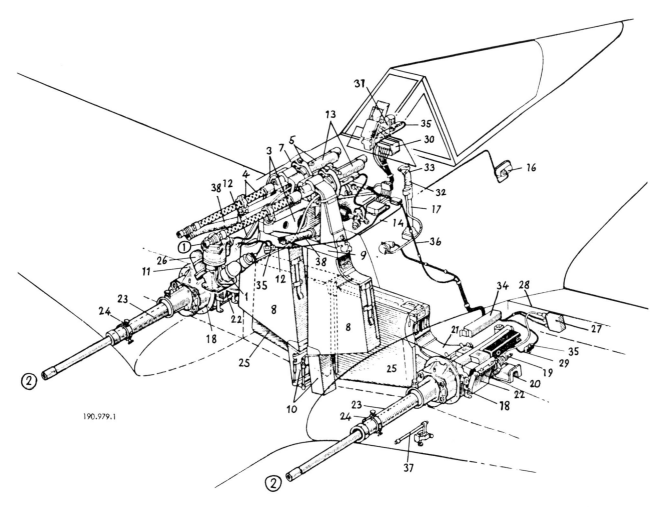

190.979.1

Fw 190F-3/R1 ground attack variant armament with two MG 17s in the fuselage and two MG 151 machine cannons in the wing roots.

1 MG 17 in fuselage
2 MG 151/20E in wing roots
3 Fuselage gun mount
4 Forward fuselage gun support
5 Aft fuselage gun support
6 Ammunition feed chute for fuselage gun
7 Ammunition discharge chute for fuselage gun
8 Ammunition belt box for fuselage guns
9 Ammunition box stays
10 Spent shell casing holders (adjustable)
11 17E controller with EKu 17
12 Wire impulse transmitter line
13 EPAD 17
14 Compressed air bottle with DHAG 4
15 Compressed air line
16 External compressed air connector
17 ADSK 2-17
18 Wing root gun forward mount
19 Wing root gun aft mount
20 Aft mount support brace
21 Ammunition feed chute for wing root gun
22 Belt and shell discharge port for wing root gun
23 Air flow sleeve
24 Barrel support
25 Ammunition belt container for wing root gun
26 Electronic dual firing controller for wing root guns
27 Wing root gun EDSK
28 Wing root armament cable
29 Electronic firing cable for wing root gun
30 SZKK 4
31 Reflexive gunsight
32 Control column
33 Fire button for fuselage and wing armament
34 Wing attachment point
35 Cable connection
36 Spark plug housing
37 Sighting calibrator
38 Cold air piping for ammunition cooling

BMW 801TR, 801TS, 801TU and 801F Engines

Engine Type	# of cylinders	stroke (mm)	bore (mm)	capacity (ltrs)	compression	length (mm)	width ∅ (mm)	height (mm)	Supercharger	type of performance	altitude m	output kW/hp	rpm ata	boost pressure	consumption rate g/hp/hr	ltrs/hr	Dry Installed Weight kg	Comments
BMW 801TR	14	156	156	41.75		2550	1360	1360	2-stage, 4-gear charger with intermediate and final cooling. 1st stage: 1st gear 4.2, 2nd gear 5.4 2nd stage: 3-d gear 6.5, 4th gear 7.25	takeoff and emergency climb	0	1470/2000	2700	1.65	414/304		1690 kg with armor	As of August, 1944 planned for Ta 152. TH follow-on development with greater max pressure alt by using a 2-stage multi-geared charger
											0	1250/1700	2500	1.45	376/276			
										takeoff and emergency climb and combat	5200	1433/1950	2700	1.65	430/316			
											5300	1227/1670	2500	1.45	392/288			
										takeoff and emergency climb and combat	8600	1294/1760	2700	1.65	465/342			
											8600	1125/1530	2500	1.45	462/340			
										takeoff and emergency climb and combat	10900	1154/1570	2700	1.65	493/362			
											11000	1029/1400	2500	1.45	435/320			
BMW 801TS	14	156	156	41.8	7.2	2006	1290	1290	1st stage 2 gears, 1st gear 6.0, 2nd gear 8.31	takeoff and emergency climb and combat	0	1470/2000	2700	1.65				Operational from Oct-Nov 1944. Compared with BMW 801D had higher performance through greater rpm and turbocharge
											0	1250/1700	2500	1.45				
											0	1080/1470	2400	1.30				
										max. cruise economy	0	786/1070	2200	1.15				
BMW 801TU	14	156	156	41.8	7.2	2006	1290	1290	1st stage 2 gears, 1st gear 5.31, 2nd gear 8.31	takeoff and emergency	600	1271/1730	2700	1.42				
										takeoff and emergency	5700	1258/1710	2700	1.42				
BMW 801F	14	156	156	41.8	7.2	2256	1290	1290	1st stage 2 gears, 1st gear 6.35, 2nd gear 9.35	takeoff and emergency climb	0	1764/2400	2700	1.65				With MW 50 1985 kW/2700 hp. flown in Apr-May 1945
											0	1617/2200	2500	1.45				

Fw 190G Long-Range Fighter-Bomber

A line of *Jabo-Rei* increased-range fighter-bombers, designated the G-series, were produced parallel to the F-series. These long-range aircraft were an attempt to fulfill the wishes of the field units and reduce - at least on the return journey - the high dropoff in performance (particularly for *Jabo-Rei* aircraft) incurred by underwing and underfuselage fittings. The aircraft were fitted with drop tanks which were attached to shrouded Messerschmitt braces comprised of a strut based frame which dropped away when the tanks were released. The aircraft were fitted with the FuG 16Z and FuG 25. The air inlet ducts were moved back inside the engine cowling. For nighttime operations, the G-2 was fitted with flame dampers. Instead of the cowl guns the aircraft only retained two MG 151 cannons in the wing roots. The Fw 190G-1, of which 50 machines were produced, was based on an A-4/U8 configuration. It had two drop tanks of 300 liters each.

The *Jabo-Rei* Fw 190G-2 was a follow-on development of the Fw 190A-5/U8 and had a slightly longer fuselage. Approximately 470 of these aircraft were built.

The Fw 190G-3 long-range fighter-bomber, production of which began in late summer 1943, was a follow-on development of the A-5/U13. The airplane was fitted with two MG 151s and a PKS 11 autopilot. The wings were carried over from the A-6. G-series aircraft from the G-4 onward were sometimes fitted with the *Kuto-Nase* in order to deflect or cut blockade balloon cables encountered during low-level flying.

The Gw 190G-3 was equipped with racks for two 300-liter drop tanks and for ordnance ranging up to 1000 kg bombs or two 250 kg bombs. With this load, the aircraft was capable of ranges of 1550 km and an endurance of up to three hours at maximum idle cruise setting. Undercarriage and tires were beefed up yet again. G-series planes occasionally carried bombs weighing up to 1800 kg for strikes against bridges - probably the greatest bomb load ever lifted into the air by a single-engined aircraft during the war. These planes needed a takeoff run of 1200 meters or more in order to get airborne. One G-3 fell into American hands after the war and became a welcome study object for engineers and military personnel. The Fw 190G-4 had a simplified intercom and the FuG 16ZY. Production began in December 1943. The Fw 190G-5 was planned for the BMW 801F, although the 801TH was later delivered in its place.

Fw 190G-3 long-range fighter-bomber with 500-kg bomb and two 300-l auxiliary fuel tanks, year of service 1944.

The Fw 190G-7 had attachment points for three drop tanks each holding 300 liters of fuel.

The final version in the G-series, also built in large numbers in 1944, was the Fw 190G-8. This variant was basically the same as the Fw 190A-8 and was fitted with hardpoints for drop tanks and virtually every other type of air-to-ground ordnance. The airplane was given an R4 conversion set with additional 115 liter long-range tanks for the GM 1 system or to increase the plane's radius of action. For this reason the FuG 16ZY and ETC 501 pylon were moved further forward. In all, a total 790 Fw 190G aircraft were manufactured at Focke-Wulf, Arado, AGO and Fieseler.

Fw 190G-8 with ETC 501 and ER 4 rack holding four 50-kg bombs.

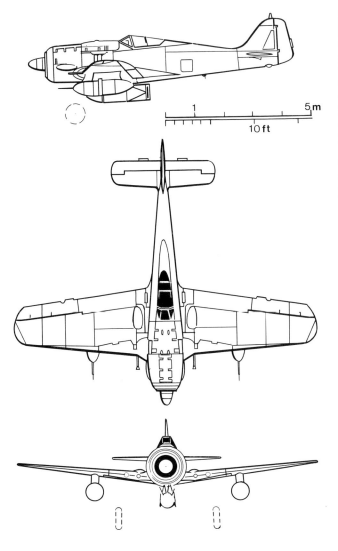

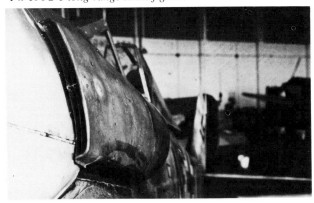

Fw 190G-3 long-range strike fighter.

Strike Fighter and *Jabo-Rei* Long-Range Fighter-Bomber Comparison

Manufacturer		Focke-Wulf	
Type		Fw 190F-2[1]	Fw-190G-1[7]
Powerplant		BMW 801D2	BMW 801D2
Performance	kW	1272	1272
	hp	1730	1730
Crew		1	1
Length	m	9.10	9.10
Height	m	3.95	3.95
Wingspan	m	10.50	10.50
Wing area	m²	18.30	18.30
Aspect ratio		6.02	6.02
Weight, empty	kg	3103[2]	3112
Fuel	kg	396	839[8]
Oil	kg	50	50
Crew	kg	80	80
Load	kg	1071[3]	918[9]
Max. permissible load	kg	1597	1887
Takeoff weight	kg	4700	4999
Wing loading	kg/m²	256.83	273.17
Weight/power ratio	kg/kW	3.69	3.93
	kg/hp	2.72	2.90
	kW/m²	69.51	69.51
	hp/m²	94.54	94.54
Max. speed	km/h	585[4]	560[10]
@ altitude	m	6400	6200
Cruise speed	km/h	530[5]	510[11]
@ altitude	m	6200	6000
Rate of climb	m/s	11.00	9.00[12]
Service ceiling	m	8500	8000
Range	km	455[6]	1040[13]
Max. flight time	hrs	0.95[6]	2.25[13]
Takeoff run	m	600	720
Takeoff run to 25 m	m	850	950
Landing run	m	550	580
Landing speed	km/h	162	170
Max. permissible load as % of takeoff weight		34	38
Payload as % of takeoff weight		23	18
Built		1943	1943

Fw 190G-3 with an experimental fitting of flash suppressors.

Ranges - A Critical View

It is always difficult to include range data in tables, as in reality these fluctuate based on the military situation at the time. This problem had been broached even as early as the Fw 190A-5/U8. The RLM often computed ranges based on a brief period of high consumption during takeoff and climb, with the remainder of the flight profile being conducted at idle cruise. In comparison with takeoff consumption, idle cruise lowered the fuel consumption rate by up to 50 percent. Bomber pilots were naturally keen to reach their target as quickly as possible and return home just as quickly, while ground attack planes attempted to fly as low as fea-

sible. Such conditions left little time for flying at idle cruise settings. As a result, ranges calculated using idle cruise showing distances of 1500 km or times of four to five hours can be reduced by 50 percent across the board.

The same applies for fighters. Every fighter pilot knows that the rearmost aircraft in a formation fly at full throttle. Where is there room for idle cruise settings when climbing, flying in formation and fighting? And in the last two years of the war, those who lazily cruised along at slow speeds over friendly territory all to easily became victims of enemy fighters. A large percentage of the more grueling missions were generally flown at higher cruise or combat settings. For these reasons the range and endurance data in the tables, where these were not common practice, were brought more into line with reality.

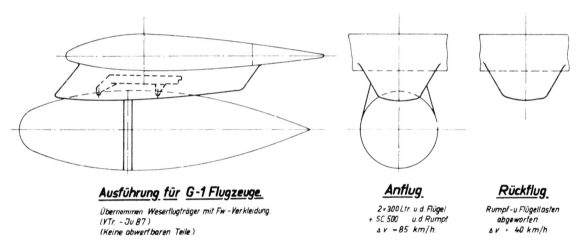

Ausführung für G-1 Flugzeuge.
Übernommen Weserflugträger mit Fw -Verkleidung.
(VTr. - Ju 87)
(Keine abwerfbaren Teile.)

Anflug.
2 × 300 Ltr. u.d Flügel
+ SC 500   u.d Rumpf
Δv ≈ 85 km/h.

Rückflug.
Rumpf-u.Flügellasten
abgeworfen.
Δv ≈ 40 km/h

Fuel tank and ordnance fitting on the Fw 190G series, particularly applicable to the Jabo-Rei *variant.*

---

[1]Heavily armed strike fighter with 500 kg bomb
[2]Empty weight includes 360 kg for armor
[3]**Payload**

2 MG 17	kg	21
2x900 rounds	kg	140
2 MG 151	kg	84
2x250 rounds	kg	96
2 MG 151	kg	84
2x150 rounds	kg	56
SC 500 bomb	kg	500
fittings	kg	90
Total	kg	1071

[4]510 km/h at sea level with 2700 rpm during takeoff and for emergency power
[5]460 km/h at sea level with 2300 rpm cruise speed
[6]At maximum permissable cruising speed(2300 rpm, 1007 kW/1370 hp) 1.20 ata and 235 g/hp/hr at an altitude of 300 m and 480 km/h; 665 km and 1.44 hrs at 495 km/h at 5000 m @ 2100 rpm, 742 kW/1010 hp, 1.10 ata and 212 g/hp/hr

[7]*Jabo-Rei* long range fighter-bomber with Kuto-nose, autopilot, FuG 16Z
[8]396 kg plus drop tanks with 2x221.5 kg = 839 kg
[9]**Payload**

2 MG 151	kg	84
2x160 rounds	kg	64
SC 500 bomb	kg	500
Kuto-nose & fittings	kg	270
Total	kg	918

[10]At 2700 rpm
440 km/h at sea level with max permissable cruise speed of 2300 rpm, 1007 kW/1370 hp, 1.20 ata and 235 g/hp/hr
[11]440 km/h at sea level with max permissable cruise speed of 2300 rpm
[12]5.5 m/sec after takeoff with landing gear and flaps extended
[13]With 2300 rpm max permissable cruise speed at 465 km/h, 2.25 hrs endurance and 360 kg of fuel consumed
With maximum economy setting of 2100 rpm(889 kW/1210 hp, 1.10 ata and 212 g/hp/hr rate of consumption) at 5400 m the range was 1545 km and endurance was 3.34 hrs

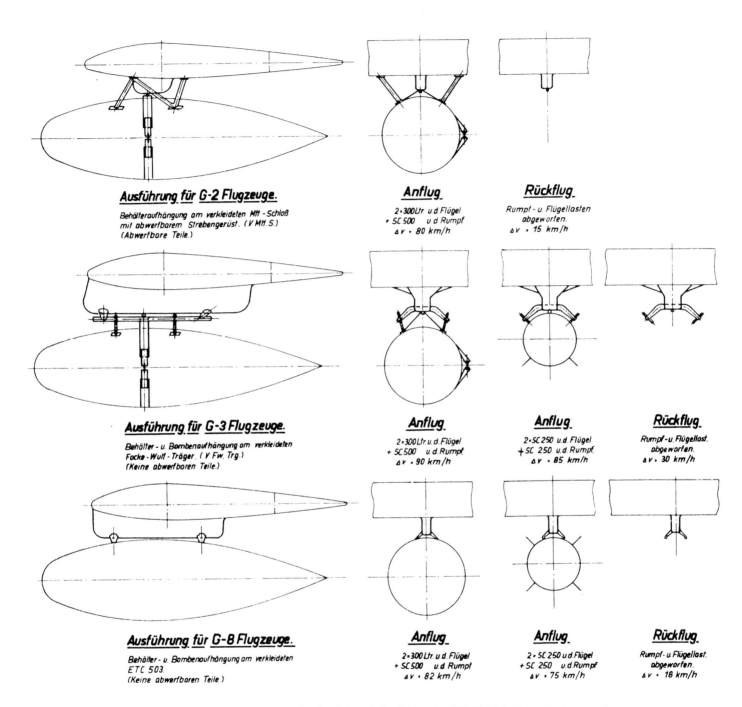

Ausführung für G-2 Flugzeuge.

Behälteraufhängung am verkleideten Mtt-Schloß
mit abwerfbarem Strebengerüst. (V Mtt.S.)
(Abwerfbare Teile.)

Anflug.

2·300 Ltr. u. d. Flügel
+ SC 500   u. d. Rumpf
Δv · 80 km/h

Rückflug.

Rumpf- u. Flügellasten
abgeworfen.
Δv · 15 km/h

Ausführung für G-3 Flugzeuge.

Behälter- u. Bombenaufhängung am verkleideten
Focke-Wulf-Träger. (V Fw. Trg.)
(Keine abwerfbaren Teile.)

Anflug.

2·300 Ltr. u. d. Flügel
+ SC 500   u. d. Rumpf
Δv · 90 km/h

Anflug.

2·SC 250 u. d. Flügel
+ SC 250 u. d. Rumpf.
Δv · 85 km/h

Rückflug.

Rumpf- u. Flügellast.
abgeworfen.
Δv · 30 km/h

Ausführung für G-8 Flugzeuge.

Behälter- u. Bombenaufhängung am verkleideten
ETC 503.
(Keine abwerfbaren Teile.)

Anflug.

2·300 Ltr. u. d. Flügel
+ SC 500   u. d. Rumpf
Δv · 82 km/h

Anflug.

2·SC 250 u. d. Flügel
+ SC 250 u. d. Rumpf
Δv · 75 km/h

Rückflug.

Rumpf- u. Flügellast.
abgeworfen.
Δv · 18 km/h

Die Geschwindigkeitsdifferenzen gelten für Steig- und Kampfleistung (n₊ · 2400 U/min) in Bodennähe bezogen auf
Flugzeug ohne Anbauten (Fw 190 A-5)

Geschwindigkeitsverlust durch ETC 501 unter dem Rumpf beträgt dabei Δv · 12 km/h!

Bad Eilsen , den 20.1.44.

Fuel tank and ordnance fitting on the Fw 190G series, particularly applicable to the Jabo-Rei variant.

150

Battle for the High Ground

Fw 190B-Series: Testbed for Pressurized Cockpit and GM 1 System

In mid 1942, with production of the Fw 190A series in full swing, the field units were soon calling for improvements to be made to the aircraft's high-altitude performance. After all, as could be seen from the British comparison flights the Fw 190 was only superior to its opponents within a certain altitude segment. Although at the time high-altitude engines were being bench tested, these were still a long way from actually entering production.

Nevertheless, in order to meet the demands of the front-line units Focke-Wulf began concerted efforts to improve the high-altitude performance of the Fw 190 in the autumn of 1942. These efforts began with the testing of pressurized cockpits and trials using the GM 1 injection system. The latter was designed to maintain the engine's full output even at heights above the maximum pressure altitude for as long as possible.

The GM 1 system was covered in detail in describing the MW 50 system for the Fw 190A-4. The MW 50 enabled a marked improvement to the motor at low and medium altitudes, while the GM 1 was designed for higher altitudes. Oxygen was added to cool the boost air and had the added benefit of reducing engine knocking as well. Increased fuel injection coincided with higher performance. Naturally, this was only an emergency solution until engines with high-altitude turbochargers and exhaust superchargers became available.

Three different testbed groups were organized in addition to work with the GM 1 system and the pressurized cockpit. A number of prototypes were to have been evaluated with the BMW 801TJ equipped with exhaust supercharger and, fitted with a pressurized cockpit and longer wings, were to have led to the B-series. A DB 603, which held promise as a high-performance high-altitude engine, was planned for a second group of prototypes. These prototypes were to have spawned the C-series.

A third group of V-types was kitted out with the Jumo 213. Initially, these aircraft were to have been tested with the Jumo 213A and receive the Jumo 213E at a later date; the latter was also a high-altitude engine with impressive performance figures. This last group was to have given birth to the D-series. Work enthusiastically began on all three group projects at about the same time in early 1943.

The company made use of three prototypes for the intended fitting of the pressurized cockpit, these being from the previously mentioned Fw 190A-3/U7 series and having Werknummer 528, 531 and 532. A sliding double canopy was developed to ensure a good cockpit seal. For this aspect of the project the engineers made good use of the experience gained from the V12(0035), which had been used for similar experiments at quite an early stage. Sealing of the aircraft's firewall, the floorboard and the sidewalls was improved and an insulating strip was fitted around the canopy. A DVL compressor was installed. There followed experiments using cockpit heating, a ventilation system and heating plates. Flight testing, however, revealed a number of problems with poor cockpit sealing and plate damages. In March and April 1943 the above named B-0 series aircraft were sent to Rechlin for testing.

The two subsequent aircraft, a fourth B-0(0049) and a B-1(811) were also fitted with pressurized cockpits and, for the first time, the GM 1 system with an 85 liter tank behind bulkhead #8, giving 17 minutes' worth of use. The radio set was moved to the baggage compartment and a new sealing bulkhead added. B-0(0049) was cleared for flight in January 1944 and was delivered to BMW in April 1944. With the B-1(811) a 115 liter fuel tank for increased range was installed on an experimental basis in place of the tank for the GM 1 system.

The engine maintained its rated power output up to about 8000 meters with the GM 1. Initially, however, the system could only be activated for brief periods and, in addition, was still too heavy; its weight roughly corresponded to that of the Fw 190's armament minus ammunition. Furthermore, the BMW 801 became more susceptible to problems with the additional stress placed upon it. For all practical purposes, no changes were made to the GM 1 system from the time it was introduced on an A-0/U12(0031) until 1944, despite the fact that initial tests also showed the same inherent problems. While the Americans began their daily routine of carpet bombing from 6000 to 8000 meters, the engineers at Focke-Wulf, the engine companies and the Rechlin test pilots all struggled to come to grips with auxiliary boost systems. Finally, after months of toilsome work

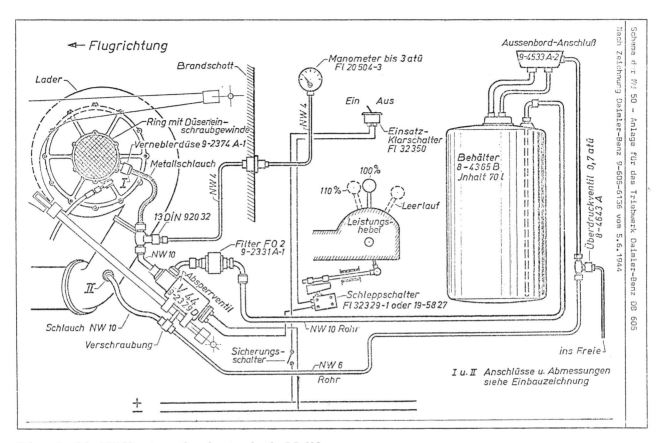

Schematic of the MW 50 water methanol system for the DB 605.

in cooperation with the manufacturers, the GM 1 injection system was finally made acceptable for the field units. Then, however, the systems were only delivered in limited numbers.

During the time work was being carried out on the GM 1 system, BMW had been expected to have delivered the first of its BMW 801TJ engines with exhaust turbocharger for trial installation in B-series airframes. But the engines never arrived. The company had been overtaken by the circumstances of the war and from then on would simply crank out quantities of engines for which there was no real need.

But back tot he B-series, which included a further two prototypes: the V45(7347) and the V47(530115). Both possessed the BMW 801D and a GM 1 system, but lacked the pressurized cockpit and also awaited the BMW 801J or TJ with exhaust turbocharger. According to a Focke-Wulf company document signed on 2 March 1944 in Bad Eilsen by Willi Kaether, Prof. Tank's assistant, the V45 and V47 were the first to be fitted with the larger wing (with an area of 20.3m2). The company's intentions with the B-series seemed entirely logical. While waiting for BMW's high-altitude engines, development and construction of a pressurized cockpit and follow-on development of the stopgap GM 1 injection system were prerequisites for high-altitude operations. For the two prototypes just mentioned, a larger wing appeared to be the next natural step.

B-1 V45(7347) had been completed by July 1943 and tested at Focke-Wulf using the GM 1 system. B-1 V47(530115), on the other hand, was not completed until 1944 and was sent to Rechlin on 18 February 1944. A later company document, dated 15 October 1944 (albeit without signature), claims that the two airplanes in question did not have the larger wings. Which of the two claims is correct seems impossible to determine, as none of the participants in the program are able to remember the details after more than 35 years. It's possible that the larger wing had been planned, but that there was reluctance to carry out the labor-intensive work because initially there was no high-altitude engine for the B-series. In all probability, this modification to the aircraft would only be carried out if and when high-altitude engines were at least made available on a trial basis.

Fw 190C-Series: Flying Engine Testbeds

The first C-series aircraft were chiefly testbeds for the DB 603 high-altitude engine and lacked the pressurized cockpit. These aircraft included the V13(0036), V15(0037) and V16(0038). The V13's airframe came from the Fw 190A-1 and had been pressed into service once before as a testbed for the BMW 801C-1. The airplane was now fitted with the DB603A-0. A larger wing, having an area of 20.3m2, was envisioned for these high-altitude aircraft. However, as mentioned earlier, this wing was not delivered in time and it was not until later that it became available for the Ta 152. The airplane was not fitted with armament and was lost in a crash as early as July 1942.

The V15 was fitted with the same DB 603A engine. This powerplant delivered 1286 kW/1750 hp at emercency and takeoff and 2700 rpm at sea level with 1.40 atas boost pressure and a fuel consumption rate of 570 liters per hour. At 10000 meters' altitude its performance was still 698 kW/ 950 hp at 2700 rpm and 0.85 atas boost pressure. It's weight/ performance ratio was 0.69 kg/kW, or 0.51 kg/hp. The DB

603A had a centrifugal supercharger which was hydraulically operated by the engine instead of mechanically. The oil cooler on the DB 603 was painstakingly shrouded as a belly cooler as it could no longer fit within the annular-type radiator. The above-named aircraft were subjected to a rigorous test program at Focke-Wulf following installation of the new engine.

Also about this time (23 July 1942) Prof. Tank wrote a letter to the RLM in which he recognized the better high altitude performance of the V13 compared with those machines fitted with the BMW 801. He believed that, with an exhaust supercharger, the DB 603 would be able to the design's high altitude performance could be boosted by up to 2000 meters. This would have made it possible for the high-flying enemy bombers to be engaged. Accordingly, that very day a priority contract was issued calling for a further six aircraft to be developed for testing high-altitude engines. These will be discussed in a later section.

The V16, coded CF+OW, was ferried to the Daimler-Benz test facility in Echterdingen on 2 August 1942. There, Flugkapitän Ellenrieder assumed responsibility for the airplane.

Fw 190 V13 engine testbed for the DB 603A (Werknummer 0036). First prototype of the Fw 190C series.

Fw 190C V13 with DB 603A and belly oil cooler.

According to Ellenrieder's report, the initial test flights showed that the coolant circulation system on the DB 603 was still unstable. As a result, the cooling system was rebuilt in Echterdingen. This consumed a considerable amount of time, delaying any further flight testing until late September/early October. Ellenrieder was able to carry out flights up to 11000 meters. These flights continued after the airplane had been fitted with a wide variety of DB 603 variants, such as the DB 603EM and the DB 603L. The DB 603 had a larger diameter turbocharger and fittings for an MW 50 and GM 1 system. The MW 50 had a 180 liter tank in addition. The DB 603EM with a volume of 44.5 liters delivered 1654 kW/2250 hp on takeoff and at emergency power with water-methanol and simultaneous fuel injection and was still capable of delivering 779 kW/1060 hp at 10000 meters. The weight per unit was just 0.56 kg/kW (0.41 kg/hp), a very favorable value. The V16, with Ellenrieder at the controls, displayed enormous potential during its Echterdingen testing, reaching an altitude of 12000 meters, 725 km/h true air speed at 7000 meters and a climb rate of about 22 meters per second with the aid of the MW 50 system. Naturally, this data would not have been applicable for a machine flying in combat conditions with full armament and external stores. Nevertheless, these figures could not be touched by the BMW 801 - even with the GM 1 injection system.

On 14 August 1944 the V16 and many other test platforms at the Echterdingen testing facility were destroyed in an American daylight bombing raid. Two months later the test facility accepted an Fw 190D-9 (Werknummer 210040 and coded TS+DN). The machine was fitted with a Jumo 213A and was to be used for evaluating a standardized DB 603 for fighters and heavy fighters. Once again, the airplane was fitted with various models of the DB 603, eventually having the DB 603 L with turbocharger and alcohol boost installed. The purpose of these tests was to determine the best standardized engine. The DB 603 LM (M stood for MW 50 injection) delivered 1544 kW/2100 hp at sea level for takeoff and emergency power and had a fuel consumption rate of 650 liters per second. Even at 15000 meters, the engine still delivered 478 kW/650 hp at 2700 rpm.

On 10 October 1944 Damler-Benz was provided with the Fw 190D-12(210043, TS+DQ), which had been converted from the V77, for experimental installation of the newly-designed DB 603G fighter and heavy fighter engine. The aircraft was handed over to field units in March of 1945.

On 18 November 1944 Daimler-Benz took over the Fw 190 V21/U1(0043, TI+IH) at Langenhagen. This machine from the A-series now boasted a pressurized cockpit, had a larger fuel capacity and was in fact quite similar to the Ta 152. Using this airplane, Ellenrieder carried out flights up to altitudes of 12000 meters as late as March of 1945. Just before the end of the war, in March 1945, Daimler-Benz received 15 Fw 190D-9s with the Jumo 213A which were to have been fitted with the DB 603G standardized engine; this was done at the instigation of the *Jägerstab*, or

Fighter Staff. Initiator of this program was the chairman of the board of directors, Dr.-Ing. Haspel. Pressured by war-time conditions, the last of these engines were converted in the forest area near Nellingen, 50 km south of Ectherdingen. The pilots test flew the modified aircraft from a tiny air-field until the Americans occupied Nellingen on 22 April 1945.

At High Altitudes with the "Kängeruh" and Hirth Exhaust Turbocharger

At the same time these efforts were underway to de-velop the DB 603 engine series for high-altitude operations, there was also an intensive parallel program focused on tur-bochargers which had their turbines driven by the engines exhaust gases. The TK 11 exhaust supercharger system, developed by DVL in cooperation with Hirth, had been made available for the Fw 190C-series.

In late 1942 a V18(0040) was fitted out with a TK 11 system as a prototype for a planned high-altitude fighter series. The system was mounted underneath the fuselage and necessitated a considerable amount of modification work. Although the aircraft initially lacked a pressurized cockpit, it was to have been fitted with a larger wing which, however, added 40 kg to the weight and pushed the load factor down to 5.1. Focke-Wulf documentation claims that the large wing had been used for the V18, while other sources maintain that the larger wing (which, incidentally, was manufactured in France) had not yet been completed by this time. The use of this wing necessitated the enlarge-ment of the tailfin and change to be made to the ailerons and landing flaps. Furthermore, a four-bladed VDM pro-peller was also fitted. This modified airplane, designated Fw 190 V18/U1 and nicknamed "Kangerüh", was sent to Daimler-Benz for evaluation on 10 December 1942.

Exhaust from the V18/U1's engine was provisionally routed throught two tubes running along the fuselage into a collector located at the extreme aft end of the system where the exhaust turbine was located. The turbine drove the su-percharger. The compressed boost air passed through a boost air cooler which was also located on the fuselage underside and, with its 0.81 m2, negatively affected the aerodynam-ics of the aircraft. The compressed and cooled air then flowed into the engine's turbocharger. The turbine itself was cooled by the airflow over the plane. Unfortunately, no data is available regarding the weight of this complicated sys-tem.

There is a wide variety of conflicting information re-garding the engine as fitted. One RLM report mentions a DB 603A-1, while another calls it the DB 603A; a Focke-Wulf company file designates it as the DB 603L and yet another source refers to the engine as a DB 603G with in-creased turbocharger rpms and higher compression. As the reports by *Flugkapitän* Ellenrieder show, these designations are only accurate for the C-series flying testbeds which were fitted with different variants of the DB 603. On the other hand, The V18/U1 and its subsequent high-altitude fighter equipped with the Hirth turbine were powered by the DB 603S, whose basic engine was the DB 603A-2 without tur-bocharger. This engine had been tagged for utilizing the Hirth TK 11 turbocharger.

In January 1943 the company gave test pilot Sander the assignment of putting the V18/U1 through its paces at Daimler-Benz's facility in Echterdingen.

After nine flights with the V18/U1, Sander's impres-sions were devastating: the aircraft had been made so tailheavy by the underfuselage system that it could no longer be trimmed out at an altitude of 7700 meters. At that alti-tude it was unstable on its axes and heavy on the controls. At speeds upward of 280 km/h the plane began to vibrate slightly. The tailheavy machine tended to set down on its tailwheel first when landing, playing havoc with the tailwheel's self-alignment and causing it to shift from side to side - ideal preconditions for a ground loop. The oil cooler's efficiency was inadequate. The turbocharger's rpms never rose above 20000, meaning that it never reached its full output potential. The blades sometimes fractured. Prob-lems with the pressurized cockpit meant that Sander was unable to fly above 10000 meters.

Many of the problems Sander had identified were cor-rectable. But after 30 flying hours the prospects still didn't look any better. During climbing, it was impossible for the exhaust turbine to reach its target rpm rate. Although the problem was eventually pinpointed and the exhaust gills were modified, the engine's maximum pressure altitude of 11400 meters was not quite attained either. The whole com-plicated turbine system with its size and weight had, quite simply, spoiled the airplane from an aerodynamic stand-point. This had an effect on the performance and - as Sand-ers had already noted - also negatively impacted the flight handling characteristics of the plane in a major way. At sea level the V18 reached 490 km/h and at 11000 meters its speed was 680 km/h. Freed from the ballast of the Hirth supercharger, another machine with a DB 603A engine and mechanically operated G-type turbocharger displayed high-altitude performance equal to or better than the V18's.

Fw 190 V30 GH+KT Kängeruh with DB 603S, TK 11 turbo-supercharger and pressurized cockpit. The aircraft was later fitted witht the Jumo 213E and subsequently served as the prototype for the H-0 series.

What was lacking were the DB 623, 626, 627 and 624 with their integrated turbochargers. What Sander didn't mention - most likely out of courtesy - were the countless problems with the TK 11 turbocharger. Trials using the V29, V30, V31 V32 and V33 prototypes, all fitted with pressurized cockpit, DB 603S engine and supercharger, showed little improvement over previous tests. For these trials, the V 32 was reputedly fitted with the larger wings and tailfin. In Kaether's opinion, although the aircraft were fitted with the larger rudder, they retained the smaller wing configuration. The V29 (Werknummer 0054) was equipped with the FuG 16Z and FuG 25a and had a pressurized cockpit. The V30 (0055), V31 (0056) and V32 (0057) all had the same engine (DB 603S), a pressurized cockpit and the same radio/navigation equipment, but the V32 and V33 were the first to be fitted with two MG 151s. The V29 was completed in March 1943 and delivered to the Hirth company in June of that year. The V30 was delivered in April 1943. Shortly afterward the turbocharger was removed and the aircraft converted into the Ta 152H. V31 was lost in a crash on 29 May 1943 during flight testing in Rechlin. The V32 was fitted with the DB 603G and turned over to Daimler-Benz for evaluation; the V 33 was also modified to Ta 152H

standards - truly an ignoble end for the "Kangerüh" and the high altitude fighters of the C-series.

A second group of prototypes comprised the V19 (0041), V20 (0042), V21 (0043) and V25 (0050), all of which came from the Fw 190A-0 series and retained their "V" designations as they were originally intended for installation of the DB 603. In actuality, they were fitted with the Jumo 213. The V19 served as the pre-production prototype. The V21, completed in March of 1943, and the V25 both served as weapons testbeds and were equipped with two MG 131s and three MG 151s (one of which was mounted above the engine). The V26 (0051) and V27 (0052), on the other hand, were evaluation airframes for the planned D-2 series. A V28 (0053) was deliberately destroyed in static structural soundness tests.

Testing of the Jumo 213 in the above named prototypes led to markedly improved results over the DB 603 for the Fw 190D. Although Tank continued to maintain that the DB 603 had more potential, he was forced to concede that, like the BMW 801TJ, this engine also needed time before it could reach production maturity as a high-altitude engine. In April 1944, therefore, the RLM stopped developmental work on the high-altitude fighter concept for the time being.

Work on the turbocharged engines was to continue, however; in the short term, these engines were only available for bombers as these types of aircraft were able to fly at set altitudes for longer periods of time at reduced throttle. The majority of testbeds and prototypes, such as the V19, V20, V21, V25 and others therefore served as prototypes for the D-series and Jumo 213 engine, which by this time had become the powerplant of choice.

High-Altitude Test Bed

Manufacturer		Focke-Wulf	
Type		Fw 190B-0 A-3/U7	Fw 190C-0 V16
Powerplant		BMW 801D2	DB 603AA with turbocharger
Performance	kW	1272	1227
	hp	1730	1670[4]
Crew		1	1
Length	m	8.95	9.50
Height	m	3.95	3.95
Wingspan	m	12.30	12.30
Wing area	m²	20.30	20.30
Aspect ratio		7.45	7.45
Weight, empty	kg	2728[1]	3440[5]
Fuel	kg	396	396
Oil	kg	50	35
Crew	kg	80	80
Load	kg	596[2]	156[6]
Max. permissible load	kg	1122	667
Takeoff weight	kg	3850	4107
Wing loading	kg/m²	189.65	202.31
Weight/power ratio	kg/kW	3.02	3.35
	kg/hp	2.23	2.46
	kW/m²	62.66	60.44
	hp/m²	85.22	82.27
Max. speed	km/h	690[3]	685[7]
@ altitude	m	6900	11800
Cruise speed	km/h	600	600
@ altitude	m	7000	8000
Rate of climb	m/s	16.00	10.00[8]
Service ceiling	m	11500	13000
Range	km	600	430[9]
Max. flight time	hrs	1.20	0.50
Takeoff run	m	300	400
Takeoff run to 20 m	m	500	600
Landing run	m	450	500
Landing speed	km/h	158	164
Max. permissible load as % of takeoff weight		29	16
Payload as % of takeoff weight		15	4
Built		1942	1943

[1]Empty weight(A-3) was 2678 kg + add'l 50 kg for increased wing = 2728 kg
[2]**Payload**

2x MG 151 w/o ammunition(prototype)	kg	84
2x MG 17 w/o ammunition	kg	42
pressurized cockpit(test), est.	kg	150
GM 1 system(test)	kg	170
Total	kg	596

[3]In clean configuration and with average flying weight; 1/2 fuel, emergency power: 550 km/h at sea level; 630 km/h at 10000 m altitude based on RLM documents
[4]1227 kW/1670 hp at 2700 rpm at sea level; 750 kW/1020 hp at 2700 rpm at 10000 m altitude
[5]**Empty weight(reinforced) (for A-3 in parentheses)**

fuselage	kg	310	(248)
landing gear	kg	289	(220)
empennage	kg	121	(96)
control system	kg	35	(27)
wings	kg	485	(330)
engine	kg	1940	(1488)
equipment	kg	260	(110)
Total	kg	3440	(2519)

[6]**Payload**

2 MG 151	kg	84
2 MG 17	kg	42
equipment testing	kg	30
Total	kg	156

[7]At emergency power (based on DB report)
[8]Continuous to 12000 m on average, 19.3 min to 12000 m
[9]At an altitude of 11800 meters

Another Brush with Death - Fuel Lines Break at Night

One evening during the late summer of 1943, Tank found himself flying an Fw 190 to Berlin in order to become familiar with the "Wilde Sau" night-fighting method perfected by Major Hajo Hermann being carried out from Döberitz. Tank's Fw 190, along with the Bf 109, was often employed for this new method of hunting down bombers. It had certain benefits over radar, in that it could not be fooled by Düppel, or chaff strips. Arriving at the unit, he met Oberst Wittmer from the staff of General Kammhuber, the commander of the entire night-fighting operations. At the time Wittmer commanded the night-fighting unit stationed at Döberitz. Tank was surprised at the results achieved by this unusual style of fighter combat which placed many demands on equipment and pilot skills: the fighters intercepted high-altitude enemy bomber formations coming over from England. Searchlight batteries searched for and acquired the bombers in clear weather, blinding their crews, while the fighter pilots pounced on their quarry from the darkness. In cloudy weather the searchlights illuminated the cloud base and revealed the bombers' silhouettes to good effect. Once more the fighter pilots had a chance to strike back under visual conditions against the bombers flying above the so-called "shroud of death". There were problems working with the flak, however: although the guns were forbidden from firing at certain altitudes, they often shot anyway when enemy aircraft were caught in a search-light beam. Thus, many a German pilot was shot down by friendly anti-aircraft fire.

Late that night, as the air raids tapered off, Tank climbed into his Fw 190 and headed back towards Langenhagen. Near the Elbe, whose silvery arm was recognizable in the clear weather even at the altitude he was flying at, it suddenly began smelling of fuel inside the cockpit. So strongly, in fact, that Tank had to crank the Fw 190's canopy open a bit just to get some fresh air. Stendal had to be in the vicinity somewhere, but below everything was black as pitch. Obviously, he couldn't land the plane in such conditions. Tank clenched his teeth. His head was in pain from the fumes and seemed as though it would explode. He cranked the canopy more and more frequently despite the fact that the force of the draft was almost unbearable. Soon his head began throbbing again and he almost lost consciousness. Tank snapped out of it, cranked again and grabbed some air - and then, far in the distance, caught a glimpse of a humble, yet familiar light. Langenhagen! With the last bit of strength he swung towards the light, throttled back, chopped his speed, lowered the undercarriage and flaps and turned in for the approach, whereupon the landing field was faintly illuminated for a brief period. He touched down, cranked the canopy half open yet again, and at the moment he shut the engine off, Tank lost consciousness. The machine rolled out and came to rest on the runway strip. Rushing up to the plane, his colleagues found Tank unconscious in the cockpit. They carried him out to some fresh air on a stretcher, where he soon regained his senses. A fuel line had begun leaking; the aircraft would have had just enough fuel for one airfield circuit. A few minutes more and the engine would have cut out. Once again, fortune had smiled on Tank.

State of Engine Development in 1942

As early as 1942 the Americans were using production exhaust turbochargers on their Flying Fortress bombers. It was not until 1942 when the Germans, within the framework of their high-altitude fighter program, began practical testing of engines with exhaust turbochargers. One could be forgiven for thinking the German engine industry had become stagnant. The former *Generalingenieur* Wolfram Eisenlohr, head of the RLM's developmental planning for engines, sketched the situation thusly during a meeting of a working team for engine planning on 4 November 1942 in Berlin:

"The neglect under which matters of engine development have long suffered have now led to a critical lack of developmental capacity. A glance at other countries shows that research into powerplant matters abroad have been handled much more favorably than here."

BMW 801 TJ high-altitude engine with exhaust supercharger was rated at 1323 kw/1800 hp and had a maximum pressure altitude of 11600 meters.

159

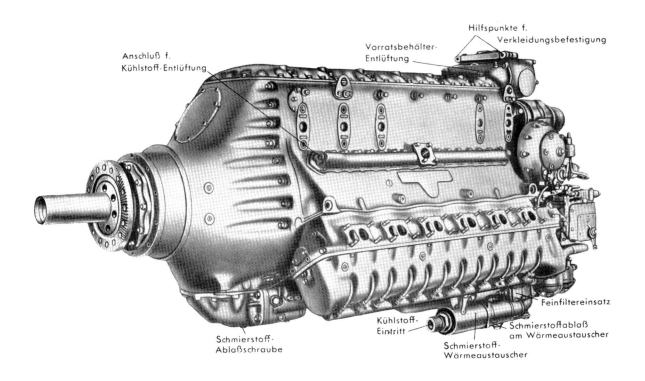

Anschluß f.
Kühlstoff-Entlüftung

Vorratsbehälter-
Entlüftung

Hilfspunkte f.
Verkleidungsbefestigung

Feinfiltereinsatz

Kühlstoff-
Eintritt

Schmierstoffablaß
am Wärmeaustauscher

Schmierstoff-
Wärmeaustauscher

Schmierstoff-
Ablaßschraube

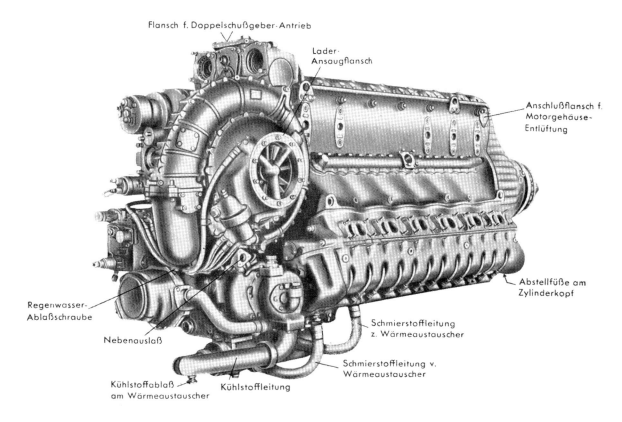

Flansch f. Doppelschußgeber-Antrieb

Lader-
Ansaugflansch

Anschlußflansch f.
Motorgehäuse-
Entlüftung

Abstellfüße am
Zylinderkopf

Regenwasser-
Ablaßschraube

Nebenauslaß

Schmierstoffleitung
z. Wärmeaustauscher

Schmierstoffleitung v.
Wärmeaustauscher

Kühlstoffablaß
am Wärmeaustauscher

Kühlstoffleitung

160

Piston Engine Planning with a Focus Toward Fighters

This summed up the situation at the time in a nutshell. In a subsequent lecture *Stabsingenieur* Helmut Schelp referred to the issue of developmental planning and the current limitations on increasing flight performance. In doing so, Schelp focused on the state of piston engines, previous developmental work and future plans. Research was geared toward the possibility of increasing operating altitudes and the dependence of engine performance capability on altitude. A motor whose output was to have maintained a constant rate of, say, 735 kW/1000 hp up to an altitude of 10000 meters required as much effort to build as a non-supercharged engine delivering 2646 kW/3600 hp at sea level. The trend in engine production promoted at the time by the RLM was toward fitting the basic variant of a certain engine with a single-stage turbocharger initially, followed eventually by a two-stage charger. For this reason, planning was not focused on exhaust turbochargers, but instead placed much more of a priority on the type of development which resulted in the success of the DB 628 and 627, among other engines. Of course, the *Amt* still promoted work on exhaust turbocharger development, as witnessed by the numerous DB engines with exhaust chargers. But the primary focus was on engines with single and two-stage boost having a maximum pressure altitude of up to 12000 meters.

This ongoing development at Daimler-Benz and other companies such as Junkers and BMW held such promise that the planning division justifiably felt that altitudes of up to 12500 meters could be attained with ease and that exhaust turbochargers for fighter engines would only be necessary at the extremely high operating altitudes between 12500 and 18000 meters. These beliefs were confirmed by the Jumo 213E with a two-stage boost and automatic triple gearing, a powerplant which delivered unusually good high altitude performance. The same applied to various Daimler-Benz engines - with the exception that the Jumo 213E had entered full-scale production by late 1944 and the first DB high-altitude engines weren't available until early 1945, and even then only in small numbers.

In this context the reader is referred to a book, titled "Flugmotoren und Strahltriebwerke", by Kyrill von Gersdorff and Kurt Grassmann appearing in the "Entwicklungsgeschichte der deutschen Luft- und Raumfahrt" published by Bernard & Graefe Verlag. Von Gersdorff and Grassmann's book contains valuable information on German aircraft engine construction and places a particular emphasis on jet and rocket engines. Accordingly, this book won't go into greater detail on aircraft engine development.

Engine construction planning within the RLM and the wisdom which this office exercised in planning for future needs was truly commendable. However, theory and practice differed considerably as a consequence of the war.

Theory and Practice

A shortage of capacity, raw materials and problems with subcontractors meeting their deadlines delayed planning by about two years, so that - as already mentioned - highly developed engines such as the Jumo 213E weren't being produced in any quantity until late 1944, with the urgently needed DB 603L only being available on a small scale from early 1945 on. The BMW 801E, with 1470 kW/2000 hp, had reached production maturity by 1943 but, as discussed earlier, could not be built before the war's end due to a lack of machining tools. Production capacity was far too small to keep up with the new demands on the industry. Even the BMW 801TJ with exhaust turbocharger was only available in single units by the end of the war. The Jumo 222 was only built in limited numbers as well, and these were all prototype variants. Development of a Jumo 224, a four-shaft 24-cylinder and 73-liter diesel engine delivering 2940 kW/4000 hp to counterrotating propellers, was completely out of the question, as was work on a 2600-3600 kW/3600-5000 hp Jumo 225 class. By the war's end an unusually high state of engine development had been attained with engines having fuel injection, performance boosting GM 1 or MW 50 injection systems and powerplants fitted with so-called Kom*mandogerät* systems, not to mention the gains achieved with jet and rocket propulsion systems. But the new engines, whose combination of MW 50 and GM 1 systems produces an extraordinarily high performance boost, didn't make their appearance until near the end of the war at a time when no more fuel was available for the airplanes to fly their missions.

Jumo 213A with an output of 1300kW/1770 hp and single-stage two-speed turbocharger, year of service 1943.

Fw 190D "Langnasen" Series

Trials with the Fw 190D-series proceeded much less dramatically than with the two other groups. Plans called for an Fw 190D-1 series lacking pressurized cockpit, to be used exclusively for testing the Jumo 213A, and an Fw 190D-2 with pressurized cockpit. When testing stopped on the Fw 190B and C-series flying engine testbeds, it freed up sufficient numbers of prototypes for converting the BMW 801 and DB 603 powerplants to the Jumo 213A. By mid 1942 Fw 190 V19(0041) had been fitted with the Jumo 213A. There followed additional V-types, all without pressurized cockpits, which had originally been designated for the C-series; these included V20(0042), V21(0043), V25(0050) and V28(0053).

In the V19 only the engine was tested; the other aircraft from the V20 onward were fitted with the complete Jumo 213A engine assembly. As the Jumo 213 was some 60 cm longer than the BMW 801, a 0.49 m plug was fitted into the fuselage ahead of the empennage to offset the engine extension which gave rise to the nickname "Langnase", or long-nose. The tailfin was enlarged. The proven annular radiator design, consisting of two half-shells surrounding the propeller gearbox, was decided upon. The cooler ring ended at its aft end with circular cooling gills which splayed open and whose position automatically controlled the cool airflow based on the radiator temperature. The V28 was used for static testing. Fitted with the Jumo 213A, V20 left the factory in November of 1943, followed by V21 in February 1944 and V 25 in April 1944.

The V25 was the first to make use of a Mk 103 firing through the propeller hub; installed, it weighed no less than 165 kg. The Jumo 213C had been designed from the outset to accommodate a centerline weapon. This arrangement had the advantage of the weapon being more along the line of sight; it also had a positive influence on the aircraft's speed and maneuverability. Furthermore, the weapon had a better concentration of fire. The disadvantage in a centrally mounted gun lay in the fact that the recoil had a greater impact on the engine and could lead to problems in this area. A V17(0039), also taken from the A-0 series, had already undergone flight testing with the Jumo 213A back in September of 1942. The engine delivered all it had promised. Similar favorable results were found when testing the

above mentioned testbeds. The Jumo 213A's high-altitude performance was better than that of the BMW 801D and in a dive the Langnase, with the reduced drag offered by the narrower radiator profile, was faster than the Fw 190 with its bullish radial engine. Nothing stood in the way of a series production.

Dora 9 D-Series, Fighter and Fighter-Bomber

The previously mentioned V17 prototype (0039) from the A-0 series had been further developed prior to the other types. Prototype V19(0041, crashed 16 Feb 1944), V20(0042, crashed 5 Aug 1944), V21(0043), V25(0050) and V28(0053), all without pressure cockpits, made up the Fw 190D-1 series. Two additional aircraft, the V26(0051) and V27(0052), which had been used for testing the DB 603, were fitted with the pressurized cockpit and belonged to the D-2 series.

Three additional testbeds, the V22(0044), V23(0045) and the V 46 received the Jumo 213C for testing an MG 151 cannon firing through the propeller arc. The engines in the above named aircraft proved satisfactory, but it hadn't been possible to adequately pressure seal the cockpit. As a result, the M*inisterium* decided against issuing a contract for a D-1 or D-2 series. At higher altitudes (6000 to 7000 meters), however, the aircraft fitted with Jumo 213s were in all cases much superior to the BMW 801D-powered A-series airplanes due to the fact that the engine had a higher maximum pressure altitude. It was therefore decided to bring out an improved D-series based on the Fw 190A-8 airframe. The V17, converted accordingly, was sent to Rechlin in mid 1944 and Focke-Wulf began flight testing two additional prototypes taken from the A-8 production line, the V53(170003, DU+JC) and V54(174024). These aircraft were converted and cleared for flight testing in June and July of 1944. Production of the D-9 was expected to begin in August 1944. However, the entire program suffered a setback when both the V53 and the V54 were damaged on the ground in bombing raids. Nevertheless, series production of the *Dora* began at Focke-Wulf in August of 1944 at their Cottbus plant, at Fieseler in Kassel-Waldau and at Arado as well.

The production version of the Fw 190D-9 revealed several improvements over the V 53 and V54 prototypes: the tailfin was enlarged chord-wise, the engine support arms were modified as was the wing-engine compartment join. The fuselage was beefed up as was the gun cover plate ahead of the windscreen. The forward fuselage tank held 167 kg (232 liters) of fuel, the aft one 210 kg (292 liters). Armament consisted of two fuselage MG 131s and one MG 151 in each of the wing roots. Ordnance release system was a single multi-purpose ETC 504 rack. The D-9 was only retrofitted with a water-methanol system. The MW 50 injection system could be utilized up to an altitude of about 5000 meters and boosted the Jumo 213A's performance to 2100 hp. The system was not to be used on takeoff, however, at least initially. Aquisition of suitable water-methanol systems was hampered by the constant bombing raids, so that a simplified system known as "Oldenburg" was initially fitted. The first production Fw 190D-9 carried the W*erknummer* of 210001. Machine #2 (210002) was retro-

fitted with its methanol injection system in Langenhagen, while the third aircraft (210043) had it installed in Cottbus.

At first, pilots in the fighter units were mistrustful of the Dora, for the Jumo 213 (like its Jumo 211 predecessor) had been laid out for use as a bomber powerplant. The maneuverability of the *Langnase* was therefore held in some doubt. But these feelings soon were revealed to be ill-founded. The aircraft were successfully employed for protecting the Me 262s. The jets were most vulnerable to enemy fighters during landing and takeoff, as they needed considerable time to get up to speed - particularly during takeoff. During landing, the Me 262 had a long, flat approach profile. In this role, for which the BMW 801-equipped Fw 190 was also used, it was found that in comparison the *Dora-9* was faster and more maneuverable and, in addition, had a better climb rate. Plus, a significant boost in performance was noted with the markedly improved MW 50 system, which by this time could be operated continuously for up to ten minutes.

Fw 190D-9 with blown canopy.

Jumo 213 installation in the Fw 190D-9.

An increased tank capacity offered the possibility of enough fuel for nearly 40 minutes of MMW 50usage. This effectively negated the advantage which the more powerful foreign engines had enjoyed in the lower altitude regime.

The use of methanol and the lack of a pressure cockpit indicated that there were no plans for using the aircraft as a high-altitude fighter. The *Hohenjäger II* high-altitude fighter program, initially undertaken with the BMW 801 and DB 603, seemed to have been stymied with the third group, the Jumo 213A D-series, as well - at least for the time being. Advances were only expected in this area once production maturity was attained for the DB 603G or DB 603L with dual supercharger, the BMW 801TJ with exhaust turbocharger, or the Jumo 213E with two-stage charger and triple gearing (which, incidentally, still delivered 1044 kW/1420 hp emergency power at an altitude of 9800 meters). As the Jumo 213E was expected to go into production as early as mid 1944 and seemed at the time to be most reliable engine

by a wide margin, the RLM used all means at its disposal to make production of this powerplant top priority. Accordingly, the *Dora* was seen as only a stopgap solution, although despite this a contract was issued in September 1944 for 2825 aircraft (instead of the originally planned 400). The Fw 190D series proved to be the best overall performing Fw 190 built during the war years. With the planned 2825 aircraft, it was hoped to bridge the time until the introduction of the Jumo 213E. This was not to occur until several months down the road due to the fact that problems were being encountered in converting from the Jumo 213A to large-scale production of the Jumo 213E. Even then, work on the DB 603's G-turbocharger had been stepped up, so that a contest began between the Jumo 213E (ready for production) and the DB 603G, at the time still in its developmental stages.

Another version was the Fw 190D-10, which was to have been fitted with the Jumo 213C with the capability of holding a gun firing through the propeller hub. This version was never built, however.

164

Fw 190D *Langnasen*

Manufacturer		Focke-Wulf		
Type		Fw 190D-9	Fw 190D-12	Fw 190D-14
Powerplant		Jumo 213A-1	Jumo 213E-1	DB 603AE[11]
Performance	kW	1300	1374	1286
	hp	1770	18706[6]	1750
Crew		1	1	1
Length	m	10.13	10.13	10.13
Height	m	3.35	3.35	3.35
Wingspan	m	10.50	10.50	10.50
Wing area	m²	18.30	18.30	18.30
Aspect ratio		6.02	6.02	6.02
Weight, empty	kg	3249[1]	3269[7]	3440
Fuel	kg	467[2]	467[2]	467[2]
Oil	kg	50	50	50
Crew	kg	80	80	80
Load	kg	424[3]	534[8]	314
Max. permissible load	kg	1021	1131	911
Takeoff weight	kg	4270	4400	4351
Wing loading	kg/m²	233.33	240.44	237.76
Weight/power ratio	kg/kW	3.38	3.20	3.38
	kg/hp	2.41	2.35	2.49
	kW/m²	71.03	75.08	70.27
	hp/m²	96.72	102.19	95.63
Max. speed	km/h	686[4]	725[9]	710
@ altitude	m	6600	11000	7400
Cruise speed	km/h	518	580	620[12]
@ altitude	m	6600	8800	7100
Rate of climb	m/s	16.00[5]	17.00[10]	16.00
Service ceiling	m	11100	12500	11750
Range	km	810	750	800
Max. flight time	hrs	1.33	1.25	1.25
Takeoff run	m	460	450	500
Takeoff run to 20 m	m	675	600	650
Landing run	m	500	500	500
Landing speed	km/h	167	170	170
Max. permissible load as % of takeoff weight		24	26	21
Payload as % of takeoff weight		10	12	7
Built		1944	1944	1945

[1]**Empty Weight**

fuselage	kg	276
armor	kg	60
landing gear	kg	257
empennage	kg	141
control system	kg	28
wings	kg	443
engine	kg	1834
equipment		
FuG 16Z + FuG 25	kg	210
	kg	3249

[2]232 liters of fuel in foreward tank and 292 liters in aft, plus 110 liters for the MW 50 = 634 liters or 467 kg

[3]**Payload**

2x MG 131	kg	40
2x250 rounds	kg	44
2xMG 151	kg	84
2x100 rounds	kg	18
weapons fittings	kg	35
MW 50 system	kg	50
other	kg	153
	kg	424

[4]580 km/h at sea level at 3250 rpm for takeoff and emergency boost

[5]Time to climb to 10000 m was 17.7 mins, equating to 9.4 m/sec average rate of climb

[6]1506 kW/2050 hp during takeoff using MW 50 injection, climb and combat performance at 3000 rpm at a height of 9600 m was 933 kW/1270 hp, two-stage turbocharger with three gears per stage

[7]Empty weight as for footnote [1] with the addition of 20 kg since the Jumo 213E was heavier than the Jumo 213A

[8]**Payload**

2xMG 151	kg	84
2x250 rounds	kg	42
1 MK 108 engine cannon	kg	58
85 rounds	kg	50
fittings	kg	30
MW 50 system	kg	50
other	kg	220
	kg	534

[9]730 km/h at 9150 m and 760 km/h at 12500 m

[10]14.5 mins to 10000 m gives an average rate of climb of 11.49 m/sec

[11]DB 603AE was an A engine with MW 50 system and having a single stage turbocharger with automatic drive via a hydraulically operated clutch having a barometric governor

[12]551 km/h at 2500 rpm at sea level
571 km/h at 2700 rpm at sea level(full load)

Junkers Jumo 213A and E for the Fw 190D and Ta 152H

Engine Type	Configuration								Supercharger	Performance and Consumption Data								
	# of cylinders	stroke(mm)	bore(mm)	capacity(ltrs)	compression	length(mm)	widthØ (mm)	height(mm)		type of performance	altitude m	output kW/hp	rpm	ata boost pressure	consumption g/hp/hr	consumption ltrs/hr	Dry Installed Weight kg	Comments
Jumo 213A-1	12	165	150	34.97	6.5	2437	776	1012	Single-stage charger with automatic two-gear clutch	takeoff & emergency	0	1301/1770	3250		256	575	920	As of August 1944. Complete engine system for Fw 190D. In production
										climb	0	1176/1600	3000		248	480		
										max cruise	0	985/1340	2700		322	350		
										emergency	6000	1103/1500	3250		286	575		
										climb	6000	1029/1400	3000		270	480		
										max cruise	5400	882/1200	2700		224	350		
Jumo 213E-0	12	165	150	34.97	8.5	2437	776	1012	Two-stage charger with three-gear clutch	takeoff	0	1374/1870	3250		232		930	High-altitude follow-on development of the Jumo 213B. As of August 1944. In production in 1944 for the Ta 152H and Fw 190D. Performance with blower air cooling
										climb	0	1250/1700	3000		202			
										max cruise	0	1029/1400	2700					
										max economy	0	823/1120	2400		190			
										takeoff	9800	1044/1420	3250		292			
										climb	9600	1014/1380	3000		254			
										max cruise	8800	838/1140	2700					
										max economy	7800	706/960	2400		227			

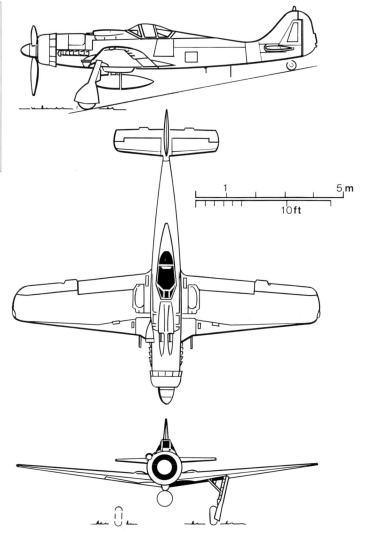

Fw 190D Field Conversion Sets

R5: Two additional soft-skinned fuel cells in each wing (D-12, planned for D-13)

R11: LGW K23 fighter navigation system, heated windscreen and FuG 125 Hermine(D-11)

R20: MW 50 high compression system (planned for D-11)

R21: MW 50 high compression system, PKS 12 and FuG 125 Hermine(planned for D-11)

R25: 130 liter add'l fuel tank in fuselage (planned for D-12)

Fw 190D-9 with blown canopy and 300-l auxiliary fuel tank.

Tank Flies the Fw 190D-9 Dora

When Tank had come to Focke-Wulf in 1932, the company employed just 150 workers. Since that time, however, numerous branches had sprung up so that by 1944 there were now a total of 35,000 people working for the company. Tank's responsibility in this giant conglomeration was that of technical director. With this workload weighing upon him, it was no longer possible for him to continue making the initial test flights of those aircraft which he'd designed. Despite this, on his business trips Tank sat at the controls of his machines himself - regardless of the weather - and was

not satisfied with his test pilots constantly just keeping him abreast of the test programs going on with the various types. Whenever time permitted, he would test fly one or another of his aircraft designs himself.

It was a warm, pleasant autumn day in 1944 when Tank called the maintenance hangar and asked that an Fw 190 Dora be warmed up and made ready for him to fly. Planned, built and made famous under his direction, the Fw 190 was known throughout the world as a stocky butcher-bird with a chunky twin radial engine. And now, from these auspicious beginnings had risen an aircraft which bore little resemblance to his early dreams. The Jumo 213A's performance was only better than the BMW 801D at higher alti-

The Fw 190D-9 revealed a new single-piece blown canopy and was fitted with the Jumo 213A.

tudes; but production of the Jumo 213E was already under-way. This was a better variant, with a two-stage turbocharger and automatic triple gearing, which held its own against the BMW 801D with a combat performance of 1000 kW/ 1360 hp at 2400 rpm and 1.32 *atas* at an altitude of 5300 meters. Even at 9600 meters it still delivered 3000 rpm, thereby paving the way for the ideal high-altitude engine. The Jumo 213A then in use was expected to be replaced by the Jumo 213E as soon as possible. Also demonstrating major improvements, the BMW 801TJ was unfortunately not yet fully ready for production. In particular, the *Ministerium* quite favored the reliable Junkers engine, whose *Kommandogerät* device was one of the most remarkable technical achievements of the German powerplant indus-try. Tank wanted to find out for himself if the *Langnase* was indeed faster than the Fw 190A-8 and its predecessors and whether it could climb and turn tighter as well. Up to this point his colleagues had had only good things to say about the machine, but now Tank wanted to put the ma-chine through its paces himself.

The hangar soon calls back: "The Fw 190D-9 is ready for takeoff." A few minutes later Tank was sitting in the machine. The maintenance director briefed him on the dif-ferences in control from the Fw 190A-series. "Just fly ac-cording to the rpms", he says, "everything else works auto-matically. You can forget about adjusting the propeller pitch,

boost pressure, cooler gills had everything else." "Does it fly itself, then?" asked Tank with a wink. "Not yet", re-torted the maintenance director with a laugh.

This time, Tank has brought a kneeboard which had the comparative values for the Fw 190A-5 and A-8 jotted down. After landing, he'll pass on the values read from the instruments during the flight to the ground crew, who will compute these into true airspeed data, etc. The engine catches without hesitation and all engine instruments quickly move to the green, for the mechanics had already warmed up and chocked the aircraft. With another glance at the trim setting and the fuel gauge, then Tank pushes the throttle forward and taxis out to the takeoff point. As he begins his taxi, Tank releases the tailwheel's self-centering feature in order to be able to turn on the ground, applies either brake and swings the tail a bit to the left and right. By doing so, Tank finds that despite the longer nose (albeit with a nar-rower profile) and the somewhat more reclined seat the view during taxiing had been improved dramatically.

At the end of the runway Tank points the airplane into the wind, puts on his oxygen mask, switches both fuel pumps on, drops the flaps to their takeoff setting and pushes the throttle in one continuous motion to full power. During taxi-ing and when building up speed on takeoff, the control stick remains centered; takeoff occurs with the tail hanging. Tank discovers to his satisfaction that so far everything is just

like the old design. No tendency to swing, the machine lifting off at 170 km/h after a run of 350 meters. "Just fly by the rpms" keeps going through Tank's mind. He also had to adjust from the BMW 801 to a liquid-cooled engine. The engine's now turning at 3300 rpm and he throttles a bit back; takeoff output is at 3250 rpm. At that rate the engine burns 620 liters - Tank has the data on his kneeboard. He applies the foot brakes to stop the spinning wheels and pushes the red landing gear knob on the left side of the instrument panel, watches the electrical indicator on the left and the mechanical indicator out on the wing which shows the current undercarriage position. The two red control lamps light up, the indicator rods on the wing disappear and the undercarriage tucks up into the fuselage.

Once the landing gear is securely closed, Tank then pushes another knob and brings the flaps in. Again, a red control lamp lights up and the marked mechanical gauge on the upper wing surface registers 0. No change in con-

Cockpit of the Fw 190D-9.

figuration, no need for retrimming! The pitot gauge shows an airspeed of 290 km/h, climbing at a rate of 16 meters per second. Tank breaks the climb off sharply, pushes the machine earthward and flies a long, level stretch at an altitude of 300 meters, following a railroad track. He keeps a constant eye on the airspeed indicator and notes the rpms are running at 3250; gradually Tank juggles the airspeed indicator from 570 to 580 km/h. "That's almost 70 to 80 km/h faster than the Fw 190A-5 or A-8" thinks Tank. He pulls back on the rpm selector lever and slowly reduces his speed to 280 km/h. Now quite low to the ground, Tank slams the throttle to takeoff power, activates a stopwatch he'd brought along and pulls up at a speed of 280 km/h. Again, 16 meters per second rate of climb; for the A-8 this was 13 to 15 meters per second. Tank holds the plane at precisely the best climbing speed of 280 km/h. The plane flies straight as an arrow through the beautiful skies. 1000 meters - the stopwatch shows one minute, 2000 meters' altitude in two minutes, 3000 meters in three minutes. At this point there's a slight bump as the rpm indicator drops. The Kom*mandogerät* automatically switches the turbocharger from low-altitude to high-altitude setting at 3300 meters. The machine continues its smooth climb, reaching 7000 meters in 7.1 minutes. The BMW 801D on the A-8 began losing performance at 5600 meters. But this engine maintains power through an altitude of 6000 meters and almost to 7000 meters.

Tank pushes the nose down into level flight and throttles back to 3000 rpm cruise setting. With each movement of the throttle lever the K*ommandogerät* maintains a constant airscrew rpm via a hydraulically powered automatic propeller pitch controller. If throttle is reduced to 2700 rpm or less, an automatic mixture controller kicks in and the engine shifts to so-called idle cruise. At cruise (3000 rpm) the fuel consumption rate is 530 liters per hour, at 2700 rpm 375 liters/hr, at 2400 rpm about 285 liters/hr and at 2100 rpm just 215 liters/hr. This range of fuel consumption hadn't generally been possible with the BMW 801D. With the tanks filled to 410 kg/569 liters, the *Dora* had an endurance of about 2.60 hrs flying time at maximum idle cruise setting (2100 rpm), although this figure dropped to 1.30 hrs when the throttle was set to climb and combat. With two 300 liter drop tanks, the aircraft had a flight time of five hours at maximum idle cruise and two hours at combat setting.

Tank bleeds off some of the altitude in his search for the best operating height for the turbocharged engine, which he finds to be around 6600 meters. Now he checks out the maximum speed of the airplane. He pushes the rpms to 3250 and keeps the climb rate indicator set to 0 for about three minutes. 686 km/h! (the calculated true airspeed is given here.)

Tank compares the Fw 190A-8 fighter variant's speed on his kneepad: at the same fuel load it was 647 km/h at 5500 meters, whereas he was now flying almost 40 km/h faster at an altitude of 6600 meters. Tank now checks the stability, the harmonizing of the control inputs, stalls the machine, spins it, loops, rolls and turns the plane as tightly as possible. With the long nose and the liquid-cooled motor out in front everything feels slightly different, yet in spite of the many changes to the plane's engine and fuselage the aircraft's good flying qualities have been fully preserved. Tank again climbs to 7000 meters, pushes the engine to climb setting (3250 rpm), starts the stopwatch and points the nose to 10000 meters. Now the plane climbs yet again, albeit this time a bit more slowly. It takes about 9.7 minutes to reach 10000 meters, a good three minutes per 1000 meters on average. Tank zealously rotates the figure on his kneeboard and thinks about the Jumo 213E, which at this altitude will still be able to deliver 1029 kW/1400 hp and offer unimaginable developmental possibilities.

With a half roll, he flips the machine onto its back and dives earthward. 3300 rpm is the maximum allowed, and Tank keeps a watchful eye on the rpm gauge. The airspeed indicator registers 450 km/h, quickly building up in the dive to 500 km/h. At 7000 meters the plane pushes 600 km/h, while at 6000 meters it hits 700 km/h; this translates to 955 km/h true airspeed. Yet again, Tank finds himself approaching the sound barrier in a dive. But the machine remains unaffected - no flutter, no vibration, nothing flying off. Slowly and carefully he begins the pullout. The needle on the g-meter shows 7 *g* after pullout. The values are nearly the same as for the Fw 190A-7 he had test flown in a dive earlier.

Tank heads back towards the airfield, throttles back to 300 km/h and lowers the undercarriage as he enters the downwind leg. To do so, he must first push a red switch on the left side panel and pull the undercarriage lever located on his left auxiliary panel. Only then does the landing gear unlock. He watches the indicator rod on the wing as it slowly extends. Now the green lamps light up. Tank turns onto the base leg, extending the flaps halfway, then as he enters on final he lowers them fully. The buttons for operating the flaps are also to be found on the left side panel. He cuts the airspeed even more and, at 220 km/h, sinks toward the ground. Holding the aircraft level for a bit, he pulls the stick slightly and at 170 km/h the machine lightly touches down.

Tank is happy with his work. High-altitude performance, speed and climb rate had been improved notably, without increasing the engine output performance. A remarkable advance in technology indeed. The Jumo 213Es to be installed in the follow-on Ta 152H will allow much better high-altitude performance to be achieved.

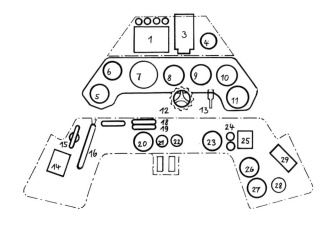

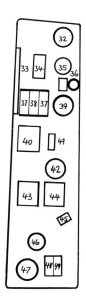

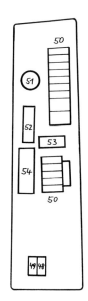

Fw 190D-9 Cockpit
1 Ammunition counter
2 Gun armed indicator lights
3 Reflexive gunsight
4 Homing indicator
5 Altimeter
6 Airspeed indicator
7 Artificial horizon
8 Variometer
9 Compass
10 Supercharger pressure gauge
11 Tachometer
12 Cooler vent control switch
13 Cold starting and windscreen washer lever
14 FuG 25a control panel
15 Manual landing gear lever
16 Fuel cock
17 Engine cut-out emergency lever
18 External stores jettison lever (wings)

19 External stores jettison lever (fuselage)
20 Fuel/oil pressure gauges
21 Coolant temperature gauge
22 Oil temperature gauge
23 Fuel supply indicator
24 Fuel remainder warning light
25 Fuel gauge selector switch
26 Oxygen flow indicator
27 Oxygen pressure gauge
28 Oxygen vent
29 Flare gun
30 W.Gr. 21 safety switch
31 W.Gr. 21 jettison switch
32 Dimmer control
33 Throttle lever
34 Primer switch
35 Emergency electronic switch
36 Supplemental systems switch (for Rüstsätze)
37 Landing gear position indicator

38 Landing flap position indicator
39 Trim position indicator
40 Landing gear-flap actuator switches
41 Horizontal stabilizer trim switch
42 FuG 16ZY mode selector switch
43 FuG 16ZY receiver fine tuning
44 FuG 16ZY volume control
45 Pilot's flight suit heater connection
46 Primer pump actuator
47 Headset R/T connection
48 Notice card
49 Component card
50 Circuit breakers
51 Clock
52 Compass deviation panel
53 Starter switch
54 Manufacturer's type plate

Fw 190D-11 Fighter and Strike Fighter

The Fw 190D-11 was designed as a fighter and ground attack plane with an MW 50 system and additional armor. No less than seven machines served as prototypes. The aircraft stemmed from the A-8 series and were taken off the production line as is, with fuselage, wings and undercarriage being changed and reinforced accordingly. These were the V55(170923), V56(170924), V57(170926), V58(170933), V59(350156), V60(350157) and the V61(350158). The D-11 was fitted with the Jumo 213F. This powerplant differed from the Jumo 213E with its two-stage boost and three-gear switchbox by deleting the boost air cooler. The D-11 had two MG 131s over the engine, two MG 151s in the wing roots and two MK 108s outboard on the wings.

Installation of a new, high-pressure water-methanol system (R20 conversion set) was planned for the Fw 190D-11/R20, production of which was to have commenced in the spring of 1945. the D-11/R21 was also to have been equipped with an autopilot. V55 and V56 were still undergoing trials at Focke-Wulf in September of 1944. V57 was flown to the Rechlin test center in November of 1944, while V58 was scheduled for weapons testing at Tarnewitz. V59 was lost in a crash on 9 October 1944. V60 underwent flight testing from November onward, and V61 was supposedly delivered to the Junkers Motorenwerke in October 1944. Despite the effort that went into this program, it seems as though the D-11 was never put into production and development did not extend beyond the prototypes.

The Fw 190D-11 strike fighter with Jumo 213F and a 30-mm Mk 108 cannon firing through the propeller hub.

Fw 190D-12 High-Altitude Fighter - at Last

Three prototypes from the A-8 series were provided for the Fw 190D-12; these were the V62(732053), V63(350166) and the V64(732254), all equipped with the Jumo 213E. This engine had a fully automatic Junkers VS 19 airscrew with feather pitch and a gun channel. The latter enabled a cannon to be fitted with the ability to fire through the propeller hub.

The difference in engine block weight and the weight of the complete assembly is worthy of note here. The engine itself had a weight of 940 kg, while the entire powerplant assembly (including propeller and fittings) weighed in at 1854 kg. Wings, undercarriage and engine assembly were the same as for the D-11. Armament consisted of one MK 108 firing through the propeller hub and an MG 151 in each wing root. The V63 and V64, which

had been converted to the D-12 standard at Adelheide along with the V62, served as weapons configuration testbeds. The aircraft were cleared for operational flying in October and November 1944. Production was planned to begin in January 1945. Half of the D-12 aircraft were armed with the MK 108 cannon, while the other half flew with the MG 151. During production, four additional fuel tanks (totaling 315 liters) were to have been built into the wings. However, this concept was not implemented until later, with the production of the Ta 152. Additionally, plans called for equipping the variant with the PKS 12 autopilot, the FuG 16Z, the FuG 125 and a heated windscreen.

Production took place at Arado and Fieseler. Again, planned conversion kits included a high-pressure system for water-methanol injection (D-12/R21), plus the R25 and the R11. In this case, the MW 50 was to have been installed in the wing vice the fuselage. As the table shows, the Fw 190D-12/Jumo 213E-1 combination had excellent performance and, with a pressurized cockpit, would have been the aircraft which the high-altitude fighter development program had been working towards two years earlier.

Fw 190D-12, rotting away in the USA.

Fw 190 Dora D-13

Two prototypes were converted from the A-8 series for the Fw 190D-13 long-nosed variant, these being V65(350165) and V71(350167). The Jumo 213F served as the powerplant for V65, while a Jumo 213E was installed in the V71. The 30 mm MK 108 was dropped; instead, a 15 mm MG 151 was fitted over the engine in Adelheide, supplemented by two additional MG 151s in the wing roots. The two prototypes were cleared for flight testing in November and December 1944, respectively, and since the majority of changes affected only the armament production was expected to have begun that December. Follow-on developments included the use of the R21 and R5 conversion sets.

Fw 190D-14 with Daimler-Benz DB 603

Surprisingly, the *Technisches Amt* suddenly expressed a renewed interest in the Daimler-Benz high-altitude engine. As mentioned earlier, this engine had made considerable progress under the direction of Dr. Haspel and had been developed into a complete engine package. The planning department recommended that the *Dora* series be allowed to continue with the D-14 onward being fitted with the DB 603E or DB 603LA. The DB 603LA was based on the E version and had an improved turbocharger giving it a maximum pressure altitude of 11000 meters. On takeoff it delivered 1543 kW/2100 hp. D-9 and D-12 airframes were used for the conversion. Designated V76(210040) and V77(210043), they were fitted with the DB engines and delivered to the flight test center at Echterdingen. The aircraft reached speeds of 700 km/h and a service ceiling of 11700 meters. The following changes were also planned:

Converting the D-12 series over to the DB 603, changes to the weapons configuration in the fuselage as needed, fitting of a special fuels injection system for the DB 603 and subsequent installation of a methanol high pressure system, new oil tank and a new engine cowling tailored to the shape of the DB engine. The aircraft would be put into production as the Fw 190D-14. Blueprints and construction documents were completed around March/April of 1945.

Fw 190D-15 Fighter-Bomber with DB 603E

In order to obtain a DB powered fighter-bomber without delay, plans were made to convert the ongoing Fw 190A-8/F series over to the DB 603E with the designation Fw 190D-15. Basically, it involved the same modifications as for the D-14, mostly as a result of the new engine. An all-weather D-15/R11 variant was to have been kitted out with the PKS 12 autopilot and the FuG 125. Conversion was to have begun in April 1945 at Focke-Wulf, Dornier and the Luther Werke.

Dora Suffers from Shortages of Pilots and Petrol

The Fw 190D-9 was being produced in numbers by August of 1944 and from this time onward many Luftwaffe units were equipped with the aircraft. With an experienced pilot at the controls the *Dora* was equal to or even better than most enemy aircraft up to about 7000 meters. It climbed better than the Fw 190A, achieved a higher airspeed, dived faster and could turn inside most enemy fighters. A clear advantage was not expected until the introduction of the Jumo 213E, however. The aircraft was nonetheless handicapped by the fact that, at this late stage there was a shortage of good pilots. Young pilots could be given the best plane in the world and they would still become victims of an experienced foe. Additionally, fuel shortages at the time often kept the *Staffeln* grounded. Therefore, although there weren't enough pilots or fuel, airplane production output increased rapidly. Production of day fighters amounted to 1900 in September 1944, yet in spite of repeated Allied bombing raids this figure had jumped to 3300 fighters per month by November of that year. This, incidentally, must be one of the most outstanding feats ever carried out by a developed industrial nation.

About 700 D-series fighters were delivered to the Luftwaffe's combat units, the major portion of which were either destroyed or damaged on the ground.

New High-Performance Fighters

Ta 152A Stays on the Drawing Board

In recognition of his valuable service to the aviation industry, in January 1943 Dipl.-Ing. Kurt Tank was named an honorary professor. In addition to many other awards, in 1938 Tank was authorized the use of *Flugkapitän* as his duty title. He was further honored by the fact that all new aircraft designed at Focke-Wulf in the future would henceforth bear his name (Ta) in their designation.

With his unique enthusiasm Tank tackled new projects. The increasing scale and frequency of American daylight bombing raids at high altitudes coupled with reports of bombers having pressurized cockpits and specialized high-altitude engines being built in both the US and England now began to make the political leadership within the Reich uneasy. As a result, the *Technisches Amt* issued a requirement to Messerschmitt and Focke-Wulf - albeit two years too late - for a new high-altitude fighter. A top priority program in two stages was recommended. The first stage would see the construction of a higher performing fighter based on a current type so as to disrupt the flow of production as little as possible; the second stage would lead to a new aircraft design altogether.

Tank immediately set his sights on an improved version of the Fw 190 and proposed that the aircraft be fitted with more powerful engines and have better high-altitude performance. The end result would be a new aircraft embodying all the experience gained up to that point. Messerschmitt proposed a dedicated Me 155B high-altitude aircraft. It soon became apparent, however, that the company lacked the capacity to develop a completely new airplane. At the instigation of the RLM the half-finished project was handed over to Blohm & Voss, where further developmental work was carried out under the designation BV 155B. Today this monster graces the halls of the National Air and Space Museum in Washington.

In accordance with the *Technisches Amt*'s vision, Tank laid the design for the new Ta 152A down in such a manner that the airframe of the Fw 190A-8, then in production, could be utilized with minimal changes. In this manner, it would have been possible to make use of available manufacturing equipment for the most part. For the Ta 152, a somewhat larger wing was designed with a wingspan of 10.71 m and an area of 19.5 m², which was a square meter larger than the wing of the A-8. The Jumo 213A was planned as the powerplant. The Ta 152A-1 was to have been a heavily armed fighter with a MK 103 engine cannon included as part of its armament configuration. In this case, it would have been necessary to have utilized the Jumo 213C as the Jumo 213E was not designed for installation of a cannon. In addition, the aircraft's design called for two MG 151s above the engine, two MG 151s in the wing root and two MK 108s in the outer wings. A second variant, the Ta 152A-2, was to have had two MG 151s above the engine, two MG 151s in the wing roots and two MG 151s in the outer wing sections - in addition to the MK 108 firing through the propeller hub. For the A-series, however, no prototype was actually ever built nor were any aircraft contracted for. The reason was plainly evident: at the time the Jumo 213 was not yet available in sufficient numbers. As a result, the entire Ta 152 planning program came grinding to a halt. Further work was not possible until early 1944, at which time the project was embraced again - but this time with much greater urgency.

Ta 152B Heavy and All-Weather Fighter

A second version, designated the Ta 152B, had in the interim been planned as a *Zerstörer*, or heavy fighter. Significant changes to the airframe had been planned for this version, which again was to have made use of an Fw 190A-8 as its foundation. The fuselage was lengthened - initially on the drawing board - the same as for the *Dora* by inserting a 50 cm plug ahead of the empennage. A new wing center section was designed and incorporated the larger wing planned for the Ta 152A, having an area of 19.5 m². The design's landing gear had a somewhat wider track as well.

The intended powerplant for the B-series was the Jumo 213E. The Ta 152B-1 was to have been fitted with an MW 50 system and an R11 all-weather conversion set. The design's armament called for installation of an engine cannon (MK 108 or MK 103) and four MG 151s, plus two WGr. 42 sets. B-2, B-3, B-4 and B-5 sub-variants were to have been created by varying the weapons combinations based on the current tactical necessities. A B-5 *Zerstörer* version would have made use of either an MW 50 or GM 1

system, depending on preference. A B-5/R11 was designed for the all-weather role.

In the event, however, the comprehensive preliminary work on the B-series had to cease. It was not until late 1944 that an Fw 190 V68(170003, a former V53) was converted as a prototype for the B-5 heavy fighter version. The aircraft would have been fitted with the Jumo 213E high-altitude engine and utilized a methanol injection system. Construction blueprints had been drawn up by January 1945 and production was to have begun in the spring of that year. A Ta 152B-5 was fitted with the R11 conversion kit, which can be found in the table along with the other R-type field conversion sets. In the end, the V68 was the only prototype for the B-series, although it was joined in January 1945 by three new V-types from the Ta 152 series: V19, V20 and V21.

By the war's end plans were in the works calling for a Ta 152B-7, a variant which was to have been equipped with a Jumo 213J having four vents per cylinder in place of three and a two-stage supercharger with three speed regimes. This engine had been designed for 1911 kW/2600 hp on takeoff at 3700 rpm and 1272 kW/1740 hp at 3700 rpm at an altitude of 10000 meters.

Ta 153 Project, High-Altitude Fighter with DB Engines

In the meantime, one of the prototypes from the Fw 190C program (V32, 0057), fitted with the DB 603A and Hirth exhaust turbocharger, had been modified in December of 1943 for the purpose of testing components of a planned Ta 153. The type was to have had a longer fuselage, probably in order to accept the high-altitude exhaust-turbocharged DB 623, DB 626, DB 627 and DB 624 engines. As a result, the airplane was to have become a flying testbed for DB high-altitude engines, having a new wing and numerous other improvements. There are references to this variant in both RLM files as well as company records from Focke-Wulf. Nevertheless, there is no concrete data on the type. It has often been claimed that the Ta 153 was a fantasy design. According to reliable information, however, RLM representatives did indeed inspect a mockup of the Ta 153 - probably the V32 -, plus documents from the Messerschmitt company dated 30 July 1943 show a comparison of the Ta 153's expected performance figures with those for the Me 209. Based on this information, the aircraft must have at least completed the design stages and would have been tested for suitability with the DB 603G and four-bladed propeller in accordance with an RLM understanding.

The longer span wing with the capability of holding additional fuel in the center section found considerable interest within the Technisches Amt. The Ministerium accordingly demanded that this wing also be used for the Ta 152. This changeover required time, however, and only later versions of the Ta 152H were able to make use of the wing. The Ta 153 was never built, apparently because the previously mentioned Daimler-Benz engines never became available. According to Focke-Wulf company records, efforts on making the Ta 153 ready for production ceased on 13 January 1944.

Ta 152H High-Altitude Escort Fighter

It was not until early 1944 that jig construction began for the manufacture of the first prototype of an entirely new design, the Ta 152H-0.

This third Ta 152 design was to be an escort fighter, specifically for protecting the Me 262 on takeoff and landing. Aside from its high speed in horizontal flight, this jet fighter namely had many faults - as quickly became obvious. These had nothing to do with the aircraft as such or its qualities, but were exclusive to the uniqueness of its engines. The jet's acceleration and deceleration were quite poor at the time due to the low excess thrust reserves. For acceleration when transitioning from a climb into level flight the airplane needed much more time and space than a piston-powered aircraft did. And when approaching a slow moving target the jet fighter also required a relatively long distance because of the lack of speed brakes. If the machine were moving at high airspeeds it tended to overshoot its target. The engine's lag response time also made it poorly suited for formation flying.

The Me 262 therefore needed protection during its long takeoff stretches and its flat approach phases, since by that time the Allies enjoyed virtually complete air superiority over Germany and enemy aircraft often were able to bring down the Me 262 during these vulnerable phases. Protection of jet fighters was naturally only one of the roles envisioned for the Ta 152H. Its primary role would be attacking enemy fighters and bombers. The designation "H" indicates H*öhe*, or altitude.

The Ta 152H differed from the A and B designs primarily by having a larger wing with an area of 23.5 m2, a span of 14.82 meters and a high aspect ratio. In addition, the cockpit would be pressurized. The design would be equipped with the GM 1 system and limit its armament to a Mk 108 engine cannon and two MG 151/20s in the wing roots in accordance with its role as a high altitude fighter. Nevertheless, for specialized tasks the plane could be fitted with supplemental armament in the fuselage or wings. The engine was to be the production Jumo 213E, now available, with the alternative being the DB 603G.

With the Ta 152 in its final form Focke-Wulf was actually able to succeed in redressing the balance which had for so long favored fighter aircraft construction abroad. What this meant for a nation which was being plowed under bit by bit beneath an incessant rain of bombs is inconceivable today. Therefore, it is worth examining this masterpiece in somewhat greater depth, despite the fact that only a relatively small number complete with armament and in its latest operational configuration were able to be delivered. At the end of the war, it was something of the penultimate single-engined piston-powered fighter plane.

Ta 152H Specifications

Fuselage

Due to the large space required for the MK 108 engine cannon and the two MG 151s at the wing/fuselage joint, it became necessary to enlarge the Ta 152 H's fuselage forward section even more. This extension was fitted to existing engine connecting points in order to limit the requirement for new construction jigs as much as possible. The wing, moved forward by 420 mm due to changes in the center of gravity, was joined to the fuselage midway along the extension section. To prevent the extended forward engine assembly from affecting the plane's stability, particularly its directional stability, the aft fuselage was fitted with a 0.5 m long cylindrical plug. The latter also served as space for housing the oxygen bottles for high altitude flight and the cannon's compressed air bottles which had to be shifted aft, again to balance the center of gravity. In turn, this extension necessitated the reinforcement of the fuselage frame which was accomplished by using steel formers in place of the previous dural formers. The fuselage center section deviated from the planned Ta 152A and B by having a pressurized cockpit. The actual cockpit itself, with a volume of about 1 m3, encompassed the entire area above the fuel cells. The plating was sealed by using a type of paste applied to the riveted surfaces. The canopy was sealed by an all-round expanding tube partially filled with foam rubber, which was inflated by a bottle of compressed air to 2.5 atu. If the canopy had to be jettisoned, it was first necessary to deflate the tube, break the seal and then fire the canopy off. A double glazing was used to reduce the chance of penetration. Silica gel capsules were used to keep the air dry. One of the most difficult problems in sealing the cockpit was feeding the instrumentation and control lines into the pressurized area.

From a structural and design standpoint the fuselage of the Ta 152A and B had already been prepared for the use of a pressurized cockpit, so that basically the H-version differed from these earlier versions only in having the sealing applied.

Undercarriage and Control Surfaces

The landing gear struts including braces and bearings were carried over from ongoing production series. The tailfin was enlarged by some 15 percent to 1.77 m2 and plans called for both a metal and a wooden version. Landing flaps were operated hydraulically, while the elevators were electrically driven. For the most part, the flying controls were taken over from the Fw 190A-series, although moving the wings forward and lengthening the fuselage meant that some of the relay points had to be modified.

Ta 152 H-0 (Werknummer 150005) with Jumo 213E and 115-l long range tanks (1945), photographed here in the compensating pit at the Cottbus factory.

An Fw 190 V30/U1 (0055) with Jumo 213E, modified to Ta 152H-0 GH-KT. Photo taken on 8/13/1944.

Ta 152H-0 (Werknummer 150003) with Jumo 213E at the Langenhagen factory, 1945.

Wings

The landing gear was moved outboard by 250 mm on either side. The plating inside the wing was reinforced as a result of the increased span and wing area. Externally, it was a purely monocoque wing design.

Engine and Equipment

The interchangeable Jumo 213E (9-8213 FM) powered the airplane, fueled initially by B_4 (87 octane) and later by C_3 (100 octane) which differed only in their octane rating. The flight performance in the table is calculated based on B_4 fuel.

A so-called barrel radiator hid beneath a radial cowl and had a frontal area of 76 dm2. The oil was cooled by a heat exchanger. As on previous versions, exhaust nozzles were utilized to turn the exhaust air into thrust. A wooden three-blade(V9) or smaller diameter four-blade(V19) Junkers variable pitch propeller was chosen. For improving performance above 8000 meters the aircraft was fitted with an 85 liter GM 1 tank in the fuselage, which was removable. By this time, the GM 1 system could easily provide 17 min-

utes of boost at an average consumption rate of 100 grams per second.

The forward fuel tank, with a capacity of 233 liters, came unchanged from production aircraft and was only moved forward to accommodate the change to the wing's position. This made possible the increase in capacity of the aft tank by 70 liters for a total of 362 liters. The aircraft's total internal fuel capacity was therefore 595 liters. In addition, the H-1 onward carried three non-armored softskinned fuel cells in the wings for an additional 454 liters/335 kg of fuel. The left inboard fuel cell could carry water-methanol, while the aft fuselage tank could be used for the GM 1 system. To improve range even further, a non-armored 300 liter drop tank could be carried beneath the fuselage suspended from a *Schloß 503* rack mounted on the underfuselage centerline. The oil tank was located on the right side next to the engine cannon; it was a simple steel plate container protected at the front by an 8 mm thick armor plating. It held 64 liters of oil.

The aircraft was equipped with heated windscreen, electric rpm indicator, instrumentation for coolant and cockpit pressure and an electrical firing counter. Radio/navigation equipment included the FuG 16ZY and FuG 25a and, with the H-2 on, the FuG 15.

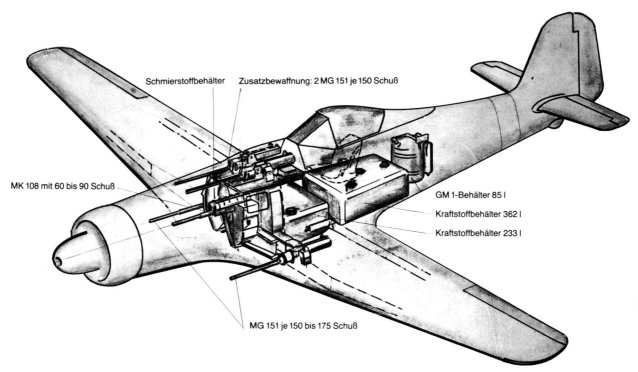

Schmierstoffbehälter   Zusatzbewaffnung: 2 MG 151 je 150 Schuß

MK 108 mit 60 bis 90 Schuß

GM 1-Behälter 85 l

Kraftstoffbehälter 362 l

Kraftstoffbehälter 233 l

MG 151 je 150 bis 175 Schuß

Fuel tank and weapons layout of the Ta 152H.

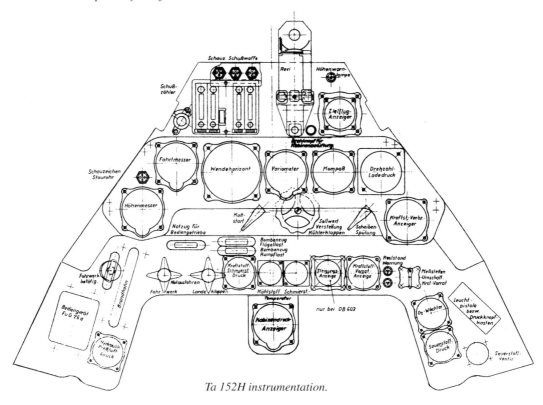

Ta 152H instrumentation.

According to Tank, the pressurized cockpit caused many problems on the previous aircraft because the entire cockpit had to be pressurized by the relatively small turbocharger. As a result, the cockpits then had to have a much better seal than today; the mass of air delivered by jet engines is vastly different than from a piston engine.

Under the auspices of the flight testing program Tank also had the opportunity to fly the Ta 152H with Jumo 213E and GM 1 system. He flew it to a ceiling of 14000 meters and at 13000 meters clocked an airspeed of 746 km/h. An aircraft had been created with which it was possible to hunt the dreaded British Mosquito without difficulty.

A new solution to the problem of supplying the cockpit with breathable air had been found for the Ta 152. For the reasons just mentioned the air for pressurizing the cockpit was not taken from the engine boost air. Instead a Knorr-Roots air compressor, lacking any type of intermediate gearing, was bolted onto the engine. Via an inlet duct, the compressor sucked in ram air and forced it into the cockpit through a relief valve. The device began operating an altitude of about 8000 meters. From this altitude and higher the cockpit pressure was maintained at a constant 0.36 atas by a pressure vent. At flight altitudes under 8000 meters, i.e. with an unpressurized cockpit, fresh air was drawn in directly from the ram air. A slider control for breathable air enabled pressurized or fresh air (or a mixture of the two) to be selected as desired, which also permitted simultaneous temperature control within the cockpit.

Ta 152 V-Types and H-0 Series

Once again, the test planes for the earlier Fw 190C-series served as prototypes for the Ta 152H; these had been fitted out as flying testbeds for the DB 603 high-altitude engines. As already mentioned, however, insurmountable problems forced a stop to the program. These planes were the V33/U1(Werknummer 0058 with DB 603 and Hirth exhaust turbocharger) and the following types with the DB 603S, all of which were fitted with exhaust turbochargers: V30/U1(0055 DB 603S with pressurized cockpit), V 29(0054 DB 603S with pressurized cockpit), V32(0057 DB 603S) and V 18/U2(0040 DB 603S). These aircraft were converted to Ta 152H prototypes at Adelheide in August 1944 to accept the Jumo 213E with its two-stage three-gear switchbox and delivering 1375 kW/1870 hp at 3250 rpm at sea level and 1595 kW/2170 hp with methanol injection.

V29/U1, V30/U1, V32/U2 and V33/U1 served as prototypes for the H-0 series, while V18/U1 was used as the prototype for the H-1 series. These ex-Kangerüh planes were not yet fitted with the larger wing and therefore also lacked the additional wing fuel tank. They were fitted with the GM 1 system and were designed for operating at high altitudes, particularly since the V29/U1 as well as the V30/U1 had pressurized cockpits. Armament was generally two MG 151s carried in the wing roots. Unfortunately, V33/U1 was lost on 13 July 1944 on its second flight, with the V30/U1 following on 23 August 1944. Although nothing is known regarding the cause of these two losses, it was almost assuredly due to the overly hasty developmental program.

The V29/U1 was cleared for flight in late September 1944 and became the initial prototype for the H-0 series. It was followed in November of that year by V32/U2. Following a brief trial period of these V-types at Langenhagen and Rechlin, manufacture of pre-production aircraft got underway in November 1944 at the Sorau plant and series production began at the Cottbus facility. The aircraft were further tested at Rechlin once they rolled off the assembly line. Approximately 20 H-0 machines were delivered to an Erprobungskommando commanded by Hauptmann Bruno Stolk for combat evaluation.

There are so many different claims regarding the number of Ta 152s actually built that it's difficult to arrive at a definitive figure. It is a known fact that the Ta 152A was never built. Only a few of the Ta 152B and C series were produced.

It was a different matter with the H-series, despite the fact that construction documentation was not available until March 1944. In a letter dated 18 July 1944 Oberst Petersen, commander of the Rechlin test center, expressed his concern at the overly hasty introduction of the Ta 152. He saw a danger for the H-series in the program's accelerated tempo. The fact that Ta 152 production began with the H-series and not with an A, B and C version, as was normal, was cause for worry in and of itself.

Petersen's concerns focused on the "four prioritized, non-production V-planes". That had not been an adequate evaluation, in Petersen's opinion. Therefore, once production was underway "delays caused by flight safety and flight handling problems as well as due to a large number of initial changes" would be encountered. In any case, the first twelve production machines would be needed for evaluation purposes." He foresaw even greater problems with production of the Ta 152C and its DB 603L and demanded 30 prototypes for this variant. "And it's not even remotely certain whether the DB 603L will even be ready for delivery in January 1945."

A Ta 152H-1 as an American war prize.

Company documents agree that series production of the Ta 152H-0 began in December 1944 at the earliest, while the H-1 entered production in mid January to February 1945 and the H-2 in March. The aircraft were all manufactured at the Sorau facility. In place of the twelve prototypes called for by Petersen, a total of 26 V-types (designated V1 through V26, 110001 through 110026) were in actual fact built. Based on planning requirements these were distributed among the various planned H-versions as determined by certain guidelines.

The H-0 series planes were powered by the Jumo 213E and, as already mentioned, were built with an extended and reinforced fuselage, a pressurized cockpit, an MK 108 engine cannon and two MG 151s in the wing roots. Undercarriage and landing flaps were driven hydraulically instead of electrically, The first 18 machines had only the 115 liter long-range tank and lacked the wing tanks. An improved navigation suite was to have been installed in a specialized Ta 152H-0/R11 all-weather fighter variant. Series production of this variant was to have begun in January 1945.

Ta 152H-1 Series

A Ta 152 V5 built in Sorau and the old V-type Fw 190 V18/U2 were prototypes fro the H-1 series. These were joined by the Ta 152 V3 and V4 from sorau. Fw 190 V18/U2 flew for the first time in October and after only a few flights was lost in a crash on 8 October 1944; Ta 152 V5 flew in December 1944. According to Focke-Wulf records (dated 10/15/1944) production of the H-1 began in January 1945 at Focke-Wulf's Cottbus facility and in March of 1945 at the Erla and Gotha plants. The prototypes had a GM 1 system or a long-range tank, the larger 23.5 m2 wing, auxiliary tanks in the wings, larger tires and a pressurized cockpit. Production H-1s were fitted with the new wing, designed to incorporate no less than six additional fuel tanks. Extremely important for boosting performance, a GM 1 system was carried in the fuselage and a water-methanol system in the wing; these could be employed independent of each other depending on altitude. The H-0, H-1 and sub-

sequent H-2 series were laid down as escort fighters, a type for which there was urgent need at the time. Of course, the aircraft could be employed in different roles, such as the use of the R21 conversion kit for fighting in inclement weather. Approximately 150 aircraft are reputed to have been manufactured at the Cottbus works before the Soviets occupied the city.

The Ta 152H-1, with its Jumo 213E and dual injection option (GM 1 and MW 50), was without a doubt the best performing fighter built by Professor Kurt Tank during the war. It need not have feared any enemy, whether at high altitudes or near sea level. To be sure, problems with stability forced a restriction on the GM 1 system for a time, and this may be a clue behind the possible reasons for the many accidents with the prototypes. The many changes to the fuel system had probably given rise to problems with weight distribution.

The H-1/R21 was given an MW 50 high-pressure injection system in the wing, while the GM 1 system was still temporarily under a ban. The GM 1 system was to be cleared for an H-1 with R31 conversion kit again, however. In exchange, the aft fuel tank was to be reduced from 350 liters to 280 liters and a 10.5 kg ballast in the engine compartment. Room also had to be made in the engine for the GM 1 compressed air bottles. Blueprints were supposedly completed in March 1945 so that production could begin in June that year.

As evidenced by the Ta 152 table, this machine's performance figures were nothing short of sensational thanks to the simply outstanding Jumo 213E-0. The engine had a relatively low rate of fuel consumption, both at low levels as well as at height. With the aid of the Ta 152's markedly higher fuel capacity provided by the wing tanks, this aircraft was capable of ranges approaching 1500 km - again, both at sea level as well as at the maximum rated altitude for the engine. Even with climb and combat settings the range at sea level was still 914 km. A 300 liter drop tank increased the range to 2200 km at idle cruise and 1230 km at full military power at sea level.

On the Ta 152 the production GM 1 and MW 50 systems finally were able to prove their worth with significant boosts in power, so that this variant would have been more than a match for even those enemy fighters equipped with exhaust turbochargers. With a service ceiling of 14800 meters and a speed of 745 km/h at 12500 meters the Ta 152H-1 was the sought-for high altitude fighter capable of threatening the Mosquito and the American Superfortress

bombers. The Ta 152 would also have been just as effective as a low-level strike platform. Although this plane wouldn't have won any wars, a night-fighter variant would have certainly blunted the worst of the British night bombing raids and the American daylight attacks. The prerequisite for all of these hopes would simply have been to put the Jumo 213E high-altitude engine as proposed by Junkers into production in 1941, making it available for Tank's Dora series; the *Dora* and eventually the Ta 152 would then have been able to go into large-scale production in 1942. The planning division within the *Technisches Amt* anticipated a monthly output of 690 Jumo 213E powered Fw 190D-9s, 1600 Ta 152s with DB 603Ls and 1000 Ta 152H-1s for the year 1945. No other aircraft, not even the Bf 109, were planned for 1945 in such large numbers. Tank's philosophy that the aircraft's flying qualities must allow the pilot to concentrate on the task at hand was now recognized by the *Technisches Amt* as the correct approach. Tank's designs were pioneers in the realization of this principle.

Ta 152C High-Altitude Fighter

Despite all the confusion wrought by the war, Tank and his colleagues worked on an even better performing design powered by the DB 603L. The DB 603L high-altitude engine, which had undergone improvements in the interim, was made available in small quantities for use in the Ta 152 in mid 1944. Nonetheless, the *Ministerium* reversed its position on the engine's use for this aircraft and insisted on sticking to the planned Jumo 213. However, after many battles Tank succeeded in August of 1944 in getting permission to install the DB 603 in a C-version of the Ta 152. No less than 15 prototypes were provided for the Ta 152C series; these included the company availing itself of the new prototypes being produced at the Sorau facility. According to Focke-Wulf records all these machines were fitted with the DB 603L excepting the V7, which was given a DB 603EM.

This engine delivered 1653 kW/2250 hp on takeoff and at 10000 meters still had an output of 780 kW/ 1060 hp. It was fitted with a 180 liter auxiliary tank for an MW 50 system. In its latest variant with two turbochargers (two-stages) and boost air cooling, the DB 603L delivered 974 kW/1325 hp at 2500 rpm at 1.30 *atas* at an altitude of 9200 meters. At 15000 meters' altitude 434 kW/590 hp at 2700 rpm could still be attained at emergency boost.

The Ta 152 V7 with Werknummer 110007 was built in Cottbus and became the prototype for the Ta 152 C-0/R11 with DB 603L engine and MW 50 injection. It was expected to enter production in March of 1945.

Prototypes V6(110006), V7(110007) and V8(110008) were made available for the Ta 152C-0. In addition, there were the V13 and V15 for the C-1 series. Due to a lack of larger wings, aircraft of the C-0 series sported the 19.5 m2 medium sized wing and, although lacking a pressurized cockpit, they did have the MW 50 system. Apparently, the better wing with a fuel cell in the center section was available for the Ta 152C-1; this variant was fitted with the DB 603L minus boost air cooler. Planned armament included the MK 108 engine cannon, two MG 151s in the fuselage and two MG 151s in the wing roots. The prototypes were to have been cleared for flight in December 1944 and production would have been able to get underway by January/February 1945. However, given the progress of the war, it seems questionable whether plans made in October 1944 could be kept three months later. Incidentally, this applied to all deadlines during the last months of the war. However, Daimler-Benz/Focke-Wulf conference reports on the Ta 152C V6 and V7's initial flights dated 13 January 1945 show that the time schedule, insofar as it affected the two prototypes, was adhered to. The V6 and V7 were cleared for flight operations in December 1944 and test flown that same month.

Included among the C-3 series prototypes were the V16 (110016), V17(110017) and V18(110018), all of which had originally been designated for the C-2 series (which was apparently never produced). They were to have been cleared for trials in February and March 1945 in order for full-scale production to begin in mid-1945. The R11 field conversion kit was intended for the C-1 and C-2.

DB 9-8603 (DB 603L) standard engine as fitted in the Ta 152 C-3.

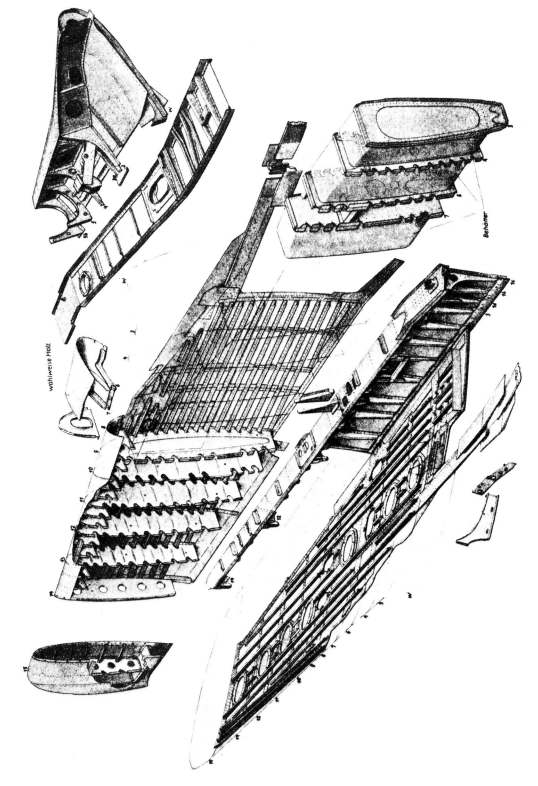

wahlweise Holz

Behälter

The steel wings of the Ta 152 C-1 was some 224 kilograms heavier than the previous duraluminum-made wings.

The V19, V20 and V21 prototypes, originally laid out as the prototypes for the C-3 series, were in fact destined to become the prototypes for the B-5 series. V19(110019) was lost in a crash in February 1945. These machines were supposedly cleared for initial testing in March 1945.

The V22, V23 and V24 were planned as the test types for the C-4 series. Deadlines for their readiness were given as February and March 1945; whether the machines were ever built is up to speculation.

Ta 152E Reconnaissance Aircraft

Two reconnaissance versions of the Ta 152 were also conceived, a Ta 152E-1 medium altitude reconnaissance fighter and a Ta 152H-10 high altitude recon platform. Prototypes for the E-1 were to have been the V9(110009) and

the V14(110014). However, both of these were most likely used for structural soundness testing and in their place appeared the Fw 190 V-32/U2, which was given the wing of the unfinished V25(110025), and the Ta 152 V26(110026), a prototype converted to the H-10 (E-2) reconnaissance standard. Both prototypes were fitted with a camera monitor having a sighting scope, plus a 300-liter drop tank. Radio and navigation equipment included the FuG 15 and FuG 25a, and it was planned to utilize an MW 50 system. Both aircraft were supposedly cleared for flight in January 1945 and were to have entered production in February 1945. The Jumo 213E was apparently fitted to both aircraft.

The H-10 or E-2 high-altitude recon fighter was the same as the E-1 with the exception of a three-stage GM 1 system and an additional MW 50 system in the wing. Both systems could be switched on during flight. A V26(110026) served as the prototype for this variant. Production was to have begun in May of 1945.

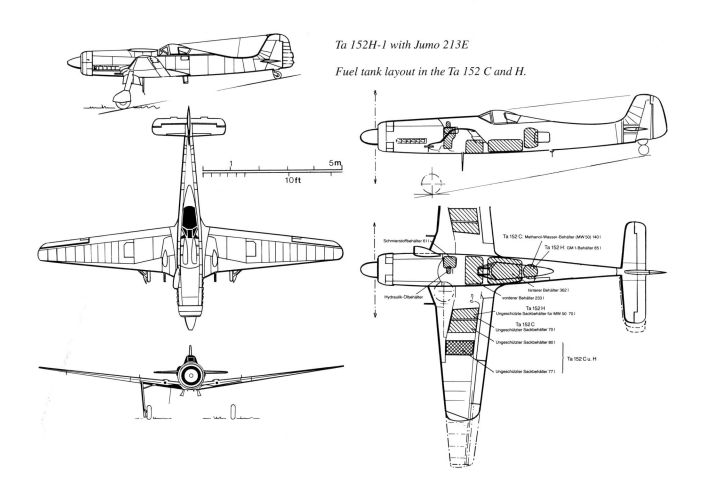

Ta 152H-1 with Jumo 213E

Fuel tank layout in the Ta 152 C and H.

Schmierstoffbehälter 61 l

Ta 152 C: Methanol-Wasser-Behälter (MW 50) 140 l

Ta 152 H: GM 1-Behälter 85 l

hinterer Behälter 362 l

vorderer Behälter 233 l

Hydraulik-Ölbehälter

Ta 152 H Ungeschützte Sackbehälter für MW 50 70 l

Ta 152 C Ungeschützter Sackbehälter 70 l

Ungeschützter Sackbehälter 80 l

Ta 152 C u. H

Ungeschützter Sackbehälter 77 l

Ta 152S-1, S-5 and S-8 Trainers

Several versions of the Ta 152 were planned as two-seaters for training purposes, similar to the Fw 190A-8/U1 trainers. However, no two-seat trainers were ever built. The Ta 152S-1 was to have been derived from the C-1 series with a Daimler-Benz DB 603L engine and converted accordingly. The fuselage was to have been modified to accommodate two seats and most of the aircraft systems would have been duplicated. Armament was dispensed with altogether. Blueprints had been completed by December 1944. Construction of the S-1 was to have begun at Blohm & Voss in April of 1945 and in August of 1945 at the Lufthansa hangars in Prague.

Ta 152 Field Conversion Sets

R1: Camera installation for recon acft (planned for E-1 and H-10)
R11: LGW K23 fighter navigation system, heated windscreen and FuG 125 Hermine(H-0 and B-5)
R21: MW 50 high compression system in wings, PKS 12 and FuG 125 Hermine(H-1)
R31: GM 1 system with compressed air and 10.5 kg counterweight (H-1)

Ta 152 Production Aircraft Built by Cottbus Focke-Wulf Works*

Type	Werknummer	Engine	Notes	
Ta-152H-	15001	Jumo 213E	19.5 m² wing	**only 115 ltr long-range tank, production from January 1945
Ta-152H-0	15002	Jumo 213E	19.5 m² wing	
Ta-152H-0	15003	Jumo 213E	19.5 m² wing	
Ta-152H-0	15004	Jumo 213E	19.5 m² wing	
Ta-152H-0	15005	Jumo 213E	19.5 m² wing	
Ta-152H-0	15006	Jumo 213E	19.5 m² wing	
Ta-152H-0	15007	Jumo 213E	19.5 m² wing	
Ta-152H-0	15008	Jumo 213E	19.5 m² wing	
Ta-152H-0	15009	Jumo 213E	19.5 m² wing	
Ta-152H-0	150010	Jumo 213E	19.5 m² wing	
Ta-152H-0	150011	Jumo 213E	19.5 m² wing	
Ta-152H-0	150012	Jumo 213E	19.5 m² wing	
Ta-152H-0	150013	Jumo 213E	19.5 m² wing	
Ta-152H-0	150014	Jumo 213E	19.5 m² wing	
Ta-152H-0	150015	Jumo 213E	19.5 m² wing	
Ta-152H-0	150016	Jumo 213E	19.5 m² wing	
Ta-152H-0	150017	Jumo 213E	19.5 m² wing	
Ta-152H-0	150018	Jumo 213E	19.5 m² wing	
Ta-152H-1	150019	Jumo 213E	23.5 m² wing	6 soft-skinne fuel cells in wings, MG-1 and MW 50 systems, produced from 1/45 to 3/45
Ta-152H-1	150020	Jumo 213E	23.5 m² wing	
Ta-152H-1	150021	Jumo 213E	23.5 m² wing	
Ta-152H-1	150022	Jumo 213E	23.5 m² wing	
Ta-152H-1	150023	Jumo 213E	23.5 m² wing	
Ta-152H-1	150024	Jumo 213E	23.5 m² wing	
Ta-152H-1	150025	Jumo 213E	23.5 m² wing	
Ta-152H-1	150026	Jumo 213E	23.5 m² wing	
V27 C-3	150027	H-0 conversion to C-3 with DB 603L, planned for production from 6/45		
V28 C-3	150030	H-0 conversion to C-3 with DB 603L, planned for production from 6/45		

*Table is not complete
**Werknummer 150001 to 1500018 had the 19.5 m² wing

Ta 152 High-Altitude Fighter and Reconnaissance Aircraft

Manufacturer		Focke-Wulf			
Type Recce		Ta 152H-1	Ta 152C-1	Ta 152 *Projekt*	Ta 152H-10 High-Alt.
Powerplant		Jumo 213E-0	Daimler Benz DB 603L	Jumo 222E	Jumo 213E-0
Performance	kW	1374	1338	1837	1374
	hp	1870[1]	1820[10]	2500	1870
Crew		1	1	1	1
Length	m	10.71	10.80	10.77	10.71
Height	m	3.36	3.38	3.75	3.36
Wingspan	m	14.44	11.00	13.68	14.44
Wing area	m²	23.50	19.50	23.70	23.50
Aspect ratio		8.87	6.20	7.90	8.87
Weight, empty	kg	3495[2]	3799[11]	4538	3495[23]
Fuel	kg	836[3]	876[12]	919[20]	836[23]
Oil	kg	55	65	61	65
Crew	kg	80	80	80	80
Load	kg	498[4]	811[13]	615[21]	704[24]
Max. permissible load	kg	1469	1832	1675	1685
Takeoff weight	kg	4964	5631	6213	5180
Wing loading	kg/m²	211.23	288.76	262.15	220.43
Weight/power ratio	kg/kW	3.61	4.21	3.38	3.77
	kg/hp	2.65	3.09	2.49	2.77
	kW/m²	58.47	68.62	77.51	58.47
	hp/m²	79.57	93.33	105.48	79.57
Max. speed	km/h	750[5]	702[14]	740	746[25]
@ altitude	m	12500	9200	12000	12500
Cruise speed	km/h	500	550	640	515[26]
@ altitude	m	7000	8400	11500	0
Rate of climb	m/s	17.50[6]	15.00[15]	22.00	16.00[27]
Service ceiling	m	14800[7]	12300[16]	15000	14200[28]
Range	km	1100[8]	1140[17]	1290[22]	1560[29]
Max. flight time	hrs	1.80[8]	2.07[17]	2.02[22]	3.32[29]
Takeoff run	m	395[9]	415[18]		405
Takeoff run to 20 m	m	600	650[19]		615
Landing run	m	500	500		500
Landing speed	km/h	155	175		156
Max. permissible load as % of takeoff weight		30	33	27	33
Payload as % of takeoff weight		10	14	10	14
Built		1945	1945	1944 project	1945

[1]1506 kW/2050 hp at takeoff with MW 50
[2]**Empty Weight Breakdown**

fuselage	365 kg
landing gear	285 kg
empennage	140 kg
control system	35 kg
wings	620 kg
engine	1930 kg
armor	120 kg
	3495 kg

[3]**Fuel Supply(B4)**

232 liter forward fuel tank		kg 172	
360 liter aft fuel tank		kg 266	
70ltrs+80ltrs+77ltrs=227 liters	l. wing	kg 167	
77ltrs+80ltrs=157 liters	r. wing	kg 116	kg 721
70ltrs MW 50	r. wing	kg 52	
85ltrs GM 1	aft fuselage	kg 63	kg 115
Total fuel			kg 836

[4]**Payload**

parachute	20 kg
armament	230 kg
equipment incl. GM 1 system	145 kg
MK 108 ammunition	36 kg
MG 151 ammunition	67 kg
	498 kg

[5]With GM 1; with GM 1 plus emergency boost it was 732 km/h at 9500 m; with emergency boost and MW 50 it was 542 km/h at sea level
[6]With MW 50 at sea level; 11.7 min to 10000 m with injection corresponded to 14.2 m/sec average rate of climb to 10000 m
[7]With GM 1
[8]At 9600 m with climb and combat performance at 3000 rpm; approx. 1550 km and 3.34 hrs at 7800 m with max economy of 2400 rpm and 706 kW/960 hp; 1530 km and 3 hrs at sea level with max economy of 2400 rpm and 823 kW/1120 hp (190 g/hp/hr at 450 km/h); 914 km and 1.8 hrs at sea level with climb and combat performance of 3000 rpm and 1250 kW/1700 hp approx. 1230 km and 4.32 hrs at 514 km/h with 3000 ltr external fuel tank at 7800 m with max economy of 2400 rpm, 1029 kW/1400 hp
[9]265 m with MW 50
[10]DB 603L had a dual turbocharger with blower air cooling, still under development in August 1944, prototype and pre-production series. 434 kW/590 hp at 1500 m and 2700 rpm takeoff performance with MW 50 1544 kW/2100 hp
[11]**Empty Weight Breakdown**

fuselage	kg	384
landing gear	kg	245
empennage	kg	136
control system	kg	27
wings	kg	557
engine	kg	2057
equipment	kg	230
ballast	kg	13
armor	kg	150
Total empy weight	kg	3799

[12]**Fuel Supply(B4)**

232 ltrs forward fuel tank	kg 172	
360 ltrs aft fuel tank	kg 266	
454 ltrs in 6 wing tanks	kg 335	kg 773
140 ltrs MW 50 aft fuselage	kg	103
	kg	876
For increased range(planned)		
300 ltr drop tank	kg	221
400 ltr in two *Doppelreiter* upper wing tanks	kg	295
	kg	1392
- MW 50 with *Doppelreiter* tanks	-103	
Max. fuel capacity	kg	1289

[13]**Payload**

parachute	kg	20
2xMG 151	kg	84
2x150 rounds	kg	51
2xMG 151	kg	84
2x175 rounds	kg	59
1xMK 108	kg	88
100 rounds	kg	60
equipment and wpns fittings	kg	365
	kg	811

[14]At 2500 rpm combat setting, 974 kW/1325 hp; with MW 50 it was 736 km/h at 10000 m with 2700 rpm
[15]Average rate of climb to 10000 m with MW 50 was 12.50 m/sec in 13.3 min
[16]Ta 152C-1 did not have the GM 1 system
[17]At 8400 m with 2400 rpm cruise, 904 kW/1230 hp at 550 km/h, range was 1630 km and endurance was 2.96 hrs. Fuel consumption rate was 400 liters per hour at 8400 m; 1120 km at sea level with combat setting of 2500 rpm, 1323 kW/1800 hp at 500 km/h
[18]Takeoff run was 360 m with MW 50 boost
[19]With MW 50 it was 585 m to clear 20 meters' altitude
[20]Fuel was 794 kg + 125 kg for MW 50
[21]**Payload**

2xMG 151/20	kg	84
2x150 rounds	kg	51
2xMG 151/20	kg	84
2x175 rounds	kg	59
equipment and wpns fittings	kg	365
other	kg	100
	kg	615

[22]At 10500 m altitude at 2700 rpm, 1029 kW/1400 hp, 280 g/hp/hr, endurance was 2.02 hr at 640 km/h; 880 km at sea level with combat setting of 2900 rpm, 1632 kw/2230 hp, 222 g/hp/hr at 550 km/h and 1.60hrs flight time
[23]As Ta 152H-1
[24]3**Payload**

2xMG 151	kg	84
2x150 rounds	kg	51
1xMK 108	kg	88
100 rounds	kg	60
equipment, navigation	kg	245
equipment, photographic	kg	176
	kg	704

[25]At combat setting with GM 1
[26]At combat setting and 3000 rpm at sea level, 1249 kW/1700 hp and 232 g/hp/hr
[27]13.66 m/sec rate of climb to 10000 m(12.2 min)
[28]With GM 1
[29]At an altitude of 7800 m with economy setting and 2400 rpm, 706 kW/960 hp, 227 g/hp/hr at 470 km/h

Daimler-Benz Fighter Aircraft Engines

Engine Type	Configuration: # of cylinders	stroke (mm)	bore (mm)	capacity (ltrs)	compression	length (mm)	width (ø)(mm)	height (mm)	Supercharger	Performance: type of performance	altitude m	output kW/hp	rpm ata	boost pressure	consumption g/hp/hr	consumption ltrs/hr	Dry Installed Weight kg	Comments
DB 603A	12	180	162	44.6	7.5	2610	830	1156	single-stage centrifugal air with automatic drive via hydraulically operated clutch with barometric governor	takeoff & emergency	0	1286/1750	2700	1.40	460	570	910	As of August 1944
										climb	0	1161/1580	2500	1.30		1080		
										max cruise	0	1010/1375	2300	1.20	214	410		
										max economy	0	735/1000	2000	1.05		320		
										emergency	5700	1191/1620	2700	1.40		530		
										climb	5700	1109/1510	2500	1.30		460		
										max cruise	5400	1029/1400	2300	1.20	216	420		
										max economy	5000	879/1170	2000	1.05	335			
										emergency	10000	698/950	2700	0.85				
DB 603E	12	180	162	44.5		2670	830	1167	larger than charger on DB 603A	takeoff & emergency	0	1323/1800	2700	1.48		580	925	As of August 1944, planned as standard engine for Ta 152 fighter and heavy fighter
										climb	0	1158/1575	2500	1.35		490	1020	
										max cruise	0	1011/1395	2300	1.25		410		
										max economy	0	698/950	1900	1.05		310		
										emergency	7000	1139/1550	2700	1.48		510		
										climb	7100	1051/1430	2500	1.35		460		
										max cruise	6700	974/1325	2300	1.25		410		
										max economy	5700	753/1025	1900	1.05		330		
										emergency	10000	779/1060	2700					

190

ð

A second variant, the Fw 190S-5 incorporating the same modifications, was to have come from repaired A-5 series planes. Blueprints were expected to have been completed by December 1944. An Fw 190S-8 was to have been developed from a converted Fw 190A-8; production of this series was planned for October 1944 at Altenburg and for November 1944 at Menibum.

Ta 152V-1 through V-26 Prototypes Built by Fock-Wulf-Werk Sorau*

Type	Werknummer	Comments
Ta 152V-1	110001	Structural testing(?)
Ta 152V-2	110002	Structural testing(?)
Ta 152V-3	110003	H-1 Jumo213E (steel wing)
Ta 152V-4	110004	H-1 Jumo213E
Ta 152V-5	110005	H-1 Jumo213E
Ta 152V-6	110006	C-0 DB 603L + MW 50, in production from 3/45
Ta 152V-7	110007	C-0/R11 DB 603L + MW 50, in production from 3/45
Ta 152V-8	110008	C-0 DB 603L + MW 50, in production from 3/45
Ta 152V-9	110009	E-1 Jumo 213E
Ta 152V-10	110010	no information
Ta 152V-11	110011	no information
Ta 152V-12	110012	no information
Ta 152V-13	110013	C-1 DB 603L + MW 50
Ta 152V-14	110014	E-1 Jumo 213E + MW 50
Ta 152V-15	110015	C-1 DB 603L + MW 50
Ta 152V-16	110016	C-3 DB 603L + MW 50, production planned from 6/45
Ta 152V-17	110017	C-3 DB 603L + MW 50, production planned from 6/45
Ta 152V-18	110018	C-3 DB 603L + MW 50, production planned from 4/45, 5/45
Ta 152V-19	110019	B-5/R11 Jumo 213E, planned for production from 5/45
Ta 152V-20	110020	B-5/R11 Jumo 213E, planned for production from 5/45
Ta 152V-21	110021	B-5/R11 Jumo 213E, planned for production from 5/45
Ta 152V-22	110022	C-4 DB 603L + MW 50
Ta 152V-23	110023	C-4 DB 603L + MW 50
Ta 152V-24	110024	C-4 DB 603L + MW 50
Ta 152V-25	110025	H-2 high-alt recce R11 Jumo 213E, not finished
Ta 152V-26	110026	H-10(E-2) Jumo 213E + MW 50 + GM 1, production planned from 5/45

*Table is incomplete

Daimler-Benz DB 603L High-Altitude Engine

Engine Type	Configuration								Supercharger	Performance and Consumption Data							Comments
	# of cylinders	stroke(mm)	bore(mm)	capacity(ltrs)	compression	length(mm)	width Ø (mm)	height(mm)		type of performance	altitude m	kW/hp output	rpm ata	boost pressure	consumption rate g/hp/hr	ltrs/hr	Dry Installed Weight kg	
DB 603L	12	180	162	44.5	7.5	2740	1008	1203	Dual charger with two-stage, blower air cooling	takeoff & emergency	0	1338/1820	2700	1.40		560	975	August 1944, prototype and pre-production standard engine
										climb	0	1231/1675	2500	1.30		500	1135	
										max cruise	0	1102/1500	2300	1.20		415		
										emergency	10000	1029/1400	2700	1.40		510		
													974					
										climb	9200	1325	2500	1.30		450		
										max cruise	8400	904/1230	2300	1.20		400		
										max economy								
										emergency	15000	434/590	2700					

Ta 152 with Jumo 222E

In mid-1943 Focke-Wulf was awarded a contract for researching whether the Jumo 222E could be fitted into a single-engined plane built by the company. This engine, mentioned earlier , was developed by Dipl.-Ing. Brandner at the instigation of Dr.-Ing. Mader; it was a liquid-cooled 24-cylinder powerplant with six rows of cylinders arranged in a radial fashion. Volume was 48.85 liters. The motor had a liquid-driven two-stage turbocharger with boost air cooling. It delivered 1838 kW/2500 hp at 3000 rpm at sea level and had a climb/combat output of 1286 kW/1750 hp at 2900 rpm at an altitude of 9400 meters. It weighed 1330 kg.

Calculations showed the fuselage of the Fw 190 to be unsuitable for this engine. On the other hand, the engine promised good performance for the Ta 152. The Ta 152H would have been a natural choice for the installation; Junkers would have first had to develop a new engine housing. A Ta 152H thus fitted would have had an empty weight of 4600 kg and a takeoff weight of 5800 kg. A wing having greater structural integrity would have been necessary, something which would have needed to have incorporated the latest aerodynamic developments. Unfortunately, the design remained the project that it was, as the Jumo 222 was not able to go into production before the end of the war.

Ta 152 Leaves Mustangs in the Dust

In late 1944 Tank took off from Hannover-Langenhagen in one of the first Ta 152H-0s (equipped with an MW 50 system) for a conference with his fellow workers in Cottbus. Shortly after leaving the runway the tower called out the warning: "Vier *Indianer am Gartenzaun*" - four Indians at the garden fence, meaning that enemy planes were approaching the airfield perimeter. Soon he spotted four Mustangs closing rapidly in his rearview mirror. Tank accordingly pushed the throttle to emergency power and activated the water-methanol system. Soon the Mustangs became smaller and smaller and eventually disappeared in the haze. The system had proven itself impeccably. This event was later reported in an American magazine, with the Americans at a loss to explain what German aircraft could have such reserves of power to be able to simply walk away from Mustangs as though they'd been standing still.

Twin-Engined Wooden Night-Fighter

Ta 154 with Tricycle Landing Gear

The English DeHavilland Mosquitos, twin-engined light bombers made entirely of wood, began appearing over Germany in 1942 and at their high operating altitudes could not be touched either by German fighters or by anti-aircraft guns. Then there was the horrible large-scale bombing raid on Cologne on 30/31 May 1942 in which a massive armada of 1046 bombers returned to England virtually unscathed. Their losses totaled just 3.8 percent. Just 26 hours later 800 British bombers struck Essen, with only 37 failing to return. On 25/26 June 1942 the British set their sights on Bremen on a full-moon night; out of 1000 bombers, just 52 were brought down. These catastrophic events forced the responsible parties within the RLM to call upon German aviation industry to develop a high-performance night-fighter. Heinkel, Focke-Wulf and Junkers were tasked with submitting proposals as soon as possible.

The focus was on a two-seat all-weather night-fighter with an endurance of two to three hours and armed with four forward-firing cannons. To facilitate a quick production, the aircraft was to be of simplified construction with minimal use of steel and alloys and be designed for available engines currently in production. And finally, the prototype was to fly within twelve months.

In September 1942, Tank accordingly had the blueprints drawn up for a two-seat, all-wood construction night-fighter with tricycle gear, for which the T*echnisches Amt* immediately issued him with a top priority contract.

Many experts within the *Technisches Amt*, however, had serious reservations about the wooden construction as there were simply no construction guidelines for wooden aircraft capable of speeds of 600 to 700 km/h and no company had experience with such designs. Tank, however, pointed to the British Mosquito and, in view of the shortage of raw materials, was able to get his way in the end. To compete with the Ta 154 the *Ministerium* issued a contract for the continued development of the Heinkel He 219, which was already available, and the development of the Ju 388J.

Ta 154 V1 TE+FE with Jumo 211 F/2 in July 1943 at Hannover-Langenhagen.

Tank flies the Ta 154 V1 in Langenhagen.

Tank assigned the construction of the aircraft to Oberingenieur Ernst Nipp. The design originated with Oberingenieur Ludwig Mittelhuber, while Oberingenieur Gotthold Mathias was responsible for its flight handling and Dipl.-Ing. Herbert Wolff concerned himself with performance calculations and airscrew design.

On 1 July 1943, a scant nine months after the contract was awarded, Ta 154 V1(100001 TE+FE, engine factory number 104129, 2426+2434) took off on its maiden flight from Hannover-Langenhagen with Hans Sander at the controls. With its two Jumo 211 F/N engines delivering 2700 rpm at 1.45 at*as*, the unarmed plane achieved a speed of 575 km/h at sea level and 635 km/h at an altitude of 6000 meters. The twin engined shoulder-wing design with tricycle landing gear had a narrow oval fuselage cross section made of wood skinning. The two-spar wooden wing was of a one-piece pass-through design and was attached to the wing by four bolts.

The entire airplane was skinned with thin sheets of laminated plywood, with only the ailerons, flaps and elevators being made of metal alloy construction. New for a Focke-Wulf design was the hydraulically activated nose gear.

The crew sat in tandem beneath a jettisonable canopy. For protection against enemy shells, the windscreen was made of 50 mm armored glass with the side panes being 30 mm thick. The crew was protected aft by a 12 mm thick armor plated bulkhead, while the sidewalls were reinforced by 8 mm armor plating. Two fuel tanks with a total capacity of 1944 liters were housed in the fuselage behind the crew; the engine nacelles accommodated two 116 liter oil tanks. As the Junkers Jumo 213A engines were not yet available in early 1943, two Jumo 211F/2s were chosen as the powerplant; this engine produced 985 kW/1340 hp at 2700 rpm at sea level and 1036/1410 hp at 2700 rpm at an altitude of 6000 meters. Planned armament included two 20 mm MG 151s and two 30 mm MK 108 cannons, located on the fuselage underside parallel to the wing leading edge.

The engineers at Focke-Wulf took an unorthodox and, by today's standards, rather adventuresome approach in obtaining reliable data on the structural soundness of the aircraft's forward fuselage section and canopy access. They made use of an experimental towing method developed by the Lu*ftfahrt-Forschungsanstalt* (Aeronautical Research Institute) Graf Zeppelin. A floating test booth was set up on Lake Alat, near Füssen, and a wooden mockup of the Ta 154's forward section was suspended from the booth's framework. A winch dragged the fuselage through the lake underwater. The thicker medium of water enabled the drag encountered during flight to be simulated with relatively little force. The experiments showed the airplane's design to be sufficiently sturdy.

On 28 July the undercarriage on the V1 collapsed after a relatively hard landing. Subsequent investigation revealed that the struts, as they were being heat-treated during the manufacturing process, had been over hardened and become brittle. Fortunately, the machine was repaired in short order.

Ta 154 V2(100002 TE+FF), the second prototype, was completed shortly after the V1's first flight and was the first to be fitted with a radar system (called a radio ranging device, or F*unkmeßgerät*, at the time), an FuG 212 Lichtenstein C-1 with four antenna. The aircraft was later used for static vibration testing.

The first pre-production Ta 154 V3(100003 TE+FG) for the 0-series was designated Ta 154A-03/U1 and was able to be fitted with the Junkers Jumo 213A engine originally intended for the design. The engines delivered 1300 kW/1770 hp at 3250 rpm near sea level and 1103 kW/1500 hp at 3250 rpm at an altitude of 6000 meters. At these ratings the fuel consumption was 256 and 286 g/hp/hr, respectively. The additional drag caused by the armament now installed in the fuselage, the Lichtenstein radar antennas and the flame dampers reduced the speed by some twelve percent compared to the unarmed prototypes, despite the more powerful engines. Nevertheless, a contract was immediately issued for 250 A-1 variants of the Ta 154.

Preparing the Ta 154 V4 for a test flight in Langenhagen.

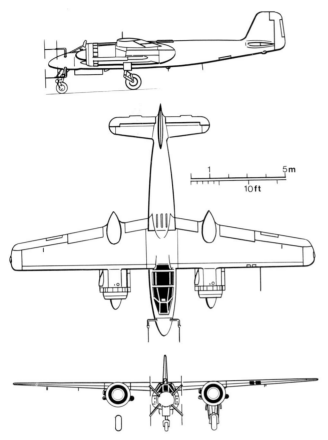

Ta 154A-0/U2 (V14).

Ta 154 V4(TE+FH), V6(TE+FJ) and V7(TE+FK) (100004 to 100007) were built at Focke-Wulf's Langenhagen facility where they were also initially test flown. V4(100004) entered into its evaluation phase on 19 January 1944, followed by V5(100005) on 25 February 1944. Both were kitted out with the Jumo 211N powerplant and subsequently ferried over to Detmold in August, where the engines were swapped for Jumo 213As. Ta 154 V6(100006) flew for the first time on 17 March 1944, was sent to Rechlin after initial flight testing and from there also went to Detmold. On the other hand, V7(100007) was destroyed on the ground after assembly due to enemy action.

The Gothaer Waggonfabrik built the first eight pre-production aircraft, Ta 154A-01 through -08, in the underground salt mine facilities at Wremen. Ta 152A-01(120001 TQ+XA/V22) was cleared for flight in June, but in August was destroyed on the ground during a strafing attack. This had been the first prototype to have been factory-fitted with the Jumo 213A. Ta 154A-02 (120002 TQ+XB) suffered the same fate as its predecessor.

In July 1944 Ta 154A-03(120003 TQ+XC/V23), also fitted with the Jumo 213A, was declared flight ready and subsequently fitted out as a night fighter in Detmold. The A-0/U2(120004 TQ+XD) yet again met an ignoble fate on the ground, as did two other A-0s (120006 and 120009). On 5 August the Jumo 211 powered Ta 154A-0(1200005 TQ+XE) suffered 30 percent damage from ground attack fighters, yet was repaired and flown to Detmold for conversion to a Jumo 213A powered night fighter within the month.

Flight testing at Langenhagen soon revealed that the undercarriage, specifically the nose gear, was causing several minor accidents; these difficulties were partially alleviated through the use of a caster-type nose gear. Despite this, however, on 18 April 1944 Ta 154A-02 TE+FM(V9) was reputed to have been lost in a crash, followed by Ta 154A-0 V8(100008, TE+FL) on 6 May.

The first two A-1 series aircraft (Werknummer 320001 and 320002) were also completed at the underground facility in Wremen, while preparations got underway at the Posen works for manufacturing the wing assemblies and empennage. Fuselage and pressurized cabin were to be produced at the Cottbus facilities, which would also be the site of final assembly and fitting of equipment.

Gauleiter Saukel, whom the Party had designated to be in charge of directing the emergency fighter program, paid a visit to the Posen works on 15 January 1944. Saukel took this opportunity to threaten works director Schnebel with internment in a concentration camp if he couldn't produce a specific number of wings and empennage assemblies in short order. This news agitated Schnebel so much that he collapsed, whereupon Gieschen, the works director from the Focke-Wulf facilities in Cottbus, briefly assumed management of the Posen works in addition to his regular duties.

The first production A-1, Werknummer 320001, flew for the first time on 13 June 1944, but apparently crashed just a few days later, on 28 June, when a wing broke.

Two days later another Cottbus-built A-1 (320003) reportedly lost its starboard landing flap on final approach. The ensuing crash presumably destroyed the aircraft and killed its operator, a test pilot by the name of Bartsch.

At the time Tank was already looking into a new type of bonding material which was of a different mixture than the glue hitherto supplied. The first prototypes built in Langenhagen made use of a Tego-Film glue developed by the Goldmann company. However, the company had been destroyed in a nighttime bombing raid; this resulted in a contract being placed with the Dynamit AG in Leverkusen for supplying a replacement material in as short a time as possible - even though that company's product was still undergoing development. From the beginning, Tank never

fully trusted this glue and arranged to have Focke-Wulf supplied with a few samples. Experiments showed a loss in bonding strength of up to 50 percent at the required values. The oxygen content of the hardener, although meeting the specification requirements of the glue, was too high, meaning that instead of the excess glue being absorbed it would soak into the wood's interior and eat away at it. At this point of the glue experiments Tank had production stopped in order to first establish the root cause of the problem.

Neither Professor Tank and his planning chief, Kaerther, nor Dipl.-Ing. Wolff (performance calculations) were able to recall the above-mentioned accidents - despite the fact that these have been repeatedly cited in both the German and international aviation press. This leads to some serious questions being raised. Company records show two hand-written notes documenting a crash landing of Ta 154 V3 on 7/12/1944 at Sorao and of Ta 154 V9(TE+FM) on 4/18/1944. Professor Tank and his coworkers have stressed that the Ta 154's production was halted because of the poor results of the bonding material experiments and not due to the aforementioned accidents. There remains the slight possibility that some of the planes reputedly lost in crashes were either destroyed on the ground by enemy aircraft or shot down as they attempted to land.

An overzealous worker now believed that Tank was sabotaging his own factory by stopping production and reported him to Gauleiter Saukel. A short time later Tank found himself in the Hotel Deutscher Kaiser in Nuremberg before a tribunal chaired by Reichsmarschall Göring, answering to the charge of sabotage. Göring took this occasion to rant and rave about the state of affairs in the loudest tones possible, until Tank was eventually able to interject and in a calm voice explain the facts leading up to the accident with the bonding material. The tribunal withdrew and the Reichsmarschall muttered something about having to act on "higher authority". Later he apologized to Tank for the whole affair.

With the Ta 154 program now being jeopardized by serious delays until the glue mixture could be improved, the RLM halted preparations for series production of the aircraft, at the same time directing that the Me 262 be produced in the underground facilities at the Wremen salt mines, as there was a much more urgent requirement for the latter machine. Nevertheless, seven Ta 154A-1s were still produced before production came to a standstill.

[1] At 4300 m; at sea level it was 985 kW/1340 hp

[2] Payload

2xMG 151	kg	84
2x 150 rounds	kg	51
2xMK 108	kg	176
2x100 rounds	kg	120
equipment	kg	365
radar system	kg	74
	kg	870

Ta 154 Twin-Engine Night-Fighter

Manufacturer		Focke-Wulf
Type		Ta 154A-0
Powerplant		Jumo 211F/2
Performance	kW	2x1036=2072
	hp	2x1410=2820[1]
Crew		1+1
Length	m	12.60
Height	m	3.60
Wingspan	m	16.00
Wing area	m²	32.40
Aspect ratio		7.90
Weight, empty	kg	6160
Fuel	kg	1600
Oil	kg	160
Crew	kg	160
Load	kg	870[2]
Max. permissible load	kg	2790
Takeoff weight	kg	8950
Wing loading	kg/m²	276.23
Weight/power ratio	kg/kW	4.32
	kg/hp	3.17
	kW/m²	63.95
	hp/m²	87.04
Max. speed	km/h	620[3]
@ altitude	m	6000
Cruise speed	km/h	534[4]
@ altitude	m	3000
Rate of climb	m/s	9.00[5]
Service ceiling	m	9500
Range	km	1600[6]
Max. flight time	hrs	3.73
Landing speed	km/h	185
Max. permissible load as % of takeoff weight		31
Payload as % of takeoff weight		10
Built		1944

[3] With Jumo 211F/2; with Jumo 213A it was 630 km/h at 8500 m; with Jumo 213E it was 750 km/h at 10500 m

[4] At max economy setting of 2250 rpm; 465 km/h at sea level with max economy setting of 2250 rpm

[5] Average rate of climb to 8000 m(14.5 min), at sea level with no add'l equipment it was 11 m/sec

[6] At 5900 m; 2750 km with two 300 liter drop tanks at economy setting at 500 km/h at an altitude of 5900 m, giving it an endurance of 5.49 hrs

Factory documents only give speed performance figures for the Jumo 213A and E fitted aircraft, although other material has been derived from comparison flights against the British Mosquito. These show the Ta 154 with Jumo 213A reaching a speed of 630 km/h at an altitude of 8500 meters, while the Mosquito with its two RR Merlin 21s attained a top speed of 620 km/h at 6300 meters' altitude. The Ta 154 could therefore only successfully attack a Mosquito if it enjoyed a significant height advantage - a poor showing indeed! Otherwise, there is no shame in comparing the speed figures of the two aircraft. On the other hand, the Jumo 213E powered Ta 154 was markedly superior to the higher-performing Mosquito and its two Merlins. The Mosquito could achieve 630 km/h at an altitude of 8500 meters and the Ta 154 approximately 740 km/h at 10500 meters. With this variant, not only would it have been possible to carry out relatively successful anti-Mosquito operations, but it also met the Technisches Amt's requirements. However, in order to deliver adequate high altitude performance the Ta 154's wing area would have required an increase to 40 m² and its span to 17.8 meters. The weight increase and drag incurred by the larger wing and a pressurized cockpit would have been offset by the use of a GM 1 system, which probably would have improved performance overall.

In the meantime, plans for follow-on developments were maturing in the design department at Focke-Wulf's Bad Eilsen facilities. A Ta 154C would have embodied a metal nose, a raised pilot's seat, ejection seats and two forward-firing 30 mm MK 108 cannons as well as the "Schräge Musik" conversion kit. As described in a previous chapter, this consisted of automatically-triggered cannons mounted in the fuselage firing at an upward angle of 65 to 70 degrees, enabling attacks to be made on bomber formations from below. Both the Ta 154A with its larger wings and

Jumo 213E and the Ta 254B with DB 603 engines would assuredly have been more than a match for the British Mosquito design. However, it seems the warnings of experienced personnel working in the Technisches Amt, claiming that such a fast high-performance machine could not be rushed into production, were entirely justified.

Shortly thereafter, some of the Ta 154A-1s built in Cottbus were evaluated by a night-fighter wing stationed in Stade. While this was going on, Focke-Wulf worked out a plan for using the remaining partially completed aircraft. This involved the well-known Mistel principle, whereby an Fw 190A-4 would be mounted above a Ta 154 on a break-free framework. The Ta 154's fuselage would be filled with explosives. The pilot of the Fw 190 would fly the joined pair towards a bomber formation and, when within firing range, release himself from the Ta 154. When the Ta 154 had reached the formation, the pilot would detonate the explosive charge via radio, causing a massive explosion. The idea was never put into practice due to the fact that much time was needed to develop and test a practical release system for the Fw 190/Ta 154 combination, and time was running out.

The plan was tackled in another way; the six remaining Ta 154s and prepared for carrying a 2000 kg explosive load and 1300 liters of fuel. When reaching the vicinity of approaching enemy bomber formations the aircraft was to be flown on a collision course, with the pilot escaping through a new type of downward-firing ejection seat just before impact. Although the six planes were indeed completed, they were never used for this purpose.

According to Tank, who frequently enjoyed flying machine, the Ta 154 was a good plane from a handling standpoint. He had the opportunity to fly the Heinkel He 219 for comparison and was somewhat disappointed with this plane - it seemed to be not so much a fighter as a bomber and, compared with the Ta 154, was heavier on the controls.

The Decisive Leap to Transatlantic Routes

Fw 200 Condor Long-Range Aircraft

A discussion of Professor Tank's works would be incomplete without mentioning his contribution to the advancement of commercial aviation. By applying creative initiative, it was in this area that he enjoyed his greatest success in peacetime aircraft development. He conceived of a four-engine design which continues to receive praise today, and in so doing became a pioneer of commercial aviation over the North Atlantic routes.

As is often the case, chance played an important role: on the return leg of a vacation in the Dolomites in March of 1936, Tank met a certain Dr. Stüssel, the technical director of Lufthansa, as they were switching trains at the Alpine station of Franzensfeste. Both were waiting for their next trains and had time for small talk. Tank took this opportu-

Prof. Kurt Tank with a model of the Fw 200 Condor, which quickly amassed a number of export contracts throughout the world. One of the first examples went to the Danish airlines Det Danske Luftfartselskab (DDL) in 1939.

Engine test run-up of the Fw 200 V1 prior to its maiden flight. At this time the aircraft still lacked its identification codes.

199

Fw 200 Condor V1 D-AERE "Brandenburg" during its flight test program in 1937.

nity to convince the Lufthansa director that technology had now advanced to the point where it was now economically feasible to consider a landplane for commercial aviation routes over the Atlantic to the USA. He even had a name chosen for such an airplane: "Condor", the best endurance glider in the South American bird kingdom. It was to be his role model. Long-span wings and high wing loading would help make long-range flight possible. Tank no longer envisioned some cumbersome, awkward flying boat, but rather an elegant, four-engined high-speed long-range aircraft.

Returning to Berlin, he assigned Ober*ingenieur* Ludwig Mittelhuber with the task of working out a design based on his ideas; once this was completed he presented it to the Lufthansa. In June of 1936 a contract was issued following discussions with Lufthansa director *Freiherr* von Gablenz and Dr. Stüssel. The Lufthansa managers were surprised at Tank's courage and his faith in the project before them. For up until this point, Focke-Wulf had only built wood and metal trainers and weather planes and the twin-engined Weihe - the "bandaid bomber". And now they were to create a four-engined passenger plane made entirely of metal?

Tank was convinced that he could have the design flying within twelve months. To the reserved Lufthansa representatives, this appeared to be a pipe dream.

Von Gablenz was so sure that Tank would not be able to meet such a deadline that he made a bet with the designer - the stakes were a crate of champagne. Yet it was hard to believe when, twelve months and eleven days later, on 27 July 1937, the Fw 200 Condor landed safe and sound in Bremen after its maiden flight with Tank at the controls. Tank was overjoyed. The aircraft had performed virtually flawlessly on its first flight and was truly worthy of the sobriquet Condor, its namesake which soared over the Andes with such effortless ease. Only the elevators were so overbalanced that Tank had required the assistance of his only other crewmember, the mechanic, to hold the control column steady. But this was an easy matter to rectify. Otherwise, Tank had no complaints with the airplane, but he had lost the bet by only a narrow margin. The next day he sent the Lufthansa's chief the promised crate of champagne. For his part, however, von Gablenz found eleven days to be inconsequential for such a project and sent him back a second crate.

Deutsche Lufthansa's Fw 200 Condor D-AMHL. Wherever the new passenger plane, the prototype for which had crossed the north Atlantic in record time, put in an appearance it was greeted with pomp and circumstance and admired by aviation experts.

Fw 200 Condor V5 "Nordmark" of the Deutsche Lufthansa (coded D-AMHC) with BMW 132G engines and Werknummer 2895. It has served as the prototype for the modern airliner, which - other than the powerplants - has seen few significant changes down to our day.

The Condor Fw 200 V1(2000) was fitted with four American 559 kW/760 hp Pratt and Whitney Hornet S 1 E-G engines. The low wing design with retractable undercarriage and equipped with landing flaps was laid out for a four-man crew and 26 passengers. The V1 weighed in at 14000 kg on takeoff and cruised at 362 km/h at an altitude of 3900 meters. The aircraft was still able to maintain flight even with two engines out on a single wing. Its range at full load capacity was about 1500 km.

Fw 200 Specifications

The Fw 200 had a three-piece wing consisting of a continuous center section with the four engines and the two outer wing sections. The middle section also housed the fuel tanks, holding between 2000 and 3000 liters. Between the ailerons were the continuous split flaps in seven sections; these were hydraulically driven. The monocoque fuselage contained the cockpit in the forward section, followed by the luggage compartment and the galley. It included two passenger compartments, a washroom, mail compartment and the baggage compartment. The control surfaces, of entirely metal construction, were of a cantilever design and the rudder and elevators all had electrically adjustable trim tabs. The wheels were mounted in forked struts and retracted hydraulically forward and upward. The tailwheel was also retractable.

The changes brought about by the flight test program of the Fw 200 V1 D-AERE "Brandenburg" were remarkably few given the fact that this was such a revolutionary new design. Elevators and tailfin were redesigned slightly, and the outer wing sections were given a somewhat greater sweep in order to achieve a better center of gravity. This in turn decreased the span from 32.97 meters to 32.84 meters and the wing area from 120 m2 to 118 m².

Tank personally carried out the dangerous vibration testing phase for the Condor as well. Such a large aircraft was not put into a vertical dive for the tests, but rather flown at a steep angle as possible. Tank nosed the Fw 200 over until the machine had reached its maximum potential airspeed. At no time did the aircraft display any dangerous vibration or flutter tendency throughout the speed regime. According to Tank, this regime lay in the area between 500 and 600 km/h.

The modifications carried out on the V1 were incorporated into the second prototype as it was being manufactured. This prototype, Fw 200 V2 D-AETA "Westfalen", was destined for Lufthansa and was powered by four BMW 132G engines, each delivering 529 kW/720 hp and driving two-bladed Hamilton airscrews whose pitch could be varied for climbing and high-speed flying.

The Fw 200 V3 D-2600 "Immelmann III" was fitted out as a governmental aircraft and a personal transport for Hitler himself. While the V2 and V3 were still under construction, Tank had the V1 converted to a long-range configuration. The entire rear compartment was fitted with extra fuel tanks, the contents of which were to gradually be pumped into the wing tanks during flight. On this occassion the airplane was given a new registration code of D-ACON and refitted with the BMW 132G engines.

Berlin-Cairo-Berlin Record-Setting Flight Ends in a Storm

The first flight which would demonstrate the airplane's capabilities to the public was planned to be a trip to Cairo with journalists on board. It was to be a Berlin-Cairo-Berlin route lasting less than 24 hours - however, Tank and his colleagues did not reckon with the three months' worth of red tape just involved in preparing for the excursion itself. The aircraft used for the flight was Fw 200A-0 (S 1) D-ADHR "Saarland" (Werknummer 2893), a machine also destined for Lufthansa's inventory. It was to be piloted by Kurt Tank, with Hans Sander acting as his copilot. The remaining crew included a radio operator (Heidfeld) and two on-board mechanics (Bolin and Nienstermann). Representing the board of directors from Focke-Wulf was Friedrich Roselius and consul Heinz Junge, and Rolf Kortlebel took part in the flight as Lufthansa's design supervisor. Ing. Rothkegel, who had made all the arrangements, also was on board. There was room for an additional twelve passengers, including Dr. Georg Böse from "Adler", Dr. Orlovius, press chief from the RLM, and eight more journalists, including two women.

On 27 June 1938 at 0:17 hrs Central European Time(CET) it was time: Tank pushed the four throttle levers on the Fw 200 forward and started off from Berlin-Tempelhof towards Cairo. The flight carried them over Czechoslovakia, Hungary, Yugoslavia, and Greece to Saloniki, where they made their first stopover at 5:00 CET after flying a distance of 1600 km. A weather front over the Balkans had forced the crew to deviate some 100 kilometers from their intended path - a frustrating loss of time since this was ultimately planned to have been a record-breaking flight monitored and confirmed by expert witnesses from the FAI. The planned 20 minute period for refueling stretched to over an hour. At 6:05 CET the "Saarland" assumed a direct heading for Cairo, where Tank landed at 10:38 hrs after covering a distance of 1555 kilometers. However, instead of the civilian airport at Heliopolis, Tank landed by mistake at the Royal Air Force base at Almaza.

The British were used to prominent pilots making such errors, for just 14 days previously Air Marshall Balbo had done the same thing. The error, coupled with another takeoff to Cairo-Heliopolis, tacked an additional 35 minutes onto his flight time.

For two hours the passengers and those Germans living in Cairo celebrated the event with representatives of Egyptian aviation. The return leg began promptly at 13:15 CET. Kicking up a huge column of dust, the Fw 200 raced across the airfield and headed yet again for Saloniki. Some of the journalists slept, while others typed out their impressions of the flight thus far. Landing, refueling and takeoff took place in Saloniki without a hitch. By 18:45 CET the wheels left the Greek airfield's surface and the Condor began climbing to altitude in order to quickly hurdle the Balkan mountains. However, a massive storm front began building up over Yugoslavia itself. Flying under it would not have been advisable due to the mountains, and without pressurization it would have been impossible to overfly it at 8000 meters' altitude. Flying around it would have meant possibly violating the airspace of other countries, which in turn may have led to diplomatic consequences; in any case, there was insufficient fuel for such a detour. Thus Tank made the decision - a typical one for him - to fly through the middle of the storm even though night was rapidly falling. Before too long, all hell broke loose.

The heavy aircraft was tossed about the skies; its joints creaked and groaned. It was only by combining all their collective strength that Tank and Sander were able to hold the plane steady on course and altitude. Lightning bolts split the darkness. Radio communications were lost. Tank, who had participated in working out the calculations for the Condor's fuselage and wing spars, knew what the plane could withstand and felt that the turbulence would surely cause the plane to pay the ultimate sacrifice, that the structural soundness of the aircraft was being stretched to its limit and that, ultimately, 15 prominent personnel were sitting in the back (not exactly enjoying themselves in such weather, it should be added). A glance at Sander, an approving nod, and it was understood what to do: Tank set a reciprocal course back to Saloniki. He was pleased to find that they had outrun the storm after only a short time.

Something began rattling as the plane landed in Saloniki and the Saarland had problems taxiing. An inspection revealed that the retraction cylinder for the tailwheel had become plugged with sand from the Egyptian airfield and the extreme rear fuselage section had been damaged. Continuing the flight was out of the question.

After weathering the excitement of the past few hours all the guests were soon sleeping soundly in improvised hotel accommodations, and the journalists were not at all upset about their two-day enforced vacation they now had to "endure". They had material to write about - not only the powerful forces of the storm, but also what an aircraft was able to withstand.

Two days later Fw 200 V2 D-AETA "Westfalen", just acquired by Lufthansa, landed in Saloniki with Lufthansa captain Graf Schack at the controls, bringing with it replacement parts for the "Saarland". It picked up the happy group of journalists and brought them back to Berlin safe and sound. Tank soon followed with Sander and the remaining crew following repairs to the "Saarland".

Despite the difficulties, the "Saarland" had nevertheless flown 3155 km in ten hours and 21 minutes for an average speed of 304.83 km/h - a notable feat for the time indeed!

Berlin-New York and Back Record Flight

At the same time, preparations continued apace for the next flight: "world record across the Atlantic". Fw 200 V1 was kitted out with auxiliary fuel tanks enabling it to cover distances of 6000 kilometers. As mentioned earlier, in place of its D-AERE registration it now carried a new code of D-ACON, under which the machine would soon become world famous. Officially, Lufthansa was responsible for the flight and provided the crew, so that Tank, to his great disappointment, was not able to participate in the flight. Instead, he flew his "Weihe" D-ALEX to Berlin-Staaken to wish the crew good luck on their flight to New York.

Following careful preparations the modified Fw 200 Condor, V1 D-ACON, lifted into the air from Staaken's runway after a long takeoff run at 20:05 hrs CET on 10 August 1938. At the controls sat Lufthansa's own Dipl.-Ing. Flugkapitän Alfred Henke; his copilot was *Hauptmann* Rudolf Freiherr von Moreau, who at the outbreak of the Spanish Civil War had ferried the Moroccan troops from Africa to Spain with the aid of a Ju 52/3m *Geschwader*. The engineer was Paul Dierberg and Lufthansa had selected the experienced Walter Kober as the radio operator. The Fw 200 landed safely at 20:41 CET on 11 August 1938 at New York's Floyd Bennett Field after covering 6371 kilometers in 24 hours, 36 minutes and 12 seconds. The average speed was 255.49 km/h. With these figures, the Condor established a new FAI-recognized world's record for long-range flights.

Fw 200 V1 D-ACON following its conversion to a long-range aircraft, shortly before its record-breaking Atlantic flight.

Fw 200 V2 D-AETA "Westfalen" was put into passenger service shortly after being built, while its V1 sister set records flying over the Atlantic.

German aviation pioneers and aircraft set milestones for today's Atlantic flights with the first east-west crossing in 1928 by Hermann Köhl, Freiherr von Hünefeld and Major Fitzmaurice in a Junkers W33 and now, ten years later, with the Condor's successful crossing of the Atlantic.

Two days later, on 13 August 1938, the Condor set out on its return journey from New York at 14:06 CET, landing safely in Berlin-Tempelhof after a flight of 6371.7 kilometers lasting 19 hours, 55 minutes and 1 second at an average speed of 320.92, where the crew was greeted with a triumphal reception.

For Tank, the successful crossing of the Atlantic in a plane which he had designed and flown in twelve months was the highpoint of his creativity as a designer and test pilot. It was what he had dreamed of: technical advancement uniting people through peaceful application of aviation. He could hardly have imagined that he would be so successful. To be sure, from a technical standpoint he found it interesting to build military aircraft, but these were to fulfill contracts which were often poorly conceived and made little sense, linked to a constant to and fro, conflicts over powerplants, armament, range and speed. The Condor, however, was a masterpiece, paving the way for aviation development over the next ten years. It bore fruit even after the war, although these benefits were to be reaped by people other than the Germans.

Record Flight Berlin-Tokyo

Three and a half months later, on 28 November 1938 at 15:55 CET, D-ACON left Berlin-Tempelhof for a four-stage flight to Tokyo. The same team crewed the plane on this flight as well, although they were joined by engineer Georg Kohne of Focke-Wulf and sales director Heinz Junge as passenger. They overflew the control line at Tokyo's Tachikawa airport at 14:13 CET on 30 November and made a safe landing. Yet again, the FAI would report another world record. The three stopover points on the journey were Bara, Karachi and Hanoi. The 13844 km route was covered in 46 hours, 18 minutes and 19 seconds, at an average speed of 192.308 km/h; this included time on the ground. Showing an interest in the Condor, the Japanese airline Nippon Koku Yuso Kabushiki Kaisha had provided the impetus for the flight to Tokyo and subsequently placed a purchase contract for five Fw 200B models. The Imperial Japanese Navy contracted for a sixth machine configured as a reconnaissance platform.

Due to a basic operator error D-ACON was forced to ditch in Manila Bay in November of 1938 while on the return trip from Tokyo to Berlin. This was a premier test of the aircraft's high quality; no one on board even had his hair rumpled and the machine itself floated like a boat.

Data and Performance Figures for Civil Variants of the Fw 200 Condor

Manufacturer		Focke-Wulf					
Type		Fw 200 V-1 D-AERE	Fw 200 F-1 D-ACON	Fw 200 V-2 D-AETA	Fw 200A-0[1]	Fw 200B-1	Fw 200B-2
Powerplant		Pratt & Whitney Hornet S1E-G[1]	BMW 132L[6]	BMW 132G[9,10]	BMW 132L	BMW 132Dc[13]	BMW 132H-1[18]
Performance	kW	4x559=2236	4x588=2352	4x529=2116	4x588=2352	4x625=2500	4x735=2940
	hp	4x760=3040	4x800=3200	4x720=2880	4x800=3200	4x850=3400[14]	4x1000=4000
Crew(+passengers)		4+26	4+6	4+26	4+26	4+16	4+26
Length	m	23.85	23.85	23.85	23.85	23.85	23.85
Height	m	6.00	6.00	6.00	6.00	6.00	6.00
Wingspan	m	32.84[2]	32.84	32.84	32.84	32.84	32.84
Wing area	m[2]	118.00[3]	118.00	118.00	118.00	118.00	118.00
Aspect ratio		9.14	9.14	9.14	9.14	9.14	9.14
Weight, empty	kg	9200	8800	9200	10925	11300	11300
Fuel	kg	1800[4]	11500[7]	1800	2600	3700	2800
Oil	kg	200	450	200	280	280	280
Crew	kg	320	320	320	320	320	320
Load	kg	2480	150	2480	2875[12]	1400	2800
Max. permissible load	kg	4800	12420	4800	6075	5700	6200
Takeoff weight	kg	14000	21220	14000	17000	17000	17500
Wing loading	kg/m[2]	118.64	179.83	118.64	144.07	144.07	148.31
Weight/power ratio	kg/kW	6.26	9.02	6.62	7.23	6.80	5.95
	kg/hp	4.61	6.63	4.86	5.31	5.00	4.38
	kW/m[2]	18.95	19.93	17.93	19.93	21.19	24.92
	hp/m[2]	25.76	27.12	24.41	27.12	28.81	33.90
Max. speed	km/h	375	310[8]	350	340	418[15]	405[19]
@ altitude	m	0	0	0	0	2600	1100
Cruise speed	km/h	355	280	320	325	376	365
@ altitude	m	1000	1000	1000	1000	3000	3000
Rate of climb	m/s	7.2[5]	3.0	6.0	6.0	6.2[16]	7.37[20]
Service ceiling	m	6100	3000	6000	6000	7400[17]	7200[21]
Range	km	1250	6500	1250	1700	2000	1700
Max. flight time	hrs	4.00	25.00	4.00	5.40	5.35	4.10
Takeoff run	m	400	1200	400	420	400	420
Takeoff run to 20 m	m	600	1600	600	600	600	630
Landing speed	km/h	105	100	105	110	118	118
Max. permissible load as % of takeoff weight		34	59	34	36	34	35
Payload as % of takeoff weight		18	1	18	17	8	16
Built		1937	1937	1937	1938	1939	1939

[1]**Pratt & Whitney Hornet S-1 E-G**
Performance and Speed

Performance	kW/hp	559/760	386/525
Speed	rpm	2250	2000

Gearing ratio airscrew: 0.66
Compression ratio: 6.5:1
Charger: 10:1

87 octane; weight 486 kg
Aircraft fitted with the Hornet S-1 E-G were:
Fw 200V-1   D-AERE
Fw 200A-0   PP-CBJ Arumani
Fw 200A-0   PP-CBI Abaitara
[2]Initial wingspan was 32.97
[3]Initial wing area was 120 m[2]

On the return journey, Henke ditched D-ACON in the marshy waters of Manila Bay, the Phillippines, when two engines on one wing shut down as a result of both pilot error and an error in judgement when switching from one fuel tank to another. No one on board had even a hair knocked out of place. The smooth water landing spoke for the quality of the aircraft.

On the day of the mishap, Tank was visiting the Paris Aero Salon and was strolling through the halls gathering the latest information. Suddenly, an acquaintance patted him on the shoulder and asked in a surprised tone why Tank was peacefully wandering about while his Condor lay in the waters of Manila Bay.

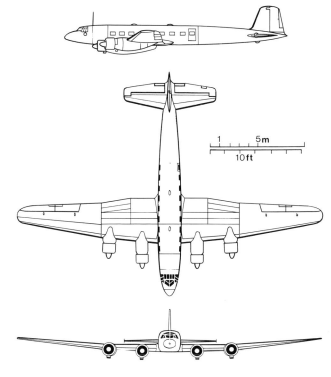

Fw 200 Condor V1.

[4]2520 kg theoretical capacity
[5]2.5 min to 1000 m
5.5 min to 2000 m
9.3 min to 3000 m
14.3 min to 4000 m
[6]D-ACON V-1 was converted to a long-range airplane from D-AERE V-1 BMW 132L engine, record-breaking Atlantic flight
See table for performance and fuel consumption at sea level
Aircraft fitted with BMW 132L were:
Fw 200A-0 D-ARHW Friesland DLH(V-7)
Fw 200A-0 D-ACVH Grenzmark DLH(V-10)
Fw 200V-1 D-ACON record-breaking Atlantic airplane
[7]Tanks for an estimated 10000 kg of fuel were located in the fuselage; the fuel was constantly being pumped into the wing center section tanks
[8]Estimated data, since this is an overloaded configuration
[9]**BMW 132G**
See table for performance and fuel consumption
[10]**Aircraft fitted with BMW 132G were:**
Fw 200V-2 D-AETA Westfalen DLH
Fw 200V-3 D-ARHU Ostmark RLM, D-2600, WL-2600, 26-00 Immelmann III, Führer's aircraft
Fw 200A-0(V-4) D-ADHR Saarland DLH
Fw 200A-0(V-5) D-AMHC Nordmark DLH
Fw 200KA-1 OY-DAM Dania DDL
Fw 200KA-1 OY-DEM Jutlandia DDL
[11]Engine for the Fw 200, Ar 197, Ju 52/3m, 87 octane, B-4 fuel

[12]**Weight Distribution:**

26 passengers with luggage	2600 kg
water	35 kg
mail	240 kg
	2875 kg

[13]With three-blade variable pitch airscrew running at constant rate rpm
[14]**BMW 132Dc**
turbocharger 1:9.15, blower centrifuge 250 mm °, dry weight 525 kg, B4 fuel, 87 octane; see table for data
Aircraft fitted with the BMW 132Dc
Fw 200B-1 D-ACWG Holstein DLH(V-11)
[15]376 km/h at sea level; all figures for average flying weight of 15500 kg
[16]8.1 min to 3000 m
[17]Ceiling with three engines was 5600 m
Ceiling with two engines was 3000 m
[18]**BMW 132H:**
turbocharger 1:7.87, blower centrifuge 250 mm °, dry weight 525 kg, 100 octane on takeoff, 87 octane in flight; turbocharger with low-blower ratio blower for takeoff; see table for data
Aircraft fitted with the BMW 132H were:
Fw 200B-2 D-ASHH Hessen DLH(V-12)
Fw 200B-2 D-AMHL Pommern DLH
Fw 200B-2 D-ASVX Thüringen DLH
Fw 200B-2 D-ABOD Kurmark DLH(V-10 CB-FB WL)
[19]385 km/h at sea level
[20]7.6 min to 3000 m
[21]5400 m with three engines
2400 m with two engines

Fw 200 Condor Civil Variant Registrations

Fw 200V-1	Fw 200V-1 modified	Fw 200V-2	Fw 200V-3	Fw 200A-0 add'l	Fw 200A-0	Fw 200 KA-1	Fw 200 B-1* D-2
D-AERE Brandenburg DLH Pratt&Whitney Hornet S-1 E-G	D-ACON DLH/RLM record-setting aircraft BMW 132L	D-AETA Westfalen DLH BMW 132G	D-ARHU Ostmark RLM D-2600 WL-2600 26-00 Immelmann III BMW 132G *Werknummer* 3099	D-ADHR Saarland DLH(V-4) BMW 132G *Werknummer* 2893 D-AMHC Nordmark DLH (V-5) BMW 132G *Werknummer* 2895 D-ACVH Grenzmark RLM(V-6) BMW 132L *Werknummer* 3098 D-ARHW Friesland DLH(V-7) BMW 132L *Werknummer* 2994	D-ASBK Holstein DLH BMW 132Dc *Werknummer* 2995 delivered to Condor in 1939 as PP-CBJ Arumani SC Condor D-AMHL later repaired following accident on 4/27/39 as D-AXFO DLH Pommern BMW 132H *Werknummer* 2996 delivered to Condor in 1939 as PP-CBI Abaitara SC Condor D-ABOD Kurmark DLH BMW 132H *Werknummer* 3324 CB+FB	OY-DAM Dania DDL BMW 132G, later G-AGAY BOAC Dx 177 RAF *Werknummer* 2894 OY-DEM Jutlandia DDL BMW 132G *Werknummer* 2993	D-ASHH Hessen DLH Fw 200B-1 BMW 132Dc *Werknummer* 0009 D- ACWG** Holstein DLH *Werknummer* 0001 Fw 200B-1 D-ASVX Thüringen DLH Fw 200D-2 BMW 132H *Werknummer* 0021 D-AMHL Pommern DLH *Werknummer* 0020 Fw 200D-2
Quantity: 1	1	1		7	2		4

Total: 16 civil

* B- and D-series had 2x2 wheels, larger fuel tank capacity, greater takeoff weight.
** Lufthansa took over the names Holstein and Pommern after these aircraft were delivered to South America and applied them to later B-1 and D-2 series aircraft.

A few weeks later the Condor's crew sat before him. It was probably the loudest tirade Tank had ever given. He was simply beside himself, because this water landing - as the crew so succinctly put it - had been completely unnecessary and was due to purely human error. Tank accused Henke of not ever having practiced flying with only two engines on one side despite Tank's urgent recommendations to do so. Thus he had been entirely helpless when two engines had died due to a blatant fuel switching error. Everything he had done was backwards. Had Henke switched to the takeoff tanks, the engines would have come back to life. Instead Henke, apparently believing the plane could not remain airworthy on just two engines, extended the flaps. And instead of lifting the "dead" wing and flying a bit into the side with the running engines, he increased the drag by dropping the flaps. Why hadn't the engineer from Lufthansa switched to the full starboard tanks when the port tanks were empty? Why was there even a second engineer from Focke-Wulf on board? With two men, one of them surely must have noticed that a grave error had been committed.

Following this dressing down, Henke flew with Tank in a Condor which had been made ready with a 14 ton takeoff weight; its total weight was far heavier than D-ACON when it had ditched in Manila. Tank climbed to 2000 meters,

Fw 200 Condor Engines

Engine Type / #cylinders	length (mm) / stroke	height (mm) / bore (mm)	width (mm)	volume (ltrs)	comp-ression	dry weight (kg) installed	takeoff rpm / kW / hp / (altitude in meters)	max cruise / kg/kW / kW / hp / (altitude in meters)	weight/performance ratio / g/hp/hr / kg/hp / (mm)	consumption rate / cruise performance	characteristics
BMW 132L / 9	1252 / 155.5	1380 / 162	1380	27.72	6.5	460	0 / 2230 / 588 / 800	0 / 2000 / 456 / 620	0.78 / 0.58	250	four- stroke, air- cooled radial
BMW 132Dc / 9	1411 / 155.5	1380 / 162	1380	27.72	6.5	525	0 / 2450 / 625 / 850	0 / 2100 / 460 / 625	0.84 / 0.62	240	ditto
BMW 132G / 9	1252 / 155.5	1380 / 162	1380	27.72	6.6	450	0 / 2050 / 529 / 720	0 / 1910 / 422 / 575	0.86 / 0.63	250	
BMW 132H-1 / 9	1411 / 155.5	1380 / 162	1380	27.72	6.5	525	0 / 2550 / 735 / 1000	0 / 2090 / 508 / 690	0.72 / 0.53	230	ditto
Bramo 323R / 9	1700 / 154	1388 / 160	1388	26.82	6.4	580 / 850	0 / 2500 / 735 / 1000	5000 / 2100 / 485 / 660	0.74 / 0.55	210	two- stage char- ger + fuel injection

shut down the two port engines, retrimmed the machine, pulled the wing with the silent engines a bit higher and demonstrated to Lufthansa's chief pilot that the plane could indeed maintain level flight in such a condition. He insisted on turning the controls over to Henke, who found that he could hold the machine level as easily as had Tank. "You've got to fly with your heart and your head, not just with brute strength", swore Tank. At the time of writing this book, Tank was still bitter about the disconcerted air of the crew, who had not familiarized themselves enough with the plane and whose negligence caused so much damage to the reputation of the Condor and the company. Henke was killed in 1940 in another Condor airplane when, in a senseless act, he dove on an airfield and pulled up sharply just before impact, whereupon a wing broke off.

A contract totaling ten Fw 200 machines was soon forthcoming from Lufthansa; there followed two aircraft for the Syndicato Condor in South America, several for courier services with the RLM, contracts for two planes for Denmarks, a further two for Finland and the previously mentioned six planes for the Japanese. It must surely be a rare occurrence in the history of aviation when an airliner prototype is able to set transoceanic records immediately followed by contracts from Europe and abroad. This success can only be compared to that enjoyed by the Junkers F 13 and Ju 52/3m during the '20s and '30s and today's Airbus.

In all, 16 civilian variants of the Fw 200 Condor were built, varying mainly in their powerplants and weight. The two tables provide sufficient details on the various types. Aircraft of the B-series had a modified empennage with somewhat smaller control surfaces. The engine nacelles were lengthened and fitted with controllable oil cooler flaps at the base of the annular cowling. The undercarriage was also strengthened and fitted with dual wheels.

Flight over the Alps - with no Power!

On 26 November 1938 a four-engined Ju 90 V2 D-AIVI crashed on takeoff in Bathurst on the West African Atlantic coast. It had been scheduled to fly an evaluation and calibration flight with Flugkapi*tän* Untucht, one of Lufthansa's best pilots, at the controls. Twelve people were killed in the crash, including the entire crew. Investigation subsequently revealed that the high temperatures had apparently caused the fuel to boil within the Ju 90's fuel lines, vaporizing it and causing the engines to either lose power or shut down completely on takeoff.

Tank wanted to avoid similar problems and decided to check the Condor's suitability for tropical climates one more time and, if needed, make any precautionary changes.

On 3 April 1939 Tank took off from Bremen in Fw 200 "Pommern" for hot climate trials in Gadames, a small desert airstrip 500 km south of Tripoli. His best designers were on board as passengers, those who had worked on the Fw 200 and played a major role in the design's success.

The weather on takeoff was miserable. 50 meter cloud base and danger of icing! Yet Tank remained unflustered as he pushed the throttle levers forward and slowly gained altitude in the fully tanked machine. After about two and a half hours' flight time, radio bearings showed that he was over the Alpine foothills. Due to the inclement weather, Tank wanted to make sure he would safely clear the Alps and therefore gradually climbed to 5000 meters. It became cold and most of the passengers drifted off to sleep; the Fw 200 was not yet fitted with a pressurized crew compartment and the high altitude made a person tired easily. Only the crew had oxygen masks. One of the passengers, Obe*ringenieur* Willi Kaether, remained alert. It was his job to carry out fuel consumption testing during the long flight. For this purpose, a special instrumentation box had been fitted into his work station with special switches through which ran all the fuel lines to the engines.

Suddenly, as Tank espied the Großglockner's summit through a break in the clouds, there was a slight bump, the rpm indicators swung wildly and dropped to zero, and all four engines sputtered and died. Tank's blood almost froze in his veins. No ground in sight and even now the Condor's nose threatened to lead the plane into a fatal glide into the mountainside. In Manila, at least Henke had visibility and water beneath him, not to mention two running engines. Tank, however, quickly mastered the situation. Thinking quickly, he switched over to the four takeoff tanks, the engines sprang back into life and the rpms slowly began to climb. But the takeoff tanks only carried a few minutes' worth of fuel. The Condor lifted its snout and leveled off, a glimmer of hope. The question pounded through Tank's skull

... what could be the problem? The entire fuel feed system must have cut out. His eyes wandered over to the tank switches next to the engineer, who called out the position of the switches as if he were reading from a checklist. Tank bellowed: "Get back and see what Kaether is doing! The engines can go out at any moment!" The engineer disappeared. Tank stayed at the controls, almost at his wits' end as he tried analyzing what could be causing the loss of fuel feed. If necessary, would he be able to make the Italian Alpine foothills? No, it was still too far away. Why, when all the switches were correctly set, did all four engines cut out simultaneously? He could not find an explanation. Already, it seemed to him that the rpm gauges were bouncing again; his eyes became transfixed by the needles. The seconds since the engineer had gone became tortuous minutes for him. Now, though, the engineer returned, his face relaxed, and with a smile he shouted into Tank's ear: "You can turn the takeoff tanks off again. Kaether became airsick and shut off the three-way switch on his instrumentation box. I turned it back on. Everything's o.k."

Tank swallowed and breathed a sigh of relief, cautiously closed the first fuel cock for the takeoff tank, and in fact the motor continued running. The second, third and fourth switches were shut off. All engines remained running smoothly at cruise setting. He could relax again. Soon the clouds parted and Tank could see the Po Valley far off in the distance. But that was still 50 km away, too far to have made it without power.

He then had Kaether come up to the cockpit. The poor man, one of his best and most reliable workers, received a tongue lashing like he'd never been given before. But in reality, all members of the crew shared in the blame. Kaether could not have known that Tank would be flying so high, and like the rest of the crew an oxygen mask should have been given to an engineer working on such important equipment from the outset of the flight.

Looping in the Fw 200

On 27 April 1939, Lufthansa reported an accident of a Condor piloted by Graf Schack: "Fw 200 Pommern, 60 damage to airframe, 40 percent crew", although in reality nothing had happened to the crew at all. As the "Pommern" had to be delivered on time to the Condor syndicate in South America, it had been fitted with the wings of the "Kurmark" then under construction and was flown to South America in June of 1939, before the breakout of World War II. Schack had flown the Condor from the hangars in Hamburg to Berlin-Staaken. Nobody had told him about the changes to the flaps on this aircraft mentioned earlier, an oversight which led to the landing accident.

One day, as Flug*kapitän* Graf Schack was bringing an Fw 200 Condor to Bremen for an overhaul, by way of announcing his arrival he buzzed the airfield and began making a loop with the four-engined giant at low altitude. *Flugbaumeister* Hans Sander was standing in front of one of the airfield's hangars at that moment, and could not believe what he was seeing. After pulling out at an altitude of about 50 meters, Schack screamed across the airfield, pulled up, lowered the gear and made a sharp turn onto final approach. Lowering the flaps, he dropped onto the runway as if the machine had been a sportplane. "Hopefully the guy's practiced this before", thought Sander. The demonstration was flawless and was in no way a spontaneous and foolhardy occurrence.

The Second World War broke out in the midst of this spate of record-breaking and marketing successes at home and abroad. As a result, exports immediately ground to a halt. The only Condors delivered were the two to Denmark and the two to South America.

Fw 200C Condor as Maritime Reconnaissance Aircraft

The reconnaissance version of the Condor which had been ordered by the Japanese Navy soon caught the attention of the R*eichsluftfahrtministerium*. Although the He 177 was planned as the premier long-range maritime reconnaissance and bomber platform, it was still a long way off from reaching production maturity. Planes which had held promise for a long-range aircraft, such as the Do 19 and Ju 89, had been scrapped years before. Now, however, the *Technisches Amt* awarded Focke-Wulf a contract for a feasibility study regarding the Fw 200's suitability for conversion to an armed maritime reconnaissance aircraft which could also engage ship targets. In doing this research, the company benefited from the experience gained in working out the details for the Condor ordered by the Japanese Navy. However, the Condor's biggest handicap was and remained its light construction - the aircraft was simply not laid out for the military role.

Focke-Wulf proposed a modified B-version to the RLM, designated Fw 200C. The ministry accordingly issued a contract for a 0-series pre-production run, for which a few of the half-completed B-types were used as these could no longer be supplied to Lufthansa due to the outbreak of the war. The first four B-series machines, as they were nearly finished, were delivered after modification to the Luftwaffe as transports with the designation Fw 200C-0. A further six aircraft from the B and D series had weapons and ordnance racks fitted during their manufacture. O*berstleutnant* Edgar Petersen, who had been tasked by the Luftwaffe's general staff to begin forming a squadron of long-range maritime recon aircraft for training crews, took delivery of these six aircraft.

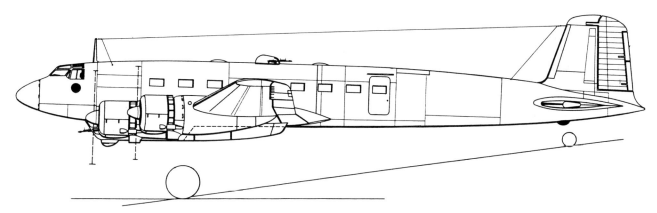

Fw 200 V10 B-2, originally built for Lufthansa, but with the outbreak of the war it was manufactured as an armed transport and delivered to the Luftwaffe.

Fw 200 C-1 Condor. A long-range reconnaissance platform was born from the airliner design.

Pre-flight checks for an Fw 200 C-2 Condor belonging to the Seeluftstreitkräfte.

In addition to these first military C-1 variants (Werknummer 0003-0008 and 0011-0014), the unit was brought up to strength by an additional delivery of six machines. A further six Fw 200s, Werknummer 0015-0018 and 0022-0024, followed as Fw 200C-2s. In early 1940 Petersen's unit was formally designated as the first *Staffel* of *Kampfgeschwader* 40. It was initially pressed into service in the transport role during the Norwegian campaign and tasked with supplying the German forces trapped in Narvik. In addition, it carried out reconnaissance flights over the North Atlantic, tracking British shipping convoys. In June of 1940 the unit was brought up to *Gruppe* strength and transferred to Bordeaux-Mérignac. By February 1941 I/KG 40 had sunk no less than 363000 tons of shipping. Soon, however, it became obvious that the Fw 200C-1 and C-2 were, from a structural standpoint, not up to the task of

flying for hours at a time at low levels and the strain of military operations. There was considerable down time due to breaks and tears in the airframe.

Following the C-2 in 1941, the C-3 (beginning with Werknummer 0025 - see table "Fw 200C through F Type Overview") was structurally reinforced and better armed accordingly. To offset the weight increase, this version was given the BMW Bramo 323R-2 delivering 735 kW/1000 hp, although with MW 50 injection it could attain 882 kW/ 1200 hp on takeoff.

With the C-3, Focke-Wulf came quite close to fulfilling the Luftwaffe's requirements for an aircraft with 14-15 hours' endurance and a range of 4500 km, adequate armament, the ability to carry mines and bombs for attacking ships as well as a radio system for communicating with submarines. The aircraft were produced at the Cottbus works; Blohm & Voss later took over production.

Fw 200 C-3/U2 long-range recon plane (1941).

From Bordeaux, the long-range machines flew out over the Atlantic, eastward past Ireland and then northward towards the southern tip of Greenland, recovering at the Norwegian airfields at Stavanger-Sola and Trondheim. After refueling, they returned via the same route. Even today, such flights put a strain on the Breguet Atlantik, one of the most modern maritime reconnaissance platforms in NATO's inventory.

The operations of I/KG 40 became much riskier when the enemy convoys began carrying catapult-launched fighters on their civilian ships. In August 1941 the first Condor was lost, shot down by fighters. In late 1941 a carrier even appeared on the scene for protecting the convoys. The Ge*schwader* suffered even more serious losses at the hands of the Grumman Wildcat fighters based on this aircraft carrier.

In the winter of 1943 I/KG 40 - rising to the occassion - reverted back to its transport role for supplying the beleaguered troops caught inside Stalingrad. But the valuable machines were not as well suited to the merciless ravages of the winter war as the robust Ju 52/3m and the Condor planes were therefore soon pulled out of Russia and transferred to Bordeaux-Mérignac and Trondheim.

Trials were carried out using the Fw 200C-6 for attacking ships with the aid of flying bombs such as the Henschel Hs 293. For this role the aircraft were fitted with special surface search radars like the FuG 203 Kehl III. Eventually, however, enemy superiority led to the Ge*schwader* ceasing operations in 1944.

Fw 200C-3 Specifications

Based on the identification sheet for type Fw 200C-3 with Bramo 323R-2 engines, eval.-no. 480, Berlin 1941:

Aside from the long range and high military payload, the most important feature of military versions of the Fw 200 was an effective defensive armament.

The A-*Stand* (A-station) above the cockpit (see drawing and caption) was fitted out with an MG 15 with 1125 rounds in a D-30 rotating turret beneath a 360° traversing plexiglas canopy (known as an LLG *Linsenlafette*). Later, the MG 131 with 1000 rounds was used from the C-3/U6 on, and the MG 151 was fitted to the C-3/U5 onward as well. Details of these weapons can be found in the table "Machine Guns and Machine Cannons Used in Focke-Wulf Aircraft" (page 126).

Fw 200C-4 with added armament, year of service 1942.

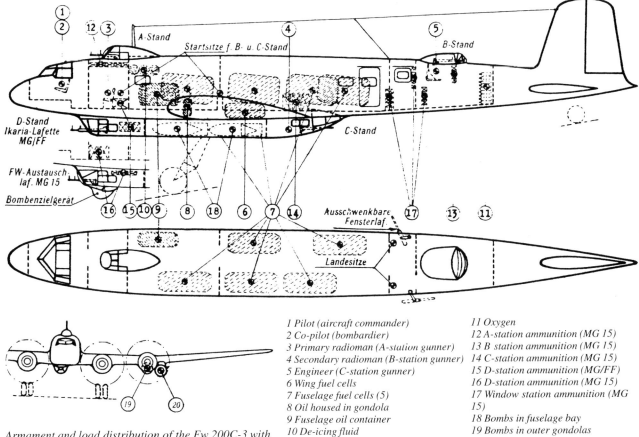

Armament and load distribution of the Fw 200C-3 with four Bramo 323R-2 engines.

1 Pilot (aircraft commander)
2 Co-pilot (bombardier)
3 Primary radioman (A-station gunner)
4 Secondary radioman (B-station gunner)
5 Engineer (C-station gunner)
6 Wing fuel cells
7 Fuselage fuel cells (5)
8 Oil housed in gondola
9 Fuselage oil container
10 De-icing fluid
11 Oxygen
12 A-station ammunition (MG 15)
13 B station ammunition (MG 15)
14 C-station ammunition (MG 15)
15 D-station ammunition (MG/FF)
16 D-station ammunition (MG 15)
17 Window station ammunition (MG 15)
18 Bombs in fuselage bay
19 Bombs in outer gondolas
20 Bombs on outer wing stations

B-Stand: MG 15 in a D-30 turret with 1125 rounds. From version C-3/U4 onward MG 131 with 1000 rounds in a D-30 turret.

C-Stand: MG 15 in a KL 15 ball mount with 1125 rounds. Version C-4/U1 onward also initially fitted with MG 131 in a KL 15 or WL 131 mount.

D-Stand: Ikaria L-FF mount with MG FF and 300 rounds; could be exchanged for LLG-Fw mount (*Linsenlafette*) and MG 15 with 1125 rounds. MG 151 first used with C-3/U4 variant, version C-3/U9 *Linsenlafette* with MG 15 and for C-5/U2 with MG 131. Each fuselage side station was armed with a flex-mounted MG 15 with 1500 rounds. Furthermore, an extra MG 15 and three machine pistols with 450 rounds were also on board.

Bombs were carried in the fuselage, on the outer engine nacelles and under the outer wing sections. The depth

charge mines (LMB + LMA), weighing up to 4000 kg, were suspended beneath the outer wings. Naturally, the aircraft's range depended on the load carried. The maximum bomb load with full tanks (6470 kg or 8986 liters without auxiliary tanks) was 1230 kg and the highest ordnance load possible was 5400 kg.

Sighting mechanisms were the GV 219d was used in the Ikaria mount, the Lotfe (*Lotfernrohr*) 7b and 7c and later the improved Lotfe 7d (from the Fw 200C-3/U4 on) plus the BZG 2L and the Revi C/12 in the cockpit for low-level attacks.

Planned photographic equipment included the RB 50/30 and RB 20/30 auto cameras and the 12.5/7x9 handheld camera.

Details of the armament and radio navigation equipment can be found listed in the table "Fw 200C through F Type Overview" (see pages 218-221).

The technical developmental progress of this interesting aircraft can clearly be seen from the table, which provides information on advances with regard to load and range associated with individual versions. All told, 20 civil versions were built and a further 263 aircraft went to the Luftwaffe.

Fw 200F Ultra-Long-Range Reconnaissance Aircraft

In mid 1943 the RLM requested that Focke-Wulf explore the possibility of increasing the range of the Fw 200C to its very limits. It was recommended that fuel be carried in the wings and fuselage, avoiding externally carried auxiliary tanks. In order to save weight, it was suggested that the forward and aft ventral gunner's stations in the fuselage be dispensed with. The increase in fuel capacity was to be linked with minimal conversion effort so that the field units might be able to carry out the work themselves if needed.

The company came to the conclusion that these requirements could only be met by a major increase in the weight. In view of the fact that this was to be a stopgap measure, authorization was given to increase the maximum allowable takeoff weight up to 25260 kg, for which it was recommended that takeoff with the Bramo 323R-2 either be accomplished using water-methanol injection or with longer takeoff runs·from hardened surface runways.

After reviewing seven different designs, Focke-Wulf recommended the Fw 200F proposal to the Mini*sterium*. This design called for the fuel load of an Fw 200C-6 to be raised by some 2000 kg/3300 liters, from 6765 kg/8600 liters to 8795 kg/11900 liters, increasing the range to 6900 kilometers. The flying weight would have increased to 25260 kg as a result. The previous five 1100 liter fuselage

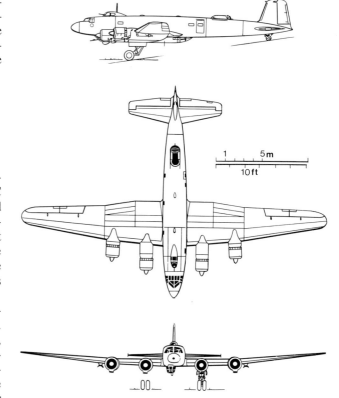

Fw 200C-2 Condor

[1]Long-range recon variant payload distribution:		
ammunition and weapons	kg	954
equipment	kg	1207
safety equipment	kg	70
bombs	kg	500
Total	kg	2731

[2]At 22.7 metric tons takeoff weight
6.25 m/sec at 17.6 tons
At 22 tons:
14 min to 3 km altitude
25 min to 4 km altitude
47 min to 6.5 km altitude
[3]8000 m with 17.6 tons takeoff weight

[4]Bomber payload		
ammunition and weapons	kg	954
equipment	kg	1209
safety equipment	kg	70
bombs	kg	4432
Total	kg	6665

[5]Configured as strategic reconnaissance platform
[6]With water-methanol injection and 4x882 kW(4x1200 hp) output of the Bramo 323R-2
[7]It is uncertain whether the Fw 200F was built as conversion was possible by field units

Fw 200 Military Variants

Manufacturer		Focke-Wulf				
Type		Fw 200 C-2 long-range recon	Fw 200 C-2 bomber	Fw 200 C-3/U4[5] *Werknummer* 0070	Fw 200 C-6 long-range recon	Fw 200F strategic recon
Powerplant		BMW 132H-1	BMW 132H-1	Bramo 323 R-2	Bramo 323 R-2	Bramo 323 R-2
Performance	kW	4x735=2940	4x735=2940	4x735=2940	4x735=2940	4x735=2940
	hp	4x1000=4000	4x1000=4000	4x1000=4000	4x1000=4000	4x1000=4000
Crew		7	7	7	7	7
Length	m	23.85	23.85	23.85	23.85	23.85
Height	m	6.00	6.00	6.00	6.00	6.00
Wingspan	m	32.84	32.84	32.84	32.84	32.84
Wing area	m²	118.00	118.00	118.00	118.00	118.00
Aspect ratio		9.14	9.14	9.14	9.14	9.14
Weight, empty	kg	12950	12950	13080	13225	13447
Fuel	kg	5948	2214	5437	6765	8795
Oil	kg	511	311	513	510	600
Crew	kg	560	560	560	560	560
Load	kg	2731[1]	6665[4]	3110	1765	1858
Max. permissible load	kg	9750	9750	9620	9601	11813[5]
Takeoff weight	kg	22700	22700	22700	22826	25260
Wing loading	kg/m²	192.37	192.37	192.37	193.44	214.07
Weight/power ratio	kg/kW	7.72	7.72	7.72	7.76	8.59
	kg/hp	5.68	5.68	5.68	5.71	6.32
	kW/m²	24.92	24.92	24.92	24.91	24.92
	hp/m²	33.90	33.90	33.90	33.89	33.90
Max. speed	km/h	378	378	380	380	360
@ altitude	m	1600	1600	5000	5000	5000
Cruise speed	km/h	306	320	325	325	300
@ altitude	m	4000	4000	5000	5000	4000
Rate of climb	m/s	4.10[2]	4.10[2]	4.10[2]	4.10[2]	3.50[2]
Service ceiling	m	6600[3]	6600[3]	6600[3]	6600[3]	6000[3]
Range	km	4500	1570	4500	5500	6900
Max. flight time	hrs	14.70	5.00	14.50	17.00	23.00
Takeoff run	m	900	900	900	900	900[6]
Takeoff run to 20 m	m	1450	1450	1450	1450	1450[6]
Landing speed	km/h	130	130	130	130	130
Max. permissible load as % of takeoff weight		43	43	42	42	47
Payload as % of takeoff weight		12	29	13	7	7
Built		1940	1940	1941	1943	1944[7]

Fw 200C through F Type Overview

Built	1939	1939/40	1940	1940	1940	1941	1941
Variant	Fw 200B-1 V-10	V-11		V-12	V-13		strategic recon
Series designator	Rowehl recon	C-1	C-1	C-2	C-3	C-3/U1	C-3U2
Werknummern	0001-0024	0002	0003-0008 0011-0014	0015-0018 0022-0024	0025-0054 0056-0063 0065-0069	0052 DE+OG	0055
Armament	*B-stand:* D 30 with MG 15 *D-stand:* LLB with MG 15	*A-stand:* LLG with MG 15 *B-stand:* D 30 with MG 15 *C-stand:* KL 15 with MG 15 *D-stand:* LLB with MG 15 or L- FF with MG FF					
Changes over predecessor			gondola with MG 15, replace- ment MG 15		*A- stand:* D-30 with MG 15		
Equipment	Telefunken S 427/1/36		FuG 10, Peil G V, Fu Bl. 1				7452 kg (10350 ltrs) fuel instead of 5800 kg; 6400 km range
Features	BMW 132H-1 engine, armed recon	armed transport		shortened nacelles, ETC racks swapped for PVC single- bomb racks, bomb load in- creased to 4900 kg; weapons tested in Rechlin	Bramo 323R-2 initial then standard fitted, could be flown with crew of just 6	Prototype for LT aerial tor- pedo system usage. Con- version not completed	Prototype for non- armored fuel tanks in gondola and outer nacelles; with or without weapons

1941	1941	1941	1941	1941	1941	1942 government transport bombs + torpedoes	1942 long-range recon with
C-3/U3	C-3/U4	C-3/U5	C-3/U6	C-3/U7	C-3/U8	C-3/U9	C-4
0064	0070-0094	0095	none given (could be modified by field units)	planned conversion	may have been converted from Werknummer 0070 by field unit	0099	0096-0098, 0100-0113, 0115-0136, 0139-0190, 0194-0225, 0229, 0231-0234
	B-stand: D 30 with MG 131 *D-stand:* L151/1 mount with MG 151 *A-stand:* DL 15 with MG 15	*A-stand:* HG 15 with MG 151 *B-stand:* D 30 with MG 131	*A-stand:* DL 15 with MG 131		*D-stand* dropped	*D-stand:* bubble-mount with MG 15; no window gun ports *A-stand:* D 30 with MG 131	*D-stand:* L151/1 mount with MG 151 *A-stand:* HD 151 with MG 151, gondola with MG 15
	FuG 10, Peil G V, Fu Bl. 1, FuG 25 short-wave transmitter					FuG 10, Peil G V, Fu Bl. 1, FuG 25 170 transmitter system	FuG 10, Peil G V, Fu Bl. 1, FuG 25 FuG 27, FuG 25
Atlas-Echolot installed in outer wing. With or without ordnance	armored fuel tanks in gondola, more weapons; engine nacelle tanks removed		DL 15 with MG 131 in *A-stand.* Interim solution for HD 151. Armored fuel tanks. 1 gondola tank removed.	converted for testing Kehl III, but apparently not completed	DL 15 MG 131 in *A-stand;* two armored fuel tanks in gondola. Otherwise as C-3/U6	armed gov't transport. Interior modified from C-3/U5	increased armament through modification of window ports with SL 131 socket mounts for MG 131

Fw 200C through F Type Overview

Built	1942	1942/43	1942	1942	1942	1943
Variant	armed gov't transport	armed gov't transport escort	testbed		Petersen long-range acft	long-range recon
Series designator	C-4/U1	C-4/U2	C-4	C-4/U3	C-4/U4	C-5
Werknummern	0137 CE+IB, 0176	0138 GE+IC 1942, 0181 GC+SJ 1943	0114 NT+BN, pulled from C-4 production	0130, 0172, 0174, 0175, 0177, 0178, 0180	0152, 0153	0201
Armament						
Changes over predecessor	*A-stand:* DL 15 with MG 151 *B-stand:* DL 15 with MG 131 *C-stand:* HL 15 with MG 131 and WL 131 *D-stand:* LLG with MG 15	window gun ports dropped, armament same as C-4/U1	*H-stand:* IID 141 with MG 151 *D-stand:* L151/1 with MG 151 *Window stands:* MG 131 flex-mounted		*A-stand:*DL 15 with MG 131	*A-stand:*HD 151 with MG 151 *B-stand:*D 30 with MG 131 *C-stand:* KL 15 with MG 131 *D-stand:*L151/1 with MG 151 *Window stations:* SL 131 with MG 131
Equipment	FuG 10, Peil G V, Fu Bl. 2 170 W transmitter			FuG 200 Rostock radar system		
Features	Escort acft with all-through cabin for 14 men. Shortened gondola; rocker tailwheel, Himmler's personal transport, exhibited at Farnborough in 1945	as C-4/U2	testbed for add'l armament; Kärcher heating FuNG 181, window de-icing, Allweiler pump, rocker tailwheel	fitted with Rostock	non-armored fuel system; 13 tanks in fuselage; 10 tanks in wings; FuNG 101; 5-man oxygen system with 5 hrs time; replacement tailwheel; Lorenz TO system; no gondola	add'l for *C-stands* and window stands

C-5/U1	C-5/U2	C-6	C-8	C-8/U10	F
1943 long-range recon	1943 long-range recon	1943 long-range recon	1943 long-range recon	1943 long- range recon	1943/1944 long-range recon
0221		230, 235-247	248-258, 262-268	259-261	project
			A-stand: HD 151 with MG 151 *B-stand:* DL 15/131 with MG 131 *C-stand:* KL 15 with MG 131 *D-stand:* MG 131 *Window stands:* SL 131 with MG 131		
B-stand: DL 15/131 with MG 131	*D-stand:* LG 131 with MG 131				*A- stand:* 4D 151/2 with MG 151
		FuG 10, Peil G V, Fu Bl. 1, FuG 27, FuG 25, FuG 200 Hohentwiel			
add'l armament for *B-stand*	add'l armament and increased armor	Henschel Hs 293 flying bomb with Kehl III in FuG 203			Fw 200F similar to Fw 200C-6. Fuel increased from 8600 ltrs to 11900 ltrs, range increased from 4900 km to 6600 km

Fw 200 production took place at the Focke-Wulf Cottbus works. As far as is known, 263 aircraft (including civil variants) were built

Weapon system designations for flexible/traversible weapons

D 30	Drehring 30 (pivot ring)	KL 15/1	Kegellafette 15 ball mount for single gun
DL 15	Drehringlafette 15 (pivot ring mount)	L	Lafette (mount)
HD 151	hydraulic powered pivot ring wtih MG 151	L-FF/1	mount for single FF machine cannon
HL	Hecklafette (tail turret)	LG 131	MG 131 mount
		LLG	Linsenlafette groß (large bubble mount)
		L 151/1	mount for single MG 151
		LT	Luft-Torpedo (aerial torpedo)
		SL	Sockellafette (sockel mount)
		WL 15	cylindrical mount for MG 15
		WL 131	cylindrical mount for MG 131

Fw 200C-6 with the latest radar systems designed for searching out submarines.

tanks were to have been supplemented by three additional tanks holding a total of 3300 liters of fuel. Housing the additional fuel in the fuselage center section had the advantage of not interfering with the design's center of gravity. The only other change was shifting the internal equipment, meaning that the conversion work could have easily been carried out by the field units. The airplane retained its full complement of defensive firepower. Only the forward dorsal gunner's station would have seen its large hydraulically driven HD 151/1 turret with MG 151 swapped for a smaller, more streamlined HD 151/2 turret. However, the events of the war forced these plans to be abandoned altogether.

With Tank at the Controls of the Fw 200C-3

Tank had devoted himself fully to the Fw 190 project over the last few months and had spent little time working on the Condor's metamorphosis from a transport into a heavily armed long-range patrol plane. One day, however, he had the opportunity to visit *Kampfgeschwader* 40 on the

Atlantic Coast and discuss the unit's successes as well as their concerns with the commander and his pilots.

According to the flyers, from a flying standpoint the modifications and additions had had little effect on the good handling characteristics of the machine. On the other hand, there had been problems because of the poor structural soundness of the design, for it was a known fact that the plane had not been intended for the hard military strain incurred by low level operations. As the pilots unanimously stated, the aircraft remained stable in all axes up to its maximum load and there were no restrictions on its suitability for instrument flying. In a stall, the aircraft nosed over at 160 km/h and 16.5 metric tons of weight without tipping over onto either wing, picked up speed and once it reached 160 km/h, nosed over again. With undercarriage and flaps extended, the plane did not nose over until the speed had dropped to 140 km/h. "Almost like my first Condor that I'd test flown myself", beamed Tank. "How would you like a flight in one of our Fw 200s?" asked Petersen, and Tank agreed without hesitation. "We have a machine ready, awaiting a post maintenance flight after having its outer starboard engine repaired. Would that suit the plane's designer and its test pilot?" Petersen called the hangar and ordered the machine be made ready for flight.

After a long interlude Tank again finds himself at the controls of a Condor and becomes reacquainted with the 91 levers and buttons in the cockpit. "Basically, it's the same as the old one", he thinks, "and on this flight we can even forget the switches for the military equipment." Next to the designer sits an Ob*erleutnant* as his copilot, while behind him an onboard engineer and radio operator find their seats. Tank adjusts his seat and makes sure he could move the rudder to its extremes without having to twist his body. He sets the coarse altimeter to the airfield's altitude and adjusts the fine altimeter to 0 meters. The engineer reports the machine ready for flight: "pages one through sixteen on the checklist have been checked off." Tank glances at the gauges for the elevator, rudder and aileron trim. Automatic and emergency switches are set, landing gear lever set to "extended", flap settings to "takeoff", de-icing for leading edges, propeller blades and control surfaces to "off", autopilot main switch is on and the directional arrow on the right control horn points to 0. He checks the fuel and oil reserves, starts each engine in sequence and taxis out to the runway. The Condor taxis smoothly without the need for brakes; the elevators are kept in neutral to avoid putting unnecessary pressure on the tailwheel.

Turning to the engineer, Tank asks "Is the fuel switching mechanism working o.k.? Are all the fuel feed pumps for the fuselage tanks switched on?" "Everything is switched properly and checked", confirms the engineer and copilot. Tank then brings the propeller settings to the 12 o'clock position, i.e. smallest pitch setting. "With six tons of fuel the machine taxis like a fully laden Condor ready for an Atlantic crossing", he muses. "A bit nose heavy and some lateral trim" (drifting to the right), retorts the Ob*erleutnant*, "everything's o.k."

Tank carried out a test flight from Bordeaux with an Fw 200C model.

Pilot's compartment of the Fw 200C.

Now Tank slowly gives it gas, countering the right drift with a bit of rudder. He lets the machine pick up speed and at 165 km/h pulls on the control column ever so slightly - the plane comes unstuck almost by itself. The gear is tucked in almost immediately, rudder and elevator trim is set to 0 and with 1.25 a*tas* boost pressure and 2250 rpm the machine begins climbing. Takeoff weight was 19 tons, the take-off run on the paved strip may have been 500 to 600 meters. The machine carries two-thirds of its total fuel capacity. The red control lamps light up as the main gear and tailwheel are fully retracted; the airspeed indicator registers 200 km/h. Now Tank shifts the lever controlling the flaps and sets a course for the ocean. 250 km/h is the best speed for climbing. The gauges show a rate of climb of 6 meters per second. Tank checks the oil temperature and the oil and fuel pressure for all four engines. All needles are in the green, even those for the outboard starboard engine which was the particular focus of his attention as it was the real purpose of this flight. After about three minutes they reach an altitude of 1000 meters. Tank brings the rpms to 2100 and the boost

pressure to 1.10 *atas*. The airspeed indicator gradually climbs to 310 km/h.

Now he turns back towards the city, situated at the mouth of the Garonne and its famous vineyards. He lets the outer starboard engine run at 2250 rpm and 1.25 a*tas*, trims the machine to compensate and monitors temperatures and pressures. He then slowly throttles it back and feathers the propeller. After cutting the ignition and shutting down the Bramo 323, he closes the oil cooler flaps. Again retrimming the machine, he enjoys the experience of flying so easily with three engines. After awhile he again adjusts the pro-peller pitch of the dead engine. Soon it begins windmilling; switching the ignition back on the engine resumes operat-ing smoothly - cruise rpms, temperatures and pressures are all within normal limits. "The motor is operating normally", says Tank to his copilot, who nods in agreement. Where-upon Tank heads back to the field for a landing.

On the downwind leg he bleeds off speed by pulling the nose up slightly, sets the propeller blades to their small-est inclination and at 200 km/h lowers the gear. After about

Cockpit control system of the Fw 200C-2.

1 Airspeed indicator
2 Rate-of-climb indicator
3 Turn-and-bank indicator
4 Artificial horizon
5 Coarse-fine altimeter
6 Coarse altimeter
7 Gyro compass
8 Gyro compass course indicator
9 Distance reading compass gauge
10 Gyro compass heater indicator
11 Gyro compass heater switch
12 Radio beacon gauge
13 Compass
14 Vacuum/pressure indicator for compass and autopilot
15 External air temperature gauge
16
17
18 Gyro support switch
19 Instrument lighting dimmer control
20 Booster motor emergency button
21 Booster motor emergency handle
22 Lateral trim indicator
23 Lateral trim control knob
24 Emergency lateral trim knob
25 Horizontal trim indicator
26 Horizontal trim control knob
27 Emergency horizontal trim knob
28 Aileron trim indicator
29 Safe/armed selector lever
30 Airspeed indicator gauge
31 Vacuum switch
32 Tachometer
33 Manifold pressure gauge
34 Oil temperature gauge
35 Fuel/oil pressure gauge
36 Climb/descent rate gauge
37 Air intake temperature gauge
38 Air intake temperature switch
39 RPM harmonization selector switch
40 Cylinder temperature gauge
41 Cylinder temperature switch
42 Gondola flap actuator
43 Fuselage flap actuator
44 Cruising fuel supply gauge
45 Cruising fuel supply selector switch
46 Takeoff fuel supply gauge

47 Takeoff fuel supply selector switch
48 Oil supply gauge
49 Oil supply switch
50 Ignition switch
51 Starter switch
52 Starter selector switch
53 Starter system signal lights
54 Electrical system shutdown
55 Landing light switch
56 UV lighting switch
57 Wing searchlight control switch
58 Wing searchlight activation switch
59 Signal light
60 Right gondola flap indicator lamp
61 Left gondola flap indicator lamp
62 Fuselage flap indicator lamp
63 Throttle
64 Mixture control
65 Throttle friction controller
66 Fuel cock lever
67 Fuel tank selector switch
68 Air intake pre-heater
69 Propeller pitch indicator
70 Split flaps indicator

71 Landing gear actuator
72 Landing flap actuator
73 Hydraulic system pressure gauge
74 Parking switch actuator
75 Emergency hydraulic pump switch
76 Emergency hydraulic pump indicator lamp
77 Landing gear/flap indicator
78 Fire extinguisher activator
79 Fire extinguisher pressure gauge
80 Pilot oxygen pressure gauge
81 Propeller de-icing lever
82 Carburetor de-icing lever
83
84 Control surface temperature gauge
85 Control surface temperature selector switch
86 Wing de-icing lever
87 Control surface de-icing lever
88 Pressure/vacuum gauge for control surface de-icing system and gyroscopes
89 Undercarriage de-icing switch
90 Fuel pump switch
91 Reserve pressure gauge

ten seconds the green lamps light up: gear and tailwheel extended and locked. Tank applies a little more trim, then turns onto the base leg maintaining a constant 190 km/h. On final he sets the flap lever to "takeoff" setting and keeps the speed to 190 km/h, then switches the lever to "land-ing". Another green lamp begins glowing, and the additional drag reduces the speed to 165 km/h. If the speed is increased to 185 km/h by throttle application the flaps would then retract automatically due to an overload cut-in safety mechanism. The change in load configuration can easily be

compensated for by minor trim adjustments. At 165 km/h Tank points the nose down for landing and flares out. The machine touches down at about 130 km/h.

During taxi he retracts the flaps again, lets the motors run for a bit in the parking area with the cooling flaps open, then pulls the throttles back and switches off the ignition. The engineer takes over closing the fuel cocks, switching off the electrical circuits and the automatic switches. "Flies itself almost like Condor V 1 D-AERE, it's just a bit heavier and more cumbersome because of it. But the aircraft has suffered little with regard to its flight handling qualities, although the fact that we didn't fly with a full military payload must naturally be taken into account." So much for Tank's assessment.

A New Generation of Aircraft

Focke-Wulf Ta 183

All the major aviation companies were working on jet aircraft designs near the end of the war. However, it was not until the end of 1944 that five companies were awarded official contracts by the Luftwaffe high command for developing a jet-powered fighter:

Junkers-Flugzeugwerke in Dessau
Blohm & Voss in Hamburg
Focke-Wulf Flugzeugwerke in Bremen
Messerschmitt AG in Augsberg
Heinkel-Flugzeugwerke, Vienna Works.

In doing so, the long-expressed desire of the bulk of aircraft manufacturers to build a jet fighter which would later replace the twin-jet Me 262 was finally fulfilled. In a gas dynamics department headed by Dr.-Ing. Pabst, Tank had already had much preliminary work carried out in the transsonic and supersonic realms as early as 1942/43.

The tiny, single-seat machine was laid out around a Heinkel He S 011 engine. There were many designs drawn up with the designations of P I through P VIII, some of these making use of the Jumo 004 engine already in series production. In working on these designs, many problems cropped up as the lower supersonic region was still unexplored territory. Which also explains the large number of designs and modifications.

Project Fw P I

The experimental Fw P I project explored the fitting of the Jumo 004, although it was chiefly geared toward the location of the large fuel tank. It had been drawn up well in advance of any jet fighter contract. A solution was found in the form of a mid-wing design having a tapered wing, a large fuselage with the engine located beneath the pilot's seat. A normal tailwheel was not the recommended choice with this design as the extremely deep layout of the air intake for the turbine would have increased the danger of sucking foreign objects in. In addition, there was the danger of burning the grass strips on takeoff.

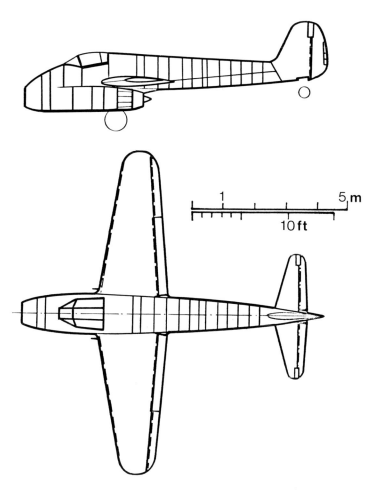

Fw P I design (March 1943).

227

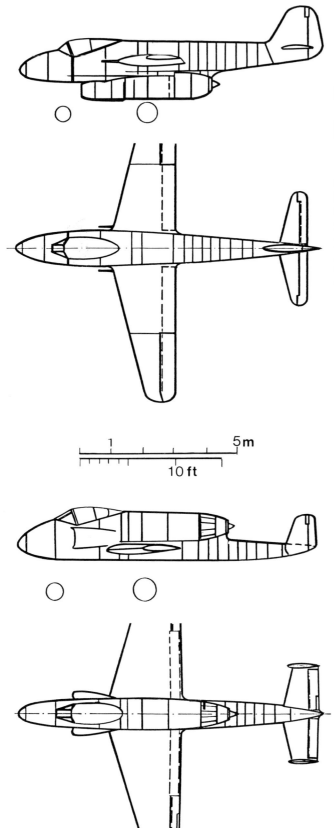

Fw P II design (November 1943).

Project Fw P II

The Fw P II project from June of 1943 succeeded in circumventing these disadvantages. It was also a cantilever mid-wing design with hydraulically retracting undercarriage. It was planned to house two large fuel tanks in the fuselage behind the cockpit. The use of a nose gear made it possible to increase the distance between the intake and the ground. The only jet engine available at the time, the Jumo 004C, had to be shifted aft under the fuselage to make room for the nosewheel. The rear section of the fuselage remained unchanged. The wing leading edge was given a slightly greater sweep. Like the P I, this design was also abandoned because of the fears of a stone being sucked into the low hanging engine. At the time, jet aircraft would still have had to operate from grass airfields.

Project Fw P III

A third design from November of 1943 envisioned an aircraft with a nosewheel, but this time the engine had been moved to the upper fuselage. The canopy was blended smoothly into the engine nacelle, and the entire unit melded into the fuselage in a refined manner. To protect the empennage from the hot engine efflux, the fuselage tapered sharply from the aft end of the engine and ended in a flat boom which supported the twin rudders. This, however, brought higher drag along with it. The side scoops or air intakes also affected performance. The wings were similar to the previous design but had a greater chord. The roll rate and ability to withstand a belly landing, on the other hand, would have been much better on this design than on its predecessor. The calculated performance figures, however, proved unsatisfactory.

Fw P III design (November 1943).

Project Fw P IV Flitzer

A fourth design was born in December 1943 calling for a central fuselage nacelle with two tailbooms and side intakes running along the fuselage. Two jettisonable RATO packs were to have been utilized for accelerating takeoff and improving climb rate. This model promised to have good handling characteristics.

At about the same time, De Havilland in England was working on a jet fighter with the same layout and design. This resulted in the DH 100 Vampire, powered by a DH Goblin centrifugal flow engine delivering 1334 daN/1360 kp of thrust. The aircraft reached production maturity in April 1945 and after the war served alongside the Gloster Meteor as the standard fighter of the Royal Air Force until well into the seventies.

Two engineering teams, working entirely independently of each other, came to the same conclusions at the same time. At the time, however, Dr.-Ing. Pabst and Mittelhuber were not satisfied with the level flight speed of the project.

Project Fw P V

The fifth design, dating from January 1944, exhibited all the characteristics of a new generation of jet aircraft. It called for the He S 011 engine from Heinkel, a development of Hans-Joachim Pabst von Ohain working at Heinkel's Stuttgart facility. The He S 011 (109-011) had a diagonal compressor followed by a three-stage axial-flow compressor. The engine's thrust ratio documentation was made available to the industry in general. At sea level, it was supposedly capable of delivering 1029 daN/1050 kp of thrust at 900 km/h. Takeoff thrust was to have been about 1568 daN/1600 kp.

Hans Multhopp, following intensive work on the numerous designs, had in the meantime come to the conclusion that all the projects hitherto drawn up had little chance in the long run. Aircraft expected to operate in the lower supersonic regions - and this was ultimately the goal of these many projects - would require a greater wing sweep and lower thickness to push the shock waves outward as the plane approached the speed of sound at high Mach num-

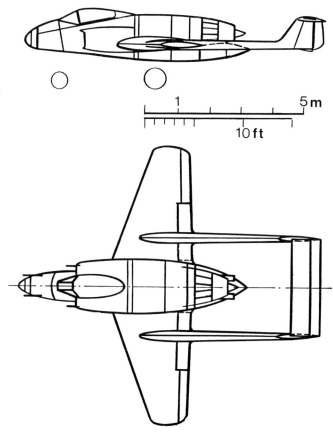

Fw P IV design, first project in the Flitzer series (December 1943).

bers. Based on this awareness, Multhopp designed an entirely new project with a more compact fuselage and central intake, approximately 40° wing sweepback and an unusual sharply swept tail with the elevators set above like a roof. The design was characterized by keeping the dimensions as small as possible and later formed the basis for the Ta 183 as well as the Pulqui II. At first, there were problems determining where to put the undercarriage; no adequate solution was found for this first design.

The engineers were also plagued by many doubts about the anticipated flutter problems and a potential tendency to tumble (Dutch roll). Due to its unique shape, the Project P V was nicknamed "Huckebein" (Lame Jack).

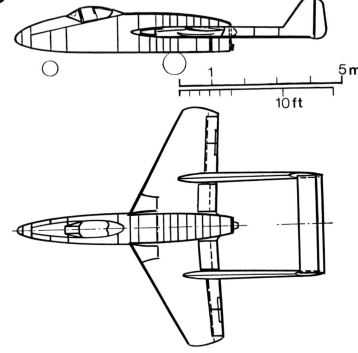

The Fw P VI "Flitzer" design (February 1944) was built in mockup form.

Project Fw P VI Flitzer

The Huckebein left so many problems unsolved that Mittelhuber decided to continue working on the Fw PIV project at the same time, as it had far fewer problems. This P VI project, too, dating from February 1944, was also to have been fitted with a high performance Heinkel He S 011 engine, but this was not yet available. Nevertheless, for improving takeoff performance a Walter HWK 109-509 liquid fuel rocket was used, delivering 1862 daN/1900 kp. The air intakes had been relocated to the wing roots. The Technisches Amt's concern regarding this arrangement was dispelled by trials carried out on test stands and in the wind tunnel. Focke-Wulf's more conventional design offered better promise with regard to the new generation of aircraft engines, for which no practical experience was yet available at this stage.

The wing fuel tanks held 175 liters of kerosene each, while 275 kg of fuel was carried in a fuselage tank. For the rocket motor, the fuselage housed a T-*Stoff* tank and two C-*Stoff* tanks were carried inside the tailbooms. Planned armament included two MG 151s in the nose and two 30 mm MK 108 guns in the wings. However, the RLM showed no interest in the design, a stance which resulted in greater emphasis being placed on the more advanced Project Huckebein.

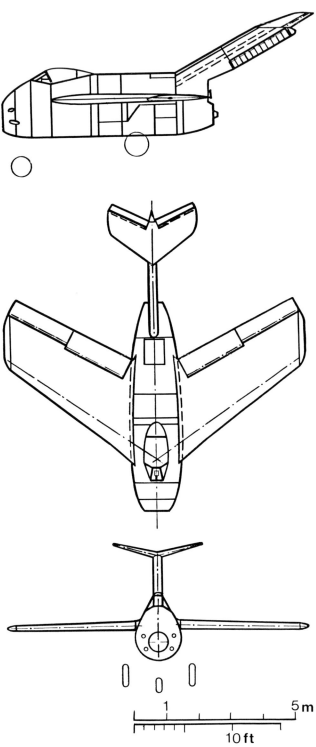

First design for the Ta 183 was the P V (January 1944). During the design stage the P V was nicknamed "Huckebein" ("Lame Jack") because of its unusual appearance.

Project Fw P VII

Nevertheless, work continued on the Project Fw P VI - although from an entirely different standpoint. By mid-1944 information showed that Heinkel was developing a turbo-prop engine, designated the He S 021, with an output of 2205 kW/3000 hp. This powerplant was to have found use in a new project based on the previous IV and VI designs already drawn up. The trend was toward a fighter-bomber with outstanding low and medium level performance. The wings, empennage, tailbooms, controls and main undercarriage were to have carried over from the planned P VI jet fighter. The expensive and dangerous twin-fueled rocket could be dispensed with and the plane would be able to operate from small grass airstrips. Given its speed and good climb rate, the P VII would have been superior to any piston powered fighter. Its armament was to have been the MG 213, a machine cannon which was copied after the war by the United States, England, France, Switzerland and the Soviet Union (see table for data and weights). In the end, however, there was concern that the elevators on the P VI and P VII designs would fail at high Mach numbers due to their lack of sweepback, and the projects were therefore dropped.

Ta 183 Huckebein I and II

In late 1944 Focke-Wulf participated in the request for tender for the development of a jet fighter called by the Luftwaffe's high command (already mentioned in the introduction to this chapter) with two improved designs based on the Huckebein project. The company submitted two proposals, the Huckebein I and the Ta 183 Type II.

Project I closely resembled the Fw P V Huckebein project; it was laid down as a shoulder-wing design and had a constant chord wing with a 40° sweep with only the leading edge tip being slightly rounded. The fuselage had an oval cross section, with the nose intake feeding air in a direct line to the engine mounted in the aft fuselage section. The upper fuselage swept upward to the tailfin, which was capped off by the swept elevators having a slight dihedral. By now, a solution had been found regarding the location of the landing gear. The nosewheel retracted rearward and the main gear forward. Armament was to have been housed in the nose.

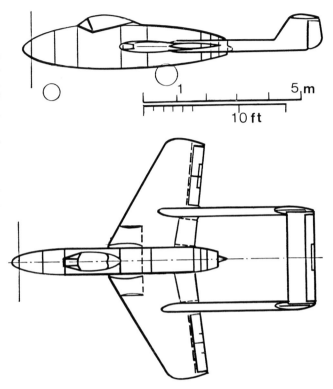

A special variant in the Flitzer series was designed as the Fw P VII (July 1944) for testing the follow-on development of the He S 011 jet engine as a turbo-prop He S 021. This variant could take off from forward airfields without the aid of rocket packs (RATO) and effectively engage piston-powered aircraft.

The Fw P VI Projekt I "Huckebein" was an advanced preliminary design for the Ta 183.

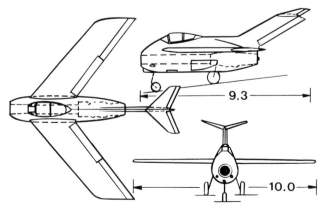

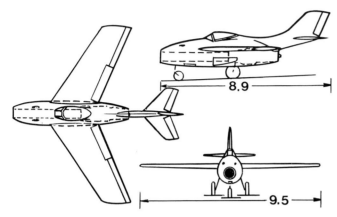

Fw Typ II, improved preliminary design for the Ta 183.

The second design called for somewhat less of a sweepback to the wings of 32°, and the shoulder-wing design gave way to a mid-wing layout. The fuselage was longer and more slender, with the cockpit set further aft. The T-tail configuration was dropped in favor of swept elevators located beneath the rudder.

Attended by representatives of the industry, several meetings took place at the DVL in Berlin in December 1944 and January 1945, the purpose of which was to correlate the various designs from the individual companies with the intent of coming to comparable results.

The best way to achieve higher speeds was found with design number I. Dipl.-Ing. Dietrich Fiecke, a participant in the meetings with the DVL, provides the following assessment of the two Focke-Wulf designs in his article "Stand der deutschen Jagdflugzeug-Entwicklung zu Kriegsende" (see Flugwelt 6/1953, pages 165 ff. and 7/1953, pages 203 ff.):

Initial Focke-Wulf Design

The design's straightforward swept wing was a good way to achieve high speeds. The poor ratio of slenderness of the fuselage and the bulbous nose could lead to compression shocks at even relatively low speeds, resulting in a large increase in drag. The cockpit layout provided good visibility. The air intake opening and the straight flow of air to the engine was probably the best solution given the location of the engine. The large surface area of the swept and upward protruding tailfin caused an enormous amount of drag buildup. Furthermore, drag could be induced by compression shocks at the elevator roots, even at relatively low speeds, despite the fact that the area of greatest thickness for the tailfin and elevators abut each other. The poor drag ratio of the fuselage and tailfin for the low maximum speed compared to the other designs. The comparatively short takeoff runs and low landing speeds shown in the calculations were based on the large wing surface area. The low wing loading proved extremely beneficial in this area as well.

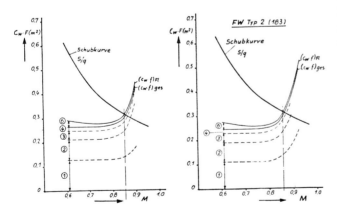

Left: Fw P VI Projekt I, right: Fw Typ II. Comparison diagrams for the two Focke-Wulf designs showing drag and thrust ratios at high speeds at 7000 meters' altitude. The numbers show: 1 - wings without leading edge slats; 2 - fuselage; 3 - control surfaces; 4 - interference, etc. 5 - leading edge slats; 6 - induced drag surfaces.

Second Focke-Wulf Design

The wing had less of a sweep than the other designs. As a result, this wing had a higher drag buildup at higher speeds despite having ten percent less area compared to the first design. The benefits gained by sweeping the wing back to offset the buildup of drag at high speeds was not as apparent here. The fuselage shape and transition to the empennage seem to have been a good choice relative to the airframe's aerodynamics. Even the form of the canopy shape was well blended into the contours of the fuselage. The wings, however, restricted vision somewhat. As on the first design, the airflow was well designed given the location of the engine. From an aerodynamic perspective the sweepback to the elevators and rudder proved to be beneficial.

Compared to the first draft proposal, the drag area was not high at higher speeds, although the drag area of the wing increased dramatically because the sweepback effect was not pronounced enough. The layout of the control surfaces produced a relatively high drag area, meaning that altogether the maximum speed was not appreciably higher than the other types. The minimal wing sweep made the flaps more effective during landing and the landing speeds were not out of limits. The good aerodynamic shape of the fuselage contributed to the good service ceiling compared with the other designs.

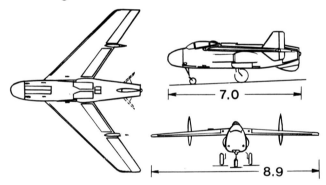

The Ju EF 128 was initially declared the winner of the competition and was to have entered production in mid-1945. Later, however, a decision was made in favor of the Fw Typ II.

[1]Payload was 2xMK 108 including 100 rounds ammunition per gun plus rescue equipment
[2]At average weight of 3700 kg. The data figures calculated by the DVL (C_w f) for the entire aircraft served as the basis for calculated flight performance:

    at Mach 0.6 = 0.2676 m²
    at Mach 0.8 = 0.272 m²
    at Mach 0.9 = 0.430 m²
[3]Time to climb to 6000 m was 3.0 min
    " 10000 m was 12.5 min
    " 13000 m was 24.0 min

Focke-Wulf Ta 183 Jet Fighter Designs

Manufacturer		Focke-Wulf	
Type		Ta 183 I	Ta 183 II
Powerplant		Heinkel He S 011A	Heinkel He S 011A
Performance	daN	1570	1570
	kp	1600	1600
Crew		1	1
Length	m	9.20	8.90
Height	m	3.86	3.45
Wingspan	m	10.00	9.50
Wing area	m²	22.50	22.80
Aspect ratio		4.45	3.96
Sweep		40°	32°
Weight, empty	kg	2705	2535
Fuel	kg	1200	1200
Oil	kg	20	20
Crew	kg	80	80
Load	kg	295[1]	315
Max. permissible load	kg	1595	1615
Takeoff weight	kg	4300	4150
Wing loading	kg/m²	191.11	182.02
Weight/power ratio	kg/daN	2.73	2.64
	kg/kp	2.69	2.59
	daN/m²	69.77	68.85
	kp/m²	71.11	70.18
Max. speed	km/h	962[2]	967[5]
@ altitude	m	7000	7000
Max. speed	km/h	875	905[5]
@ altitude	m	0	0
Rate of climb	m/s	24.2[2]	21.5[5]
Service ceiling	m	14400[3]	14400[6]
Range	km	1740[4]	1800[4]
Max. flight time	hrs	2.03	2.03
Takeoff run	m	670	725
Takeoff run to 20 m	m	1050	1115
Landing speed	km/h	164	166
Max. permissible load as % of takeoff weight		37	39
Payload as % of takeoff weight		7	8
Built(project)		1944	1944

[4]With full thrust at 13000 m,
at sea level 560 km; at 7000 m 990 km/h
[5]With an average weight of 3350 kg
[6]Time to climb to 6000 m was 5.6 min
    " 10000 m was 11.3 min
    " 13000 m was 20.0 min

P II, P VI and P VII Jet Projects

Manufacturer		Focke-Wulf	Focke-Wulf	Focke-Wulf
Type		Fw P II jet fighter project	P VII project with turboprop	Fw P VI Flitzer project
Powerplant		Jumo 004C	Heinkel He S-021	Heinkel He S 011/ Walter HWK 109-509 rocket
Performance	daN	882	2205	1274
	kW		+1862=3136	
	kp	900	3000	1300[9]
	hp			+1900=3200
Crew		1	1	1
Length	m	9.85	9.00	10.55
Height	m	3.20	2.65	2.35
Wingspan	m	9.70	8.00	8.00
Wing area	m²	15.00	17.00	14.00
Aspect ratio		6.27	3.76	4.57
Weight, empty	kg	2135	3208[5]	2705
Fuel	kg	665	1128	570
Oil	kg	15	20	+936[9]
Crew	kg	80	80	80
Load	kg	455[1]	564	476
Max. permissible load	kg	1215	1792[6]	2062
Takeoff weight	kg	3350	5000	4767
Wing loading	kg/m²	223.33	294.12	340.50
Weight/power ratio	kg/kW kg/daN	3.79	2.27	1.52
	kg/hp kg/kp	3.72	1.67	1.48
	daN/m²	58.80	129.71	224.00
	kp/m²	60.00	176.47	228.57
Max. speed	km/h	825[2]	825	830
@ altitude	m	6000	0	6000
Cruise speed	km/h	750	700	
@ altitude	m	6000	0	
Rate of climb	m/s	20.00[3]	40.00	107[10]
				13.20
Service ceiling	m	12400	15200	13000
Range	km	425[4]	550[7]	570[11]
Max. flight time	hrs		40[8]	56
Takeoff run	m	400	360	400
Landing run	m	600	500	650
Landing speed	km/h	170	145	180
Max. permissible load as % of takeoff weight		36	36	43
Payload as % of takeoff weight		14	11	23
Built		1943	1944	1944

[1]**Payload breakdown**

2 MK 108 in fuselage	150	kg
2 MG 151 in wing roots	125	kg
ammunition	160	kg
rescue equipment	20	kg
Total	455	kg

[2]800 km/h at sea level

[3]At sea level; 11 m/sec at 6000 m

[4]At 6000 m; 585 km at 10000 m; 315 km at sea level

[5]**Empty weight breakdown**

fuselage	kg	420
armor	kg	140
landing gear	kg	270
empennage	kg	108
control system	kg	52
wings	kg	455
engine	kg	1330
fuel system	kg	200
equipment	kg	190
radio-navigation equipment	kg	43
	kg	3208

[6]**Max permissible load with payload**

crew	kg	80
fuel	kg	1128
oil	kg	20
	kg	1228

Payload

2xMG 213 fuselage	kg	191
2xMG 213 wings	kg	186
ammunition	kg	187
	kg	564
+	kg	1228
max permissible load	kg	1792

[7]1460 km at 10000 m

[8]At sea level; reduced throttle gave 70 min

[9]Including Walter HWK 109-509 rocket engine

[10]Average rate of climb to 7500 m with rocket engine

[11]At 11600 m

Fiecke summed up his report on the two Focke-Wulf designs as follows:

"The large spread of the fuel tank inside the fuselage brought difficulties with the longitudinal stability along with it. The low wing loading compared to the other designs made for better maneuverability and takeoff and landing performance. The tail's play had a negative effect on the rudder, the stability in a turn and the weathercocking stability. The reduced sweep of the second version had a positive effect on the operation of the ailerons and flaps. This was reinforced even further by the taper ratio of the wings."

Of the eight designs which the Deutsche Versuchsanstalt für Luftfahrt (DVL) in Berlin-Adlershof explored and compared in late 1944 and early 1945, only one was actually built - and this was the Focke-Wulf project. And it was built twice - once in the Soviet Union and once by former members of the Focke-Wulf team in Argentina.

This seemed to indicate that the Focke-Wulf design was the best.

The Luftwaffe High Command, however, decided in favor of the Junkers design, to be produced with the greatest priority; it was a tailless shoulder-wing design with wings swept at 45°, with the rudders located midway along each wing trailing edge. The elevators were replaced by flaps along the wings. Production was to have begun in mid 1945. Apparently, however, there was a change of heart during the last weeks of the war and it was decided to go ahead with the construction of the Ta 183. For Tank clearly remembers a meeting in Bad Eilsen to which he summoned those companies participating in the RLM jet fighter competition and at which the RLM representative explained that the Ta 183 was to be built as the Me 262's successor. As a result, Tank immediately had mockups of the Ta 183 constructed and began preparations for full scale production.

Long-Range Aircraft Bound for New York

Fw 300 Transatlantic Aircraft

As already indicated, following the occupation of France Tank had managed to wrangle permission from the RLM to have a group of Focke-Wulf engineers work on a better version of the Fw 200 Condor in conjunction with the French company of SNCASO. This improved model, designated the Fw 300, was to be designed for trans-Atlantic commercial aviation. Dipl.-Ing. Bansemir moved to Paris

with a staff of technical experts and there, together with French designers, began working on the Fw 300 program. After two years the project was completed, once again in cooperation with Lufthansa. But then permission was never given for Focke-Wulf to produce the airplane.

The design envisioned four DB 603 engines, each delivering 1433 kW/1950 hp, having variable-pitch propellers and a fuel capacity of 19600 liters. 30 to 40 passengers would have traveled comfortably from Berlin to New York in the Fw 300's pressurized cabin.

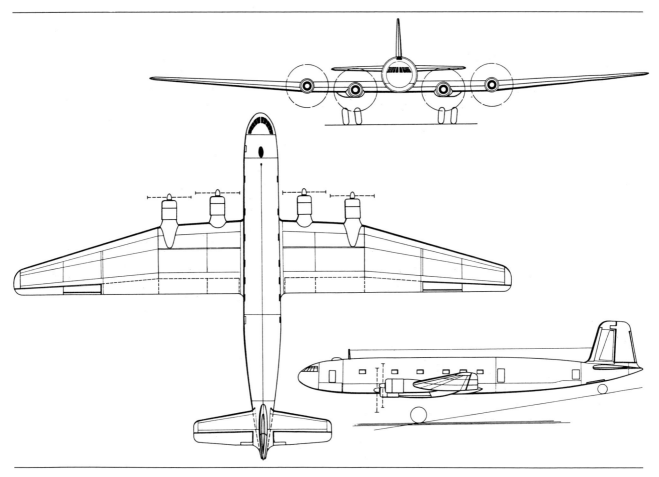

The Fw 300Design, drawn up in close cooperation with SNCASO in Paris during the war, was to have led to a successor to the Fw 200 which Lufthansa wanted to employ on Atlantic routes following the war.

Fw 300 Compared to DC-4 and DC-6

Manufacturer		Focke-Wulf	Douglas	Douglas
Type		Fw 300	DC-4	DC-6
Powerplant		Jumo 222E[1]	P&W Twin Wasp 25D-13G	P&W Double Wasp CA 15
Performance	kW	4x1470=5880	4x1080=4320	4x1566=6264
	hp	4x2000=8000	4x1470=5880	4x2130=8520
Crew(+passengers)		5+32	5+30(44)	5+40(52)
Length	m	31.34	28.50	30.95
Height	m	7.80	8.50	8.75
Wingspan	m	46.80	35.80	35.80
Wing area	m²	227.20	135.00	136.00
Aspect ratio		9.64	9.49	9.42
Weight, empty	kg	27324	18343	26732
Fuel	kg	15080	9789	11560
Oil	kg	1200	800	1000
Crew	kg	400	400	400
Load	kg	3496	3778	4580
Max. permissible load	kg	20176	14767	17540
Takeoff weight	kg	47500	33110	44272
Wing loading	kg/m²	209.06	245.26	325.53
Weight/power ratio	kg/kW	8.08	7.66	7.07
	kg/hp	5.94	5.63	5.20
	kW/m²	25.88	32.01	46.04
	hp/m²	35.21	43.55	62.65
Max. speed	km/h	620	430	504[3]
@ altitude	m	6400	6350	6220
Cruise speed	km/h	437	390	446
@ altitude	m	6200	6350	6000
Rate of climb	m/s	4.50	5.40	3.30
Service ceiling	m	11000	7000	7600
Range	km	7000	5300[2]	7168[2]
Max. flight time	hrs	16.00	14.00	16.00
Takeoff run	m	1000	1200	1550
Takeoff run to 15 m	m	1500	1700	2000
Landing speed	km/h	120	141	160
Max. permissible load as % of takeoff weight		42	46	40
Payload as % of takeoff weight		7	11	10
Built		1941	1947	1949

[1]The Jumo 222 was expected (after an estimated two years of design work on the Fw 300) to provide 1654 kW/2500 hp, plus an additional 1029 kW/1400 hp with a two-stage liquid-powered turbocharger at an altitude of 10800 m. Fuel consumption was to have been 280 g/hp/hr. In 1942 the engine produced 2205 kW/3000 hp during test run-ups.
[2]Ranges are estimated
[3]Performance figures with a takeoff weight of 38140 kg

This German equivalent of the DC-4 or DC-6 was a four-engined cantilever low-wing design with retractable tailwheel. The machine had been laid out with an anticipated range of 7000 km and a cruising speed of 430 km/h. It was capable of carrying a payload of 3500 kg. Once it had completed two-thirds of its journey, it would still have been able to reach its destination on just two engines.

Aside from the DB 603, the Jumo 222 was also initially considered as a powerplant. In 1940 there was no way that Bansemir could have known that, of the engines chosen, the Jumo 222 would not have reached production status even by 1945. In order to provide an overview of how the Fw 300's dimensions, weights and performance compared with its potential DC-4 and DC-6 rivals, data for these American planes is also included in the table.

Focke-Wulf Ta 400: Bombs Vice Passengers

With the Fw 300 project completed, Focke-Wulf was given a contract by the RLM for a long-range bomber which would have been able to carry a 10000 kg payload over a distance of 4000 km to 5000 km. The thinking behind this was its use as a so-called Amerika-Bom*ber*.

Messerschmitt and Junkers also were awarded a similar contract at the same time. Work on the Ta 400 probably continued at Bad Eilsen, since for security reasons no military designs were allowed to be worked on in France.

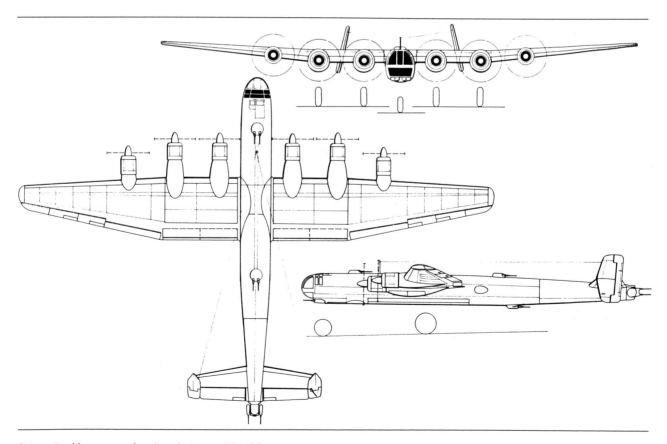

Six-engined long-range bomber, designated Ta 400.

Comparison of Me 264, Ju 390 and Ta 400 Long-Range Aircraft

Manufacturer		Focke-Wulf	Messerschmitt	Junkers
Type		Ta 400	Me 264A	Ju 390
Powerplant		BMW 801D	BMW 801D	BMW 801D
Performance	kW	6x1323=7938	4x1323=5292	6x1323=7938
	hp	6x1800=10800	4x1800=7200	6x1800=10800
Crew		8	8+1	8
Length	m	28.18	21.33	31.10
Height	m	6.58	4.28	6.90
Wingspan	m	41.91	43.00	50.00
Wing area	m²	188.50	127.70	254.40
Aspect ratio		9.31	14.48	9.84
Weight, empty	kg	33860	21150	38330
Fuel	kg	14000	29340	22680
Oil	kg	1500	1260	1500
Crew	kg	640	720	640
Load	kg	10000	3530[1]	10000
Max. permissible load	kg	26140	34850	34820
Takeoff weight	kg	60000	56000	73150
Wing loading	kg/m²	318.30	438.52	287.54
Weight/power ratio	kg/kW	7.56	10.58	9.22
	kg/hp	5.56	7.78	6.77
	kW/m²	42.11	41.44	31.20
	hp/m²	57.29	56.38	42.45
Max. speed	km/h	535	545	450
@ altitude	m	5700	5100	5500
Cruise speed	km/h	480	350	420
@ altitude	m	5700	5100	5400
Rate of climb	m/s	2.16	2.00	3.50
Service ceiling	m	7500	6200	6200
Range	km	5280	15000	7340
Max. flight time	hrs	11.00	45.00	17.00
Takeoff run	m	1550	2100[2]	
Takeoff run to 15 m	m	2000		
Landing speed	km/h	140	160	120
Max. permissible load as % of takeoff weight		44	62	48
Payload as % of takeoff weight		17	6	14
Built		1942	1942	1943

[1]**Me 264A payload breakdown**

armor	kg	1000
wpns+ammo	kg	1200
photo equip	kg	210
provisions	kg	100
GM 1	kg	600
other	kg	420
	kg	3530

[2]Takeoff in this overloaded configuration was only possible with jettisonable rocket boosters(RATO) having 6000 kp thrust

The Ta 400 was laid out as a cantilever, mid wing design with six engines. Follow-on developments called for a Jumo 004 jet engine to be mounted below the two outboard engines, which would assist in temporarily boosting the plane's speed from 535 to 720 km/h.

In the end, Messerschmitt and Junkers were awarded the final contracts for construction of prototypes. Messerschmitt had already developed the Me 264 long-range bomber, a plane which had completed its maiden flight back in late 1942. It had provisionally been fitted with four Jumo 211J engines. Within the framework of this new contract it was to have been enlarged and equipped with more powerful engines. When the BMW 801E never got beyond the bench testing stage, Messerschmitt redesigned the machine for the BMW 801D. Due to a lack of capacity, however, the company was never fully able to develop the Me 264.

The victor in this race finally turned out to be the Junkers-Werke, which only had to enlarge and fit its production Ju 290 with six engines in order to meet the requirements with regards to range and payload. This time, Tank was left empty-handed, because the other two aircraft could already be displayed while he was still at the drawing board. Accordingly, their development was much further along. The Ju 390 V1 flew as early as mid-1943, and during field testing the V2 prototype even flew across the Atlantic to within 20 km of New York and returned back to base safe and sound.

Focke-Wulf Projects

The design department at Focke-Wulf was responsible for drawing up a great number of varied and interesting projects. Because his area of responsibility had expanded enormously, however, Tank was only able to work on a handful of these many projects himself. This book focuses primarily on discussing those projects and aircraft on which Professor Tank had a predominant influence, whether it be during the testing phase under his direction, or whether he inspired the development of these aircraft or was involved in the details of the design. This short overview shows how advanced and future-oriented most of these designs were. Often these charted entirely new territories with their choice of powerplant and their layout.

Fw 206, a German DC-3

Success with the Fw 200 Condor established a good relationship between Focke-Wulf and Lufthansa. This relationship included both partners agreeing on the definition of future projects and the aircraft manufacturer then working out the designs. Work was carried out on these designs until well after the beginning of the war.

Accordingly, Lufthansa found itself looking for a Ju 52/3 replacement and - spurred by the Americans' success with the DC-3 - leaned towards a reliable, twin-engined short and medium range machine which was up to the task of performing a variety of roles. Lufthansa's requirements encompassed the following five areas:

°Cargo capacity was expected to be 2000 to 2500 kg

°The plane must be able to remain airworthy with one engine out and be able to maintain altitude in order to guarantee reaching its destination

°The plane must also be able to carry out a missed approach with extended gear on only one engine as well

°Payload distribution was recommended as follows: 14 to 18 passengers and luggage, 1400 to 1800 kg

°Range was be 1200 km including reserves

The result of these requirements was a design showing a cantilever twin-engined all-metal low-wing aircraft with retractable landing gear, tailwheel and flaps which had an all-up weight of 10000 to 13000 kg. The aircraft was designed to carry 15 passengers and 620 kg of luggage ofer 1200 kg. At first, it was planned to utilize the 735 kW/1000 hp Bramo 323R-2 engines which had proven so reliable with the Fw 200C-1 and C-2. Later, a projected BMW 800 was to have been fitted, which would have provided improved performance in the neighborhood of 882 kW/1200 hp. The final design showed the aircraft having the ability to climb at a rate of 1.5 meters per second at a weight of 10160 kg up to an altitude of 800 meters. With an idle cruise setting the machine could be expected to maintain a 1 meter per second climb rate up to 2000 meters. In February 1941 Lufthansa representatives were invited to inspect a mockup

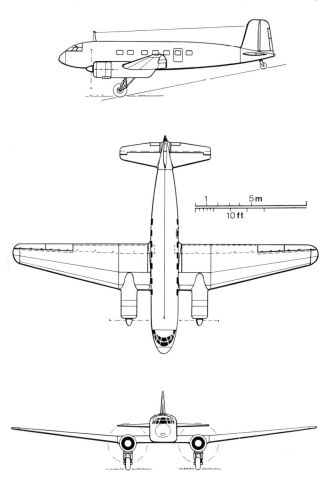

Fw 206, a design study for a short-range commuter plane carrying up to 15 passengers.

of the Fw 206. Negotiations were begun for an initial contract for six aircraft.

Shortly afterward the Bremen works turned the project over to the French SNCASO company in Paris-Chatillon, where (as already mentioned) Dipl.-Ing. Bansemir was working on a follow-on development of the Fw 200 Condor. There work continued on the Fw 206 - including the manufacturing of all jigs - up to the point where production could begin. However, on the instructions of the RLM all work was to cease effective 1 October 1942 and production was to be postponed until after the war.

Fw 206 Twin-Engined Commercial Airliner Project

Manufacturer		Focke-Wulf
Type		Fw 206
Powerplant		Bramo 323-R
Performance	kW	2x735=1470
	hp	2x1000=2000
Crew(+passengers)		3+15
Length	m	19.43
Height	m	5.45
Wingspan	m	27.40
Wing area	m²	85.50
Aspect ratio		8.78
Weight, empty	kg	7490[1]
Fuel	kg	900
Oil	kg	80
Crew	kg	240
Load	kg	1890
Max. permissible load	kg	3110[2]
Takeoff weight	kg	10600
Wing loading	kg/m²	123.98
Weight/power ratio	kg/kW	7.21
	kg/hp	5.30
	kW/m²	17.19
	hp/m²	23.39
Max. speed	km/h	370
@ altitude	m	2400
Cruise speed	km/h	325
@ altitude	m	2600
Rate of climb	m/s	4.80[3]
Service ceiling	m	8200[4]
Range	km	1150
Max. flight time	hrs	3.9
Takeoff run	m	400
Takeoff run to 20 m	m	600
Landing run	m	350
Landing run from 15 m	m	650
Landing speed	km/h	115
Max. permissible load as % of takeoff weight		29
Payload as % of takeoff weight		18
Built(project)		1940/41

[1]**Empty weight breakdown**

fuselage	kg	1592
landing gear	kg	587
empennage	kg	463
control system	kg	161
wings	kg	1745
engines	kg	2156
equipment	kg	786
Total	kg	7490

[2]**Max. permissible load breakdown**

15 passengers	kg	1200
luggage	kg	300
freight and mail	kg	240
crew	kg	240
crew luggage	kg	60
de-icing fluid	kg	16
steward facilities	kg	44
water	kg	30
fuel	kg	900
oil	kg	80
Total	kg	3110

[3]2000m   7.0 min
4000 m   14.9 min
6000 m   25.0 min
[4]2300 m on single engine

Focke-Wulf Fw 238H

One of the many projects which came from this time period was the Fw 238H long-range bomber. It was laid out in accordance with the guidelines which had been specified for the Ta 400 and Ju 390. With the appearance of the first American "Flying Fortresses", at the time it was felt that a suitable warning would be to drop a few bombs on New York. To this end, an aircraft was needed which would have a range of 15000 km and a payload of five tons.

The Technis*ches Amt*'s guidelines from March 1941 placed an enormous emphasis on range and payload and could only be realized if the RLM would accept a safe maneuvering load factor of 1.75 during the initial leg of the flight. This seemed justified insofar that the weight percentage taken up by the fuel was quite high and on the outbound journey the fuselage tank could be flown dry. This would enable a safe maneuvering load factor amounting to about 3.2 at the target, i.e. at half the aircraft's range. The mid-wing design's four engines extended outward from the wing leading edge.

Each of the BMW 803 engines on the 238 was to have driven two counter-rotating propellers. The tailfins were designed to cap the horizontal stabilizers on each end in order to provide a clear field of fire aft. The gargantuan machine was to have been made entirely of wood. Details

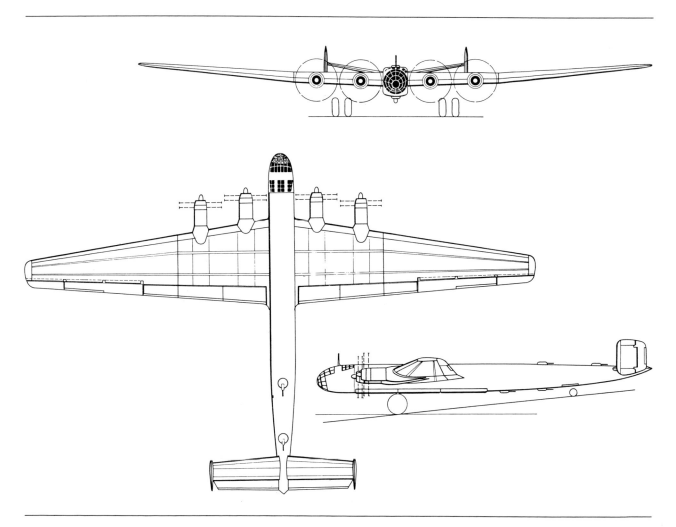

Fw 238 long-range airplane with a range of 14000 km and powered by four BMW 803 engines (rated at 2867 kW/3900 hp) driving counter-rotating propellers.

15000 km Long-Range Aircraft Projects

of the aircraft's layout can be seen in the drawing and the table provides comprehensive weight, geometric data and performance figures.

Manufacturer		Focke-Wulf	
Type		Fw 238H	Fw 238
Powerplant		BMW 801D	BMW 803
Performance	kW	4x1323=5292	4x2866=11464
	hp	4x1800=7200	4x3900=15600
Crew		4	5
Length	m	30.60	35.30
Height	m	5.80	8.70
Wingspan	m	50.00	52.00
Wing area	m²	240.00	290.00
Aspect ratio		10.41	9.32
Weight, empty	kg	24834	55620
Fuel	kg	28750	49500
Oil	kg	1900	3200
Crew	kg	360	450
Load	kg	5256[1]	5760[1]
Max. permissible load	kg	36266	58910
Takeoff weight	kg	61100	114530
Wing loading	kg/m²	254.58	394.93
Weight/power ratio	kg/kW	11.55	9.99
	kg/hp	8.49	7.34
	kW/m²	22.05	39.53
	hp/m²	30.00	53.79
Max. speed	km/h	400	670
@ altitude	m	5700	8000
Cruise speed	km/h	310	500
@ altitude	m	5400	8000
Rate of climb	m/s	7.8[2]	7.00[2]
Service ceiling	m		
Range	km	15000[3]	14100[3]
Max. flight time	hrs	48	29
Takeoff run	m	775[4]	1000[4]
Takeoff run to 20 m	m	1000[4]	1300[4]
Landing speed	km/h	110	130
Max. permissible load as % of takeoff weight		60	51
Payload as % of takeoff weight		9	5
Built(project design)		1941	1941

[1]256 kg for defensive weapon ammunition
[2]At half fuel capacity and with 46 metric ton takeoff weight
[3]9000 km range with 15 metric ton payload
[4]With 6 RATO packs having a combined thrust of 6x14.71 N(1500 kp)

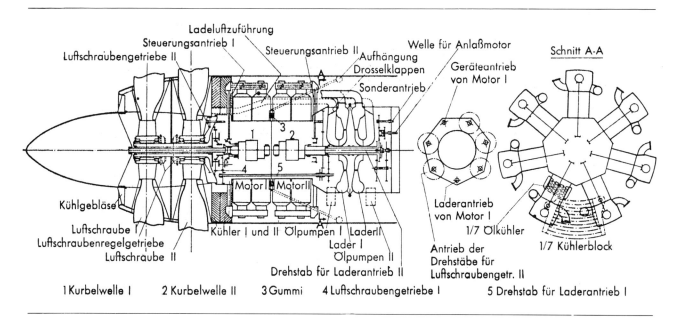

Cutaway of the four-chambered BMW 803 radial engine for the Focke-Wulf Fw 238. The motor powered counter-rotating four-bladed propellers which had full variable-pitch functionality. The engine weighed about 3000 kilograms.

Fw 195(249) Heavy Lift Transport

In 1941, at the instigation of the *Technisches Amt*, work also began on designs for "super freighters" capable of carrying 30 to 40 ton payloads. These projects intended to make use of the Jumo 222 , which as a precautionary measure was rated lower at 1646 kW/2240 hp instead of its standard 1838 kW/2500 hp.

The design for the Fw 195(249) transport, an all-metal low-wing aircraft with six engines, was laid down using a 30 payload capacity as its basis. The aircraft would have been able to carry 300 soldiers over a distance of 1500 kilometers, while the larger eight-engined Fw 95 could carry up to 400 soldiers over the same distance. The design's retractable tricycle landing gear would have ensured a problem-free horizontal loading configuration. The aircraft's cargo hold was laid out in accordance with the European gauge railroad. Both machines had an aft fuselage floor ramp which could be lowered for loading and unloading. As the ramp was quite steep, vehicles could be pulled into the cargo

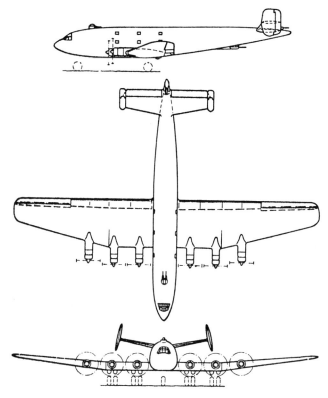

Focke-Wulf Fw 195 heavy-lift transport with a capacity of 30 metric tons.

Fw 195 and Fw 95 Super Freighter Projects

Manufacturer		Focke-Wulf	
Type		Fw 195(249)	Fw 95(249)
Powerplant		Jumo 222	Jumo 222
Performance	kW	6x1646=9876	8x1646=13168
	hp	6x2240=13440	8x2240=17920
Crew		7	7
Length	m	43.00	47.00
Height	m	11.50	11.80
Wingspan	m	56.00	58.00
Wing area	m²	400.00	460.00
Aspect ratio		7.84	7.35
Weight, empty	kg	47750	60000
Fuel	kg	8000	9500
Oil	kg	750	1000
Crew	kg	700	700
Load	kg	30800	40800
Max. permissible load	kg	40250	52000
Takeoff weight	kg	88000	112000
Wing loading	kg/m²	220.00	243.48
Weight/power ratio	kg/kW	8.91	8.51
	kg/hp	6.55	6.25
	kW/m²	24.70	28.63
	hp/m²	33.60	38.96
Max. speed	km/h	450	490
@ altitude	m	3600	3600
Cruise speed	km/h	370	400
@ altitude	m	3600	3600
Rate of climb	m/s	4.07	4.70
Service ceiling	m	6700	7100
Range	km	1500	1500
Max. flight time	hrs	4.00	4.00
Takeoff run	m	775	800
Takeoff run to 20 m	m	1340	1400
Landing speed	km/h	130	135
Max. permissible load as % of takeoff weight		46	46
Payload as % of takeoff weight		35	36
Built(project)		1941	1941

Fw 261 Planned Replacement for the Fw 200C

Manufacturer		Focke-Wulf	Focke-Wulf
Type		Fw 261 long-range recon	Fw 200F long-range recon
Powerplant		BMW 801E	Bramo 323R-2
Performance	kW	4x1470=5880	4x735=2940
	hp	4x2000=8000	4x1000=4000
Crew		7	7
Length	m	26.10	23.85
Height	m	6.00	6.00
Wingspan	m	40.00	32.84
Wing area	m²	187.00	118.00
Aspect ratio		8.55	9.14
Weight, empty	kg	27840	13447
Fuel	kg	18800	8795
Oil	kg	1600	600
Crew	kg	700	560
Load	kg	4660	1858
Max. permissible load	kg	25760	11813
Takeoff weight	kg	53600	25260
Wing loading	kg/m²	286.63	214.07
Weight/power ratio	kg/kW	9.12	8.59
	kg/hp	6.70	6.32
	kW/m²	31.44	24.92
	hp/m²	42.78	33.90
Max. speed	km/h	455	360
@ altitude	m	6700	5000
Cruise speed	km/h	380	300
@ altitude	m	6700	4000
Rate of climb	m/s	3.10	3.50
Service ceiling	m	6300	6000
Range	km	8500	6900
Max. flight time	hrs	22.00	23.00
Takeoff run	m	1000	900
Takeoff run to 20 m	m	1670	1450
Landing speed	km/h	144	130
Max. permissible load as % of takeoff weight		48	47
Payload as % of takeoff weight		9	7
Built(project)		1942	1944

hold by means of an onboard winch. When ferrying troops, the plane could be fitted with an interim floor at a height of 3.40 meters, enabling both soldiers and cargo to be carried on two decks.

To maintain a clear field of fire aft, it was planned to make use of twin rudders. Only tried and true construction techniques and proven accessories were to have been employed in order to ensure a speedy developmental process without any setbacks.

Fw 261 Long-Range Maritime Reconnaissance and Submarine Hunter

By 1942 the enemy had developed improved detection and defensive methods which seriously hampered the effectiveness of the German U-boot force. At the same time, losses had risen considerably. The German Kriegsmarine therefore demanded that the Luftwaffe provide it with a reconnaissance aircraft which could search further out into the Atlantic than the Fw 200C, enabling the submarines to

better find and approach the enemy's convoys. In addition, the aircraft would have to be capable of attacking naval targets on its own and ward off the enemy antisubmarine patrol aircraft which by then were becoming more and more numerous.

Given these requirements, Focke-Wulf developed a four-engined long-range bomber, a mid wing design with a central fuselage and two tail booms extending backward from the two outboard engine nacelles. In addition, the Fw 261 was fitted with a particularly effective aft-firing defensive weapons system. The design's unique twin-boom rudder configuration was laid out in accordance with the requirement to have as unrestricted a field of fire for the tail gun as possible.

The aircraft was a "flying fortress" in its own right with an enormous amount of defensive firepower. In addition to the crew and gun stations, the fuselage was designed to carry about 25 percent of the total fuel capacity along with bombs/depth charges. The nose was completely glazed, providing excellent visibility. The undercarriage configuration called for either four compressed strut oleos or two twin-wheeled legs retracting aft into the outer engine nacelles, the nose gear rotated through 90 degrees as it retracted to the rear.

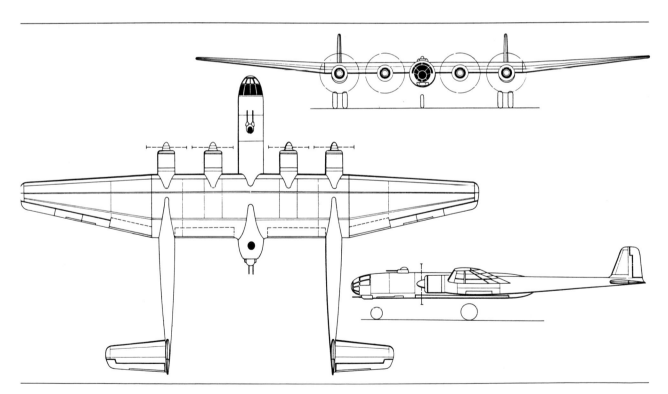

Project study of an Fw 261 long-range reconnaissance aircraft, planned as the replacement for the Fw 200C.

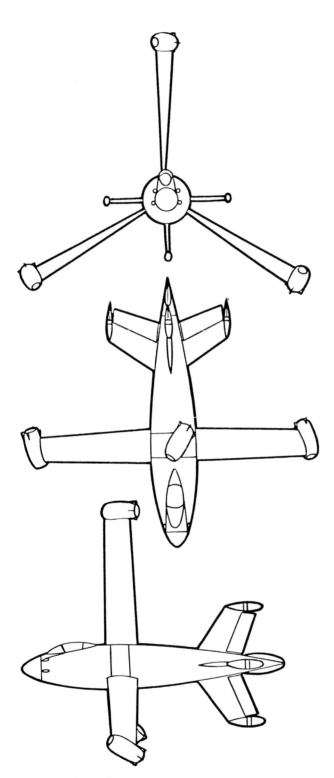

Powerplant was to have been the BMW 801E, an engine which would also have boosted the Fw 190's performance considerably. This engine, with an improved supercharger, new piston design and an improved oil system with de-foaming centrifuge, reached production maturity in July of 1942. However, as mentioned earlier, the 801E never actually entered production due to the fact that the war prevented the tooling equipment from ever being delivered. Thus, construction of this urgently needed powerplant was prevented. In the end, lack of facilities also prevented construction of the Fw 261. This was probably the reason that Focke-Wulf was given a contract for the development of the new Fw 200F version discussed previously. According to company records, by the way, the field units would have been able to carry out the necessary conversion work on the Fw 200C themselves.

Fw Project 1000x1000x1000

A high-speed jet bomber design was conceived in 1944. It was to have been capable of carrying a 1000 kg payload at a speed of 1000 km/h over a distance of 1000 km, and therefore was given the appellation of Fw 1000x1000x1000. Two proposals were worked out - one conceived of a twin-engined aircraft with sharply swept wings and a narrow area-ruled fuselage center section while the other was a delta-winged aircraft with two jet engines buried in the wings.

Triebflügel Aircraft with Lorin Ramjets

A vertical takeoff aircraft, designed by *Flugbaumeister* Dipl.-Ing. V. Halem, was also in the works. The fuselage stood upright and rested on a single mainwheel supported by several outrigger wheels. Three propeller-like blades with Fw-Lorin ramjets on each tip rotated around the fuselage center section at a speed of about 220 rpm. Each ramjet was expected to have provided 808 daN/825 kp, giving a total available thrust of 2428 daN/2475 kp.

Once it had taken off vertically, the aircraft would transition to horizontal flight whereby the thrust wings would act like an oversized, slow-spinning propeller.

Focke-Wulf design for a VTOL aircraft with rotating wings powered by Lorin jet engines.

Jet-Powered Night and All-Weather Fighter

In addition to the two jet fighter projects(Ta 183) already discussed in detail, the design department was also involved in the development of several night and all-weather jet fighter programs. As late as March 1945 the RLM issued a request for tender to Arado, Blohm & Voss, Dornier, Gotha and Focke-Wulf for such a project. The requirements called for the aircraft to be able to cruise at low altitude for over three hours at extremely slow speeds in addition to being able to deliver high speeds and have great range. Focke-Wulf fulfilled this requirement with a design for a twin-jet fighter having low wing loading and utilizing two 1472 daN/1500 kp He S 011 turbojet engines.

The *Entwurf II* design portrayed a mid-wing aircraft with two jet engines buried in the fuselage beneath the pilot seats. The pressurized cockpit would have accommodated a crew of three. The air inlet was located in the nose of the aircraft and the nose gear retracted into the fuselage. All-up weight was calculated at 12000 kg.

By utilizing a smaller fuselage the designers hoped to fulfill the requirements with the *Entwurf III* layout. In this case the takeoff weight would have been just 10500 kg.

The fourth design was similar to its three predecessors in concept, that is, a mid-wing layout with tricycle gear, but was powered by three jet engines. Two were situated beneath the wings and the third was housed in the fuselage beneath the cockpit.

Another attempt was made with the *Entwurf V*, which envisioned two engines under the cockpit and the third in the extreme aft fuselage section. The takeoff weight was calculated at 19000 kg for both designs IV and V.

Materials which would have been used to construct the designs included wood and metal. For all types, wing sweep was approximately 30 degrees and wing chord ranged from 10 to 12 percent. Load factor was 4.5. Two-thirds of the fuel - 6000 kg - was carried in the fuselage, with the remaining one-third in the wings. Data for the anticipated performance of the five designs, which were drawn up shortly before Germany's collapse, are not available.

Focke-Wulf Rocket Fighter

A smaller, less-refined version of the Ta 183 having a skid in place of the undercarriage was planned as a rocket fighter; powerplant was to have been the Walter HWK 109-509 engine delivering 1668 daN/1700 hp. The aircraft would have taken off with the aid of a takeoff trolley and then have been able to accelerate to 650 km/h. In a nearly vertical climb, it would have been able to climb to an altitude of 16500 meters in just 100 seconds. At this point it would have still had 180 kg of fuel on board for pressing home the attack, after which it would glide back to its base.

Piston and Jet Aircraft Projects

Focke-Wulf also developed another 25 or so projects, including a self-destruct airplane. Personally, Tank took a dim view of Asiatic combat philosophies and it was therefore quite difficult for him to carry out this project which had been assigned to his company by the *Technisches Amt*. He deliberately avoided butting heads with the Amt because he was convinced that, at this late stage of the war, none of these projects would ever come to fruition. Nevertheless, the work carried out during this period was not in vain. The last projects described briefly on these pages show the transition from highly developed piston aircraft to a new era of jet aircraft design, an era in which Tank would play a significant role in just a few short years with his work abroad.

Puqui II: Star in South America's Skies

After the war Professor Dr.-Ing. E.h. Kurt W. Tank and many of his colleagues found a new home in Argentinia. In late 1947 Tank had managed to escape to South America in a rather adventurous manner. At the time, the Argentinians had ingenious methods for helping numerous engineers to flee from occupied Germany.

Tank settled in at the I.A. Fabrica Militar de Aviones in Cordoba with a staff of about sixty of his former colleagues. There, supported by qualified personnel in the company's well-equipped facilities, he continued work on his Ta 183.

I.A. Fabrica Militar de Aviones had been established in 1927 and had built foreign aircraft and engines - such as Focke-Wulf's Stieglitz and the Siemens Sh 14 engine - under license. It began working on its own designs in 1932 and produced two- and three-seat trainers, followed by a twin-engined commercial airliner in 1933. In 1946 the company employed 6000 workers and was the largest aircraft manufacturer in South America. At this time, the name of the company changed to Instituto Aerotécnica de Córdoba. In 1952 the company merged with the Industrias Aeronáuticas u Mecánicas del Estado(IAME) and in 1956 reverted back to its original name of Fabrica Militar de Aviones.

Just after the war, the company had "acquired" the famous French aviation designer Dewoitine. In Cordoba, Dewoitine built South America's first jet aircraft, the IAe 27 Pulqui I (Arrow I), which flew for the first time in 1947. But the type had neither sufficient power nor acceptable handling characteristics; flight testing was therefore terminated in 1950.

Then Kurt Tank and his colleagues stepped in; they were given a contract for developing a jet aircraft with better performance. This resulted in the Pulqui II, which embodied much of the experience with the Ta 183 in its design. South America's first jet-powered swept wing airplane took off on its maiden flight on 27 June 1950. Six of these machines were built before production ceased in 1954. At this time the company was forced to severely curtail its aircraft production and take up the manufacturing of automobiles.

In place of the He S 011A engine originally intended for the Ta 183, Tank was given use of a Rolls Royce Nene II jet engine delivering 2271 daN/2315 kp of thrust and fitted with a double-flow centrifugal compressor. The en-gine had been sent to Cordoba after being tested by the British. The Pulqui II made use of a NACA profile: NACA 001108-1.1-40 at the wing root, NACA 000797-0.825-40 at the tip, interpolated across the span, so that the actual chord dropped off progressively and in a linear profile.

In Bad Eilsen the design team had already "flight tested" models of the Ta 183 with the aid of small fireworks rockets - a low-wing t-tail version and a twin-fuselage model. Multhopp, who had drawn up the plans, was satisfied with the low-wing design. The twin boom flying model came from Ludwig Mittelhuber, who had had a major influence on virtually all Focke-Wulf designs since 1930. It bore a passing resemblance to the DeHavilland Vampire and had better flight handling characteristics than the low-wing Ta 183 design, which, although it had a tendency to tumble (Dutch roll), was also better performing. The models had been built by Ingenier Stampa. The evaluation report on the Multhopp model's flight handling, compiled by Gotthold Mathias (Focke-Wulf's flight characteristics expert), was not very favorable. The Dutch roll problem was not alleviated until the positive sweep of the model's elevators had been flipped around and flown with a negative sweep.

For the Pulqui II Tank relied on the better-performing Multhopp version of the Ta 183. However, the wings were set higher on the fuselage, turning the Pulqui II into a shoulder wing design sitting much lower on its landing gear and having its lengthened fuselage underside much closer to the ground. For the Argentinians, the aircraft also had a higher wing sweepback angle than the Ta 183 in order to more easily broach the sound barrier. The fuselage had to be lengthened to accommodate the larger engine and achieve good damping. Rudder and elevator design were brought into line with the new layout and the air intake more smoothly blended in to the fuselage shape. Tank used a t-tail for the first time, as this offered the optimal solution with regards to weight and drag.

Proceeding cautiously, Tank first had a 1:1 scale flying model of the Pulqui II built. To the amazement of his Argentinian colleagues, he had himself towed to an altitude of 2000 meters behind a twin-engined Calquin light bomber, released the cable and flew the Pulqui as an engineless glider. During the flight, he checked out its stability, aileron control and handling characteristics. Over the course of sev-

An exciting event: just prior to the Pulqui II's maiden flight.

eral flights he found no major faults with the design. Already well acquainted with the airplane, shortly afterward he flew the first Pulqui II V1 on its maiden flight.

It's remarkable to note that this jet made no use whatsoever of hydraulic controls. All control surfaces were driven solely and directly through stick and rudder pressure from the pilot. Using these controls (derived from experience with the Fw 190) the machine remained fully controllable up to Mach numbers over 0.9 and dynamic pressures of 6000 kg/m2 (corresponding to 1030 km/h at low level). For ease of control the force ratio between control stick and elevator could be manually adjusted during flight to 2:1.

Captain Weiss of the Argentinian Air Force carried out the first flight in the Pulqui II V1 on 16 June 1950 and was quite pleased with its flight handling characteristics.

Superstall with the Pulqui II

The maiden flight of the Pulqui II V1 took place on 16 June 1950 flown by an Argentinian pilot, Captain Weiß, who had gained experience with jet aircraft on the Gloster Meteor then being operated by the Argentinian Air Force. He put on a flawless demonstration of the Pulqui II, concluding the show by making a powered landing with a smooth touchdown. His impression after 28 minutes of flight time: "A high-performance, fast, maneuverable airplane that can climb well and is easy to fly." The former *Oberstleutnant* Behrens, who had followed Tank to Argentina, carried out the second flight on 19 June 1950. After being in the air 24 minutes, he pulled up following a steep descent and made a soft landing with the machine. However, during taxi it began bouncing due to the undercarriage not yet having enough shock absorption and was damaged.

Continued flight testing of the Pulqui II was now in Tank's hands. He took off on his first flight on 23 October 1950 and over the course of the next few weeks conducted all the major test flights himself, as he had often done formerly. During one of these flights, the Pulqui II almost cost him his life as Tank evaluated the aircraft's behavior during stalled flight. Tank had evaluated several designs, both of his own creation as well as from other manufacturers, in such a configuration and did not feel he had any reason to mistrust the Pulqui - a classy, attractive plane capable of reaching speeds of 1000 km/h, racing skyward at 30 meters per second and having a wing loading of just 300 kg/m2, unusually low for such a fast machine. Here follows his report of this memorable flight:

"I climbed to about 8000 meters' altitude in barely six minutes and was a bit proud to have launched what was probably the fastest fighter in the world at the time together with my colleagues so far away from home. We were able to realize what we'd only been able to dream of long before with our Ta 183 model experiments at Focke-Wulf. I trimmed the airplane for level flight and pulled the throttle back to idle, checked my bearings and found that I was near the airfield at an altitude of 9000 meters. Another tug on the safety harness and a glance at the canopy eject lever. It took awhile for the speed to bleed off. Slowly I approached stall speed. However, with the Pulqui II a stall didn't announce itself by a shudder or sudden drop off onto one wing or any type of unusual behavior at all. I held the stick, but the machine never nosed over to pick up speed. Suddenly, I had no control effect whatsoever. The stick could be moved around freely as though the plane were on the ground. An eery silence pervaded the cockpit. Only two of the gauges were behaving crazily: the climb rate indicator and the altimeter. The climb rate needle twitched at "falling", while the altimeter unwound rapidly - 8000 meters, 7000 meters ... It became clear to me that I was falling almost straight down like a rock with the plane in a perfectly normal flight attitude - nowadays we call this a superstall - and the aircraft failed to react to any inputs ... 6000 meters, I moved the stick around, nothing ... 5000 meters. "Bail out" went through my mind. But before that another try at the engines; the turbines were still running - they could easily have gone out during the rapid descent. I slowly pushed the throttle forward, then pulled it back - then the machine began pumping. I noticed a bit of pressure on the ailerons, but the airplane still didn't respond to controls. Once again, I pushed the throttle forward and pulled it back, forcibly

Tank comments on his experience gained while making a test flight (Dr.-Ing. Otto Pabst is seen here on the right).

This time there were some problems during the flight. Tank's colleagues seem quite interested in his findings.

pulled the stick to one side, the wing lifted and the machine dropped over onto its side, nosed over, picked up speed and I was able to pull out as though nothing had happened. I climbed out to 500 meters in order to reflect on the cause of this unusual behavior. I would have to repeat the whole spectacle, for only in this way would I be able to get to the root of the matter. Was it chance, or did this fall happen as a result of a particular flight attitude? I pushed the throttle lever forward and climbed to an altitude of 9000 meters. Again I put it into a stall and I was at once whistling straight down like a rock with the plane still maintaining a level attitude. But this time I immediately began pumping the throttle and quickly regained control of the machine. One thing was obvious to me: the tail must have fallen in the airflow's dead zone and downdraft, for the airplane refused to react to anything. As I landed, I became aware of the fact that for the first time I'd built an airplane which could be deadly."

Tank searched for the cause of the Pulqui II's odd behavior and eventually came across an article in the magazine ZFM from 28 May 1931, volume 10, written by Dr.-Ing. Peterson of the Kaiser-Wilhelm-Institut für Strömungsforschung on downdraft effect behind wings with airflow separation. Peterson's observations applied to angles of attack ranging from 15 to 60 degrees. He discovered that an airplane having an angle of attack of 20 to 60 degrees became nose heavy when the airflow separated and, picking up speed, subsequently continued flying in the normal direction of flight. In the 15 to 20 degree realm, however, situations cropped up which could prove quite dangerous. The airflow has separated completely and even flows forward against the direction of flight. And it was in this realm that Tank had ventured with the Pulqui II.

As we know today, even with unswept wings a design having elevators which are set high on the tail is prone to the effect of superstall. The Lockheed F-104 Starfighter had the same characteristic which proved quite difficult to overcome. In rare cases it is possible to avoid the flight condition with a stable equilibrium at angles of attack between 30 and 40 degrees by making the center of gravity relatively far forward. One effective solution is the application of electronics technology, e.g. on the F-104 the control stick automatically moves forward as the airflow nears the point of separating. On the Pulqui II, the tendency to rear up during landing (flare) led to a sharp-profiled leading edge to the wing near the fuselage in order to permit the airflow to separate sooner. Wind tunnel testing, however, revealed that this profiled edge did not fully rectify the problem. So, in addition, for the same reason ballast was used in the nose section to shift the center of gravity forward. Combined, both measures corrected the problem and eliminated the dangerous tendencies of the plane during a stall.

Tank was thus able to retain the T-tail design, a feature which offered several advantages. The rudder deflected less with the same effect and could be set further aft, which in turn resulted in better stability.

The care which Tank devoted to testing the airplane following the changes is evidenced by his flight book, which showed no less than 28 test flights up until 31 May 1951. On that date, Captain Manneval flew the Pulqui II V1 into the mountains to test the aircraft's aerobatic handling. During these maneuvers, the plane lost a wing and he crashed to his death.

The Pulqui II also claimed a second victim, this time from Tank's own team. It was Oberstleutnant a.D. Behrens, who had formerly been so enthusiastically involved in the Fw 190 program. As already mentioned, Behrens had followed Tank to Argentina and soon became one of his most trusted coworkers. Problems with his flight accident insurance, which to him seemed to be too low for test flying the Pulqui, led to him being grounded for a period of time.

Oberstleutnant a.D. Behrens (right) after a flight in the Pulqui II.

"It's a good thing I didn't bail out", calls out Tank to his colleagues. During the flight his instrument panel lit up with the warning: "engine fire". He pulled up into a turn, checked his rear-view mirror, temperature, and everything seemed to be in order. The engine was running smoothly. He flew back to base and landed. Here he has just discovered that a false indicator in the warning system had been taunting him.

Tank saw to it that he was given adequate coverage. Some time later, when the head of state Peron requested a visit to the factory, Tank instructed Behrens: "Now really fly the Pulqui well, get familiar with the machine again and put on a demonstration for Peron when he visits us." Behrens did not have to be told twice. Soon he was in the air and began putting the Pulqui through its paces in Córdoba's blue skies. Once he felt comfortable in the machine, he raced back down towards the airfield, pulled up into a spiral turn and suddenly found himself in an inverted spin. Behrens was able to recover the plane, but in order to do so had to put the plane into a steep dive. As he pulled up his wing brushed the ground - to the horror of all the members of the Córdoba team who had turned out to watch Behrens' aerobatics. As a result, the plane came apart and its pieces flew

across the field with unimaginable force. Behrens met a pilot's death in the accident.

Despite this, Tank and his colleagues did not become discouraged. The team continued unflinchingly with their work on the Pulqui II, trying to boost its performance - particularly in the area of range. The relatively low wing loading meant that the flying mass could be increased without difficulty. A second prototype, the Pulqui IIe, was designed and built with tightly riveted wings housing an additional 900 liters/729 kg of kerosene. In all, the wings and fuselage now held 3200 liters/2600 kg of kerosene. Takeoff weight climbed to 6875 kg, endurance to 2.83 hrs at 900 km/h at 9000 meters' altitude, with the range increasing to 3090 km. The prototype was flown and tested with full load. Corresponding data is found in the table.

Pulqui II V3 Flight Log

Otto Behrens filed a flight report on the Pulqui II V3, which Dipl.-Ing. Wolff recorded via radio. It is provided here as a fitting tribute to a faithful member of Tank's team:

8/26/1952, Otto Behrens takes off in Córdoba at 1338 hrs, landing 1412 hrs (34 minutes).

1338 hrs takeoff, takeoff run 22 seconds; 1339 hrs everything o.k., all lamps illuminated. Takeoff a bit longer than standard; 1341hrs autopilot must be reset. 1343 hrs flying on autopilot, machine handles well and flies straight and cleanly without need for rudder. Va 600 km/h (V_a = indicated airspeed), altitude 2000 m, engine 11200 rpm; 1347 hrs, 10 min flight time, everything o.k.; 1350 hrs coming from the direction of Pajas Blancas, altitude 4000 m; 1353 hrs everything o.k.; 1354 hrs, doing barrel rolls, 700 km/h, altitude 4200 m; 1355 hrs V_a 680 km/h, altitude 4000 m, 10000 rpm, turning @ 3.5 g, same characteristic in tight turn as before, turns become increasingly tighter (turn instability, aircraft pulls into the turn), rudder at V_a 600 km/h at 4000 m altitude is more pleasant than at lower altitudes, while elevators seem more effective than at 2000 m, V_a 500 to 600 km/h; 1358 hrs, 20 minutes flight time, extend brakes, 1359 hrs airplane turns right when brakes extended, quite pleasant handling when extended; 1400 hrs temperature in the cockpit is 28 degrees Celsius, outside temperature 21 degrees Celsius, altitude 1500 m; 1403 hrs 24 minutes flight time, enter the airfield circuit; 1407 hrs fantastic ventilation when canopy opened a bit, V_a 350 to 400 km/h - canopy can be opened; 1408 hrs 30 minutes flight time, landing approach; 1412 hrs landing.

Pulqui IIa during takeoff.

Prof. Kurt Tank playing with his daughter in Argentina.

Comparison of Ta 183, Pulqui I, Pulqui IIa and Pulqui IIe

Manufacturer		Focke-Wulf	I Ae	I AE	I AE
Type		Ta 183 Project Type II	Pulqui I I Ae 27	Pulqui IIa I AE 33	Pulqui IIe[7] I AE 33
Powerplant		Heinkel He S 011A	Rolls Royce Derwent 5	Rolls Royce Nene II	Rolls Royce Nene II
Performance	daN	1570	1780	2271	2271
	kp	1600	1814	2315	2315
Crew		1	1	1	1
Length	m	8.90	9.96	11.60	11.60
Height	m	3.45	3.39	3.35	3.35
Wingspan	m	9.50	11.25	10.62	10.62
Wing area	m²	22.80	19.70	25.10	25.10
Aspect ratio		3.96	6.42	4.49	4.49
Weight, empty	kg	2535	2420	3554[4]	3736[8]
Fuel	kg	1200	970	1875	2600
Oil	kg	20	10	15	15
Crew	kg	80	100	80	80
Load	kg	315	100	464[5]	444
Max. permissible load	kg	1615	1180	2434	3139
Takeoff weight	kg	4150	3600	5988	6875
Wing loading	kg/m²	182.02	182.74	238.57	273.90
Weight/power ratio	kg/daN	2.64	2.02	2.63	3.03
	kg/kp	2.59	1.98	2.59	2.97
	daN/m²	68.86	90.36	90.48	90.48
	kp/m²	70.18	92.08	92.23	92.23
Max. speed	km/h	967[1]	850	1040	1057
@ altitude	m	7000	5000	4800	4000
Cruise speed	km/h	905[1]	750	962	954
@ altitude	m	0	5000	8000	6500
Rate of climb	m/s	21.50[1]	25.00	30.00	25.50
Service ceiling	m	14400[2]	15500	15000	14200
Range	km	1800[3]	800	2030[6]	3090[9]
Max. flight time	hrs	2.03	1.00	1.75[6]	2.83[9]
Takeoff run	m	725	700	740	920
Takeoff run to 15 m	m	1115	1100	1080	1200
Landing speed	km/h	166	170	178	180
Max. permissible load as % of takeoff weight		39	33	41	46
Payload as % of takeoff weight		8	3	8	6
Built		1944	1947	1950	1952

[1] At an average weight of 3550 kg

[2] Time to climb to 6000 m   5.6 min
                  10000 m   11.3 min
                  13000 m   20.0 min

[3] At full thrust at an altitude of 13000 m; 560 km at sea level; 990 km at 7000 m.

Political Confusion Scatters Tank's Team to the Four Winds

After the fall of Peron, the Argentinian head of state, in 1956, the Fabrica Militar de Aviones in Córdoba ceased developmental work on new aircraft for a period of time. Although the airplane manufacturer was prepared to continue the employment of German engineers it was only able to offer simple jobs which were unable to satisfy a developmental engineer. Despite this, a few of Tank's colleagues accepted the Argentinian offer. Others went to Republic Aviation in the United States, while still others followed Multhopp, who was gainfully employed at Martin in the USA, and a few found positions at Lockheed and Boeing. Tank himself, expecting the worst, had established ties with both the Federal Republic (briefly) and India in order to continue keeping his team active in aircraft design and construction. In 1956 he decided on India because at the time the Federal Republic's position remained unclear with regards to re-establishing new German aircraft production, something which had been forbidden for years after the war. It was not until 1955 that such production resumed, and even then it was carried out with many restrictions still in place. Nevertheless, at the time this was the first chance that the rest of Tank's coworkers had for working in their chosen profession in their own country.

[4]**Empty weight breakdown**

fuselage	kg	810
rudder	kg	112
tailplane	kg	74
landing gear	kg	344
wings	kg	705
flaps	kg	26
ailerons	kg	54
engine+tanks	kg	1066
seat	kg	54
equipment	kg	246
hydraulics	kg	63
Total	kg	3554

[5]**Payload breakdown**

4xOerlikon 20	kg	274
ammunition	kg	170
parachute	kg	20
	kg	464

[6]At 10000 m

[7]Pulqui IIe had sealed wing compartments which held 900 ltrs/729 kg of fuel

[8]Due to the fuel tank system the wings of Pulqui IIe were 182 kg heavier

[9]At 11500 m altitude; at cruising rpm at 14000 m altitude the fuel consumption rate was 550 kg/hr + 700 kg for climbing + 10% reserves

Tank Builds the Marut for India

New Plans at HAL

In early 1955 the Indian government was looking for a German aircraft designer to assist the country in developing its own projects. Kurt Tank had already heard of these efforts while still in Argentina when, during a stay in Germany, he was invited to a reception in Bonn by the Indian minister of war Mahavir Tiagy. It therefore came as no surprise when the minister invited him to continue his work in India. Yet he was still hesitant.

Because of the unstable political situation in Argentina Tank had already begun working on establishing German connections; in addition, he had little knowledge of Indian aviation and its future work prospects.

A short time later Tank landed in Bangalore, visited the Hindustand Aeronautics Limited (HAL) and was impressed with what he found there. At the time, the government of Schleswig-Holstein was favorably inclined towards building an aircraft works in Kaltenkirchen. The Krupp firm also seemed to be interested. Thus, he was reluctant to make any final decision before paying a visit to Kaltenkirchen. But when Tank learned that the Bundestag would not be making a decision on whether to support the project for another six months, he knew he would not be able to delay his decision on the Indian offer for so long and therefore determined to go to India.

HF-24, Ground Attack and Interceptor

As early as February 1956 Kurt Tank met with 14 engineers in Bangalore. Tank's role - given him by Air Force Chief Krishna Menon - was to develop an interceptor which would also be suited to a ground attack role.

The planned engine was to have been two Bristol Orpheus 12-SR turbines with an output of 3728 daN/3800 kp thrust and 4905 daN/5000 kp with afterburning. But since this powerplant was still under development, for the testing phase it was agreed to make use of the 1962 daN/2200 kp

Orpheus 703, the engine powering HAL's license-built version of the Folland Gnat. Some two years later Bristol sent a message that the Orpheus 12 had been dropped from the NATO program and would not be delivered. However, Bristol stood ready to continue developmental work on the engine for 4.7 million pounds sterling. This seemed too high a sum for the Indians, and thus began a long and weary search for a suitable powerplant. Krishna Menon, now the country's defense minister, opened negotiations with the Soviet Union which eventually led to an agreement on license building the MiG-21 and the Tumanski engine powering it. However, as the Soviets were not able to meet the deadline for supplying the parts and engines, it was not until eight years later that work on the first machine could begin. In all, 100 of these MiG-21s were built, the last being delivered to the Indian Air Force in 1973. At the time of this writing, production of the MiG-21M is ongoing, powered by a Tumanski R-11 T2 S-300 engine with 5843 daN/5956 kp with afterburning.

Soviet Engine for the HF-24?

Defense minister Krishna Menon had been fair enough with Tank by notifying him of the negotiations with the Soviets at an early stage. Additionally, he cautiously sounded the designer out regarding the possible use of a Russian turbine for the HF-24 if no suitable powerplant could be found in the West. Visibly relieved that Tank had no reservations, Menon named him an engine whose performance lay between the Orpheus 703 and the Orpheus 12, delivering about 3434 daN/3500 kp thrust without afterburning. He purchased a few of these engines from the Soviet Union and Tank had these thoroughly bench tested in order to gather reliable technical data. The engines ran well and met the manufacturer's performance claims. However, during subsequent negotiations, the Soviets informed their partners that the engine was not yet ready and a series of tests with the afterburner were still needed. Tank had the engine bench tested yet again, running it both with and without afterburning, and found no problems.

HAL HF-24 Mk 1 with two Bristol Orpheus 703 engines.

HAL HF-24 Mk 1 (factory number 015) with two fuel drop tanks.

By this time, Tank wanted some facts. He invited the Russian engineers to a private meeting to determine for himself what concerns they had against the use of their engine in the HF-24. But instead of this, all he heard was praise for his airplane which the Soviet guests incessantly enthused over. It dawned on Tank that if the engine in question were used in the HF-24, it may result in an airplane superior to the MiG-21 and destroy the business deal in progress. And it now became clear to him why the Soviet engineers were so keenly interested in the HF-24 during their visits - they wanted to discover the performance capabilities of the aircraft when married with the Russian powerplant. And apparently the HF-24 compared quite favorably with the MiG-21.

During a later meeting the Soviets informed their partners that the engines they were offering had a service life of just 50 hours. The Indian experts were surprised by this, for all the British engines they had bought or license built delivered 500, 1000 or, in the case of the Rolls Royce Dart, even 2000 hours. Even Tank now had serious reservations and the Indians decided to break off further negotiations for this powerplant.

At the time the Americans attempted to block the Indian deal with the Soviet Union by offering to convert the 3048 daN/3107 kp Rolls Royce RB 153-61 R to suit the HF-24 and finance the program to boot. The Indians sent a delegation to Rolls Royce to inspect the engine for themselves and gather information on the planned conversion as well as the anticipated performance figures. The delegation members returned with a very favorable impression of the RB 153, which would have offered a significant performance boost to the HF-24. However, the Americans included a proviso with the deal: construction of the MiG-21 would have to be abandoned. But the Indians had already signed the contract with the Russians and could not accept the American offer under such conditions.

In the spring of 1964 Air Marshal Ranjan Dutt welcomed to Bombay one Ferdinand Brandner, the famous designer of the Junkers Jumo 222. After the war, he and his team had built for the Soviets the most powerful turboprop engine in the world, delivering 8820 kW/12000 hp. It was used in the Tu-114 and was notable for having a fuel consumption rate of just 160 g/ph/hr at 11000 meters. At the time, he had just developed the E 300 for the Egyptians, a turbojet engine with 3237 daN/3300 kp non-afterburning thrust and 4709 daN/4800 kp with afterburner. This powerplant was intended for the Ha 300, a swept-wing interceptor being built for the Egyptians by Messerschmitt.

Brandner E 300 Engine for the HF-24

Professor Tank had visited Brandner at the Egyptian EGAO works (Egyptian General Aero Organization) in Helwan in 1963. He came to the conclusion that the E 300 would make the ideal powerplant for the HF-24 and accordingly recommended to the Indians a joint project with the Egyptians. Soon thereafter, Brandner found himself together with the directors of the EGAO in India, where their hosts offered them the HF-24 in exchange for supplying India with the E 300. It would have been a sensible solution for both countries - the Egyptians would have had a production aircraft in short order and the Indians an urgently needed engine. But Egypt had already signed a deal with Messerschmitt for the construction of the Ha 300 and India was progressing with the negotiations for the MiG-21 with the Soviets.

Nevertheless, the Indians agreed to supply the EGAO with an HF-24 and necessary personnel free of charge to be used as a testbed for evaluating the E 300. In 1965 two Antonov An-10 transports ferried an HF-24 in carefully packed crates to Helwan. It was not until 1966, however, that the HF-24 made its first flight, powered by an original Orpheus 703 and an E 300. Tank was present at the event.

The HF-24 subsequently completed 80 flying hours with the two engines under the direction of Indian Wing Commander Chopra. No serious deficiencies were noted during these flights, which included a thorough high-altitude evaluation, acceleration testing, flights using afterburner, fuel consumption rate testing, stall and spin handling. On the ground, the HF-24's E 300 ran for about 15 minutes with its afterburner on. Afterwards, Tank touched the skin of the aft fuselage with his bare hand without burning his fingers - the cooling airflow was that good. Tank came to the conclusion that the E 300 was a viable engine which would provide the HF-24 with outstanding performance. But once the E 300 was ready for production, the Egyptians informed the Indians that the engine could not be delivered. For the Indians, this decision was as inconceivable as the Indian choice of the MiG-21 was for Tank.

In the meantime, Tank had made much more progress with his HF-24 than the Indians with their MiG-21 copy. After five years, Tank's first machine was already flying with the less powerful Orpheus 703. The HF-24 Marut was a low-wing design with thin wings having a pronounced

An engine-less full-scale wooden flying model of the HAL HF-24. It was towed to altitude by a DC-3 in order to study its flight handling characteristics.

sweep of 45°. The oval fuselage was area-ruled and had two air intakes located on the sides aft of the cockpit area. On the fuselage underside were two downward extending hydraulically powered speed brakes situated behind the undercarriage. The conventional style control surfaces were of a swept layout, with the tailplanes joined to the lower edge of the fuselage. The elevators were hydraulically activated, while the trim controls were adjusted either hydraulically or electrically. The pilot had the option of selecting either manual or hydraulic rudder operation. The Dowty-Rotel tricycle landing gear was retracted hydraulically.

The fuselage fuel tanks held 2500 liters. An additional four drop tanks, each holding 450 liters, could be carried beneath the wings; furthermore, an additional 400 liter tank could be fitted in the fuselage. A zero-zero Martin Baker ejection seat was planned for the pilot; this type of seat could

be fired while the aircraft was still on the ground, propelling the pilot to such a height that there was sufficient time for the parachute to deploy. Thus a pilot was able to save himself even if an accident were to occur at extremely low altitudes.

The Indians wanted to prevent Tank from test flying the aircraft at any cost. If he were to become involved in a mishap there would have been no one else to continue working on the project. After much debate and argument, Tank reluctantly agreed to this.

Tank now resumed work, taking extreme caution in his approach. He had several 1:10 scale models built for tests in the wind tunnel at the Indian Institute of Science. Slow-speed flight handling characteristics with the sharply swept wing could therefore be checked out in detail. Tank accordingly had cotton threading attached to the model so that the separation of airflow could be measured visibly in

261

the wind tunnel. In addition, he arranged for the construction of a 1:1 scale engine-less flying model. The pilot who would later assume responsibility for the flight testing phase of the program would then be able to familiarize himself with the machine's characteristics without risk to himself. To the amazement of the Indians, on 21 March 1959 the lifesize model was first towed to a height of 9000 meters behind a DC-3 with high-altitude engines and, like a sailplane, glided back to base where it landed.

Cotton threading was now applied to the flying model in the same areas as on the wind tunnel model for the purpose of comparing theory and practice. In so doing, it was discovered that, despite the same lift ratios, the results in no way matched up with each other. According to the readings from the wind tunnel, Tank should not have designed the wings with so much taper; the airflow separated too early. However, the flying model revealed good airflow under the same conditions. This therefore showed that the Reynolds number was not valid for sharply tapered wings.

Maiden Flight Hop

With the prototype Mk I now complete and following a thorough ground test - particularly with regard to the undercarriage, Wing Commander Suri taxied out to the runway for the aircraft's maiden flight. Tank was on hand to witness the happy event. He would have preferred to have flown the machine himself; instead he was forced to subject himself - wreathed in garlands - to an Indian ceremony prior to its first flight. He was given a large gourd which had a facial mask carved into it - the god of wind. Tank was supposed to swing this gourd wildly and throw it on the ground in front of the aircraft with such force that it would shatter. He followed this ritual and threw the gourd with all his might down on the ground in front of the machine. Lemons served as brake chocks in front of the wheels, and the airplane had to roll over these before clearance was given for the maiden flight. Suri climbed into the cockpit once Tank had given him a few last minute pointers and prepared for takeoff. During this discussion, Suri seemed to Tank to lack confidence and be concerned about something. He closed the canopy, powered up the turbines and waited for the all-clear to be given after a thorough check of the systems. Then he pushed the throttle levers forward and began rolling. The runway undulated somewhat, first rising and then dropping in the center section, so that it was not possible to get a clear view of the takeoff itself. The HF-24 quickly reached the "summit" and disappeared over the downward sloping side of the runway. But it never rose up again; it should have appeared on the horizon and begun its outward climb a long time ago! Tank jumped into his car and raced along the runway until he reached the vertex. There he saw the airplane lying on its belly. A fine kettle of fish!

The pilot had retracted the landing gear before pulling up, whereupon the airplane naturally dropped onto its belly. Suri's wife was at least partially to blame for the disaster; she and her five children dropped to their knees before the pilot that morning and pleaded with him not to fly at the planned time - the spirits were opposed to it. Suri's horoscope, which he had read earlier, also said the same thing. As a result, his soul was so troubled before the takeoff that there was no way for the first flight to have been successful.

The behavior of the Indian workers soon made Tank forget his wrath. They sent their foreman to Tank, who consoled him by claiming the affair was not as bad as it seemed, promising to have the machine ready for flight again within 14 days. The designer was moved by the involvement of the team, who seemed to have grown just as attached to the plane as was Tank. Nevertheless, he was forced to disappoint the foreman; although Tank fully believed the group could have the plane repaired in two weeks, all the equipment on board would first have to be removed, bench tested again and then reinstalled. Which meant that repairs took four weeks.

Following repairs, the foreman again came to Tank and reported the machine flight ready. The workers, however, would not let it out of the hangar if Suri were to be the pilot again. Tank was able to calm the man and tell him that the Chief of the Air Force had apologized for the unnecessary mishap and planned to have Group Captain Das make the first flight.

Group Captain Das, a Bengal, was married to an Englishwoman who had nothing to do with spirit worship. He flew teh HF-24 on its maiden flight on 17 June 1961, exactly five years after Tank and his 14 engineers had made the first lines on the drawing board. The airplane lifted off after a short run, climbed out, and Das flew the machine as though he had been testing it for months. After landing, he deplaned and walked over to Tank with his face beaming: "Outstanding flight handling, remarkably easy to fly. May I do aerobatics with it?" Tank responded: "Why not, the machine was laid out with the intention of being fully aerobatic!" Das subsequently climbed back into the cockpit and flew a full aerobatic program for the astounded crowd, causing the group to break out in a wave of enthusiasm.

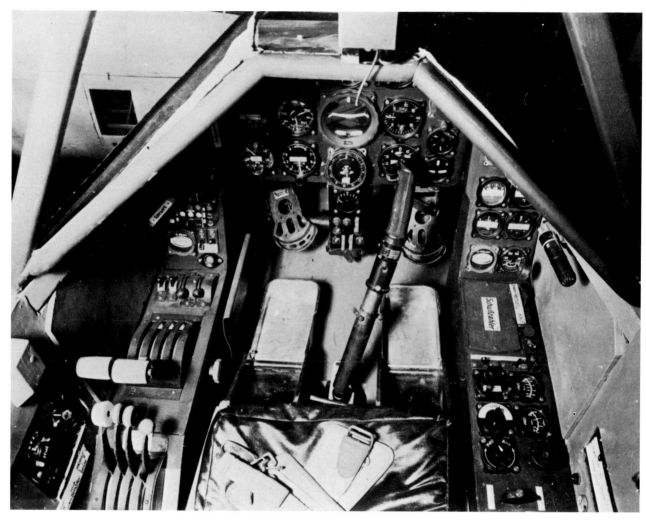

Cockpit of the HF-24.

HF-24 Marut Mk I Specifications

The first of 18 pre-production HF-24 Marut Mk 1s flew in March of 1963, with the Indian Air Force taking delivery of its first two aircraft on 10 May 1964. There followed an additional twelve machines, of which a single example - Mk TA - was fitted with afterburning Orpheus engines. The first production plane flew on 15 November 1967. 125 aircraft had been delivered to the Indian air force by 31 January 1977. In the war against Pakistan in December of 1971 the HF-24s acquitted themselves admirably, destroying nearly all the tanks which had broken through the lines without suffering a single loss to themselves.

The HF-24 has been let down in its developmental program by the lack of a suitable engine. The Orpheus 703 engine currently in use only provides the performance and characteristics of a ground attack plane and not those of an air-superiority fighter, a role for which the aircraft was also designed. According to Tank, the HF-24 flies quite peacefully and problem-free in the lower transsonic regions, an area which is usually crossed quite rapidly in jet-powered aircraft due to the unpleasant flight handling characteristics generally associated in this speed regime. At Tank's request, the HF-24 was thoroughly evaluated in the speed regions around Mach 1.2.

HAL HF-24 and Project HF-73

Manufacturer			HAL	HAL	HAL
Type			HF-24 Mk 1 fighter	HF-24 Mk 1 strike	HF-73 project[6]
Powerplant			Bristol Orpheus 703	Bristol Orpheus 703	RB 199 34R[7]
Performance	daN	dry	2x2160=4320 with afterburner	2x2160=4320	2x3561=7122 2x6681=13362
	kp	dry	2x2202=4404 with afterburner	2x2202=4404	2x3630=7260 2x6810=13620
Crew			1	1	1
Length	m		15.87	15.87	15.13
Height	m		3.60	3.60	3.60
Wingspan	m		9.00	9.00	9.00
Wing area	m²		28.00	28.00	28.00
Aspect ratio			2.89	2.89	2.89
Weight, empty	kg		6195	6195	6565
Fuel	kg		2018	2754[4]	3850
Crew	kg		80	80	80
Load	kg		407	1879	2105
Max. permissible load	kg		2505	4713	6035
Takeoff weight	kg		8700	10908	12600[8]
Wing loading	kg/m²		310.71	389.57	450.00
Weight/power ratio	kg/daN		2.01	2.53	0.94
	kg/kp		1.98	2.48	0.92
	daN/m²		154.29	154.29	477.18
	kp/m²		157.28	486.43	
Max. speed			Mach 1.5[1]	830 km/h	Mach 2.00
@ altitude	m		6000	0	11000
Cruise speed	km/h				1067[9]
@ altitude	m				0
Rate of climb	m/s		29.00[2]	22.00	91.50[10]
Service ceiling	m		16000	12000	18000
Range	km		480[3]	280[5]	650[11]
Takeoff run	m		850	1450	870
Takeoff run to 15 m	m		1300	1878	960
Landing run	m		820	1125	800
Landing run from 15 m	m		1100	1450	1000
Landing speed	km/h		250	250	270
Max. permissible load as % of takeoff weight			29	43	48
Payload as % of takeoff weight			5	17	17
Built			1961	1961	project

[1]Mach 1.5 to 12000 m; Mach 0.9 at 16000 m
[2]Average climb rate to 12000 m(7 min): rate at 2000 m was 65 m/sec; rate at 4000 m was 55 m/sec with 540 kg fuel on board
[3]760 km range with 2x455 ltr/369 kg external fuel tanks; with four 454 ltr external fuel tanks ferry range was 1450 km at 9000 m; 800 km at low altitude
[4]2018 kg in addition to 2x455 ltr(368 kg) = 2754 kg
[5]At low level

[6+7]A study calculated the performance of the HF-24 with the RB 199 34R, the powerplant used in the Tornado. The project was designated HF-73
[8]Could be increased to 16000 kg
[9]Minus afterburner
[10]300 m/sec at sea level; climbed to 16000 m in 2.1 min
[11]At 740 km/h at sea level with 2000 kg external load

HF-24 Marut Mk IT

After the Indian air force had initially determined that a two-seat version was superfluous, it was later decided to indeed proceed with the construction of a trainer version. The first MK IT took off on its first flight on 30 April 1970. The conversion was straightforward: the firing system for the MATRA missiles located inside the fuselage was removed and replaced by a second Martin-Baker MK 84 C ejection seat with dual controls. The difference in performance when compared to the single-seat Marut is minimal.

An air combat study designed to clarify what developmental potential the HF-24 offered was carried out with the focus on using two RB 199s, the same engine fitted in the Tornado, delivering 3110 daN/3170 kp and 6220 DaN/6340 kp with afterburner. Powered by this engine, the HF-24 would have been able to attain speeds of Mach 2.0 and at an altitude of 11,000 meters and Mach 1.5 would have had a velocity along the flight path of more than 300 meters per second. With the RB 199 the HF-24 would have been one of the best performing fighters of its day and would have been a match for any contemporary airplane in the West or East - including the MiG-25 - until well into the 'eighties.

The Return Home

With the completion of the HF-24 Tank's work in India had come to a close. Since the 'sixties he had felt the land of his birth beckoning him to return. As always, aviation continued to intrigue Tank. He had fulfilled his dream in life just as much as he now filled his restless years of retirement. He had given himself over to aviation, and from all appearances it seems that aviation had given itself over to him. Things had worked out as planned.

Tank found a new role as a consultant to MBB, but soon became seriously ill and passed away on 5 June 1983 in Munich-Harlaching.

Air Marshall Kartre, director of the Hindustan Works in India, paid a condolence visit to Frau Sigrid Tank shortly thereafter. In recognition of the service her husband had rendered to India Frau Tank requested that a HF-24 Marut be donated to the Deutsches Museum. Kartre agreed to her request without hesitation and one day a Marut, carefully packed in crates, arrived safe and sound in Munich. The Deutsches Museum brought it to Oberschleißheim where it will be given a place of honor once it is mounted in the Museum's planned facilities under construction.

Table Index - Engines and Equipment/Personnel Index/Key Word Index

Index of Key Personnel

Index by Subject